[

# Mind, Brain, and Education in Reading Disorders

One of the key topics for establishing meaningful links between brain sciences and education is the development of reading. How does biology constrain learning to read? How does experience shape the development of reading skills? How does research on biology and behavior connect to the ways that schools, teachers, and parents help children learn to read, particularly in the face of disabilities that interfere with learning? This book addresses these questions and illuminates why reading disorders have been hard to identify, how recent research has established a firm base of knowledge about the cognitive neuroscience of reading problems and the learning tools for overcoming them, and, finally, what the future holds for relating mind, brain, and education to understanding reading difficulties. Connecting knowledge from neuroscience, genetics, cognitive science, child development, neuropsychology, and education, this book will be of interest to both academic researchers and graduate students.

KURT W. FISCHER is Charles Warland Bigelow Professor of Education and Human Development and Director of the Mind, Brain, and Education Program in the Graduate School of Education at Harvard University. He is founding president of the International Mind, Brain, and Education Society and founding editor of the new journal *Mind, Brain, and Education*.

JANE HOLMES BERNSTEIN is a developmental neuropsychologist who divides her time between teaching, writing, and research responsibilities at the Children's Hospital Boston and the establishment of a National Child Development Program in Trinidad and Tobago.

MARY HELEN IMMORDINO-YANG studies the neuroscience of emotion and its relation to cognitive, linguistic, and social development at the Brain and Creativity Institute, University of Southern California. She recently received her doctorate from the Graduate School of Education at Harvard University.

*Cambridge Studies in Cognitive and Perceptual Development*

The aim of this series is to provide a scholarly forum for current theoretical and empirical issues in cognitive and perceptual development. As the twenty-first century begins, the field is no longer dominated by monolithic theories. Contemporary explanations build on the combined influences of biological, cultural, contextual, and ecological factors in well-defined research domains. In the field of cognitive development, cultural and situational factors are widely recognized as influencing the emergence and forms of reasoning in children. In perceptual development, the field has moved beyond the opposition of "innate" and "acquired" to suggest a continuous role for perception in the acquisition of knowledge. These approaches and issues will all be reflected in the series, which will also address such important research themes as the indissociable link between perception and action in the developing motor system, the relationship between perceptual and cognitive development and modern ideas on the development of the brain, the significance of developmental processes themselves, dynamic systems theory, and contemporary work in the psychodynamic tradition, especially as it relates to the foundations of self-knowledge.

Titles published in the series

# Mind, Brain, and Education in Reading Disorders

*Edited by*

Kurt W. Fischer, Jane Holmes Bernstein,
and Mary Helen Immordino-Yang

CAMBRIDGE
UNIVERSITY PRESS

CAMBRIDGE UNIVERSITY PRESS
Cambridge, New York, Melbourne, Madrid, Cape Town, Singapore, São Paulo

Cambridge University Press
The Edinburgh Building, Cambridge CB2 2RU, UK

Published in the United States of America by Cambridge University Press, New York

www.cambridge.org
Information on this title: www.cambridge.org/9780521854795

First published 2007

Printed in the United Kingdom at the University Press, Cambridge

*A catalogue record for this publication is available from the British Library*

*Library of Congress Cataloguing in Publication data*
Mind, brain, and education in reading disorders / edited by Kurt W.
Fischer, Jane Holmes Bernstein, and Mary Helen Immordino-Yang.
    p.   cm. – (Cambridge studies in cognitive and perceptual development; 11)
Includes bibliographical references and index.
ISBN-13: 978-0-521-85479-5 (hardback)
ISBN-10: 0-521-85479-2 (hardback)
1. Reading disability.   2. Reading disability – Pathophysiology.   3. Reading –
Physiological aspects.   I. Fischer, Kurt W.   II. Bernstein, Jane Holmes, 1947–
III. Immordino-Yang, Mary Helen, 1971–   IV. Series: Cambridge studies in
cognitive perceptual development; 11.
    [DNLM:   1. Dyslexia – physiopathology.   2. Dyslexia – psychology.
3. Dyslexia – therapy. WL 340.6 M664 2007]
RC394.W6M562   2007
616.85'53 – dc22
2007000299

ISBN  978-0-521-85479-5 hardback

To our late colleagues and friends who made fundamental contributions to this book – Ann Brown, Robbie Case, Jeanne Chall, and Samuel P. Rose

# Contents

**Part I   What is Reading, and What are Reading Disorders?
Looking to Neuroscience, Evolution, and Genetics**

**Part II   Reading and the Growing Brain: Methodology
and History**

## Part IV   Reading Skills in the Long Term

# Figures

# Tables

# Contributors

JANE ASHBY, Ph.D., is a researcher at the University of Massachusetts at Amherst and teaches at Hampshire College.

FRANCINE MARY BENES, M.D., Ph.D., is Professor of Psychiatry at McLean Hospital.

JANE HOLMES BERNSTEIN, Ph.D., is Senior Associate in Psychology/Neuropsychology at the Children's Hospital Boston.

BENITA A. BLACHMAN, Ph.D., is Trustee Professor of Education and Psychology at Syracuse University.

SUSAN A. BRADY, Ph.D., is Professor of Psychology at University of Rhode Island and a Senior Scientist at Haskins Laboratories.

JOSEPH C. CAMPIONE, Ph.D., is Professor of Education (Emeritus) at the University of California at Berkeley.

ROBBIE CASE (deceased) was Professor of Education (Emeritus) and Director of the Institute of Child Study at the University of Toronto.

VERNE S. CAVINESS JR., M.D., D.Phil., is the Chief of the Division of Pediatric Neurology at the Massachusetts General Hospital and the Joseph and Rose Kennedy Professor of Child Neurology and Mental Retardation at Harvard Medical School.

TERRENCE W. DEACON, Ph.D., is Professor of Biological Anthropology and Linguistics at the University of California at Berkeley.

FRANK H. DUFFY, M.D., is Associate Professor of Neurology at Harvard Medical School and Director of the Clinical Neurophysiology Laboratory at the Children's Hospital Boston.

ROSALIE P. FINK, Ed.D., is Professor of Literacy at Lesley University.

KURT W. FISCHER, Ph.D., is Charles Warland Bigelow Professor and Director of the Mind, Brain, and Education Program at the Harvard Graduate School of Education.

ALBERT M. GALABURDA, M.D., is the Emily Fisher Landau Professor of Neurology and Neuroscience at Harvard Medical School and Chief of the Division of Behavioral Neurology at Beth Israel Deaconess Medical Center.

MARY HELEN IMMORDINO-YANG, Ed.D., holds a joint Postdoctoral Fellowship at the Brain and Creativity Institute and the Rossier School of Education at the University of Southern California.

E. JULIANA PARÉ-BLAGOEV, Ed.D., is a Research Scientist at The MIND Institute and Assistant Professor at the University of New Mexico Department of Psychology.

DAVID H. ROSE, Ed.D., is Co-Executive Director of the Center for Applied Special Technology (CAST).

L. TODD ROSE is a doctoral candidate at the Harvard Graduate School of Education.

SAMUEL P. ROSE, Ph.D., (deceased) taught at the University of Colorado.

SANDRA PRIEST ROSE is a founding trustee of the Reading Reform Foundation.

GORDON F. SHERMAN, Ph.D., is Executive Director of the Newgrange School and Education Center in Princeton, NJ.

H. GERRY TAYLOR, Ph.D., is Professor of Pediatrics at Case Western Reserve University.

MARTIN H. TEICHER, M.D., Ph.D., is an Associate Professor of Psychiatry at Harvard Medical School and Director of the Developmental Biopsychiatry Research Program at McLean Hospital.

ROBERT W. THATCHER, Ph.D., is Director of the NeuroImaging Laboratory at the Bay Pines VA Medical Center and an adjunct Professor of Neurology at the University of South Florida College of Medicine.

JOSEPH TORGESEN, Ph.D., is the W. Russell and Eugenia Morcom Chair of Psychology and Education at Florida State University and Director of the Florida Center for Reading Research.

DEBORAH WABER, Ph.D., is Director of Research in the Department of Psychiatry at Children's Hospital Boston and Associate Professor (Psychology) in the Department of Psychiatry, Harvard Medical School.

MARYANNE WOLF, Ed.D., is Director of the Center for Reading and Language Research and Professor of Child Development at Tufts University.

# Acknowledgements

This book and the collaborations that it reflects grew out of the creative efforts engendered by Mind, Brain, and Behavior (MBB), the Harvard Interfaculty Initiative to promote cross-disciplinary dialogue about cognitive science, biology, and society. Supported by this broad effort, several faculty from Harvard and other Boston universities met regularly as a study group focusing on the development of brain and behavior, especially in the educational arena and other culturally important domains. Beyond networking, MBB provided logistic and financial support for a conference in which researchers and practitioners from more distant institutions came to Harvard to discuss the issue that is the focus of this book – analyzing reading skills and problems by combining biology, cognitive science, and education to inform research and practice. From this group and the conference the approach grew that we now call Mind, Brain, and Education (MBE). This book is the first publication from our group that articulates this new approach.

We (the editors) especially thank the working group on brain and behavior development that started this effort: Francine Benes, Jerome Kagan, Deborah Waber, Maryanne Wolf, and two of us (Fischer and Bernstein). Equally essential were the doctoral students who helped convince the Harvard community that the Mind, Brain, and Education approach was both worthwhile and sorely needed for children and schools – Donna Coch, Michael W. Connell, Juliana Paré-Blagoev, Kimberly Sheridan, and one of us (Immordino-Yang).

For the logistics of the conference and book, Erma Larson provided energetic, sensitive support for the attendees and the editors. Stephanie Prady and Nancy Rosenthal organized the logistics of the conference. Todd Rose diligently cleaned up the manuscript. Elizabeth Knoll of Harvard University Press made cogent suggestions for organizing the book. Sarah Caro of Cambridge University Press supported our efforts to finish the book together through the various delays and tribulations that come inevitably from coordinating scholars and practitioners from many diverse perspectives. Mary Kiesling did heroic work preparing the final manuscript and coordinating efforts among contributors. Jane Haltiwanger, Leonard Bernstein, and Kyle Yang provided emotional support to the editors.

The students in our classes and training programs played an essential role in stimulating ideas for approaches to building connections between biology, cognitive science, and education. Most of all, they unknowingly supported us with their confidence in the MBE endeavor and their energy and flexibility in pursuing it.

Funding sources and intellectual support that helped sustain this work include the Mind, Brain, and Behavior Initiative, Mr. and Mrs. Frederick P. Rose and Sandra P. Rose, the Harvard Graduate School of Education, the Children's Hospital Boston, and NICHD.

Most of all, we thank the authors of the papers in this volume and the colleagues who participated in the dialogue that shaped these papers at the conference and in the MBB group. All the authors worked with us to create intellectual coherence in the volume and to begin to fulfill some of the promise of the new approach that connects mind, brain, and education to illuminate reading skills and problems.

*Part I*

What is Reading, and What are Reading
Disorders? Looking to Neuroscience, Evolution,
and Genetics

# 1 Toward a grounded synthesis of mind, brain, and education for reading disorders: an introduction to the field and this book

*Kurt W. Fischer, Mary Helen Immordino-Yang, and Deborah Waber*

This is a new era in the fields of education, neuroscience, and cognitive science – a time to bring together mind, brain, and education. The advent of powerful new in vivo brain imaging technologies, the power of the burgeoning discoveries in genetics, and the general excitement in society about biology make possible a new alliance relating biology, cognition, and education (*Educational Leadership*, 1998). Hidden brain and genetic processes are becoming increasingly visible (Gage, 2003; Lyon & Rumsey, 1996; Thatcher, Lyon, Rumsey, & Krasnegor, 1996), and in a few tantalizing cases, researchers and educators can even begin to observe the functional neuropsychological effects of educational interventions. It is an exciting time! This book is designed to promote the dialogue that is essential to creating the best integration of biology, cognitive science, and education.

The burgeoning new knowledge and the focus of society on biology lead to expectations that sometimes upset the balance between scientific knowledge and meaningful use in practice, raising numerous new ethical and educational issues (Battro, 2000; Bruer, 1997, 1999; *Scientific American*, 2003). The best research and the best educational practice require a two-way interaction between the scientific research and the knowledge of educators working to help children learn. Research in neuroscience and genetics, for instance, gains new significance and controversy as educators and clinicians work to translate it into practice, dealing with the strengths and weaknesses of real children learning in schools. This translation to practice should, in turn, filter back down to shape new scientific questions. In this era of translation across disciplines, no longer can neuroscience and cognitive science research remain in the ivory tower, and no longer can educational practice escape scientific scrutiny (Shonkoff & Phillips, 2000; Snow, Burns, & Griffin, 1998). Each discipline has so much to learn from the other!

## Connecting mind, brain, and education

As educators, cognitive scientists, and neuroscientists, we have a responsibility to children to establish and maintain dialogue among our respective fields. To be maximally productive, this dialogue must go both ways. New information about the development and functioning of the brain awaits interpretation and judicious application in the classroom, while educational input and practical insights are essential in shaping new brain research. Indeed, the disciplines of education and neuropsychology are growing increasingly interdependent, and like the cousins from the country and the city, scientists cannot carry out good research, nor can educators carry out good practice, without interweaving these perspectives.

Society has great expectations, perhaps unrealistic ones, about the benefits of bringing biology into education. Scientists and educators are clamoring to make the connections in many ways, some of which will be productive and some of which may be disastrous (Bailey, Bruer, Symons, & Lichtman, 2001; Bruer, 1999). One important trap to be avoided is the assumption that laboratory science by itself will provide answers that can then be applied to education. A productive relation of education, biology, and cognitive science does not start in the laboratory, with direct application of scientific findings to classrooms and students.

What is required instead is a reciprocal process in which education informs biological research as much as biology informs educational research and practice (Battro, 2000; Gardner, 1983). The process should be similar to that in medicine, where medical practice informs biological research as much as biology informs medical practice. In education, reading a textbook is distant from reading a string of words in a reaction time study in a laboratory that measures brain activity with functional magnetic resonance imaging (fMRI). Results from such a different laboratory context seldom apply felicitously to the classroom. That is why so much laboratory research has failed when scientists have attempted to apply it to education.

Educational settings and tasks are essential for useful research in mind, brain, and education, just as medical settings and tasks are essential for useful research in biology and medicine. Laboratory research plays an important role in analyzing fundamental processes, but research in the settings of practice is key, and it is needed right now! Some scientists believe that it is premature to relate biology to education, that education needs to wait for scientific breakthroughs that solve the deep questions of mind and brain. We believe instead that research from education will help to shape the breakthroughs of the future by informing basic biological and cognitive research about human learning and behavior in schools and homes where children develop and learn.

How do educational interventions affect processing in the brain, and how can curricula be designed to make optimal use of developmental plasticity? Conversely, what are the educational implications of neuroscientific findings about processing of language and text, and how should these implications inform educational research and practice? To begin to address these and related questions, we must move into an era of partnership of education with neuroscience and cognitive science, in which we examine and treat educationally relevant capacities and skills from both perspectives.

In the service of promoting optimal connections of mind, brain, and education, this book is meant for neuroscientists, cognitive scientists, and educators alike. Although readers will undoubtedly be drawn initially to the chapters by their disciplinary colleagues, we urge you to delve into the chapters representing approaches other than your own. We hope that you will be inspired to many productive and innovative discussions that challenge assumptions and make connections across the fields of biology, cognitive science, and education.

## Reading and learning disorder

Toward these goals, this book is conceived as a first attempt to systematically bring together the latest neuropsychological, genetic, and educational perspectives on a cognitive skill that is of central importance in both the neurosciences and education: reading. Reading is an excellent place to begin this interdisciplinary dialogue. Long traditions of cognitive neuroscientific research have attempted to pin down the component processes of reading and reading problems (Benes & Paré-Blagoev; Galaburda & Sherman; Immordino-Yang & Deacon; and Paré-Blagoev, this volume). Simultaneously, long traditions of educational research and practice have analyzed literacy instruction and interventions for teaching reading and helping students with reading difficulties (Snow *et al.*, 1998; Case; and Wolf & Ashby, this volume).

Reading has been studied in far greater detail than any other area of academic competence, and reading disorders provide the most extensive, detailed, and methodologically sophisticated research literature of any learning disorder. For all these reasons and because literacy is so fundamental to our society, reading provides an ideal common focus for researchers and practitioners from diverse disciplines and perspectives to examine the interface of mind, brain, and education.

The book deals not only with reading, but it focuses especially on learning disorders. Following the long localization tradition in neuroscience, scientists and educators look to atypical as much as typical functioning to infer the component processes and developmental principles involved in reading (Geschwind, 1965; Huttenlocher, 2002; Neville & Bavelier, 1998; Pennington,

2002; Teuber & Rudel, 1962; Benes & Paré-Blagoev; Duffy; Galaburda & Sherman; Immordino-Yang & Deacon; and Paré-Blagoev, chapters in Part III, this volume; and see D. Rose, this volume, for another perspective). At the same time, understanding atypical and typical functioning requires going beyond simplistic brain–behavior correspondences to analyze how brain functioning relates to the ways real children learn and grow. When functions break down or fail to develop as expected, researchers and practitioners are afforded a unique opportunity to learn about the ways in which the brain and mind organize themselves over time, such as the ways that children functionally compensate for their neurological deficits.

The fundamental premise of this book combines biological and cognitive with educational methods and concepts to produce a new kind of disciplinarity – one that keeps a foot in each of its parent disciplines but the head in the middle. The major goals of this book are to foster meaningful interdisciplinary thinking about reading and learning disorders, and to spark discussions about how the principles derived from this thinking can be extended to other skill areas. For example, instead of considering phonological awareness independently from two perspectives – the educational perspective of reading curricula and the neurological perspective of auditory and temporal processing – we seek to bring the two together to investigate the reciprocal connections of neurological deficits with reading instruction techniques (Benes & Paré-Blagoev; Paré-Blagoev; Wolf & Ashby, this volume). Similarly, researchers and educators can explore the reciprocal connections of oral and written language comprehension with developmental changes in brain organization and cognitive capacities (Case; Fischer, Rose, & Rose; Immordino-Yang & Deacon, this volume).

### Both brain and education

In working to orchestrate an innovative synthesis that furthers both education and cognitive neuroscience, the authors who contribute to this book focus on two complementary themes that run through the book, which are central to good research and practice on learning disorders. The *first theme* is the development of the relation between brain and behavior and the role of experience in shaping their functional organization. This cutting-edge issue dominates both neuroscience and education. Neuroscientists see the shaping effects of experience on brain process and organization and emphasize neural plasticity (Gage, 2003; Huttenlocher, 2002; Neville & Bavelier, 1998; Sur, Angelucci, & Sharma, 1999). Educators and developmental scientists see the behavioral manifestations in the remarkable achievements of children with major neurological problems or histories of traumatic experiences (Battro, 2000; Fischer, Ayoub, Noam, Singh, Maraganore, & Raya, 1997; Teicher, this volume).

What is the ontogeny of the sculpted functional neural networks seen in adults? Contemporary neuroscience has yet to tell what will be a fascinating story, which will ultimately be one of the most fruitful tools for applying the emergent neuroimaging technologies. How does the modularity that is characteristic of brain–behavior relations in adults develop in children, where modularity is not so evident? In children individual skills or components of skills emerge from more global developmental frameworks, within which boundaries can be initially indistinct, emerging over time.

Understanding the principles that govern localization processes in children and adults requires a concurrent educational analysis of children's evolving skill profiles in relation to the cognitive experiences created by reading instruction. This requirement underscores the essential contribution of an educational perspective to the neuropsychological study of reading disorders. While the methods of neuroimaging necessitate a focus on deficits in individual component processes, educational methods can contribute the dynamic, in situ analyses that reveal the bigger picture (Campione; Fink; Fischer, Rose, & Rose; D. Rose, this volume).

Thus the *second theme* of the book is more pragmatic – the feedback of neuroscientific and behavioral findings into educational policy and practice. At the neuropsychological level, what are learning disorders, and who has them? What neuropsychological strengths might be used to remediate weaknesses? At the educational level, what should be done for those with reading disorders in terms of assessment, instruction, and motivational techniques, and how can we characterize a successful outcome? What does a diagnosis of learning disorder mean for the broader context of a person's life?

In thinking about these questions from an interdisciplinary perspective, we come to understand reading disorder as but one manifestation of a neuropsychological profile that often can underlie difficulties in multiple domains of developmental adaptation, such as communication, social skills, and organization of goal-directed behavior (Bernstein; Case; D. Rose, this volume).

### Plasticity and constraint

In the book these themes play out in the dynamic tension between plasticity and constrain in brain–behavior relations, especially in children. The structural properties of the configuration of neural networks and systems will constrain the plasticity with which children develop reading abilities and overcome reading disorders. There are no isomorphic relations between unitary structures and functions, but instead there are architectural constraints, governing the neural configuration that gives rise to behaviors and skills in a learning environment. The skills of reading, which have no evolutionary precedent to ground them firmly in neuroanatomy, are distributed within the complex networks of systems that make up the systems for visual and oral language and comprehension (Immordino-Yang & Deacon, this volume).

A striking consistency is becoming apparent between modern functional neuroimaging studies (PET (positron emission tomography), fMRI) and the inferences drawn from years of neuropsychological observation of individuals with focal lesions, and so the architecture of language and reading networks is likely to have universal properties (Benes & Paré-Blagoev; Duffy; Paré-Blagoev, this volume; Shaywitz, Shaywitz, Fulbright, Skudlarski, Mencl, Constable *et al.*, 2003). However, the greatest contribution of the functional neuroimaging studies to date is likely to be the confirmation that mental functions are associated with dynamic neural systems, not static brain regions. For example, recovering victims of brain damage, especially that incurred during infancy and childhood, demonstrate the flexibility of these networks. The interplay between this flexibility and the architectural constraints on network configuration is central to the study of reading disorders.

On a moment to moment basis, the neurological networks involved in reading are recruited in the service of several concurrent behavioral goals. Reading is thus a remarkably complex process, requiring effective timing and integration of multiple networks to be efficient. We suspect that the relatively subtle processing inefficiencies seen in children identified as learning disabled compound into debilitating reading difficulties based on the children having certain kinds of educational experiences and not others. As scientists and practitioners have widening opportunities to apply functional imaging techniques to the problem of reading disorder, the focus will evolve from the current emphasis on specific skill deficits to a dynamic analysis of the functional neural networks used in real-life learning contexts – which will facilitate analysis of the true nature of the disorder.

What are the range and limits of plasticity, and how are they mitigated by experience, such as by different kinds of reading instruction? Learning disorders entail relatively subtle individual variations in efficiency and efficacy of various cognitive functions. Not only their source but most especially their potential for change in response to interventions are uncertain. Moreover, the relative balance in emphases is likely to shift with the child's development (Bailey *et al.*, 2001; Neville & Bruer, 2001; Newman, Bavelier, Corina, Jezzard, & Neville, 2001; Case; Fischer, Rose, & Rose, this volume). These issues of plasticity and constraint cut to the heart not only of our appraisal of the scientific evidence about structure–function relations, but equally importantly to our ethical beliefs about human potential and rights of the individual. To what extent should the goal of intervention for children with learning disorders be normalization of performance, and to what extent should it be helping the child to identify and prepare for a niche within which he or she can be productive and experience success? What can we reasonably expect the educational system to provide?

In the arena of these very pragmatic questions, advocates of plasticity and constraint have often collided, and there is no one obviously correct resolution of this tension.

The issues that this book addresses are not the easy ones for which answers come in black and white, but the difficult ones that reside at the boundary where plasticity and constraint meet practical educational considerations. This is one reason that we invited several neuroscientists to contribute, including some with no special expertise on learning disorders – to help frame the broad questions that need to be asked about brain, development, and learning. Some of them have contributed chapters, and some have written shorter essays to describe a relevant topic, such as brain growth cycles or the effects of traumatic experience on the brain. Effective framing of questions about brain bases of learning disorders requires dealing with questions of brain growth patterns, brain bases of language, the role of experience in shaping brain development, and genetics. After all, the ultimate goal of this interdisciplinary discussion is to tease apart the effects of experience, anatomy, and genetics on functional brain organization, to relate these principles to the case of reading, and to think about what the patterns of findings all mean for a real, developing child.

## Conceptual organization of the book

In accordance with these themes and goals, the book connects mind, brain, and education throughout, although some chapters contribute more heavily to one or the other area. The book moves from the biological foundations of reading in Part I through developmental analyses of mind, brain, and education for reading and learning disorders in Part II to analyses of individual children's skill patterns in Part III. It concludes by placing reading and learning disorders in the broader context of society and lifelong development in Part IV.

### *The biology of reading*

The first section of the book works to define the phenomena of reading disorder by placing the brain bases of reading development into a broadly biological perspective, including neuroscience, evolution, and genetics. The second and third chapters focus especially on the biological constraints of species and genes that are built into the neuropsychological capacities recruited for reading. The Immordino-Yang and Deacon chapter lays out a nested model of reading-related skills for understanding the relations between genes, brain functions, and behaviors. It also cautions against the search for one-to-one correspondences between genes and complex cognitive pursuits like reading. In the essay embedded in the chapter, Caviness describes the newly emerging study of brain volume in living brains, because differences in brain volume play a prominent role in many neuroscientific models of learning disorders. The Galaburda and Sherman chapter makes a case for a genetic basis for dyslexia and outlines connections between genetically specified neurological abnormalities and low-level perceptual and cognitive deficits that are associated with the development of reading problems.

Taken together, these chapters present the state of the field on evolutionary and genetic research and provide tools with which to interpret new findings, but they purposely leave open the relation between top-down and bottom-up processes in the dyslexic profile – for example, the relations between attentional and phonological aspects. These relations have important implications for research on reading disorders, but sophisticated research and debate about analyzing developmental pathways and going beyond genetics alone is required to unpack the connections among higher- and lower-level processes involved in reading.

*Brain, development, and reading*

The second section of the book picks up the debate by working to define the various low- and high-level features of dyslexia and their relations to brain functions and developmental processes of reading and instruction. The authors provide perspectives on the history of neuroscientific and educational approaches and on important methods for analyzing the development of reading, examining existing models of reading disorder in terms of previous research and the latest findings with the new methods of cognitive neuroscience and development. The discussion centers on several key issues that cut to the core of the relation between etiology, phenotype, and development of reading disorders. These issues include reconciliation of neurological and behavioral aspects of dyslexia, analysis of variability in dyslexic profiles, and implications for the design of educational assessments and interventions.

Wolf and Ashby tackle these issues by focusing on analyses of "whole language" versus "phonological" approaches to reading instruction as well as processes of slow naming of visual stimuli in dyslexics. Case relates the study of learning disorders to the classical approaches to development and learning – empiricism, rationalism, and the sociohistorical approach – and shows how these approaches have illuminated processes behind disorders, the cognitive structures and stages involved in reading and disorders, and the cultural grounding of reading and disorders, respectively. For Fischer, Rose, and Rose, dynamic models provide a key to analyzing and supporting children's neurological and cognitive development within a common cyclic framework of brain and cognitive growth. In an essay embedded in the chapter, Thatcher describes evidence for growth cycles in neural networks in the brain.

Focusing on neuroscience, Paré-Blagoev discusses the contributions and potential of the new brain-imaging tool of fMRI in reading research. Through a historical analysis, Benes and Paré-Blagoev present neurological explanations for some of the heterogeneity of dyslexic profiles discussed by Wolf and Ashby, and they describe the connections between the written and oral language systems of the brain. Duffy uses the electroencephalogram (EEG) to analyze cortical connections in children with learning problems, showing reduced connectivity between certain regions of the brain, a finding that may well have implications for Thatcher's and Fischer's work, as well as for work on phonological aware-ness. In an embedded essay, Teicher discusses the relations between childhood maltreatment and brain functioning, which demonstrate dramatically how spe-cific experiences can reshape brain organization.

## Analyzing reading and related skills

In the third section of the book, theory is brought into practice, as neuro-psychologists and educators in turn present their assessments and understand-ings of four boys' reading and related behaviors. (Transcripts of the boys' testing sessions can be found in the Appendix.) While the chapters in the second section focus on the cognitive skills and brain processes relevant to reading, the chap-ters in this section work from the videos of four boys to define and debate how their skills actually present in real-life learning contexts. Bernstein provides a broad framework for neuropsychological analysis of learning differences and disorders in these and other children, underscoring the necessity of analyzing children's interactions and contexts as well as their performance on standardized measures. Brady suggests that better understanding of dyslexic children requires fuller analysis of the relations between written and oral language skills and of the fit between neuropsychological analyses and educational practices. Blach-man and Torgesen both discuss a need to better understand how different neuro-psychological skills manifest and interact in different educational contexts, with Blachman focusing on fluency of reading while Torgesen emphasizes the need to understand secondary deficits such as comprehension. Taylor emphasizes the relation between environmental and neurological influences, suggesting a bottom-up approach in which low-level cognitive weaknesses reveal a profile of core deficits with implications for education.

## Reading skills in life

In the final section of the book, the authors emphasize long-term trajectories for reading and learning problems, broad issues of reading in schools and society, and implications for educational practice. Theory and practice from neuro-psychology and education come together with a unique goal in mind – to bring life-span and societal issues to bear on the neuropsychological and educational debates about the nature and process of reading. Coming full circle back to Immordino-Yang and Deacon (Chapter 2), Campione emphasizes that in the search for the low-level neuropsychological causes of dyslexia, researchers and educators lose sight of the most immediate, important, high-level repercussions for children – reading comprehension problems and lack of access to printed ideas and information. Because this lack of access is a problem not only for true dyslexics but for any population of children with poor reading skills, future research should investigate the similarities and differences between dyslexics and other populations whose reading is poor, such as many poor urban and rural schoolchildren.

Fink describes another important group, people who have dyslexic difficulties but can nevertheless read and comprehend with great skill. She studied highly successful dyslexic adults who had difficulty learning to read in the early school years. Even with continuing difficulties with decoding words, many people become excellent readers, motivated by a passion for learning about topics that especially interest them. Such affective and strategic aspects of learning to read are certainly as important as decoding and are essential to successful compensation for dyslexic problems.

This emphasis on the diversity of reading problems and skills highlights difficulties with the term *learning disability*, which embodies some of the unfortunate consequences of society's practical use of a concept that can have precise meaning in scientific research. In this book, we editors have deliberately avoided using the term, choosing instead to speak of *learning disorder*. Learning disabilities are often assumed to involve a discrete and identifiable set of children, typically assessed by a measured gap between intelligence-test scores and learning performance. Political and legal ways of defining services for them are usually based more on practical concerns than scientific evidence (Snow *et al.*, 1998; Stuebing, Fletcher, LeDoux, Lyon, Shaywitz, & Shaywitz, 2002; Bernstein; Torgesen; Wolf & Ashby, this volume).

There has emerged a troubling disconnection between the scientific community and the educational gatekeepers, who must make the difficult decisions about allocation of finite resources to the most deserving children. Equally complicated is the implementation of legislative mandates such as the Americans with Disabilities Act. The scientific goal is to ascertain how to decide who does and does not merit this diagnosis, in a reliable and valid fashion, unconstrained by pragmatic limitations. Because of these real-world exigencies, diagnostic classifications are made routinely, with significant institutional consequences, even though scientists may be well aware of the tenuous nature of some of these decisions.

This conundrum must also affect the dialogue in this book: how are scientists and practitioners to discuss a diagnostic entity when they cannot reliably agree on what it is or who has it? The term *disorder* is invoked as an attempt to sidestep this issue, to call attention to the ambiguity, and to emphasize that at the present time it refers to a fuzzy set of individuals.

Building on the social problems and practical difficulties created by work on learning disabilities, David Rose warns us against overly constricting our research on reading to skills associated only with print, as we would surely be misrepresenting the problem and missing important opportunities to engage children with information in other formats. That is, reading skills are rarely the only set of skills that differentiate dyslexics; there are usually also social and physical correlates of dyslexia, as well as a characteristic set of relative strengths. In addition, overly focusing on remedial decoding would mean ignoring the affective and strategic aspects that, writes Fink, are often a major part of successful compensation.

## Conclusion: reading and learning disorders

To conclude, learning disorders must be viewed as a set of relatively subtle phenomena in a range of developmental neurobehavioral syndromes that include more dramatic disorders such as mental retardation, schizophrenia, and autism. Not only is a learning disorder subtle, but it engages social and affective considerations and debate to a far greater degree than the more dramatic, less subtle disorders, because the boundaries, definitions, and causes are less clear. With a view to helping clarify these edges, the book triangulates converging neuroscientific, cognitive, developmental, clinical, and educational perspectives on the study of learning disorders, focusing on reading. This triangulation helps to define the areas of inquiry and debate that are most current and likely to be most fruitful.

The book ranges far, from neuropsychological and educational analyses of specific cases of boys performing standardized assessment tasks of reading and related skills to cognitive scientists seeking relations between developmental processes and reading to neuroscientists describing how neural networks grow in cycles, how genetics and evolution shape reading, and how neuroanatomical development relates to brain functioning and learning experience. Within and between the main arguments, themes, and debates in the book, we hope to provide some insight into the question of why learning disorders have been so hard to pin down, why interdisciplinary discussions are so essential, and what the future holds for mind, brain, and education. We hope too that you will find your mind to be fertilized by new sets of questions and novel perspectives on learning disorders, and maybe even some productive perplexities. In our judgment, that will mark this book as a success.

## REFERENCES

Bailey, D. B., Jr., Bruer J. T., Symons, F. J. & Lichtman, J. W. (eds) (2001). *Critical thinking about critical periods*. Baltimore, MD: Paul H. Brookes Publishing.

Battro, A. (2000). *Half a brain is enough: The story of Nico*. Cambridge, UK: Cambridge University Press.

Bruer, J. T. (1997). Education and the brain: A bridge too far. *Educational Researcher*, 26, 4–16.

Bruer, J. T. (1999). In search of . . . brain-based education. *Phi Delta Kappan*, 180, 649–54.

*Educational Leadership* (1998). Special Issue: How the brain learns. 56(3: November).

Fischer, K. W., Ayoub, C. C., Noam, G. G., Singh, I., Maraganore, A. & Raya, P. (1997). Psychopathology as adaptive development along distinctive pathways. *Development and Psychopathology*, 9, 751–81.

Gage, F. H. (2003). Brain, repair yourself. *Scientific American*, 289(3), 47–53.

Gardner, H. (1983). *Frames of mind: The theory of multiple intelligences*. New York: Basic Books.

Geschwind, N. (1965). Disconnection syndrome in animals and man (Parts I, II). *Brain*, 88, 237–94, 585–644.

Huttenlocher, P. R. (2002). *Neural plasticity: The effects of environment on the development of the cerebral cortex*. Cambridge, MA: Harvard University Press.

Lyon, G. R. & Rumsey, J. M. (eds) (1996). *Neuroimaging: A window to the neurological foundations of learning and behavior in children*. Baltimore, MD: Paul H. Brookes Publishing Co.

Neville, H. J. & Bavelier, D. (1998). Neural organization and plasticity of language. *Current Opinion in Neurobiology*, 8, 245–8.

Neville, H. J. & Bruer, J. T. (2001). Language processing: How experience affects brain organization. In D. B. Bailey, Jr., J. T. Bruer, F. J. Symons & J. W. Lichtman (eds), *Critical thinking about critical periods*, 151–72. Baltimore, MD: Paul H. Brookes Publishing.

Newman, A. J., Bavelier, D., Corina, D., Jezzard, P. & Neville, H. J. (2001). A critical period for right hemisphere recruitment in American Sign Language processing. *Nature Neuroscience*, 5, 76–80.

Pennington, B. F. (2002). *The development of psychopathology: Nature and nurture*. New York: Guilford Press.

*Scientific American* (2003). Special Issue: Better brains: How neuroscience will enhance you. 289(3).

Shaywitz, S. E., Shaywitz, B. A., Fulbright, R. K., Skudlarski, P., Mencl, W. E., Constable, R. T., Pugh, K. R., Holahan, J. M., Marchione, K. E., Fletcher, J. M., Lyon, G. R. & Gore, J. C. (2003). Neural systems for compensation and persistence: Young adult outcome of childhood reading disability. *Biological Psychiatry*, 54, 25–33.

Shonkoff, J. P. & Phillips, D. A. (eds) (2000). *From neurons to neighborhoods: The science of early childhood development*. Washington, DC: National Academy Press.

Snow, C. E., Burns, M. S. & Griffin, P. (eds) (1998). *Preventing reading difficulties in young children*. Washington, DC: National Academy Press.

Stuebing, K. K., Fletcher, J. M., LeDoux, J. M., Lyon, G. R., Shaywitz, S. E. & Shaywitz, B. A. (2002). Validity of IQ-discrepancy classifications of reading disabilities: A meta-analysis. *American Educational Research Journal*, 39(2), 469–518.

Sur, M., Angelucci, A. & Sharma, J. (1999). Rewiring cortex: The role of patterned activity in development and plasticity of neocortical circuits. *Journal of Neurobiology*, 41, 33–43.

Teuber, H.-L. & Rudel, R. G. (1962). Behavior after cerebral lesions in children and adults. *Developmental Medicine & Child Neurology*, 4, 3–20.

Thatcher, R., Lyon, G. R., Rumsey, J. & Krasnegor, N. (eds) (1996). *Developmental neuroimaging: Mapping the development of brain and behavior*. New York: Academic Press.

# 2    An evolutionary perspective on reading and reading disorders

## *Mary Helen Immordino-Yang\* and Terrence W. Deacon*

*Overview:* An evolutionary perspective on reading can contribute to understanding dyslexia and other learning disorders. Human beings evolved speech over many thousands of years, but writing and reading are recent inventions, only a few thousand years old. People perform reading by a kludge of processes that evolved for other purposes, with wide variation in component processes across people and languages. Research on brain anatomy and function shows strong localization of spoken language functions, but an evolutionary approach suggests that localization will be much more variable for reading. Also, children process language across many more brain regions than do adults, suggesting that dyslexia in children may involve more brain systems as well. Processes involved in reading vary from lower-level, modality-specific processes such as vision and hearing, to mid-level linguistic processes, to higher-level processes of memory and attention. Spoken language involves a tighter integration across levels than does reading, and reading requires a greater contribution from higher-level processes because of its recent origin. One tool for investigating how these processes develop and function is analysis of brain volume in living humans by the use of modern brain-imaging tools, discussed by Verne Caviness in an essay for this chapter.    *The Editors*

In a time when learning styles, individual differences, variation in development, and separate intelligences are coming to the fore in education (Fischer & Bidell, 1998; Fischer, Rose, & Rose, this volume; Gardner, 1983; D. Rose, this volume; Rose & Meyer, 2002), practitioners and researchers are looking to explain the cognitive and neuropsychological processes that underlie scholastic achievement. To this end, it is increasingly important not only to study the observable behaviors associated with scholastic skills, but to consider these skills as deriving from systems of neuropsychological capacities with evolutionary histories and constraints (Christiansen & Kirby, 2003). In particular, basic literacy competence is fundamental to scholastic success, yet a significant percentage of

\* The first author's work was supported by a Research Training Grant from the Spencer Foundation.

children, despite sufficient general intelligence, do not attain this goal. How can thinking about reading as a task recruiting various evolutionarily derived neural systems help to shed light on this problem?

This essay attempts to outline some consequences and predictions of taking an evolutionary perspective on developmental dyslexia. Though perhaps far more theoretical and speculative than empirical or prescriptive, these remarks may help to focus attention on aspects of the problem that have been given less attention than warranted. In bringing an evolutionary perspective to bear on a localization tradition of research, we aim to bring some of the diversity of findings and explanations into a more unified view, as well as to suggest future areas of research.

## Evolution and the history of reading

Reading is a complex skill, and unlike spoken language, it is a skill for which there is no evolutionary background. The earliest conventional written symbols date from about 3500 BC, long after the evolution of anatomically modern Homo sapiens, who appeared about 200,000 years ago, and of oral language, which probably gradually evolved over as much as 2.5 million years. The evolutionary "maturity" of our faculty for spoken language is reflected in our numerous human specializations for vocal-oral and syntactic processing, by the integration of diverse language adaptations (e.g. vocal tract changes, discourse predispositions), and by the marvelously predictable and robust nature of language acquisition (Deacon, 1997, 2003, 2004; Hauser, Chomsky, & Fitch, 2002).

In contrast, phonologically based reading is totally immature in an evolutionary sense. Though various logographic (i.e. partially or wholly iconic) systems of representation have been discovered independently by different peoples around the world, the only known discovery/ invention of the alphabetic principle was in Greece, around 1000 BC (for a concise overview see Crystal, 1997; see also Wolf & Ashby, this volume). Thus, the alphabetic principle is a recently available tool and not a built-in organic function of the brain. As a result, reading in an alphabetic system is not an intuitive task, nor is it an automatic extension of spoken language. It does not develop spontaneously, and without explicit instruction it will not develop at all. Most importantly for this discussion, unlike oral language competence, literacy competence is exceedingly variable from individual to individual and full literacy may remain unachievable for a significant fraction of the otherwise normal population (worldwide estimates hover just below 10 percent), despite educational support.

It is not clear why written forms of communication only appeared at the very most recent end of human evolution, when it is likely that our oral language capacity is so old. Perhaps, as today, the recording of specific speech acts was never of sufficient reproductive consequence for most hunter-gatherer or primitive agricultural peoples. Whatever the reason, the non-organic status of written communication underscores the fact that searching for biological bases for reading competence or for dyslexia is unlike looking for the cause of organic disorders, such as congenital blindness or diabetes, in a number of important respects. For one, we know of no genes that code for reading or writing alone, and we should not expect to find any (see Galaburda & Sherman, this volume). The neural systems recruited for these skills and the genes that produce these systems almost certainly have homologues, or corresponding genes, in most primates and probably in most mammals (Deacon, 2004). If we do happen to find genes that are correlated with developmental dyslexia or agraphia (writing disorder), the chances are great that those genes will not even be unique to humans, much less unique to reading and writing. Secondly and more importantly, because reading is not a unitary biological function, shaped and organized by natural selection into a unified system, it is also not likely that there will be any unitary underlying biological cause for dyslexic syndromes. Instead, we should anticipate that although some congenital neural defects may interfere more seriously than others with the acquisition of this skill, there will be an array of potential contributors to reading disability that have cumulative or interactive effects of varying severity on susceptibility to dyslexia. This suggests that many possible inherited disturbances could interrupt literacy acquisition because such a post hoc collaboration of brain systems is likely to be more vulnerable to a wider range of disturbances: genetic, developmental, and even experiential.

So from an evolutionary perspective, one implication of this post-evolutionary status of literacy is that any reductionist effort to approach dyslexia as a simple genetic disorder will likely oversimplify the problem. In a biological context, developmental dyslexia is not a biological abnormality; instead, it is a class of special conditions within the normal variation – an unlucky coincidence of traits, only some of which would otherwise be deleterious. Taken together, these traits may affect the development of reading preferentially simply because of the biological fragility of this skill. Like the canary in the mine, reading may be more sensitive to minor insults than other cognitive and sensorimotor skills.

Another implication of the evolutionary perspective is that there will be no necessarily "natural" course of literacy development common to all children. In other words, even if it is the case that there is a modal age in which children can begin to acquire certain reading skills, this is not because of a developmental bioprogram with respect to reading, but rather because reading must piggyback on other capacities developing for other reasons according to their own schedules. Indeed, given the biologically ad hoc nature of this behavioral capacity, diverse developmental trajectories might be expected for the development of reading (Fischer & Immordino-Yang, 2002).

This leads to a further caution: dyslexia expressed in adults, or acquired due to insult in adulthood, may not provide a firm basis for retrospective deduction about the organization of reading skills in children's brains. Lacking developmental "canalization," reading skill may develop along diverse trajectories and still converge upon similar endpoints in adult brain organization (Fischer & Bidell, 1998; Fischer, Rose, & Rose, this volume). Children's brains are less differentiated, less efficient at certain tasks, and in transition toward mature anatomical development. Neural mechanisms critical for a well-learned reading competence in adults may not be available in immature brains, and the process of initially acquiring this skill may itself transiently depend on systems not critical for the mature capacity. In addition, there may be shifts in the dependence of this skill on specific brain systems during development. Though localization data from adults with acquired and developmental dyslexia offer essential clues to brain areas important for reading in adults, these data are likely to underrepresent the essential systems developmentally. Alternatively, we suggest that in order to apply such data retrospectively to children, we need first to determine if there is any change of distribution of functions from young novice to adult expert reader, as well as to elucidate the nature of this proposed developmental reorganization.

## The localization perspective

Modern neuropsychology has succeeded in giving us confidence that brain function is comprehensible in large part because it has provided extensive evidence that the brain can be analyzed into parts that contribute discrete sub-functions for perceptual, motor, and mnemonic processes of the whole. The assumption that the substrates for functions such as color discrimination or verbal short-term memory are "located" in a center or circuit in the brain, and that these centers or circuits are similarly located across most individuals' brains, has been the basis for extraordinary advancements in the neurosciences and neurology. But does it make sense to search for the reading center or centers in the brain? This enterprise has been on the whole quite successful, even if – unlike color discrimination and other functions – reading cannot be treated as an evolved function for which the brain's architecture was designed. Obviously, every function that is dependent on the working brain must be performed by a structure located in the brain, and the brain is not homogeneous nor are functions so deeply distributed that they do not have local correlates (Lieberman, 2002). Every activity of a brain has some locus or loci. The question is whether reading uses many structures diversely or just a few focal regions.

### Evidence of brain problems or disconnection

In the late nineteenth century, aphasiologists suggested that reading abilities might be localized in the brain with respect to the connections between the component functional centers involved, e.g. vision and audition. They reasoned that acquired reading problems might be the result of an interruption in the neurological pathways connecting occipital and left superior temporal cortical areas. In a classic case, Dejerine (1891) described a patient with what he termed "pure word blindness without agraphia." This patient presented with an inability to read despite apparently intact speech. On autopsy, the patient's brain demonstrated posterior corpus collosal and left parietal damage. Dejerine explained the patient's symptoms in terms of disconnection between visual areas and language areas, arguing that neither eye could send visual information to the left hemisphere Wernicke's area for language. This approach did not posit a reading center per se, but did predict that communications between centers for more basic functions would be essential for reading to be possible.

Modern neuroanatomical research efforts to understand dyslexia along similar lines, such as the work of Geschwind (Geschwind, 1982, 1983, 1984) and Galaburda (Galaburda & Livingstone, 1993; Galaburda & Sherman, this volume), built on the work of these nineteenth-century aphasiologists. They suggested that dyslexia in children, like acquired alexia in adults from brain damage, might also be the result of disconnection between, or discrete damage to, parts of the brain devoted to the component visual and auditory analysis centers of the cerebral cortex. In one of the pioneering studies of anatomical correlates to developmental dyslexia, Galaburda and Kemper (1979) found that at autopsy the brains of people with lifetime dyslexia had apparently congenital abnormalities of the cerebral cortex that were located in critical language-specialized areas as well as intermodal areas. This finding implied that inherited difficulties with reading might be traceable to congenital variants of organization of cortical cells in regions that correlate with adult acquired aphasia and alexia.

In a similar vein, following initial work by Galaburda and colleagues (see Galaburda, Rosen, & Sherman, 1990; Galaburda, 1995), a number of studies found associations between dyslexia and extensive asymmetries in the superior temporal cortex, suggesting that abnormal lateralization might also be a risk factor for dyslexia (e.g. Kushch *et al.*, 1993; Rumsey *et al.*, 1997). What exactly such atypical asymmetries of surface areas and volumes of these brain areas on the two sides of dyslexic brains would contribute is less obvious than for the case of cytoarchitectural anomalies, and studies failing to replicate these results have left these correlations uncertain (but see discussion by Schultz *et al.*, 1994). More recently, studies of size of cortical components (morphometry) have also included analyses of global cortical organization and development. Case studies have widened the range of structures implicated in dyslexia, extending to differences in frontal versus posterior cortical growth, and particularly differences involving the growth of the insula (Benes & Paré-Blagoev, this volume; Pennington *et al.*, 1999).

One common feature shared by these localization findings is that most have been focused on cortical areas specialized for language. Yet dyslexia often occurs in the absence of expression or comprehension problems involving speech. Reading difficulties secondary to language difficulties are not considered primary reading deficits, and may be more easily correlated with anatomical abnormality and damage. In fact, left hemisphere damage in the early stages of reading acquisition (i.e. middle childhood) does tend to lead to difficulties in learning to read, but recent research suggests that such reading difficulties may be a consequence of secondary linguistic or cognitive deficits rather than of an isolated reading problem per se (Pitchford, 2000).

## Differences between children and adults

Research makes it increasingly clear that the cortical areas we associate with *adult* language functions are not necessarily the areas responsible for oral language processing in *children*. Rather than being localized from the beginning, early oral language seems to be much more globally distributed in the brains of children than in adults (see review by Bates, 1992). Focal brain injury in infants in the early stages of language learning leads to patterns of disruption of language learning that are distinct from brain damage associated with language processing problems in adults. In particular, both left and right hemisphere damage can lead to significant language delays in infants, with no obvious effect of lesion size (Marchman, Miller, & Bates, 1991). What is more, in infants language comprehension deficits are associated with right hemisphere injury, not with injury to Wernicke's area in the left hemisphere (Wulfeck *et al.*, 1991), while the severity of expressive deficits is linked to left posterior injury rather than injury to Broca's area in the left temporal lobe (Thal *et al.*, 1991).

Children also tend to show more plasticity than adults in response to brain damage (Aram, 1999; Huttenlocher, 2002; Satz *et al.*, 1990). In extreme cases of early brain damage, either hemisphere can develop language function, with the extent of language being determined by the extent of compensation by the non-damaged hemisphere (Mills *et al.*, 1994; Vicari *et al.*, 2000). In one extreme case, an adolescent boy who underwent a complete left functional hemispherectomy at age eleven temporarily lost but later recovered close to normal language function (Immordino-Yang, 2004). In addition, children with early focal lesions often do not show long-term impairment of reading or oral language (Aram, Gillespie, & Yamashita, 1990), suggesting that the compensatory brain reorganization to support oral language resulted in a system that could later support reading as well. In all, such evidence suggests that early reading skill is not localized or fixed in children to nearly the extent that it appears to be in adults. This evidence gives cause to question the direct applicability of adult localization findings to the study of reading disorders in children.

Localization logic also suggests that, aside from issues around primary language deficits and localization, disturbances of basic auditory and visual centers and their interconnections should be relevant. It goes without saying that blindness or inability to analyze word sounds would directly block reading, as would inability to associate visual information with phonological information. Therefore, secondary limitations in using these modalities can be expected to contribute severe impediments as well.

Although this relation clearly holds with adult brain damage, there is a question about how it applies to young brains and to a skill that seems to involve the contributions of many more systems in children than in adults. Analysis requires paying attention to developmental patterns of reorganization and specialization, such as the dynamic redistribution of function that may occur as part of the learning process in children. One possibility is greater plasticity in children. Another is that these basic systems are relatively impervious to neural work-arounds or individual developmental compensations via neural plasticity, because they involve specialized modalities and are relatively mature by the time children begin to encounter written material in school. Thus, modality-specific processing weaknesses may either constitute a limit to the level of automatization possible or else provide only a degraded signal for higher-order processors. These linked questions of developmental change and neural commitment are important to understanding the neurobiology of reading difficulties and may provide windows into intervention approaches not obvious from localization logic (Deacon, 2000). As mentioned above, we cannot ignore developmental patterns of reorganization and specialization, or the dynamic redistribution of function that likely occurs as part of the learning process. Assuming that the component functions involved in reading are equivalently organized in adults' and children's brains may lead us to miss important factors.

In addition, the reading task itself may be very different during learning and afterwards. Because beginning readers are struggling to pick out and process the relevant cues involved in reading, the task for them likely recruits a widely distributed set of diverse functional systems. They must rely heavily on attentional and mnemonic strategies to sort out ambiguities and manage alternative ways of processing what they read. As they mature and gain reading skill and experience, the burden can shift from effortful higher-order and global processes to automated processes carried out in more specialized areas. This presents yet another reason to expect global functioning to be more critical in early reading acquisition, with specialized processing becoming more prominent later.

In fact, such a suggestion parallels evidence from adult skill learning. For instance, there is some evidence from electrical stimulation work in adult neurosurgery patients that brain functions in language and reading become localized as literary proficiency develops. Specifically, patients with low verbal IQ and relatively poor reading skills tend to show stimulation-induced reading disruption in a wider range of brain locations than do high verbal IQ patients (Ojemann, 1979, 1991). Such findings imply that with the development of reading fluency, the functions involved in reading might become progressively more localized, only reaching mature patterns late in the development of reading skill.

Also relevant is evidence from adults that the brain regions used to initially acquire new skills are often not the most active when the same skill becomes thoroughly mastered (for example, with a word-association task studied by Raichle et al., 1994). That is, tasks that are difficult because they are novel at first produce stronger, more global activation of cerebral cortex, and later produce weaker, more localized, and more subcortically prominent activations as the tasks become more familiar and less effortful.

But while evidence for a global to local processing shift is fairly well understood in skill automation learning in adults, this process is not yet well documented in children. It seems clear that for reading to become efficient, the component tasks involved must be sufficiently automated. Future research in this area could provide insight into the role of automation of processing in normal and dyslexic reading acquisition. For example, there is evidence that the cerebellum may be involved in the cross-neuron summing that enables automatization and hence localization with multiple encounters with a particular task, and dyslexic children have been demonstrated to show cerebellar weaknesses (Fawcett et al., 1996; Fawcett & Nicolson, 1999). However, the role of the cerebellum in automation of reading skill has not been well documented as yet. In dyslexics, cerebellar dysfunction appears mainly to have been studied in the context of motor learning and sequencing problems.

Another source of disruption in the automation process could stem from abnormalities of the magnocellular layer subdivision of the visual system, as described by Galaburda and Livingstone (1993). Galaburda suggests that this primary neurological deficit is a main anatomical locus of difficulties in dyslexia, which is also consistent with a related correlate that has been systematically investigated by Tallal and colleagues with respect to timing and rate of information processing (see review in Tallal et al., 1998; also Wolf & Ashby, this volume). Such processing deficits could impede the ability to automate low-level visual processing, forcing the reader to maintain effortful visual attention in order to actively compensate for the processing weakness. Automation of low-level perceptual processing is important for fluent reading, so that high-level attentional processing can be devoted to semantic and strategic functions (Wolf & Katzir-Cohen, 2001).

In sum, while the localization argument has provided a fruitful initial approach to analyzing brain correlates of dyslexia, it can be misleading to use data from adults with acquired or developmental dyslexia to simply reverse engineer predictions about children's brains. Adults with acquired neurological conditions affecting reading have completed their primary learning of language

and reading, yet it may be in large part the learning process that primarily orga-
nizes the brain into the functional modules found in adults. If the representation
of function changes significantly during development, as we suggest it does,
then applying adult data to children requires first understanding the change of
distribution of function. Analyzing the problem of reading acquisition through
a lens focusing on the evolutionary histories of the brain systems may be a
useful way of interpreting the meaning and application of localization findings
for children.

### Integrating evolutionary perspectives

Because people have no evolutionary specializations that are reading specific,
learning to read means recruiting and organizing diverse brain systems to
function in specialized capacities uncharacteristic of their evolutionary design
(Deacon, 1997). In this way, reading is a "kludge," a clumsy work-around system consisting of components designed for other tasks. The systems we use to
process and produce written language could be considered the neuropsychological equivalents to Rube Goldberg machines in that they combine various
components designed for other tasks into one fragile, complex system. The
combinatorial nature of this system means greater variance in the ways people
process written than oral language as well as a tendency toward idiosyncrasy.
This produces a continuum of reading abilities that reflects the variation in
individuals' cognitive profiles. Add to this existing variation the possibility
of inherited disturbances in any component of the system, and the potential
for reading problems grows exponentially. Certain combinations of genes may
produce reading difficulties because, in a combinatorial system, even small,
localized disturbances can result in interaction effects that impair the functioning of the system as a whole.

Due to its combinatorial nature, reading is a complex and changing activity
in which the workload must be dynamically distributed between systems of different levels. This complexity means that certain reading difficulties can derive
from high-level processes, such as a specific linguistic processing problem
or high-level attentional or mnemonic dysfunction. Other reading difficulties
could arise from sensory processing problems, including attentional problems
in scanning, problems with short-term memory for visual information, or basic
perceptual problems registering the shapes or relative positions of letters. However, the term "dyslexia" does not distinguish between these different levels of
disability. To account for these diverse sources of disability and to describe their
respective impact on the functioning of the reading system, we suggest thinking
of reading competence and dyslexia in terms of a nested model that takes into
account evolutionary and systemic considerations in addition to level-specific
processing problems (Figure 2.1).

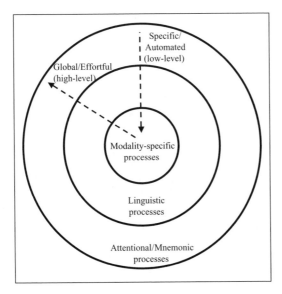

Figure 2.1 A nested model of dyslexia. In this model, low-level, modality-specific processing is nested within linguistic processing, which is in turn nested within high-level, attentional, and mnemonic processing. Processing problems originating in the center circles will result in the burden being passed up to the next intact level. High-level processing problems, on the other hand, will cause the entire system to appear disorganized and dysfunctional.

In a nested model of reading, the process of learning to read requires the person to successfully automate lower-order skills and integrate or "nest" them into higher-order ones as subroutines. Modality-specific processing, such as visual or auditory, is considered the lowest level and under normal circumstances the most automated. Alternatively, the most global processing systems, those associated with high-level mnemonic and attentional processes, are considered the highest level and least automated. These systems function to organize and direct the lower-level systems, as well as to evaluate and assign meaning and context to the text. Language-specific factors, such as phonological and syntactic analysis, fall at an intermediate level, which includes processing that is usually automated but can be brought to conscious attention in certain circumstances, such as learning new words or parsing the speech of a dysfluent foreigner.

This model leads us to ask, how do other components compensate when there is a neuropsychological disturbance somewhere in the kludged system that decodes and recodes written text? For the kludge to function with a weak link, the workload must be redistributed among the other nested constituents of the system, depleting their processing resources. We see this redistribution as occurring according to two organizing principles that follow from a developmental and evolutionary logic. First, in general, the more automated the processing the fewer attentional resources it should require (arrow pointing inward in Figure 2.1), and the more conscious the processing the more attentional resources it should require (arrow pointing outward). Because lower-level, modality-specific processes would tend to be the most automated, while higher-level processes would tend to be the most conscious and effortful, the more modality-specific the cause of reading difficulty, the easier it may be to naturally develop (or train) a work-around that allows at least some level of reading competence. On the other hand, the more global the underlying problem (e.g. working memory, sequence analysis, automatization, etc.), the more difficult it may be to surmount the initial stages of learning to read, thus blocking access to many possible alternative strategies.

Second, the model is hierarchical in that lower-level disturbances will result in the burden of processing being passed up to the next level, where the task becomes more effortful. Since there is a limit on higher-level processing resources, this shift from largely automatic to more conscious processing will bog down the higher-level systems by depleting attentional resources. The more significant the dysfunction in automated processing, the more high-level resources will be devoted to compensating for lower-level analysis. This characteristic hampers or, in serious cases, prevents higher-level processing, such as interpreting the meaning or context of the written passage. Conversely, higher-level deficits will result in failure to regulate the relations between lower-order automated functions.

In this way, children with lower-level reading problems, such as problems of visual processing, may place more workload on phonological analysis by having to read aloud. That is, these children will be forced to reconstruct through linguistic means what the visual system did not fully process. Likewise, problems with automated linguistic processing will cause the task to be passed up to the attentional system. As processes that should be automated become increasingly effortful and conscious, fewer attentional resources will be left for meaningful interpretation or expression of ideas, and the phonological and linguistic aspects of reading will become an effortful chore that is increasingly devoid of ideological content. Analogous problems would be apparent as well in such children's writing, as the effort involved in retrieving orthographic representations of phonemes could overwhelm the executive functions to the point that the child could no longer hold in mind the content they wished to express. In addition, should there be disturbances at the attentional/mnemonic level, the system will not be well organized, leading to repercussions ranging from problems with comprehending and expressing meaning to problems recruiting and directing even intact lower-level, automated processes. Thus, just as the components of the reading process are hierarchically nested, early successes and failures involving these components are nested in that later reading experiences build on earlier ones.

The above scenarios underscore the crucial role of high-order attentional processes in learning to read. Because reading is a multi-modal skill, involving multiple sensory modalities and visuo-motor skills, precise control of attention is critical to recruit and manage the diverse functions needed to become skillful. Coordinating the visual flow of incoming text with the auditory processing of the words it represents, while keeping the special demands of each from interfering with the other, requires considerable attentional resources. In addition, a fluent reader must maintain visual attention in a linear cycle to follow the stacked lines of text, while systematically attending to relevant and passing over irrelevant features in the orthographic flow. If attentional systems are bogged down with the burden of compensating for lower-level processing, meaningful reading will be exceedingly hard to accomplish. Likewise, if the attentional system itself is weak, it will be compromised in its ability to perform the unifying, organizing, and evaluative functions necessary to organize and regulate the components of the system.

In fact, one reason why normal children do not generally begin to read until the age of five or six may be that attentional and mnemonic capacities are not sufficiently developed until then. It is interesting to note that many dyslexic children overcome their reading fluency problems as adolescents (Fink, 1993, this volume), when a maturational spurt in executive functions may provide the additional attentional resources needed to compensate for such lower processing problems (Case, 1991; Fischer, 1980; Fischer, Rose, & Rose, this volume). This time lag between learning to speak and learning to read has another consequence that we hinted at earlier: literacy skill is generally parasitic on oral language abilities.

Despite attentional considerations, there are certain cases, notably hyperlexia, in which the developmental dependency between oral and written language is not so asymmetric. That is, some children may acquire phonological decoding skills of text at an unusually young age (Rispens & Van Berckelaer, 1991). However, these children's reading shows an apparent disjunction between phonology and semantics, in which poor comprehension and abstract thought are coupled with exaggeratedly good and sometimes compulsive phonological decoding of text (Aram, 1997). Thus, while hyperlexic children may be able to read aloud proficiently, they are less adept at relating this skill to the oral language and narrative skills that they should be developing (Nation, 1999). This pattern suggests that without sufficient attentional resources, the only way to read may be to focus exclusively on one narrow aspect of the task, i.e. translating the written word into spoken sound. True reading, reading for comprehension, requires the coordination of several nested levels of processing, not just phonological decoding of text.

## Conclusion: implications for practice

Thinking about dyslexia from an evolutionary and neural systems standpoint contributes two potentially useful insights, not always considered.

First: textual codes are recent technologies lacking in specific evolutionary support. This means that the brain systems that are recruited to analyze them are kludges and should be expected to exhibit considerable individual variation. The message for practice is that we should not expect there to be one central disorder underlying all forms of dyslexia, nor should we expect to find one successful therapeutic approach. Moreover, reading skills are parasitic on neural adaptations for spoken language, which are themselves comparatively recent and unprecedented modifications on a much older basic mammalian and primate brain plan. The historical recency of reading suggests that diagnostic and therapeutic approaches that carve the problem according to an evolutionary-anatomical logic are likely to be more effective than those based exclusively on either a linguistic or general learning theory paradigm.

Second: the kludginess of reading skill also means that its neural supports are more diversely distributed within the brain and involve many loosely linked systems. This diversity of components makes it more dependent than other more evolutionarily entrenched functions on attentional and working memory systems for coordinating and integrating the component sub-functions. Thus, reading may be particularly susceptible to disturbances at higher levels of general processing even while it is also subject to problems from lower-level processes (such as visual, auditory, or even language-specific processing).

The nested model of dyslexia has several implications for diagnosing and teaching dyslexic children. It suggests that rather than studying reading behavior linguistically, or even from the perspective of the requisite sensory integration, we need to assess the components of the system hierarchically from the top down, and from early to late in the learning process. Apparent problems with visual recognition or coding transfer between modalities may be strongly influenced by automation or working memory. Even an intact low-level process will appear disorganized and ineffectual without the attentional system selectively regulating its operation and its integration with other component processes.

With regard to possible genetic factors in dyslexia, inherited global attentional problems will be likely to consistently cause reading difficulties, whereas lower-level disturbances may or may not have repercussions for reading in a particular generation or individual, because distributive neural work-arounds will be possible. In general, given the inevitably distributed multi-system nature of reading processes, serious, persistent deficits will typically involve multiple system impairments at multiple levels, which complicates the analysis of inherited risk factors. Multi-level and multi-system disturbances undermine the possibility of redistributing functional load, which would allow more robust systems to compensate for more fragile ones. Again, this consideration suggests that multiple modalities of therapy, not a single technique, may be essential for successful intervention in cases of severe dyslexia.

In conclusion, from an evolutionary perspective, it is not dyslexia that stands out as deviant, but rather reading ability itself. Given the lack of evolutionary adaptations for reading combined with the serendipitous origins of this technology, it is in many ways a miracle that reading is possible at all, much less with the automatic ease that many readers develop. Perhaps part of the credit for the surprising success of most people at acquiring this skill lies in the social evolution of textual coding systems themselves, many of which have undergone a considerable change toward "user-friendliness." The gradual replacement of many early logographic and incompletely coded phonetic systems with systems that sacrifice content representation for mere speech representation has better enabled the already evolutionarily streamlined oral language adaptations to carry more of the analytic load involved in reading. Nonetheless, the study of dyslexia should be expected to show wide variation in the timing and patterns of acquisition of reading skill. We should look to this variation to teach us about the logic of the developmental organization of language functions more generally and of reading more specifically in the young child's brain and mind.

# Essay: Brain volume and the acquisition of adaptive capacities

*Verne S. Caviness*

*Connection:* Brain, language, and other human capacities develop in patterns shaped by both evolution and culturally defined experiences, including language and literacy. New tools for characterizing brain development provide means for analyzing development of different brain regions in relation to abilities such as speech and reading. Many classical neural imaging techniques assess the volume of particular brain regions in brains of people who have died, but newer techniques, such as magnetic resonance imaging, assess volume in brains of living people. Because volumes of different brain tissues change in diverse ways when people die, the new techniques provide the first good data on brain volume of living brains. Many hypotheses about learning disorders involve differences in size of specific areas of brain tissue, such as regions for phonological analysis in many dyslexic children (Galaburda & Sherman; Paré-Blagoev; Benes & Paré-Blagoev, this volume). With data on volume in living brains being so recent, the principles relating brain volume to development, learning, and evolution remain to be determined. Evidence has already shown that different people show different volumes for the same brain areas, and that areas which share functioning seem to covary in their volume, even when they are in widely separated brain regions.

*The Editors*

There appear to be powerful constraints selected through evolution that act to set the total volume of neocortex to a narrow species-specific value (Filipek *et al.*, 1994; Caviness *et al.*, 1999). Within these constraints other mechanisms, operating through individual experience, adaptively modulate the volumes of specific brain regions. In particular, such adaptive mechanisms must operate to modulate the volume of cortical structures that support the development of cognition, memory, and language, including reading, as well as other functions for which the cortex is indispensable.

### Individual variation in brain volume

This general perspective arises from the more fundamental thesis that volume reflects basic properties of brain tissue. In support of this thesis, on the evolutionary scale, there are regular principles that relate the volume of brain, or a component of the brain, to the body plan and mean size of animals for a given species. The implementing and constraining processes of development within species work to minimize individual variation in volume of the brain and certain of its principal structures, for example the volume of total cortex. Yet more elementary components of principal structures may be greatly variable from individual to individual.

By illustration, in an earlier study we found the coefficient of variation of the mean volume of cortex to be less than 10% for a set of normal young adults with equal male and female representation (Kennedy *et al.*, 1998). In contrast, the mean coefficient of variation of cortex surmounting the standard gyri (prominent folds or ridges on the surface of the cortex) of the normal brain was well over 20% and greatly variable across the full set of gyri. From this analysis we proposed a computational model that identifies a non-linear factor, interactive between individual person and specific gyrus, as the determinant of approximately 70% of this variance. In other words, this huge factor involves individual variation in size of cortical regions. One part of this variance is a difference between males and females, but it is small in magnitude, estimated as the source of less than 1% of gyral volume variance. Most of the variance is across individuals independent of gender.

The determinants of variance in volume are potentially of critical significance for all early learned, adaptive capacities. The fact that volume variance shows so much variability across individuals agrees with and may even be predictable from other types of investigations. Particularly relevant are observations indicating that the volumes of specific areas of cortex involved in highly overlearned motor skills and acoustic capacities are significantly larger than the volumes in individuals without such experience or skills. Specifically, the primary motor cortex of keyboard artists (Amunts *et al.*, 1997) and the acoustic cortex of the temporal plane of musicians with pure pitch (Zatorre *et al.*, 1998), both trained from early childhood, are large relative to the corresponding areas in the general population.

In like manner, highly repetitive and augmented activities associated with "enriched environments" in experimental animals are associated with increased volume of cortex and other cerebral structures (Diamond, 2001; Huttenlocher, 2002; Uylings *et al.*, 1978). In experimental animals the increased volume has been correlated with overall enlargement of neurons, both their cell bodies, dendritic arborizations, and increase in dendritic spines. Presumably, changes in volume in human neocortex also occur at this level of cellular components. These are the cellular foundations of the relative enlargement of a component of the neural system – the specific gyrus in the cortex interacting with individual experience.

## Volume of related parts of neural systems

The structure-by-structure view of the brain, including the gyrus-by-gyrus view of the cortex, obviously ignores the larger context of neural systems organization. For example, it takes much more, structure-wise, than primary motor cortex or primary acoustic cortex to provide neural support for excellence in keyboard or other musical skills. These aptitudes reflect the coordinated operation of a neural system distributed to all levels of the central nervous system (Mesulam, 1990, 1998), as well as the coordinated operation of this system with other systems and the linking of associative mechanisms that dominate the landscape of forebrain structure. One reasonably inquires, "What about the other processing outposts of the primary system?" or "What about the intervening and linking associative processors?" Moreover, one may well wonder, "Which structures pay the costs of enlargement of cortical fields driven by experience, such as enlargement of motor or acoustic fields?" If total cortical volume is closely constrained, enlargement of one field or a system of fields will lead to reduction in the volume of other fields. What are the implications of these relations for functioning of brain and behavior?

Much more observation is needed in order to support and develop theory about brain volume and its relation to skill and learning. Already in hand, however, is the observation that morphometry (measurement of volumes or areas of the nervous system) of the mainline structures of the human visual system, including optic tract, lateral geniculate, and primary visual cortex, covary strongly, with Pearson correlation coefficients approaching 0.8 (Andrews *et al.*, 1997): the size of one part of the neural structure for vision in one person strongly predicts the sizes of the other parts in that person. The same kind of correlation seems to hold for many brain structures. The variance does not relate much to total brain volume. Raw volumes of larger brain structures do vary more on average than smaller structures, but this relation virtually disappears when volumes are placed on the natural logarithmic scale. Within the brain itself we have found through principal-component analysis and through simple pair-wise correlations that associatively linked structures and systems covary (some positive, some negative in sign) at both cortical and subcortical (striatal and thalamic) levels (Caviness *et al.*, 1999).

A more specific thesis arises from these observations, plausible yet requiring substantially more inquiry: structures in a neural system seem to have related sizes, but the specific correlations (volumetric covariance) vary as a function of the exclusiveness of the linkage and the distance between synapses (Friston, 1998; Mesulam, 1998). Such volumetric covariance becomes a parameter by which to explore the previously uncharted relationships among diverse and widely distributed brain regions. These explorations naturally arise from functional and structural magnetic resonance imaging and provide a valuable tool for analyzing human capacities and disorders. Research on brain bases of learning disorders will benefit from analyzing these relations of size among parts of the brain systems involved in relevant abilities, such as speech and reading systems for reading disorders.

## REFERENCES

Amunts, K., Schlaug, G., Jaencke, L., Steinmetz, H., Schleicher, A., Dabringhaus, A. & Zilles, K. (1997). Motor cortex and hand motor skills: Structural compliance in the human brain. *Human Brain Mapping*, 5, 206–215.

Andrews, T., Halpern, S. & Purves, D. (1997). Correlated size variations in human visual cortex, lateral geniculate nucleus, and optic tract. *Journal of Neuroscience*, 17, 2859–68.

Aram, D. M. (1997). Hyperlexia: Reading without meaning in young children. *Topics in Language Disorders,* 17(3), 1–13.

Aram, D. M. (1999). Neuroplasticity: Evidence from unilateral brain lesions in children. In S. Browman & J. Fletcher (eds), *The changing nervous system: Neurobehavioral consequences of early brain disorders*, 254–73. New York: Oxford University Press.

Aram, D. M., Gillespie, L. L. & Yamashita, T. S. (1990). Reading among children with left and right brain lesions. *Developmental Neuropsychology*, 6(4), 301–317.

Bates, E. (1992). Language development. *Current Opinion in Neurobiology*, 2, 180–85.

Case, R. (ed.) (1991). *The mind's staircase: Exploring the conceptual underpinnings of children's thought and knowledge.* Hillsdale: Erlbaum.

Caviness, V., Lange, N., Makris, M., Herbert, M. & Kennedy, D. (1999). MRI-based brain volumetrics: Emergence of a developmental brain science from a tool. *Brain Development*, 21, 289–95.

Christiansen, M. & Kirby, S. (eds) (2003). *Language evolution: The states of the art.* Oxford, UK: Oxford University Press.

Crystal, D. (1997). *The Cambridge encyclopedia of language, second edition.* Cambridge: Cambridge University Press.

Deacon, T. W. (1997). *The symbolic species: The co-evolution of language and the brain.* New York: W. W. Norton and Company.

Deacon, T. W. (2000). Evolutionary perspectives on language and brain plasticity. *Journal of Communication Disorders*, 33(4), 273–91.

Deacon, T. W. (2003). Universal Grammar and semiotic constraints. In M. Christiansen & S. Kirby (eds), *Language evolution: The states of the art*, 111–39. Oxford, UK: Oxford University Press.

Deacon, T. W. (2004). Monkey homologues of language areas: Computing the ambiguities. *Trends in Cognitive Sciences*, 8(7), 288–90.

Dejerine, J. (1891). Sur un cas de cécité verbale avec agraphie, suivi d'autopsie. *Mémoires de la Société de Biologie*, 3, 197.

Diamond, M. C. (2001). Response of the brain to enrichment. *Annals of the Brazilian Academy of Sciences*, 73, 211–20.

Fawcett, A. & Nicolson, R. (1999). Performance of dyslexic children on cerebellar and cognitive tests. *Journal of Motor Behavior*, 31(1), 68–78.

Fawcett, A., Nicolson, R. & Dean, P. (1996). Impaired performance of children with dyslexia on a range of cerebellar tasks. *Annals of Dyslexia*, 46, 259–83.

Filipek, P. A., Richelme, C., Kennedy, D. N. & Caviness, V. (1994). The young adult human brain: An MRI-based morphometric analysis. *Cerebral Cortex*, 4, 344–60.

Fink, R. (1993). How successful dyslexics learn to read. *Teaching, Thinking and Problem Solving*, 15(5), 1–6.

Fischer, K. W. (1980). A theory of cognitive development: The control and construction of hierarchies of skills. *Psychological Review*, 87, 477–531.

Fischer, K. W. & Bidell, T. R. (1998). Dynamic development of psychological structures in action and thought. In R. M. Lerner (ed.), *Handbook of child psychology: Theoretical models of human development*, 5th edn, Vol. 1, 467–561. New York: Wiley.

Fischer, K. W. & Immordino-Yang, M. H. (2002). Cognitive development and education: From dynamic general structure to specific learning and teaching. In E. Lagemann (ed.), *Traditions of scholarship in education*. Chicago: Spencer Foundation.

Friston, K. (1998). Imaging neuroscience: Principles or maps? *Proceedings of the National Academic of Sciences (USA)*, 95, 796–802.

Galaburda, A. M. (1995). Anatomic basis of cerebral dominance. In R. Davidson & K. Hugdahl (eds), *Brain asymmetry*, 51–73. Cambridge: MIT Press.

Galaburda, A. M. & Kemper, T. L. (1979). Cytoarchitectonic abnormalities in developmental dyslexia: A case study. *Annals of Neurology*, 6, 94–100.

Galaburda, A. M. & Livingstone, M. (1993). Evidence for a magnocellular defect in developmental dyslexia. In P. Tallal & A. Galaburda (eds), *Temporal information processing in the nervous system: Special reference to dyslexia and dysphasia*, Vol. 682, 70–82.

Galaburda, A. M., Rosen, G. & Sherman, G. (1990). Individual variability in cortical organization: Its relationship to brain laterality and implications to function. *Neuropsychologia*, 28(6), 529–46.

Gardner, H. (1983). *Frames of mind: The theory of multiple intelligences*. New York: Basic Books.

Geschwind, N. (1982). Why Orton was right. *Annals of Dyslexia*, 32, 13–30.

Geschwind, N. (1983). Biological associations of left-handedness. *Annals of Dyslexia*, 33, 29–40.

Geschwind, N. (1984). The brain of a learning-disabled individual. *Annals of Dyslexia*, 34, 319–27.

Hauser, M. D., Chomsky, N. & Fitch, W. T. (2002). The faculty of language: What is it, who has it, and how did it evolve? *Science*, 298, 1569–79.

Huttenlocher, P. R. (2002). *Neural plasticity: The effects of environment on the development of the cerebral cortex*. Cambridge, MA: Harvard University Press.

Immordino-Yang, M. (2004). A tale of two cases: Emotion and affective prosody after left and right hemispherectomy. Unpublished doctoral dissertation, Harvard University Graduate School of Education, Cambridge, MA.

Kennedy, D., Lange, N., Makris, N., Bates, J. & Caviness, V. (1998). Gyri of the human neocortex: An MRI-based analysis of volumes and variance. *Cerebral Cortex*, 8, 372–85.

Kushch, A., Gross-Glenn, K., Jallad, B., Lubs, H., Rabin, M., Feldman, E. & Duara, R. (1993). Temporal lobe surface area measurements on MRI in normal and dyslexic readers. *Neuropsychologia*, 31(8), 811–21.

Lieberman, P. (2002). On the nature and evolution of the neural bases of human language. *American Journal of Physical Anthropology*, 119(S35), 36–62.

Marchman, V., Miller, R. & Bates, E. (1991). Babble and first words in children with focal brain injury. *Applied Psycholinguistics*, 12, 1–22.

Mesulam, M.-M. (1990). Large-scale neurocognitive networks and distributed processing for attention, language, and memory. *Annals of Neurology*, 28, 597–613.

Mesulam, M.-M. (1998). From sensation to cognition. *Brain*, 121, 1013–1052.

Mills, D., Coffey-Corina, S. & Neville, H. (1994). Variability in cerebral organization during primary language acquisition. In G. Dawson & K. Fischer (eds), *Human behavior and the developing brain*, 427–55. New York: Guilford Press.

Nation, K. (1999). Reading skills in hyperlexia: A developmental perspective. *Psychological Bulletin*, 125(3), 338–55.

Ojemann, G. A. (1979). Individual variability in cortical localization of language. *Journal of Neurosurgery*, 50, 164–9.

Ojemann, G. A. (1991). Cortical organization of language. *Journal of Neuroscience*, 11, 2281–7.

Pennington, B. F., Filipek, P. A., Lefly, D., Churchwell, J., Kennedy, D. N., Simon, J. H., Filley, C. M., Galaburda, A., Alarcon, M. & DeFries, J. C. (1999). Brain morphometry in reading-disabled twins. *Neurology*, 53(4), 723–9.

Pitchford, N. (2000). Spoken language correlates of reading impairments acquired in childhood. *Brain and Language*, 72(2), 129–49.

Raichle, M. E., Fiez, J. A., Videen, T. O., MacLeod, A. M., Pardo, J. V., Fox, P. T. & Petersen, S. E. (1994). Practice-related changes in human brain functional anatomy during non-motor learning. *Cerebral Cortex*, 4(1), 8–26.

Rispens, J. & Van Berckelaer, I. A. (1991). Hyperlexia: Definition and criterion. In R. Malatesha (ed.), *Written language disorders. Neuropsychology and cognition*, Vol. 2, 143–63. Dordrecht, Netherlands: Kluwer Academic Publishers.

Rose, D. & Meyer, A. (2002). *Teaching every student in the digital age*. Alexandria, VA: American Association for Supervision & Curriculum Development.

Rumsey, J. M., Donohue, B. C., Brady, D. R., Nace, K., Giedd, J. N. & Andreason, P. (1997). A magnetic resonance imaging study of planum temporale asymmetry in men with developmental dyslexia. *Archives of Neurology*, 54(12), 1481–9.

Satz, P., Strauss, E. & Whitaker, H. (1990). The ontogeny of hemispheric specialization: Some old hypotheses revisited. *Brain and Language*, 38, 596–614.

Schultz, R. T., Cho, N. K., Staib, L. H., Kier, L. E., Fletcher, J. M., Shaywitz, S. E., Shankweiler, D. P., Katz, L., Gore, J. C., Duncan, J. S. & Shaywitz, R. A. (1994). Brain morphology in normal and dyslexic children: The influence of sex and age. *Annals of Neurology*, 35(6), 732–42.

Tallal, P., Merzenich, M. M., Miller, S. & Jenkins, W. (1998). Language learning impairments: Integrating basic science, technology, and remediation. *Experimental Brain Research*, 123(1–2), 210–19.

Thal, D., Marchman, V., Stiles, J., Aram, D., Trauner, D., Nass, R. & Bates, E. (1991). Lexical development in children with focal brain injury. *Brain and Language*, 40, 491–527.

Uylings, H. B., Kuypers, K., Diamond, M. C. & Veltman, W. A. (1978). Effects of differential environments on plasticity of dendrites of cortical pyramidal neurons in adult rats. *Experimental Neurology*, 62, 658–77.

Vicari, S., Albertoni, A., Chilosi, A., Cipriani, P., Cioni, G. & Bates, E. (2000). Plasticity and reorganization during language development in children with early brain injury. *Cortex*, 36(1), 31–46.

Wolf, M. & Katzir-Cohen, T. (2001). Reading fluency and its intervention. *Scientific Studies of Reading*, 5, 211–39.

Wulfeck, B., Trauner, D. & Tallal, P. (1991). Neurologic, cognitive and linguistic features of infants after focal brain injury. *Pediatric Neurology*, 7, 266–9.

Zatorre, R., Perry, D., Beckett, C., Westbury, C. & Evans, A. (1998) Functional anatomy of musical processing in listeners with absolute pitch and relative pitch. *Proceedings of the National Academic of Sciences (USA)*, 95, 3172–7.

# 3    The genetics of dyslexia: what is the phenotype?

*Albert M. Galaburda and Gordon F. Sherman*

*Overview:* Dyslexia has a genetic basis, but a major question is the developmental relation between genes and behaviors, especially complex, culturally mediated behaviors such as reading. Moreover, because the dyslexic behavioral and anatomical phenotypes are still debated, interpreting correlations between brain and behavior is difficult. Using research involving animal models, postmortem studies of dyslexics' brains, and genetic studies of dyslexics' families, Galaburda and Sherman attempt to isolate genotypes and phenotypes for dyslexia. The research illuminates genetic differences between dyslexics and normals, as well as the low-level cognitive, sensory, and perceptual correlates of these differences. The authors focus especially on the functional and anatomical implications of ectopias, small malformations of the cortex resulting from altered neuronal migration during fetal development. Certain kinds of ectopias have been associated with dyslexia and could represent a basic, genetically influenced abnormality that through development may relate to important characteristics of dyslexics.    *The Editors*

Attempts to relate specific genes to specific human cognitive functions have not revealed any genes that control cognitive behavior in humans. We do not know, for instance, what the genetic basis for language in humans is, and why it is, genetically speaking, that even our closest relative – the chimpanzee – does not have anything approximating human language, even though we share over 95 percent of our genes with this species. This state of affairs, after 150 years of neurological research on language, and nearly 50 years since the discovery of the genetic code, should not be surprising. The distance between the genotype – what the genetic code is – and the phenotype – the biology of language as disclosed by psycholinguistic research – is so enormous in terms of both level and developmental time, that a bridge is hard to visualize, let alone demonstrate. From the point in time and space at which a gene is expressed and a protein synthesized, until the finished product consisting of a huge network of interconnected neurons performing some language function, there is a great deal of building, shaping, and reshaping to be done. Understanding the relationship between a single gene or even a handful of genes and the anatomy of language – what the system is – is difficult enough, as the language system is very large and genes are only responsible for single proteins; but language is what the system does, so there has to be a leap between structure and function, with all the discontinuities this implies. To effect this leap, i.e. to get from what the system is to what it does, is a daunting task, which has so far been achieved with relatively small ensembles of neurons supporting extremely primitive functions in lower animals (cf aplysia and some elementary memory functions). Similarly to get from a gene mutation to a disorder of cognitive function requires a long pathway where the actions of other genes as well as epigenetic influences complicate understanding.

Development and learning present other complications in understanding the relationship between genotype and phenotype, especially when the phenotype is one of the complex human cognitive functions (Immordino-Yang & Deacon, this volume; Pennington, 2002). Thus, for instance, it is possible that a gene in question, which is critical to the construction of a cognitive network, was expressed during a critical window of time in embryonic development and never again in the life of the network. The gene, then, might be found by linkage analysis and positional cloning, but the expression of the gene leading to the development of the system would be difficult to discover without having some knowledge about when the expression of this gene takes place. Furthermore there is the learning that takes place during the developmental period, which through epigenetic mechanisms continues to change the structure and function of the phenotypes. Thus, a gene may participate in building a structure that is capable of learning a certain kind of information, say phonology, by virtue of its architecture. As the structure learns the sounds of the native language, it changes such that the anatomical phenotype that is described subsequently is not the result of gene function alone, but also of the (epigenetic) effects of learning on the structure (Fischer, Rose, & Rose, this volume). If the focus is on a part of the structure that is plastic with respect to learning, it will be hard to establish linkage to a gene, especially if the learning experience is variable in the population. These are not insurmountable problems, but they will take a long time to solve.

The most important issue for linking gene to function, however, is the fact that in order to build a complex neural structure capable of a complex cognitive function, there must be literally hundreds (maybe thousands) of genes involved, expressed in specific combinations and developmental sequences. It is untenable to think of a single gene for language, or even a single gene for derivational morphology, or for phonology, or for syntax. So what do people do when they study the genetics of human cognitive disorders?

Essentially, genetic studies of complex behaviors in humans are studies of disorders (Pennington, 2002). This is equally true for developmental as for degenerative disorders. In this case, it is easily conceivable that, even though complex systems may not be built by single genes, an abnormal single gene could wreak havoc with the building of a whole system, in the case of developmental disorders, or in the maintenance of the system, in the case of degenerative disorders. One could imagine that studying disorders is a good way to get indirectly at genes used to build and/or maintain brain structures. The rationale is that if the failure of a gene leads to the failure of building or maintaining a system, then the gene participates in the process. However, this conclusion could be erroneous if, in fact, the damaged or deleted gene affects development or maintenance in a most indirect way – via epigenetic influences. So, for instance, patients with Alzheimer Disease, who accumulate amyloid containing senile plaques and show memory and language problems, may carry an allele (Apo E-4) that predisposes to the disorder by dysregulating the metabolism of amyloid protein in the brain. The protein appears to be toxic to brain cells, and many believe that its accumulation leads to neuronal loss in the hippocampus and (particularly) association cortex, which ultimately results in Alzheimer Disease. It could not, however, be argued convincingly that the amyloid protein reveals anything about the building of the structure, or its maintenance; in other words, that the culprit allele is a gene for the hippocampus, or the association cortex, or any brain region where the amyloid toxin accumulates; even less so, that the gene codes for memory or word retrieval. Instead, it is clear that the environment created by the culprit allele exerts epigenetic effects upon structures involved in memory and language. There are similar examples in developmental disorders. For instance, pregnant women who contract rubella may have babies with abnormal brain development. It would be difficult to argue that the genes of the baby have anything to do with the abnormal development of the brain. It is fair to say that the developing brain can be damaged by effects originating totally outside the brain, even the organism, whereby the genes that build the brain are not directly implicated.

The problem we have outlined above constitutes one of the many difficulties with linking genes to complex behaviors and abnormal genes to abnormal behaviors. The problem is somewhat ameliorated when it is possible to make shorter bridges among the intervening steps between gene and behavior. Thus, for instance, one would want to identify a gene that codes for a receptor that exists on the membrane of a particular type of neuron that is found in a particular interconnected system that activates every time a subject solves a particular cognitive task. In the pathological case, a genetic disorder may lead to lack of expression of the receptor on a particular cell with alterations in connectivity and physiology within a system leading to lack of activation of the system with the same task. Attempts are under way to achieve this type of correlation in Williams Syndrome, a condition in which there are specific cognitive deficits, physiological and anatomical changes, alterations in the expression of specific molecules in the brain, and the loss of a number of genes through a deletion (for a review see Ashkenas, 1996).

The determination of the genetic basis of developmental dyslexia presents all of these problems and in their most unwieldy form. In dyslexia we are dealing with a complex cognitive function – reading. This function is not spontaneously acquired. In order to learn to read (with ease) it is necessary first to become consciously aware of the sound structure of the language, which in turn has to be taught. Therefore, the influence of culture is immense. Socioeconomic issues, school systems, and parental literacy are some of the social issues that play a role. Moreover, there is some evidence that the structure of the language and of the writing system play a role too. Languages that depend on tonal changes for determining meaning produce psychophysical experiences that are different from those that pack meaning into formant transitions, and would be vulnerable to different pathologies affecting the brain. The reading of kanji characters in Japanese, which are not organized syllabically, requires different mechanisms from those for reading kana, the syllabic form of Japanese writing. It is clear from the outset, therefore, that a study of the genetic basis of dyslexia ought not to contain individuals whose native languages are as different as Japanese and English, and it is not known how much (or little) difference between languages is tolerated. Frith and colleagues (Landerl *et al.*, 1997) have pointed out that irrespective of genetic influences, phonological dyslexia has to be less common in German than in English on the basis of the differences between these two languages in orthographic consistency.

Geneticists working on dyslexia have to simplify the behavioral phenotype by focusing on a relatively simple task dyslexics cannot do (or do well) and then trying to link this behavior to the genotype (see below). Usually the characterization of the phenotype involves the measurement of phonological or orthographic deficits.

As with any phenotype, the task of determining the genetic nature of developmental dyslexia began with the determination of familiality, heritability, mode of transmission, and chromosome linkage. Genetic studies on dyslexia have clearly documented familiality and heritability. The mode of transmission, however, is complicated and not yet completely understood. There have been several susceptibility loci identified on chromosomes 1, 2, 3, 6, 7, 18, and X (Grigorenko, 2003), and two candidate genes have now been identified, although there is still debate concerning DYX1C1 (Taipale *et al.*, 2003; Scerri *et al.*, 2004; Wigg *et al.*, 2004). The next giant steps involve specifying the exact gene loci, and then cloning and sequencing the gene(s). Determining their function and defining their relationship to the phenotype would be next. A short summary of the genetic studies on dyslexia follows.

Shortly after dyslexia was identified, its familial nature was noted (Stephenson, 1907). A hallmark study in 1950 showed strong heritability of this trait –

dyslexia was present in 50 percent of the offspring from 90 families that had one parent with dyslexia (Hallgren, 1950). Modern studies using more accurate diagnostic measures and better controls confirmed these earlier studies (e.g. Finucci *et al.*, 1976; Gilger *et al.*, 1991; Vogler *et al.*, 1985; Yule and Rutter, 1975).

Of course, the documentation of dyslexia within families does not prove a genetic basis due to the confound of shared environments and other epigenetic factors common to families. In order to establish a link between genetics and a trait, twin studies comparing concordance between monozygotic and dizygotic twins are essential. Pennington and Smith (1983) reviewed the published twin studies and found that the concordance rate for dyslexia was significantly higher in monozygotic twins (70%) than in dizygotic twin pairs (31%). More recent reports from the study of twins and adopted children confirm that both reading and spelling disabilities are significantly heritable (Davis *et al.*, 2001; DeFries *et al.*, 1987; DeFries *et al.*, 1991; Wadsworth *et al.*, 2002).

The exact characteristics of the transmission of dyslexia are not clear. The best transmission study to date combined a complex segregation analysis with the use of strict experimental controls and showed a sex-influenced mode of inheritance compatible with a major locus transmission model, with complete penetrance in males, but incomplete in females (Pennington *et al.*, 1991). The penetrance difference may account, in part, for the 1.5:1 sex ratio seen in favor of male dyslexics (Wadsworth *et al.*, 1992; Rutter *et al.*, 2004).

As pointed out earlier in this article, it is difficult to link genes to complex human behaviors. This is true for dyslexia because the phenotype is not accurately described, there is substantial variance in the expression of the phenotype, and there are numerous epigenetic factors that interact to shape the characteristics of the disorder. Further, dyslexia is probably genetically heterogeneous and likely to be caused by multiple genes (Smith *et al.*, 1990).

In spite of these complicating factors progress has been made and a number of laboratories have shown significant chromosome linkage to dyslexia. Many of these studies used sibling pairs or twins with one sibling having a deviant score on a measure related to dyslexia. The small number of identified loci have been conceptualized as susceptibility, not disease loci, and are described as quantitative trait loci (QTL) that contribute to transmission of both dyslexia and normal reading variation (Pennington, 1995).

The first evidence for linkage of dyslexia was published in 1983. A lod score analysis was performed on data obtained from a small sample of nine families and indicated that a region on the long arm of chromosome 15 was associated with reading disability (Smith *et al.*, 1983). Additional testing of one family member not represented in the first study reduced the lod score to non-significance (Rabin *et al.*, 1991). Subsequently, kindreds were added to the study and using a non-parametric analysis of sibling pairs weak linkage was reestablished to chromosome 15 (Smith *et al.*, 1991).

This study also revealed linkage to the short arm of chromosome 6 (Smith *et al.*, 1991). A larger study by this group used a non-parametric analysis of two independent samples of sibling pairs and localized a QTL to 6p21.3, although a lod score analysis was not significant (Cardon *et al.*, 1994). Significant linkage was also confirmed using a sibling pair analysis of a sample of 50 dizygotic twins and their families, later corrected to 46 pairs due to the mistaken inclusion of 4 pairs of identical twins (Cardon *et al.*, 1995). This region on chromosome 6 contains the human leukocyte antigen complex and is a locus for schizophrenia and juvenile myoclonic epilepsy. The gamma-aminobutyric acid (GABA) B receptor gene is located at this site (Goei *et al.*, 1998). GABA is the primary inhibitory neurotransmitter in the brain.

Non-parametric affected pedigree member analysis (APM) of six extended families containing at least four individuals with dyslexia per family (a total of 94 individuals) yielded significant linkage of the phonological awareness phenotype to the same approximate region of chromosome 6 reported above (Grigorenko *et al.*, 1997). A lod score analysis, however, was not significant. Weaker, but statistically significant, linkage to chromosome 15 using the lod score method was shown for single word decoding, replicating the earlier study of Smith *et al.* (1983).

Chromosomes 6 and 15 also have been analyzed for spelling disability (Schulte-Korne *et al.*, 1998). No linkage was seen for chromosome 6, but positive linkage was seen for chromosome 15 at the marker location previously reported above for single word reading deficits (Grigorenko *et al.*, 1997).

The consistency of linkage to chromosome 6 and 15 suggests that we may be approaching the identification of genes that contribute to the various phenotypic characteristics of dyslexia. However, Field and Kaplan (1998) have challenged the linkage finding to chromosome 6. Using an APM method and lod score analyses of 79 families with at least 2 members having a phonologically based reading disability, they found no evidence of linkage to the chromosome 6 regions previously linked to dyslexia. Further they suggested that the APM method used in the previous studies leads to erroneous results because of its sensitivity to marker allele frequencies chosen for the analyses. They cautioned against using the APM method due to the generation of false-positive results. However, this study only analyzed a single dichotomous variable (impaired phonological coding) as opposed to most of the previous studies (Fisher *et al.*, 1999).

The Fisher *et al.* and another recent study, however, continue to offer support for linkage to chromosome 6. Gayan *et al.* (1999) used a lod score analysis of a sample of 126 sibling pairs and confirmed linkage between dyslexia (both orthographic and phonological processing components) to a 5cM area on chromosome 6 as specified in earlier studies. In addition, Fisher *et al.* (1999) studied 181 sibling pairs from 82 families and also confirmed a QTL at 6p21.3 for the reading of irregular words and non-words. This study implicated linkage of both phonological and orthographic skills to this locus.

Weak linkage has also been reported for chromosome 1 (Rabin *et al.*, 1993), but further study has discounted this finding (see Smith *et al.*, 1998).

## What is the behavioral phenotype?

Before we delve into the anatomical phenotype, which is the focus of our genetic research, we want to discuss further the behavioral phenotype, since dyslexia is recognized as a set of behaviors and not as a set of anatomical findings. Dyslexia research today considers whether the condition arises from a primary developmental disorder of language processing, either linguistic per se or metalinguistic (cognitive), or from a fundamentally sensory/perceptual failure (Wolf & Ashby, this volume). If linguistic/cognitive, does the problem affect more than just language? For instance, are there significant and contributory problems in high-level visual processing? If sensory/perceptual, what modalities might be involved – auditory, visual, motor, others? How peripheral is the problem – the cochlear nuclei, the retina? Furthermore, to what extent is the problem longitudinal as well as parallel, i.e. it involves multiple processing stages (sensory perceptual and cognitive) as well as multiple types of processing (visual as well as auditory)?

Those who argue that dyslexia is a linguistic/cognitive matter claim that no sensory/perceptual deficit so far described in dyslexics could account for the difficulties in phonological processing exhibited by the dyslexic patients. And, in fact, there has been an explosion of new findings implicating very low-level sensory/perceptual dysfunction in dyslexia (e.g. Eden *et al.*, 1996b; Fitch *et al.*, 1997; Galaburda, 2002; Galaburda *et al.*, 1994; Livingstone *et al.*, 1991; Paré-Blagoev; Wolf & Ashby, this volume). Opponents of the sensory/perceptual explanation may not deny that these problems exist; rather, they assert that they are irrelevant to the process of learning to read in dyslexia and cite a sticky problem. Thus, one of the problems with the low-level hypothesis is that it fails to account for how well dyslexics speak and comprehend spoken language by comparison to their written language abilities.

The low-level hypothesis argues that deficient low-level processing of some types of sounds that would be useful for establishing normal representations of the phonology of the language lead to secondary phonological problems, and third-hand metaphonological (metalinguistic; cognitive) problems. It continues with the suggestion that if the phonological representations are corrupted, it will be more difficult to apply metaphonological strategies prior to reading. The objection to this account is that if the phonological architecture is corrupted from any cause, then it should be measurable, not only in reading, but in all tasks that depend on this phonology, including oral language comprehension and speech production. Therefore, those in the opposite camp argue that there could not be anything significantly wrong with the phonological architecture in dyslexic brains, irrespective of what its cause might be, even if it is a problem with low-level processing. Instead, they argue that the problem is purely metaphonological and consists of a difficulty with consciously segmenting words into phonemes, which is a prerequisite for learning to read. A reasonable counterargument is that the demands on the phonological representation may be greater in reading.

As we know it, the anatomy of the brain is topographically unambiguous regarding the parts of the cerebral cortex dedicated to sensory/perceptual as opposed to linguistic/cognitive activities. Structures close to the sensory organs in the brainstem, the thalamus, and the primary and adjacent association cortex are involved in sensory/perceptual processing, whereas those many synapses downstream, e.g. in the anterior temporal and prefrontal cortex, participate in cognitive tasks. It would make sense, therefore, to examine brain structures in the dyslexic that are involved in sensory/perceptual behaviors and those that are involved in linguistic/cognitive behaviors. We could compare these to the equivalent structures in non-dyslexic brains in an attempt to draw some conclusions about which are anomalous and which are not. This is, of course, a first pass, since we realize that sensory/perceptual and linguistic/cognitive behaviors are subject to bottom-up and top-down influences during learning, and their respective anatomical substrates, too, are subject to trophic or antitrophic influences from connected structures upstream and downstream, especially during early development. There is, therefore, no reason to think that only one stage of processing or one type of processing and their corresponding anatomical substrate will be abnormal, as there is a great deal of interaction among these during development, making it likely that if one is affected, the others will be also. Of course, too, the discovery of single or multiple anatomic anomalies would not permit conclusions about causality, but we could at least state whether cognitive areas, or sensory/perceptual areas, or both, are or are not abnormal in the dyslexic brains. Observation on autopsied dyslexic brains and recent research on anatomical models have helped to get us closer to the answers to these questions, and have revealed interesting facts about developmental plasticity, including a previously unsuspected sex difference.

### More on behavioral findings in dyslexics

It is well established that dyslexics, at least the bulk of dyslexics, have difficulties with phonological tasks, e.g. pseudoword reading, phoneme segmentation, rhyming, phoneme deletion tasks (Bradley and Bryant, 1981; Bryant *et al.*, 1998; Liberman and Shankweiler, 1985; Morais *et al.*, 1984; Torgesen; Wolf & Ashby, this volume). They have also been shown to have problems with some aspects of perception (e.g. Eden *et al.*, 1996b; Fitch *et al.*, 1997;

Galaburda, 2002; Livingstone *et al.*, 1991). We showed that, as evidenced by evoked potentials, dyslexics had difficulties processing rapidly changing, low contrast checkerboard patterns presented on a computer monitor (Galaburda *et al.*, 1994; Livingstone *et al.*, 1991). The abnormalities were visible before and up to 100 msecs from the presentation of the stimulus, which indicated involvement of early visual processors anatomically placed before or up to the primary visual cortex. Others have shown dysfunction of the motion perception area (Eden *et al.*, 1996a), which is also a rapid perceptual processor, only one or two synapses beyond the primary cortical visual input zone. There had also been previous, psychophysical, evidence that the peripheral visual system was abnormal in dyslexics. However, all these data together could not establish to everyone's satisfaction that any abnormality of the visual system was relevant, particularly not abnormalities in low-level visual processing.

In the auditory system, too, dyslexics and other developmentally language impaired children have shown difficulties processing rapidly changing sounds (Anderson *et al.*, 1993; Merzenich *et al.*, 1996; Tallal, 1977; Tallal *et al.*, 1995; Tallal and Piercy, 1973; see also Wolf & Ashby, this volume; Wolf & Bowers, 1999), which suggested to Tallal and colleagues that this was the primary reason for the phonological problems dyslexics exhibit. The argument went as follows. During language acquisition dyslexics never hear certain sounds and therefore cannot represent a full set of phonemes for a given language, i.e. they have a corrupted or anomalous phonological module. Further, if dyslexics have an abnormal phonological module, they could not segment words into the proper phonemes, and they could not map these linguistic units onto the graphemes of written language – hence the difficulty with acquiring reading. However, if indeed they have a corrupted phonological module, how then do dyslexics speak so well and comprehend spoken language? Perhaps comprehension can make use of contextual information and predictions, but speaking must make use of the phonological module. Thus, at the very least, the problem is more likely to be beyond the phonological representations themselves, and instead in metacognitive operations working on these representations for the purpose of parsing the phonetic stream.

The sensory/perceptual hypothesis implicates early stations in the sensory pathway, which include sensory organs, brainstem nuclei, thalamic relay nuclei, primary cortices (visual, auditory) and adjacent association areas. The linguistic/cognitive hypothesis, on the other hand, implicates stations further downstream in the anterior temporal cortex, inferior parietal lobule, and frontal lobe.

## Neuroanatomical findings in dyslexics

The anatomy of dyslexia is complex. There is reason to believe that to the extent that there is behavioral variability among dyslexics, there will also be anatomical variability. We do not know how uniform some of the brain changes that have been described in dyslexia are in the population of dyslexics. There is also the issue of the multiplicity of types of brain changes. The dyslexic brain differs from the non-dyslexic brain in more than one way. There are changes in the patterns of asymmetry in a language area. There are instances of focal abnormal development of the cerebral cortex. There are changes in cell sizes in structures not limited to the cerebral cortex. There are male–female differences.

One way to facilitate the decision of what anatomical phenotype to focus on in genetic studies is by creating a testable hypothesis and focusing on the first event in the processing chain described by the hypothesis. The goal is to identify the simplest and earliest occurring anatomical change and attempt to link that to the dyslexia genotype. In the following sections we will describe the work in our laboratory that led to the genetic studies we have carried out thus far.

There are two types of findings made on autopsied dyslexic brains, which bear on the debate outlined above, and one of these is particularly relevant. The first has to do with alterations in the pattern of cerebral asymmetry. For instance, the planum temporale, a region on the upper surface of the temporal lobe, which is asymmetric in two-thirds of the population, fails to show asymmetry in dyslexics in most published studies (Galaburda *et al.*, 1985; Hynd *et al.*, 1990; Morgan and Hynd, 1998; Steinmetz *et al.*, 1991; see also Benes & Paré-Blagoev, this volume). The asymmetry in question is caused at least in part by an asymmetry of posterior temporal area Tpt. This cortex is one synapse or two away from the primary auditory cortex, and still unimodal enough to be mainly involved in sensory/perceptual and early cognitive tasks. Area Tpt is just as far from the primary auditory cortex as area MT, one of the motion perception areas, is from the primary visual cortex. Lack of Tpt asymmetry may have some implications concerning early sound and phonological processing in dyslexics, although this is not as yet specified.

A second finding is the presence of focal cortical malformations consisting of nests of ectopic neurons and glia in the first cortical layer, which alter focally the architecture of the affected cortical areas (Galaburda *et al.*, 1985). The malformations, termed 'ectopias', represent altered neuronal migration to the cortex. They are present mostly in perisylvian locations, i.e. the superior temporal gyrus (which contains Wernicke's area) and the inferior premotor and prefrontal cortex (which contains Broca's area), but do not typically affect parts of the brain associated with reading and writing, i.e. the inferior parietal lobule and occipital lobe. Clearly, some of these ectopias affect cortical areas involved in linguistic/cognitive functions that are many synapses away from sensory input stations (Frenkel *et al.*, 2000). Over 100 ectopias have been seen in our dyslexia specimens. There is an indication that more ectopias are present in the left than in the right hemisphere, especially in males. Similar ectopias have been seen in other developmental disorders in humans, including the fetal alcohol syndrome and many mental retardation syndromes (Friede and Mikolasek, 1978), although the appearance, distribution, and numbers of the malformations are not equivalent.

Further, we have gathered evidence in dyslexic brains to show that some thalamic nuclei exhibit changes in the size of neurons (Galaburda *et al.*, 1994; Livingstone *et al.*, 1991). Changes have been seen in the LGN, a nucleus connected to the retina and to the primary visual cortex, and in the MGN, a nucleus connected to the primary auditory cortex and to auditory brainstem nuclei. These nuclei either have smaller neurons or a shift in the proportion of small to large neurons, in favor of smaller neurons. Since smaller neurons conduct nerve impulses more slowly, smaller neurons in visual and auditory relay nuclei in the thalamus may be interpreted as one possible anatomical substrate underlying slower visual and auditory perceptual processing in dyslexics. The primary visual cortex also shows an alteration in neuronal sizes and a change in the normal pattern of cellular asymmetry (Jenner *et al.*, 1999).

### Help from animal models

Determining causal links in dyslexics between genetic and anatomical differences and functional problems is dependent on the development of animal models. The cortical ectopias seen in dyslexics have been modeled in rats and mice (Humphreys *et al.*, 1989; Sherman *et al.*, 1988; Tamagawa *et al.*, 1989). In certain inbred strains of mice ectopias occur spontaneously (Figure 3.1), which has enabled us to search for genes that relate to their production (see below). In rats the malformations can be experimentally induced, which can help us with questions regarding causality and for determining exact anatomical and developmental characteristics.

Ectopias arise developmentally before the completion of the period of neuronal migration to the neocortex, which in humans takes place roughly between 16 and 20 weeks of gestation, and in mice and rats it includes one or two days after birth. The time of ectopia formation is long, and therefore the anomalies contain neurons born at different times during histogenesis of the cortex (Rosen *et al.*, 1996). The significance of this finding is that it sets up the possibility for wide-ranging connectivity between neurons in the ectopia and other cortical and subcortical areas. In fact, we have shown that ectopias may be abnormally connected to the thalamus, ipsilateral cortex, and contralateral cortex (Jenner *et al.*, 1995; Jenner *et al.*, 1997; Rosen, 1996; Rosen and Galaburda, 1996). Thus, by virtue of their connectivity, these anomalies are poised to affect the development of other brain areas to which they are connected, including the thalamus. This may account for the cell size changes noted in the thalamus of dyslexics (see previous section).

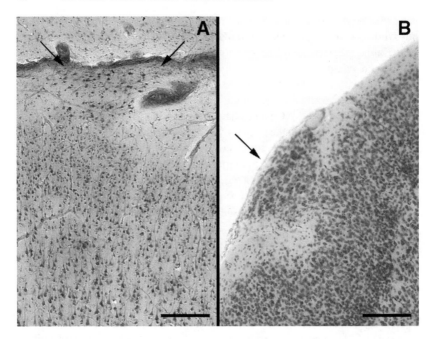

Figure 3.1  Ectopias in mice.

Further, we have shown that in mice with ectopias there is an alteration in the pattern of asymmetry in the primary visual cortex. Normally, as the coefficient of asymmetry increases (more asymmetry), the left plus right volume decreases. This suggests that asymmetry is a curtailed form of symmetry, rather than one overgrown side (see, for a review, Rosen, 1996). In the presence of ectopias, the degree of asymmetry diminishes, but, in addition, the inverse relationship between asymmetry and volume disappears (Rosen *et al.*, 1989). This suggests that in dyslexic brains, manifestation of asymmetry is not only decreased, but is also anomalous. One could propose, for instance, that left-handed dyslexics are not equivalent to left-handed non-dyslexics.

Further, the neuronal changes in thalamic nuclei and primary cortex in dyslexics could explain the sensory/perceptual problems. Ectopias and anomalies of asymmetry affecting linguistic/cognitive areas (as well as sensory/perceptual areas) could account for the linguistic/cognitive deficits. The ectopias contain enough connectivity during development to influence development of other areas, including sensory/perceptual areas. If this indeed happens, one could propose that sensory/perceptual deficits are secondary to changes downstream in the pathway, or that linguistic/cognitive changes are secondary to changes upstream in sensory/perceptual areas. Since the migrational changes, causing ectopias, arise early in development, and changes in cell size can occur at any time in life, we have thought it more plausible that the ectopias, if at all, cause the changes in the thalamus. A corollary hypothesis is that the earlier presence of ectopias than thalamic changes means that phonological and other linguistic/cognitive changes come first and sensory/perceptual changes result from secondary changes in the thalamus. This is the opposite picture to that suggested by the sensory/perceptual hypothesis and would instead support the linguistic/cognitive hypothesis.

These hypotheses can be tested in experimental animals in which one can produce cortical malformations in high-level association cortex and watch for changes in the thalamus, for instance. We used experimental rats to induce migrational anomalies similar to those seen in the dyslexic brains (Herman *et al.*, 1997; Rosen *et al.*, 1997; Rosen *et al.*, 1989). The anomalies were induced in the prefrontal, parietal, or occipital cortices, bilaterally. Control animals received sham surgery with no resulting anomalies. We were able to demonstrate that the induction of cortical anomalies produced changes in neuronal sizes in thalamic nuclei – an excess of small neurons was in the MGN and LGN of the rat, which mimicked the situation in the human dyslexic. Thus, we demonstrated that the thalamic changes could be a consequence of the cortical anomalies. The complementary experiment – to cause shrinkage of thalamic neurons and observe for the presence of ectopias – presents difficulties that we have not overcome as yet, although it seems unlikely that such a finding would be made.

Animals with cortical anomalies and secondary changes in the neuronal sizes in the MGN performed abnormally on a task that required them to process fast, rapidly changing acoustic stimuli (Fitch *et al.*, 1994). In other words, the animals with the ectopias and the thalamic findings, which paralleled the situation in the human dyslexics, behaved similarly on a temporal processing auditory task. Yet, we still could not tell with certainty that the temporal processing deficit was caused by the thalamic changes and not the cortical ectopic changes. However, an unexpected discovery helped us better to understand the role of the cortical anomaly versus the thalamic changes in the functional deficit.

It was noted that, while the male rats slowed down after induction of the cortical anomalies, the females performed normally on the auditory task. A closer look at the data showed that, whereas males showed secondary changes in neuronal size in the MGN, females, despite identical induction procedures and the development of identical cortical malformations, did not show the thalamic changes (Herman *et al.*, 1997). This indicated that it was the secondary thalamic changes and not the primary cortical malformations that were likely responsible for the changes in auditory task performance. The cortical changes themselves may be responsible for other behavioral anomalies seen in animals with malformations (Boehm *et al.*, 1998; Boehm *et al.*, 1996; Denenberg *et al.*, 1988; Denenberg *et al.*, 1991; Schrott *et al.*, 1992; Waters *et al.*, 1997).

Moreover, since females did not show the same response in the thalamus to anomaly induction in the cortex, they appeared to be spared. Since sex differences may be the result of hormonal actions, we exposed pregnant rats to the male hormone testosterone and again examined the male and female offspring after induction of cortical anomalies. Daughters of rats receiving testosterone now showed changes in the thalamus (Rosen *et al.*, 1997). The study of the behavioral effects of this manipulation is ongoing.

## Genetic studies in animal models

The description of the anatomical phenotype in the human dyslexic brain, complemented by the mechanistic and causal research in the animal models, lead us to consider the ectopias as the most proximate anatomical alteration in developmental dyslexia. For us, it was natural to propose that one of the earliest effects of an abnormal gene(s) was to lead to the formation of these ectopias. A study of the genetics of ectopias, therefore, appeared reasonable, even though we were not making an obligatory link between ectopias and dyslexia. Rather, we were considering ectopias as a risk factor for developing dyslexia, as long as other factors were also present. The number, nature, and extent of these other factors are not known, but clearly there appeared to be some influence by sex hormones. As stated at the beginning of this chapter, other factors, including developmental, linguistic, and social factors, are likely to play a role as to whether ectopias do or do not lead to the clinical expression of dyslexia. In this section we will outline what is known about the genetics of ectopias in animal models.

For the most part, the human genetic studies indicate that progress is being made in understanding the genetic contribution to dyslexia. However, our lab has chosen a different and complementary approach – one that depends on an animal model and skirts the difficulties related to accurately describing complex cognitive processing in humans. Instead we use a putative anatomical marker for dyslexia. This marker is the early produced cortical ectopias. Strains of mice that spontaneously develop this type of cortical disruption during the prenatal period have been used successfully to study the neurochemical, connectional, and behavioral attributes of this type of malformation. Since ectopias are the phenotype associated with dyslexia that can be easily and accurately identified in the postmortem tissue, it may be reasonable to assume that the determination of the genetic influence on ectopia formation will be more successful than the identification of genes related to complex cognitive traits associated with dyslexia. Further, if a gene is indeed involved, the production of the prenatal ectopias is developmentally closer to the action of the defective gene. Also, advances in mouse genetic techniques and the increased density of microsatellite marker maps in mice make this an easier task.

Two inbred strains of mice that consistently exhibit ectopias are the New Zealand Black (NZB/BlNJ) and BXSB/MpJ. Both strains have ectopias in about 50 percent of the cases and both males and females are affected. Usually one ectopia is seen in each brain, although multiple ectopias are not rare. In the NZB most ectopias are found in the primary somatosensory cortex, whereas ectopias in the BXSB are present in the prefrontal and motor cortices. The ectopias are located in the molecular layer of the cortex and may also extend through the basal lamina, past the pial membrane into the subarachnoid space. They vary in size, with the smallest containing as few as 10–50 neurons and the largest containing hundreds of neurons and measuring 300 μm in diameter. Large ectopias are visible with the naked eye on the surface of the brain.

Ectopias are recognizable as early as embryonic day 14. Neurons born throughout the period of neuronal proliferation go on to populate the ectopias. The most likely mechanism for the ectopic migration of the neurons is a breach in the superficial pial membrane that allows neuroblasts to migrate too far into the cortical plate. We have been trying to determine the cause of this breach. Initially we suspected an epigenetic etiology. NZB and BXSB mice develop severe autoimmune disease, and we hypothesized that small autoantibodies could cross the placenta and damage the fetal brain. We tested this hypothesis by designing an embryo transfer experiment in which autoimmune embryos were transferred to normal host uteri, while normal embryos were transferred to autoimmune host uteri. The presence of ectopias in the normal embryos and lack thereof in the autoimmune embryo would have supported the transplacental damage hypothesis. In fact, autoimmune embryos developed ectopias at the same frequency as non-transferred cohorts, and normal embryos failed to develop ectopias. It appeared, therefore, that some factor intrinsic to the embryo itself, probably in its genes, was playing the decisive role in the formation of ectopias.

Following the aforementioned results, we shifted our focus to a genetic etiology and carried out a series of breeding manipulations to identify the genetic contributions to ectopia formation. The initial breeding studies showed no ectopias in the F1 offspring from the cross of NZB and control strains and suggested a recessive mode of transmission.

Next, we wanted to determine whether one or several genes were responsible for the trait. Therefore, we examined 15 recombinant inbred (RI) strains that used NZB and SM progenitors (Eicher and Lee, 1990). The RI method is a breeding technique by which the genes of the original mouse are segregated among many lines of inbred mice. If several genes need to act together for the formation of a trait, it is likely that none of the lines or few of them will express the phenotype. If, however, the gene is single, or two adjacent genes are involved, it is likely that several lines will express the phenotype.

A histopathological analysis of mice from these 15 RI strains showed that 8 strains had ectopias and 7 did not (Sherman *et al.*, 1994). The highest frequency of ectopias (80%) was seen in the NXSM-D strain. The observation that at least 50% of the strains contained ectopic mice indicated that it was unlikely that the ectopic phenotype was produced by a large number of genes. Strains without ectopias could not be unambiguously scored as affected or not because of low penetrance and variability in the size of ectopias. Therefore, a genetic comparison among these RI strains was not helpful for establishing linkage of this trait.

To determine the mode of inheritance and generate mice for a linkage analysis we began a Mendelian breeding study. NZB mice were reciprocally crossed with the DBA/2 non-ectopic strain (Sherman *et al.*, 1994). The F1 progeny of this mating did not have ectopias – confirming recessive transmission. When these F1 progeny were backcrossed to the NZB strain, ectopias were present in about 15% of the offspring. This frequency did not differ statistically from that expected (about 20–25%) when only one gene is involved. Offspring from the F1 backcross to DBA did not have ectopias above background levels (1–2%).

DNA samples obtained from the affected offspring from the backcross of F1 mice to NZB mice were used for linkage analysis. There was an indication of weak ectopia linkage to chromosome 11. However, this was not statistically strong and we did not have a large number of affected backcross mice to test. We then carried out a linkage study on the NXSM-D strain because over 80% of these mice have ectopias. As in the previous study using NZB mice, NXSM-D mice were bred with control DBA mice and their offspring backcrossed to either DBA or NXSM-D. No DBA progenitor, F1 offspring, or F1 × DBA backcross progeny had ectopias above the background levels (1–2%) seen in control strains – again confirming ectopia inheritance to be recessive. Ectopia prevalence in the F1 × NXSM-D backcross progeny was 24%. This figure differed from the predicted prevalence (40%), if the predisposition to ectopias is inherited as a monogenic trait, thus implicating more than a single gene (cf NZB results above).

Linkage analysis was carried out on genomic DNA obtained from the NXSM-D backcrosses using PCR-amplification of 96 MIT microsatellite markers distributed throughout the genome. Loci that strongly segregated non-randomly in affected mice were found on chromosomes 4 and 8. Weaker, but significant, linkage was also seen to chromosomes 2 and 9.

The next step was to develop congenic strains using the NXSM-D and DBA progenitor strains. The goal of this technique is to breed a suspected gene into an unaffected strain, and to breed a wild type gene into an affected strain. Unlike the knock-out and knock-in techniques, congenic strains are prepared when the exact gene is not known, but a suspect region needs to be investigated further (for detailed explanation of congenic strains see Silver, 1995). These congenic experiments would introduce the linked area on either chromosome 4, 8, or 4 and

8 of ectopic strains into an ectopia-free genetic background. The appearance of ectopias in the new congenic strain would suggest causality between the linked chromosome segments and the trait. It would also enable us to generate mice for further characterization of the linked region in preparation for positional cloning experiments to identify the gene.

We created three congenic strains: 1) NXSM-D Chr. 4 introgressed into DBA (DBA.NS.D4), 2) NXSM-D Chr. 8 into DBA (DBA.NS.D8), and 3) NXSM-D Chrs 4 and 8 into DBA/2J (DBA.NS.D4/8). The incidence of ectopia in the DBA.NS.D4 and DBA.NS.D8 congenic lines was approximately 10%, while the incidence of the DBA.NS.D4/8 lines was 25%. These results suggest that genes located on Chrs 4 and 8 interact epistatically to modulate neocortical ectopias (Rosen *et al.*, 2003).

The identification of candidate genes in these mice could help guide the human genetic studies on dyslexia. At the present we have not seen homology between the loci that have been shown in humans with the mouse loci. This may reflect the possibility that ectopia formation may have several genetic origins. Thus, for instance, if ectopias result from injury to the external limiting membrane (see above), several agents, each linked to a different gene or to epigenetic effects, may be involved in the injury. A genome-wide screen has not been done yet in the human, and it is possible other genes will emerge, including a gene that is homologous to the mouse genome regions described in this chapter.

### Summary and conclusions

The research results presented here indicate that the central nervous system of dyslexics is affected at multiple stages and in at least two modalities. In other words, there are changes in the visual and auditory systems, and in zones that process low-level information and zones that process high-level information. Furthermore, we can learn from experimental models that changes in low-level sensory processors in the brain may be the consequence of earlier developmental changes taking place in higher-order cortices. Moreover, based on the discovery of these anatomical changes, it is possible that the sensory/perceptual deficits described in dyslexics, both in the visual and auditory modalities, could be the consequence rather than the cause of cognitive deficits, because the latter occur first. Also, it appears that the primary injury to the cortex may be relatively well tolerated for tasks involving temporal processing, but that it is the secondary changes in the thalamus which produce the temporal processing difficulties. Instead, the cortical changes may be responsible for other cognitive behaviors that have been described both in animals and in dyslexics. Thus, we can be reasonably certain that there are cognitive deficits and perceptual deficits in dyslexics, but we cannot provide good evidence for the idea that the perceptual deficits are causally related to the reading difficulty. Further, there appears to be a sex difference in rats with induced malformations of the cortex, whereby females, which do not develop secondary thalamic changes, do not show functional deficits in rapid auditory processing, whereas males, which develop secondary thalamic changes, do exhibit temporal processing deficits. We believe that the ectopia, as the initiating event in the cascades of events leading to the building of anomalous systems involved in vision and language at multiple levels, is most proximate to the genetic abnormality. However, the gene for ectopia is not the same as the gene for dyslexia, which raises the question of whether the gene for dyslexia per se really exists.

REFERENCES

Anderson, K. C., Brown, C. P. & Tallal, P. (1993) Developmental language disorders: Evidence for a basic processing deficit. *Current Opinion in Neurology & Neurosurgery* 6:98–106.

Ashkenas, J. (1996) Williams syndrome starts making sense. *American Journal of Human Genetics* 59:756–61.

Boehm, G. W., Sherman, G. F., Hoplight, B. J., Hyde, L. A., Bradway, D. M., Galaburda, A. M., Ahmed, S. A. & Denenberg, V. H. (1998) Learning in year-old female autoimmune BXSB mice. *Physiology & Behavior* 64:75–82.

Boehm, G. W., Sherman, G. F., Hoplight, B. J., Hyde, L. A., Waters, N. S., Bradway, D. M., Galaburda, A. M. & Denenberg, V. H. (1996) Learning and memory in the autoimmune BXSB mouse: Effects of neocortical ectopias and environmental enrichment. *Brain Research* 726:11–22.

Bradley, L. & Bryant, P. (1981) Visual memory and phonological skills in reading and spelling backwardness. *Psychological Research* 43:193–9.

Bryant, P., Nunes T. & Bindman, M. (1998) Awareness of language in children who have reading difficulties: Historical comparisons in a longitudinal study. *Journal of Child Psychology and Psychiatry* 39:501–10.

Cardon, L. R., Smith, S. D., Fulker, D. W., Kimberling, W. J., Pennington, B. F. & DeFries, J. C. (1994) Quantitative trait locus for reading disability on chromosome 6. *Science* 266:276–9.

Cardon, L. R., Smith, S. D., Fulker, D. W., Kimberling, W. J., Pennington, B. F. & DeFries, J. C. (1995) Quantitative trait locus for reading disability: correction [letter]. *Science* 268:1553.

Davis, C. J., Gayan, J., Knopik, V. S., Smith, S. D., Cardon, L. R., Pennington, B. F., Olson, R. K. & DeFries, J. C. (2001) Etiology of reading difficulties and rapid naming: The Colorado Twin Study of Reading Disability. *Behavior Genetics,* 31, 625–35.

DeFries, J. C., Fulker, D. W. & LaBuda, M. C. (1987) Evidence for a genetic aetiology in reading disability of twins. *Nature* 329:537–9.

DeFries, J. C., Stevenson, J., Gillis, J. & Wadsworth, S. J. (1991) Genetic etiology of spelling deficits in the Colorado and London twin studies of reading disabilities. *Reading and Writing* 3:271–83.

Denenberg, V. H., Sherman, G. F., Rosen, G. D. & Galaburda, A. M. (1988) Learning and laterality differences in BXSB mice as a function of neocortical anomaly. *Society for Neuroscience Abstracts* 14:1260.

Denenberg, V. H., Sherman, G. F., Schrott, L. M., Rosen, G. D. & Galaburda, A. M. (1991) Spatial learning, discrimination learning, paw preference and neocortical ectopias in two autoimmune strains of mice. *Brain Research* 562:98–104.

Eden, G. F., Vanmeter, J. W., Rumsey, J. M. & Zeffiro, T. A. (1996b) The visual deficit theory of developmental dyslexia. *Neuroimage* 4:S108–S117.

Eden, G. F., Vanmeter, J. W., Rumsey, J. M., Maisog, J. M., Woods, R. P. & Zeffiro, T. A. (1996a) Abnormal processing of visual motion in dyslexia revealed by functional brain imaging. *Nature* 382:66–9.

Eicher, E. & Lee, B. (1990) The NXSM recombinant inbred strains of mice: Genetic profile for 58 loci including the Mtv proviral loci. *Genetics* 125:431–46.

Field, L. L. & Kaplan, B. J. (1998) Absence of linkage of phonological coding dyslexia to chromosome 6p23- p21.3 in a large family data set. *American Journal of Human Genetics* 63:1448–56.

Finucci, J. M., Gurthrie, J. T. & Childs, B. (1976) The genetics of specific reading disability. *Annals of Human Genetics* 40:1–23.

Fisher, S. E., Marlow, A. J., Lamb, J., Maestrini, E., Williams, D. F., Richardson, A. J., Weeks, D. E., Stein, J. F. & Monaco, A. P. (1999) A quantitative-trait locus on chromosome 6p influences different aspects of developmental dyslexia. *American Journal of Human Genetics* 64:146–56.

Fitch, R. H., Miller, S. & Tallal, P. (1997) Neurobiology of speech perception. *Annual Review of Neuroscience* 20:331–53.

Fitch, R. H., Tallal, P., Brown, C., Galaburda, A. M. & Rosen, G. D. (1994) Induced microgyria and auditory temporal processing in rats: A model for language impairment? *Cerebral Cortex* 4:260–70.

Frenkel, M., Sherman, G. F., Bashan, K. A., Galaburda, A. M. & LoTurco, J. J. (2000) Neocortical ectopias are associated with attenuated neurophysiological responses to rapidly changing auditory stimuli. *Neuroreport: An International Journal for the Rapid Communication of Research in Neuroscience,* 11:575–9.

Friede, R. L. & Mikolasek, J. (1978) Postencephalitic porencephaly, hydranencephaly or polymicrogyria. A review. *Acta Neuropathology (Berlin)* 43:161–8.

Galaburda, A. M. (2002) Anatomy of the temporal processing deficit in developmental dyslexia. In E. Witruk, A. D. Friederici & T. Lachmann (eds), *Basic functions of language, reading, and reading disability*, 241–50. Dordrecht: Kluwer Academic Publishers.

Galaburda, A. M., Menard, M. T. & Rosen, G. D. (1994) Evidence for aberrant auditory anatomy in developmental dyslexia. *Proceedings of the National Academy of Sciences* 91:8010–13.

Galaburda, A. M., Sherman, G. F., Rosen, G. D., Aboitiz, F. & Geschwind, N. (1985) Developmental dyslexia: Four consecutive cases with cortical anomalies. *Annals of Neurology* 18:222–33.

Gayan, J., Smith, S. D., Cherny, S. S., Cardon, L. R., Fulker, D. W., Brower, A. M., Olson, R. K., Pennington, B. F. & DeFries, J. C. (1999) Quantitative-trait locus for specific language and reading deficits on chromosome 6p. *American Journal of Human Genetics* 64:157–64.

Gilger, J. W., Pennington, B. F. & DeFries, J. C. (1991) Risk for reading disabilities as a function of parental history of learning problems: Data from three samples of families demonstrating genetic transmission. *Reading and Writing* 3:205–17.

Goei, V. L., Choi, J., Ahn, J., Bowlus, C. L., Raha-Chowdhury, R. & Gruen, J. R. (1998) Human gamma-aminobutyric acid B receptor gene: complementary DNA cloning, expression, chromosomal location, and genomic organization [see comments]. *Biological Psychiatry* 44:659–66.

Grigorenko, E. L. (2003) The first candidate gene for dyslexia: Turning the page of a new chapter of research. *Proceedings of the National Academy of Sciences* 100(20):11190–2.

Grigorenko, E. L., Wood, F. B., Meyer, M. S., Hart, L. A., Speed, W. C., Shuster, A. & Pauls, D. L. (1997) Susceptibility loci for distinct components of developmental dyslexia on chromosomes 6 and 15. *American Journal of Human Genetics* 60:27–39.

Hallgren, B. (1950) Specific dyslexia: a clinical and genetic study. *Acta Psychiatr Neurol Scand Suppl* 65:1–287.

Herman, A. E., Galaburda, A. M., Fitch, H. R., Carter, A. R. & Rosen, G. D. (1997) Cerebral microgyria, thalamic cell size and auditory temporal processing in male and female rats. *Cerebral Cortex* 7:453–64.

Humphreys, P., Rosen, G. D., Sherman, G. F. & Galaburda, A. M. (1989) Freezing lesions of the newborn rat brain: A model for cerebrocortical microdysgenesis. *Society for Neuroscience Abstracts* 15:1120.

Hynd, G., Semrud-Clikeman, M., Lorys, A., Novey, E. & Eliopulos, R. (1990) Brain morphology in developmental dyslexia and attention deficit disorder/hyperactivity. *Archives of Neurology* 47:919–26.

Jenner, A. R., Galaburda, A. M. & Sherman, G. F. (1995) Connectivity of cortical ectopias in autoimmune mice. *Society for Neuroscience Abstracts* 21:1712.

Jenner, A. R., Galaburda, A. M. and Sherman, G. F. (1997) Thalamocortical and corticothalamic connections in New Zealand Black mice. *Society for Neuroscience Abstracts* 27:1365.

Jenner, A. R., Rosen, G. D. & Galaburda, A. M. (1999) Neuronal asymmetries in the primary visual cortex of dyslexic and non-dyslexic brains. *Annals of Neurology* 46:189–96.

Landerl, K., Wimmer, H. & Frith, U. (1997) The impact of orthographic consistency on dyslexia: a German-English comparison. *Cognition* 63:315–34.

Liberman, I. Y. & Shankweiler, D. (1985) Phonology and the problems of learning to read and write. *Remedial and Special Education* 6:8–17.

Livingstone, M., Rosen, G., Drislane, F. & Galaburda, A. (1991) Physiological and anatomical evidence for a magnocellular defect in developmental dyslexia. *Proceedings of the National Academy of Sciences* 88:7943–7.

Merzenich, M. M., Jenkins, W. M., Johnston, P., Schreiner, C., Miller, S. L. & Tallal, P. (1996) Temporal processing deficits of language-learning impaired children ameliorated by training. *Science* 271:77–80.

Morais, J., Luytens, M. & Alegria, J. (1984) Segmentation abilities of dyslexics and normal readers. *Perceptual and Motor Skills* 58:221–2.

Morgan, A. E. & Hynd, G. W. (1998) Dyslexia, neurolinguistic ability, and anatomical variation of the planum temporale. *Neuropsychology Review* 8:79–93.

Pennington, B. F. (1995) Genetics of learning disabilities. *Journal Child Neurology* 10:S69–S77.

Pennington, B. F. (2002) *The development of psychopathology: Nature and nurture.* New York: Guilford Press.

Pennington, B. F., Gilger, J. W., Pauls, D., Smith, S. A., Smith, S. D. & DeFries, J. C. (1991) Evidence for major gene transmission of developmental dyslexia. *Journal of the American Medical Association* 266:1527–34.

Pennington, B. F. & Smith, S. D. (1983) Genetic influences on learning disabilities and speech and language disorders. *Child Development* 54:369–87.

Rabin, M., Elston, R. C., Gross-Glenn, K. *et al.* (1991) Molecular genetics of developmental dyslexia. *American Journal of Human Genetics* 49:355.

Rabin, M., Wen, X. L., Hepburn, M. & Lubs, H. A. (1993) Suggestive linkage of developmental dyslexia to chromosome 1p34–p36. *Lancet* 342:178.

Rosen, G. D. (1996) Cellular, morphometric, ontogenetic and connectional substrates of anatomical asymmetry. *Neuroscience Biobehavioral Review* 20:607–15.

Rosen, G. D. & Galaburda, A. M. (1996) Efferent and afferent connectivity of induced neocortical microgyria. *Society for Neuroscience Abstracts* 22:485.

Rosen, G. D., Grasso, E. A., Gray, W. E., Palmieri, S. E., Galaburda, A. M. & Sherman, G. F. (2003) Genetic analysis of focal cerebral cortical malformations in mice using congenics and recombinant inbred strains. *Society for Neuroscience Abstracts.*

Rosen, G. D., Herman, A. E. & Galaburda, A. M. (1997) MGN neuronal size distribution following induced neocortical malformations: The effect of perinatal gonadal steroids. *Society for Neuroscience Abstracts* 23:626.

Rosen, G. D., Sherman, G. F. & Galaburda, A. M. (1996) Birthdates of neurons in induced microgyria. *Brain Research*, 727:71–8.

Rosen, G. D., Sherman, G. F., Mehler, C.., Emsbo, K. & Galaburda, A. M. (1989) The effect of developmental neuropathology on neocortical asymmetry in New Zealand Black mice. *International Journal of Neuroscience* 45:247–54.

Rutter, M., Caspi, A., Fergusson, D., Horwood, L. J., Goodman, R., Maughan, B., Moffitt, T. E., Meltzer, H. & Carroll, J. (2004) Sex differences in developmental reading disability: new findings from 4 epidemiological studies. *Journal of the American Medical Association* 291:2007–12.

Scerri, T. S., Fisher, S. E., Francks, C., MacPhie, I. L., Paracchini, S., Richardson, A. J., Stein, J. F. & Monaco, A. P. (2004) Putative functional alleles of DYX1C1 are not associated with dyslexia susceptibility in a large sample of sibling pairs from the UK. *Journal of Medical Genetics*, 41, 853–7.

Schrott, L. M., Denenberg, V. H., Sherman, G. F., Rosen, G. D. & Galaburda, A. M. (1992) Lashley maze learning deficits in NZB mice. *Physiology & Behavior* 52:1085–9.

Schulte-Korne, G., Grimm, T., Nothen, M. M., Muller-Myhsok, B., Cichon, S., Vogt, I. R., Propping, P. & Remschmidt, H. (1998) Evidence of linkage of spelling disability to chromosome 15. *American Journal of Human Genetics* 63: 279–82.

Sherman, G. F., Rosen, G. D. & Galaburda, A. M. (1988) Neocortical anomalies in autoimmune mice: A model for the developmental neuropathology seen in the dyslexic brain. *Drug Development Research* 15:307–14.

Sherman, G. F., Stone, L. V., Denenberg, V. H. & Beier, D. R. (1994) A genetic analysis of neocortical ectopias in New Zealand Black mice. *NeuroReport* 5:721–4.

Silver, L. M. (1995) *Mouse genetics: Concepts and applications.* New York: Oxford University Press.

Smith, S. D., Kelley, P. M. & Brower, A. M. (1998) Molecular approaches to the genetic analysis of specific reading disability. *Human Biology* 70:239–56.

Smith, S. D., Kimberling, W. J. & Pennington, B. F. (1991) Screening for multiple genes influencing dyslexia. *Reading and Writing* 3:285–98.

Smith, S. D., Kimberling, W. J., Pennington, B. F. & Lubs, H. A. (1983) Specific reading disability: Identification of an inherited form through linkage analysis. *Science* 219:1345–7.

Smith, S. D., Pennington, B. F., Kimberling, W. J. & Ing, P. (1990) Familial dyslexia: Use of genetic linkage data to define subtypes. *Journal of the American Academy of Child and Adolescent Psychiatry* 29:204–13.

Steinmetz, H., Volkmann, J., Jancke, L. & Freund, H.-J. (1991) Anatomical left-right asymmetry of language-related temporal cortex is different in left- and right-handers. *Annals of Neurology* 29:315–19.

Stephenson, S. (1907) Six cases of congenital word-blindness (inability to learn to read). *Ophthalmoscope* 5:482–4.

Taipale, M., Kaminen, N., Nopola-Hemmi, J., Haltia, T., Myllyluoma, B., Lyytinen, H., Muller, K., Kaaranen, M., Lindsberg, P. J., Hannula-Jouppi, K. & Kere, J. (2003) A candidate gene for developmental dyslexia encodes a nuclear tetratricopeptide repeat domain protein dynamically regulated in brain. *Proceedings of the National Academy of Sciences* 100(20):11553–8.

Tallal, P. (1977) Auditory perception, phonics and reading disabilities in children. *Journal of the Acoustical Society of America* 62:S100.

Tallal, P., Miller, S., Fitch, R. H., Stein, J. F., McAnally, K., Richardson, A. J., Fawcett, A. J., Jacobson, C. & Nicholson, R. I. (1995) Dyslexia update. *Irish Journal of Psychology* 16:194–268.

Tallal, P. & Piercy, M. (1973) Defects of non-verbal auditory perception in children with developmental aphasia. *Nature* 241:468–9.

Tamagawa, K., Scheidt, P. & Friede, R. L. (1989) Experimental production of leptomeningeal hetertopias from dissociated fetal tissue. *Acta Neuropathological* 78:153–8.

Vogler, G. P., DeFries, J. C. & Decker, S. N. (1985) Family history as an indicator of risk for reading disability. *Journal of Learning Disabilities* 18:419–21.

Wadsworth, S. J., Corley, R. P., Hewitt, J. K., Plomin, R. & DeFries, J. C. (2002) Parent-offspring resemblance for reading performance at 7, 12 and 16 years of age in the Colorado Adoption Project. *Journal of Child Psychology & Psychiatry & Allied Disciplines,* 43:769–74.

Wadsworth, S. J., DeFries, J. C., Stevenson, J., Gilger, J. W. & Pennington, B. F. (1992) Gender ratios among reading-disabled children and their siblings as a function of parental impairment. *Journal of Child Psychology & Psychiatry & Allied Disciplines* 33:1229–39.

Waters, N. S., Sherman, G. F., Galaburda, A. M. & Denenberg, V. H. (1997) Effects of cortical ectopias on spatial delayed-matching-to-sample performance in BXSB mice. *Behavioral Brain Research* 84:23–9.

Wigg, K. G., Couto, J. M., Feng, Y., Anderson, B., Cate-Carter, T. D., Macciardi, F., Tannock, R., Lovett, M. W., Humphries, T. W. & Barr, C. L. (2004) Support for EKN1 as the susceptibility locus for dyslexia on 15q21. *Molecular Psychiatry* 9(12):1111–21.

Wolf, M. & Bowers, P. (1999) The "Double-Deficit Hypothesis" for the developmental dyslexias. *Journal of Educational Psychology* 91:1–24.

Yule, W. & Rutter, M. (1975) The concept of specific reading retardation. *Journal of Child Psychology & Psychiatry and Allied Disciplines* 16:181–97.

*Part II*

Reading and the Growing Brain: Methodology
and History

# 4     A brief history of time, phonology, and other explanations of developmental dyslexia*

*Maryanne Wolf and Jane Ashby*

*Overview:* Throughout the history of the study of reading disabilities, research has been plagued by the heterogeneity inherent in individuals with dyslexia and the apparent contradictions in findings that this variability produces. In this thematic review of historical and current approaches, the authors transform this view of variability to show how it is a key source of information about development of the normal reading process and sources of reading problems. The new emphasis on connecting mind, brain, and education requires relating neurological and behavioral aspects of dyslexia in its varied forms. In their work the authors focus especially on understanding how reading disability relates both to processes underlying the slow retrieval of names for common visual stimuli, such as letters, numbers, and colors, and also to phonological processes. They discuss the educational implications of their findings for the historical conflict between "whole language" and "phonological" approaches to reading instruction. Looking to the future, they suggest that only through considering the complexity of the reading process and the variability present in reading disability profiles can progress be made in unlocking the true nature of this disorder.         *The Editors*

The title of this paper, "A brief history of time, phonology, and other explanations of developmental dyslexia," was meant not only to evoke the title of Stephen Hawking's book, *A Brief History of Time* (1988), but also to underscore the similarly Sisyphean nature of both endeavors. It is presumptuous in the extreme to attempt to summarize, in so abbreviated a form, the history of a field of research that, even when one is generous, is best described as "intrinsically untidy." There are many reasons for this untidiness, but the principal reasons

* Direct correspondence to Maryanne Wolf, Center for Reading and Language Research, Tufts University, Miller Hall, Medford, MA 02155. Electronic mail may be sent to Maryanne. Wolf@Tufts.edu.

    We wish to thank all past and present members of the Tufts Center for Reading and Language Research, particularly Wendy Galante and Linda Whitaker for help with this manuscript. The first author is grateful to NICHD grant HD/OD 30970 for support for the ongoing research in this chapter.

are the phenomena of study themselves: reading represents one of the most complex acts the brain has ever been called upon to learn; its failures are no less complex. This becomes readily apparent in any examination of the central explanations for reading failure that dominate in the different decades of dyslexia research. Just as Norman Geschwind (1965) used the original writings of early neurologists Broca, Wernicke, Dejerine, and Orton to reflect on the etiology of aphasia and alexia, an examination of Cattell (1886), Huey (1908), Dejerine (1892), Orton (1928, 1937), and Geschwind (1965, 1982) himself can be similarly helpful in chronicling the range of hypotheses about reading disabilities.

There are several essential reasons for the "brief history" of dyslexia found in this chapter that relate both to the untidiness of past research and to the complexity of reading. To paraphrase one of the most famous quotations about reading by Sir Edmund Huey (1908): "If we were able, with all our sophistication, to capture all the complex component processes, subprocesses, and underlying neurophysiological mechanisms involved in the act of reading, it would be the acme of a psychologist's accomplishments." The leitmotiv of this chapter is that the history of many a psychologist's attempts to explain reading failure provides an unexpected analogue to the componential complexity of reading. Further, the same principle applies to the extensively documented heterogeneity of reading disabilities. Whatever can go wrong in this complex system of reading sometimes does – in one or more groups of children with disabilities. The heterogeneity of reading disabilities is, therefore, another reflection of the reading processes' multiple component parts.

In other words, we wish to use the history of the field of reading disabilities to illumine once more the need to look not at a single source of disability, but at the stunning variety of ways that reading or written language can be disrupted. Perhaps more than any other human function, reading represents the brain's remarkable capacity to forge new pathways and *connections* among existing cognitive, perceptual, motor, and linguistic systems, any one of which might impede the development of reading, particularly since they were originally designed to do other things. Reading is an exquisite example of the brain's capacity to rearrange its original circuits to learn something new. It is hardly surprising in such a relatively recently evolved examplar of the brain's "rearrangement" that there will be a variety of ways reading can fail to develop. The punch line of this chapter will be that current efforts in reading disabilities research must go beyond the present largely unidimensional notions of dyslexia, if we are to go beyond the past history to incorporate our burgeoning understanding of the complexities of the reading brain. The field's history and the heterogeneity of impairments *and* strengths in our reading-disabled children are two manifestations of the extraordinary neuronal circuitry that underlies the reading act.

Table 4.1. *History of names for dyslexia.*

* *Wortblindheit* or word-blindness
* Congenital word blindness
* Psycholexia
* Bradylexia
* Legasthenia & word amblyopia
* Amnesia visualis verbalis
* Analphabetia partialis
* Linear dyslexia
* Cortical & subcortical word blindness
* Strephosymbolia
* Specific reading disability
* Specific dyslexia
* Primary & secondary reading retardation
* Auditory dyslexia
* Developmental dyslexia

### Early history

A quick look at the sheer variety of names used over the history of research on reading failure is a useful way to begin to look at the range of hypothesized sources for reading breakdown in the first 70 years (see Table 4.1). It may appear that the field is lurching from one explanation to another, but a closer look at the names themselves – word-blindness, amnesia visualis verbalis, strephosymbolia – yields a different conclusion, whereby all the newly named sources represent a collection of lenses, each scrutinizing only one piece of the whole. The metaphor of the blind men's individual descriptions of an elephant has been a frequent and useful metaphor for the early and middle history of dyslexia research, but there are more systematic patterns that emerge than this metaphor suggests – patterns that will be useful in our charting of the reading process over time.

The early history of developmental dyslexia actually begins with a grounding in the acquired alexia cases of Dejerine (1892). Dejerine described what came to be thought of as classic alexia with and without agraphia in adults. His first well-documented case of acquired reading loss was caused by an unusual set of discrete lesions in the left visual area and in the splenium tracts linking the right and left visual areas. Following a first stroke, the patient, a well-educated French businessman, was unable to read words. After a second stroke in the angular gyrus area, the patient lost all ability to write and function with written language. Geschwind (1974) later highlighted the role of the angular gyrus in dyslexia and alexia, but this area has also received renewed attention in current imaging studies (Shaywitz, Shaywitz, Pugh, Fulbright, Constable, Mencl, Shankweiler,

Liberman, Skudlarski, Fletcher, Katz, Marchione, Lacadie, Gatenby, & Gore, 1998; Poldrack, 2002), all of which buttress Geschwind's earlier insights into Dejerine's classic case in the nineteenth century.

In 1895, Hinshelwood (1895) wrote a paper on visual memory and word-blindness, which prompted Pringle Morgan (1896) to publish one of the first cases of childhood dyslexia. Morgan used Kussmaul's (1877) concept of *Wortblindheit* or word-blindness in adults to describe his child patient, and "congenital word-blindness" was adopted as the first term for "difficulty in storing visual impressions of words" (what we might today discuss as orthographic representations). Interestingly in light of later work, Morgan also thought the left angular gyrus area was responsible for this condition, a hypothesis more than likely based on Morgan's familiarity with Dejerine's case of classic alexia with and without agraphia.

Hinshelwood (1900, 1917) provided rich descriptions of congenital word-blindness and like Morgan emphasized a failure in the storage of visual images. Lucy Fildes (1921) was the first to suggest not only visual storage problems, but also the possibility of auditory involvement in reading failure. Her observation that letter reversals were prevalent among reading-disabled children was confirmed and extended in the clinical studies of Samuel Orton and Anna Gillingham.

The work of neurologist Samuel T. Orton (1928, 1937) was the best-articulated and most comprehensive work in the early history of dyslexia. In a gesture that would prove emblematic of the field, Orton (1928) renamed reading disability "strephosymbolia" or "twisted symbols." The choice of this name emphasized his hypothesis that the normal pattern of hemispheric dominance for language processes does not occur or is developmentally delayed in a reading-disabled child. He suggested that letters and words are stored as engrams (again we would refer to these as orthographic representations) in both hemispheres and that in normal lateralization the dominant hemisphere selects the correct orientation of a letter like *b* or *d* or of a letter pattern in a palindromic word like *not* and *ton*. Orton theorized that the normal pattern of hemispheric dominance for language processes does not occur or is developmentally delayed in reading-disabled children, and this anomaly interferes with selecting the correct letter orientation. Thus, he argued, abnormal lateralization leads to visual spatial confusion with reading, spelling, and handwriting, a conclusion that has gained unanticipated partial support in the imaging work of Eden, Zeffiro, and their colleagues (see Turkeltaub, Gareau, Flowers, Zeffiro, & Eden, 2003). (For a more careful examination of Orton, Geschwind's (1982) "Why Orton was right" exhumes many of the less-known insights by Orton, including his emphasis on the importance of comorbid, emotional factors in children with dyslexia.)

With an uncanny feeling of historical déjà vu, we also want to include in this paper one of Orton's more powerful observations: namely, that children taught with the "older phonics methods" have lower rates of reading disability than children taught with the "new whole-word" methods. The Orton-Gillingham method of teaching systematic letter-sound rules was the product of this observation. One can only speculate upon what might have been saved had this conclusion been more accepted in American education. Indeed, although not the focus of this chapter, it appears that almost each epoch comes to a similar conclusion about pedagogy as Orton's and then reverts back: that is, the assertion that systematic explicit instruction of letters and sounds is essential for struggling readers, to be followed by a period of contention and struggle negating that conclusion. In the middle period, for example, Chall (1967) completed a comprehensive meta-analysis of reading method studies in *Learning to read: The great debate*, and came to the same conclusion as Orton. Despite the overwhelming evidence Chall amassed and analyzed, however, the period between the 1970s and 1990s was marked by holistic methods that ran conceptually counter to Orton's and Chall's findings. Unsurprisingly, Orton's early conclusions about explicit instruction of the alphabetic principle have again been proven by more current large-scale analyses, particularly for children with any form of reading difficulty (see Adams, 1990; Foorman, Francis, Winikates, Mehta, Schatschneider, & Fletcher, 1997).

To summarize this early period, the first hypothesized sources of reading disability were rooted in the visual system with a prescient set of emphases by Orton on the importance of orthographic representations, hemispheric lateralization, emotional variables, and phonics-based methods.

### Middle history

By the 1940s, dyslexia research was no longer mainly within the purview of medical researchers. Educators, psychologists, and sociologists were increasingly drawn into dyslexia research as they investigated reasons for school failure. This entrance of researchers from various disciplines changed the field of reading research in several ways. Previous terminology and methods common to the field of medicine were replaced by a proliferation of new terms and research methods. Further, as each discipline developed its own particular terminology to describe reading disorders, a wide range of unknown variables was uncovered in the process.

The middle period, therefore, brought forth different perspectives on the etiology of dyslexia, which competed with classical neurological accounts. The new perspectives emphasized multifactorial explanations of reading disorders that included neuroses, poverty, and pupil motivation. Robinson's (1946) proposal of twelve separate causes of dyslexia is one of several approaches in this vein. Such perspectives were important, but ultimately may have marginalized neurological findings that appear accurate in hindsight. For example, Schilder

(1944) astutely described the dyslexic reader as one who can identify letters by name, but who is able neither to relate the letters with their sounds nor to differentiate the spoken word into its sounds. This description is a fair accounting of the absence of phoneme awareness in dyslexic children, which is central to current theory. Unfortunately, Schilder's observations went unrecognized by researchers in disciplines other than neurology for several decades.

Theories about the causes of reading failure in this middle period abounded. Although many of the actual explanations were eventually discarded, almost every perspective was attempting to explain some aspect of behavior in dyslexia that is still under investigation today. Furthermore, parts of several theories formulated during this period provided a foundation for future advances in dyslexia research. Schilder (1944) essentially described the now well-understood phonological deficits exhibited by readers with dyslexia. Bender (1956) anticipated another significant line of contemporary research in her description of temporal processing deficits in children with reading disorders. Rabinovitch (1959) operationalized the distinction between children with dyslexia and other impaired readers and initiated the use of IQ testing to identify reading disorders. Birch (1962; Birch & Belmont, 1964) emphasized the importance of intersensory or cross-modality processing and what he called the visual-auditory-kinesthetic connections. The latter proved to be a cornerstone of effective instruction for some reading-impaired students. Clements and Peters (1962) sought to understand the neurological basis that would explain various perceptual problems and their purported relationship to reading disabilities.

The writings of Critchley (1964), along with Johnson and Myklebust (1964), accelerated interest in the role of auditory processes in reading and the implications of this research for more precise forms of intervention. For example, in his insightful book *Developmental dyslexia* (1964), Critchley located the central problem of dyslexia in "the recognition of the visual form of a symbol and its *acoustic properties.*" Johnson and Myklebust (1964) described both visual and auditory forms of dyslexia and along with Critchley began a new emphasis on the idea of reading subtypes in dyslexia, with varied forms of disability.

Myklebust *et al.* (1969), in particular, emphasized that children with reading disabilities are deficient in learning *despite* adequate intelligence, hearing, and vision. His definition reflected the paradigm shift of this decade that would be completed later in the 1970s by Vellutino (1979): a discarding of perceptual-deficit explanations of dyslexia in pursuit of theories involving deeper linguistic and cognitive processes that included more general factors like temporal processing, sequencing, and seriation (see also Bakker, 1972; Zurif & Carson, 1970; Blank, Berenzweig & Bridger, 1975).

The middle period, then, appears as a formative time of development in the field of dyslexia. Although the fundamental question of etiology was not resolved, research emphases in the middle of the century provided a foundation for the pivotal developments of the modern period: the multi-dimensional nature of reading disabilities; the roles of underlying linguistic and cognitive systems in reading; and the particular contribution of phonological deficits to dyslexia. Each of these current strands of inquiry can be traced back to the observations of mid-century researchers.

### Recent history

What we will call the recent history of dyslexia research is marked by far greater consensus and more systematic lines of research than earlier periods. Based largely on an increased understanding of cognitive and linguistic systems, two of the major directions in more recent research have their starting points in the early 1970s: that is, the psycholinguistics-based theories of reading disorders developed by Isabelle Liberman and Donald Shankweiler, and the reexamination of the neurophysiological basis of reading disorders initiated anew by Geschwind (1965, 1974). A third direction is a major change from all other epochs and involves the systematic study of what intervention works best for which child under what conditions.

The first direction is dominated by the work of Liberman, Shankweiler, and their psycholinguistics colleagues who explored the relationship of speech and reading development across three decades of studies (e.g. Liberman, 1971; Shankweiler & Liberman, 1972; Liberman, Shankweiler, Fischer, & Carter, 1974; Brady, Shankweiler, & Mann, 1983; Shankweiler & Liberman, 1989). For example, findings from an early study of proficient deaf readers indicated that those few deaf readers who were able to learn to read beyond the fifth grade level demonstrated facility with sound segmentation and phoneme manipulation (see Hanson, Liberman, & Shankweiler, 1984). Because many children who are deaf never go beyond third grade reading level, this finding was pivotal and propelled these researchers to examine in great depth a range of phonological processes. They began by distinguishing, for example, the more abstract concept of *phonological analysis* from the *auditory perception* of speech sounds, and went on to build an entire program of research based on the importance of the phoneme's representation in the language development of every reader.

Since the landmark studies by Shankweiler and Liberman (1972), over two-and-a-half decades of research on phonological processing has resulted in the most systematically studied body of work in the history of reading research (Adams, 1990; Bradley & Bryant, 1983; Brady & Shankweiler, 1991; Byrne, 1998; Catts, 1996; Chall, 1983; Foorman *et al.*, 1998; Goswami & Bryant, 1990; Kamhi & Catts, 1989; Lyon, 1995; Olson, Wise, Connors, Rack, & Fulker, 1989; Perfetti, 1985; Siegel & Ryan, 1988; Stanovich, 1986, 1994; Torgesen, Wagner, & Rashotte, 1994; Tunmer, 1995; Vellutino, 1979; Vellutino & Scanlon, 1987; Wagner, Torgesen, & Rashotte, 1994). Based on these cumulative data, we now know that a child's ability to represent the individual phonemes (*phoneme awareness*) of a language is critical for learning the grapheme–phoneme correspondence rules that are the foundation for decoding, fluency, and comprehension (see review in Adams, 1990). The centrality of phoneme awareness in early reading development makes it a superb diagnostic predictor of reading difficulties, a key component in tracing heritability patterns, and the critical core of many reading intervention programs for increasing phonological awareness and decoding skills (see Foorman *et al.*, 1997; Torgesen, Wagner, & Rashotte, 1994). Stanovich (1990) has frequently described this entire direction of phonological-based research as one of the most successful science stories in modern research history.

The second major development in dyslexia research during the modern period involved a reexamination of the neurophysiological basis of developmental reading disorders. Several current research directions in the neurological bases of dyslexia can, in fact, be traced to Geschwind's (1965) monograph, "Disconnection syndrome in animals and man." With this paper, Geschwind inspired several productive trajectories in aphasia, alexia, and dyslexia research. For example, two lines of current research include: 1) a renewed emphasis on the contribution of particular cortical, subcortical, and cerebellar areas that are necessary for oral and written language; and 2) an unexpected conceptualization of word-retrieval or naming speed as one of the most important tasks in reading prediction across many languages.

Geschwind's early emphasis on the neurological basis of reading failure was the basis for two decades of groundbreaking studies into the underlying neuroanatomy of dyslexia by Galaburda and his colleagues, Rosen (Galaburda, Menard, & Rosen, 1994; Galaburda & Sherman, this volume; Rosen *et al.*, 2001) and Livingstone (see Livingstone, Rosen, Drislane, & Galaburda, 1991). As Benes (this volume) discusses, these researchers investigated and demonstrated specific areas of abnormal neuronal migration and distribution patterns in a small number of autopsied brains of dyslexic readers. Although their sample size prevents generalization, these studies provided the first concrete evidence for neuronal differences in the language-related cortical and subcortical areas of dyslexic readers, a finding strongly supported by current brain imaging studies of reading and reading failure (Eden & Zeffiro, 1998; Shaywitz, Fletcher, & Shaywitz, 1996; Turkeltaub *et al.*, 2003). These preliminary findings also provided an additional impetus to find those areas responsible for the critical functional deficits in dyslexia like phonology.

For example, Livingstone *et al.* (1991) and Galaburda *et al.* (1994) found substantial differences at the cellular level (i.e. specifically, the magnocellular systems) in two areas of the thalamus that are responsible for the rapid coordination of visual and auditory processes. Discussed in Benes (this volume), the magnocellular systems are devoted to smooth *rapid* neuronal transmission and quick inhibition of previous stimuli. The potential importance of finding magnocellular differences in the thalamic medial and lateral geniculate nuclei of dyslexic persons is that these data may indicate a neuronal foundation for the well-documented lack of smooth automatic functioning in phonological and orthographic systems (Galaburda *et al.*, 1994; Livingstone *et al.*, 1991). We will speculate in the next section that the findings in the magnocellular system in the lateral geniculate nuclei might also be related to naming-speed deficits.

Geschwind was infamous for novel ideas that were semi-correct, because many of them spawned whole new lines of research. One of these ideas in the "Disconnection" monograph was that a child's early color naming might be the best predictor for later reading (Geschwind, 1965). Hearkening back to Dejerine's study of classic alexia, Geschwind reasoned that because both color naming and reading processes share subprocesses responsible for attaching a linguistic label to a visually presented, abstract symbol, then color naming (which develops earlier) would be a good predictor of later reading skills. This simple concept would later be investigated by his student, pediatric neurologist Martha Denckla, who designed a set of serial, continuous naming tasks called Rapid Automatized Naming (RAN) tests. With Rita Rudel, Denckla (Denckla & Rudel, 1974, 1976a,b) demonstrated that it was not color naming per se, but rather the *speed* of naming colors, letters, numbers, and objects in serial naming that differentiated dyslexic children from other learning-disabled and average reading children.

This finding, in turn, became the basis for our own work and those of many others on the unexpected role of naming-speed processes in reading (Ackerman, Dykman, & Gardner, 1990; Badian, 1994, 1995, 1996; Blachman, 1984; Bowers, Steffy, & Tate, 1988; Bowers, 1993; Bowers, Golden, Kennedy, & Young, 1994; Felton, 1993; Kirby, Parilla, & Pfeiffer, 2003; McBride-Chang & Manis, 1996; Parilla, Kirby, & McQuarrie, 2004; Spring & Capps, 1974; Wolf, 1979; Wolf & Bowers, 1999; Wolf, Bowers, & Biddle, 2000; Wolff, Michel, & Ovrut, 1990; Young & Bowers, 1995). Each of us sought to understand why the speed of processing visually presented linguistic material differentiates dyslexic readers from most average reading persons, as well as other learning-disabled populations. Research over the last 15 years has demonstrated in cross-sectional, longitudinal, and cross-linguistic studies that dyslexic readers are slower than average readers at every age in naming speed, particularly for letters and numbers. Data in German (Wimmer, 1993; Wolf, Lotz, & Biddle, 1994), Spanish (Novoa, 1988), Dutch (van den Bos, 1998), and Finnish (Korhonen, 1995) are even more supportive. In these languages, where the orthography or writing system is more transparent, naming speed is a stronger predictor of reading achievement than is phonological awareness. Perhaps the most interesting cross-linguistic evidence to date is that naming-speed tasks appear to be the best predictor of later reading in Chinese (Ho, Tsang, & Lee

2002) and in Hebrew orthographies (Breznitz & Berman, 2003), findings that point to the relative universality of the phenomenon.

In English, naming speed also appears to differentiate *subgroups* of children with reading disorders. The careful subtyping study by Morris, Stuebing, Fletcher, Shaywitz, Lyon, Shankweiler, Katz, Francis, and Shaywitz (1998) indicated a range of specific subtypes of reading disability; a finding reminiscent of Johnson and Myklebust's (1964) and Benton's (1978) anticipation of multiple syndromes. Further, Morris *et al.* (1998) found that among their major subtypes, it was the co-occurrence of phonological, naming speed, and short-term memory deficits that marked their most impaired readers, a finding replicated by Berninger and her colleagues (Berninger & Richards, 2003).

One underlying question is why slow naming speed is related to reading disorders. Although there are good a priori reasons for understanding why phonological tasks are predictors of reading skill, there are no such transparent reasons connecting naming speed and reading. In an alternative conceptualization of dyslexia, the double-deficit hypothesis, Wolf and Bowers integrate previous research in the cognitive and neurosciences and view naming speed as an ensemble of perceptual, cognitive, linguistic, and motoric processes, any of which could impede speed in naming *or* reading (which share many of the same processes). By reanalyzing all their previous data on dyslexic children in two countries and dividing the children into groups with scores one standard deviation below the mean on naming speed or phoneme awareness, Wolf and Bowers found both some unsurprising and surprising results. They found that most of their samples exhibited *two* major core deficits in reading disorders – phonological decoding and naming speed – with three dominant subtypes: two dissociated, single-deficit subtypes (i.e. either singular phonological or single rate deficits) and one combined or *double*-deficit (Wolf & Bowers, 1999; Wolf, Bowers, & Biddle, 2000). The phonological-deficit subtype child had particular difficulties in phoneme awareness, word attack, and spelling, but was relatively unimpaired in naming speed. Conversely, the naming-speed deficit child was relatively spared in word attack and phoneme awareness skills, but had significant problems in all speed or timed aspects of naming and reading. Comprehension difficulties were found in both single deficits, but via different pathways. It was the combination of both or *double* deficits that characterized the most severe forms of reading disabilities, with pervasive breakdown in word attack, word identification, and comprehension – presumably because no compensatory routes are available. These types seem also to relate to the distinct developmental pathways for reading problems described by Fischer, Rose, and Rose (this volume).

Studies from an extensive range of research now support the presence of naming-speed deficits among most dyslexic children. Torgesen *et al.* (1998) found evidence of the co-occurrence of both deficits in his most impaired readers. Wood (1995), Meyer and Felton (1998), and Felton (Felton & Brown, 1990; Felton, 1993) have consistently reported the enduring aspect of rapid naming deficits in their clinical populations of impaired readers. Morris and his colleagues wrote in their paper: "These results suggest that serial naming deficits and more general rate-based factors must be considered in examining reading outcomes for children with learning disabilities" (Morris et al., 1998, p. 25).

Recently, imaging studies have begun to elucidate the multiple component systems that are activated during rapid naming (Misra, Katzir, Wolf, & Poldrack, 2004; Turkeltaub et al., 2003) and the overlap of these systems with reading. In a series of articles, Wolf, Bowers, & Biddle (2000) described several hypotheses that attempt to explain possible relationships between serial naming speed and reading. Both hypotheses are based on a model of naming speed that depicts the multiple components that are incorporated within it and that overlap with components in reading (see Wolf & Bowers, 1999). Hypothesis One links findings from the visual process (e.g. flicker-fusion research) and orthographic representation difficulties in dyslexic readers (Chase & Jenner, 1993; Lovegrove & Williams, 1993) to those of cytoarchitectonic studies (Galaburda et al., 1994; Livingstone et al., 1991). Flicker-fusion studies indicate that when presented with two rapidly successive stimuli, dyslexic readers cannot detect that there are two stimuli at the same rate as average readers. The argument here is that aberrant development in the magnocellular system in the lateral geniculate nucleus may impede the development of lower-spatial frequency components in the visual system. These components are equally critical in the rapid recognition of visual features, for example in orthographic letter patterns, and in the serial processing demands of fluent reading. Wolf and Bowers hypothesized that decreased speed of processing in these magnocellular and lower-level spatial processes could slow down the induction of stable orthographic representations, as well as slow down serial naming speed. In this scenario, naming speed would be largely an index of aberrant development in lower-level processes that are involved in serial movement and in orthographic pattern recognition – a different explanation for Orton's (1937) similar observations.

In their Hypothesis Two, naming speed is conceptualized as part of a cascading (i.e. more domain-general) system of rate or processing-speed difficulties. Within such a characterization the combination of several implicated components and their underlying structures (e.g. across magnocellular systems in lateral and medial geniculate nuclei; see Galaburda et al., 1994) could affect both orthographic and phonological processes, as well as rapid retrieval processes. This combination, in turn, would impede the variety of reading behaviors from word attack and word identification to comprehension. Alternatively, a severe breakdown in any one central subprocess in naming speed (including phonology) or in a single timing mechanism could explain such widespread and general disruption (e.g., the thalamic intralaminar nucleus, see Llinas, 1996; or some other "precise timing mechanism," see Ojemann, 1983). There is at present no clear resolution to what "causes" naming speed deficits. Imaging research, however, illumines why. Findings from Misra *et al.* (2004) and Turkeltaub *et al.* (2003) illustrate the complex, multiple sites required to name a letter, any one of which could result in slowed retrieval. Like reading failure, deficits in naming speed can result from more than one cause.

One of the major contributions of this direction of research is its highlighting of both the complex nature of reading fluency at the level of the letter, word, and connected text and the critical role that time plays in the reading process. Wolf and Katzir-Cohen (2001) have argued, for example, for a figure–ground shift in the conceptualization of fluency and its relationship to comprehension. They describe a developmental model of fluency with contributions from many linguistic sources of information.

Some of the most important implications of both the recent fluency work and the phonological-based research in the modern period relate to the significant implications for changes in classroom practice (Felton, 1993; Tunmer & Nesdale, 1985), the third major research direction. For example, work on phonological processes made an inestimably important impact on the way reading is taught, particularly to children with severe reading disabilities (Brady & Shankweiler, 1991; Torgesen, Wagner, & Rashotte, 1994). As discussed earlier with regard to Orton's (1937) and Chall's (1967) earlier conclusions, there is now overwhelming evidence supporting systematic, decoding-based reading instruction for young children learning to read. This evidence undercuts the assumptions of what is called the "whole-language movement," in particular the unfortunate assumption that all children possess a "natural ability" to induce the rules of English orthography without being directly taught. Although more than half of our children learn to read regardless of reading method, many children critically need help in learning to master the especially difficult letter–sound or grapheme–phoneme correspondence rules in the English language (National Reading Panel, 2000).

There are similarly significant implications from the emerging research on processes underlying naming speed and reading fluency. The double-deficit hypothesis was intentionally developed to expand a more unidimensional emphasis on phonology to include a new emphasis on automaticity, processing speed, and fluency in assessment and reading intervention. Fluency represents a new/old dimension of reading (see Cattell, 1886; Huey, 1908; Wolf, 2001; Wolf & Katzir-Cohen, 2001) that is largely unaddressed in most phonological-based methods (Blachman, 1994). It is now highlighted as a major, critical component of intervention research in several new research curricula and initiatives (Kame'enui, Simmons, Good & Horn, 2001; Morris, Lovett, & Wolf,

1996; Torgesen, Rashotte, & Alexander, 2001). For example, the RAVE-O program (Wolf, Miller, & Donnelly, 2000) is a fluency-based program based in part on Wolf and Katzir's developmental, multi-component conceptualization of fluency and comprehension, which in turn emerged directly from the extensive work on the processes underlying naming speed. Preliminary results from this work indicate that the once-considered intractable problems of fluency are amenable to change. Taken together, the combined research of the recent period on the various sources of reading failure has moved the field toward more consensually shared diagnostic batteries, more precise definitions of dyslexia, some of the most successful, comprehensive efforts at intervention to date, and a stunning depiction of the complexity of the reading brain (Heim & Keil, 2004).

In summary, this review is a necessarily truncated, inevitably selective history of a very complex field; it cannot, of course, be otherwise in a brief chapter format (see, for example, excellent reviews of neurological and computational perspectives in Chase, 1996; Demb, Poldrack, & Gabrieli 1999; Klein & McMullen, 1999; Posner & Raichle, 1995). That said, most reading researchers would agree on the necessary requirements for researchers in the *next* phase of our history: 1) a working knowledge of the attentional, perceptual, cognitive, linguistic, and neurological systems underlying reading; 2) an understanding of the rich complexity of reading through its changes in development; 3) a willingness to keep a semi-permeable membrane around the research paradigms we each adhere to; 4) a very open eye to the multiple characteristics of children with reading disabilities, so that intervention can best reflect this diversity; and 5) a deeper understanding of the *history* of this field's research. For, it has been our experience that if we look hard enough at this untidy history of reading disability, it is the complexity of written language and the heterogeneity of reading-disabled children that are staring us in the face.

REFERENCES

Ackerman, P. T., Dykman, R. A. & Gardner, M. Y. (1990). Counting rate, naming rate, phonological sensitivity and memory span: Major factors in dyslexia. *Journal of Learning Disabilities*, 23, 325–37.

Adams, M. J. (1990). *Beginning to read: Thinking and learning about print*. Cambridge, MA: MIT Press.

Badian, N. (1994). Do dyslexic and other poor readers differ in reading related cognitive skills? *Reading and Writing*, 6(1), 45–63.

Badian, N. (1995). Predicting reading ability over the long-term: The changing roles of letter naming, phonological awareness and orthographic knowledge. *Annals of Dyslexia: An Interdisciplinary Journal,* XLV, 79–86.

Badian, N. (1996). Dyslexia: A validation of the concept at two age levels. *Journal of Learning Disabilities,* 29, 102–12.

Bakker, D. J. (1972). *Temporal order in disturbed reading-development and neuropsychological aspects in normal and reading-retarded children*. Rotterdam: Rotterdam University Press.

Bender, L. (1956). Problems in conceptualization and communication in children with developmental alexia. *Proceedings of the American Psychobiological Association*.

Benton, A. L. (1978). Some conclusions about dyslexia. In A. L. Benton & D. Pearl (eds), *Dyslexia: An appraisal of current knowledge*, 451–526. New York: Oxford University Press.

Berninger, V. & Richards, T. (2003). *Brain literacy for educators*. New York, NY: Academic Press.

Birch, H. G. (1962). Dyslexia and the maturation of visual function. In J. Money (ed.), *Reading disability: Progress and research needs in dyslexia*, Ch. X. Baltimore: Johns Hopkins Press.

Birch, H. G. & Belmont, L. (1964). Auditory-visual integration in normal and retarded readers. *American Journal of Orthopsychiatry*, 34, 852–61.

Blachman, B. A. (1984). Relationship of rapid naming ability and language analysis skills to kindergarten and first-grade reading achievement. *Journal of Educational Psychology*, 76, 610–22.

Blachman, B. A. (1994). What we have learned from longitudinal studies of phonological processing and reading, and some unanswered questions: A response to Torgesen, Wagner, and Rashotte. *Journal of Learning Disabilities*, 27, 287–91.

Blank, M., Berenzweig, S. S. & Bridger, W. H. (1975). The effect of stimulus complexity and sensory modality on reaction time in normal and retarded readers. *Child Development*, 46, 133–40.

Bowers, P. G. (1993). Text reading and rereading: Predictors of fluency beyond word recognition. *Journal of Reading Behavior*, 25, 133–53.

Bowers, P. G., Golden, J., Kennedy, A. & Young, A. (1994). *The varieties of orthographic knowledge. Vol. I: Theoretical and developmental issues*. Dordrecht, The Netherlands: Kluwer Academic Publishers.

Bowers, P. G., Steffy, R. & Tate, E. (1988). Comparison of the effects of IQ control methods on memory and naming speed predictors of reading disability. *Reading Research Quarterly*, 23, 304–9.

Bradley, L. & Bryant, P. E. (1983). Categorizing sounds and learning to read-a casual connection. *Nature*, 301, 419–21.

Brady, S. & Shankweiler, D. (1991). *Phonological processes in literacy: A tribute to Isabelle Y. Liberman*. Hillsdale, N.J.: Lawrence Erlbaum Associates.

Brady, S., Shankweiler, D. & Mann, V. (1983). Speech perception and memory coding in relation to reading ability. *Journal of Experimental Child Psychology*, 35, 345–67.

Breznitz, Z. & Berman, L. (2003). The underlying factors of word reading rate. *Educational Psychology Review*, 15(3), 247–65.

Byrne, B. (1998). *The foundation of literacy: The child's acquisition of the alphabetic principle*. East Sussex, UK: Psychology Press.

Cattell, M. (1886). The time it takes to see and name objects. *Mind*, 2, 63–85.

Catts, H. W. (1996). Defining dyslexia as a developmental language disorder: An expanded view. *Topics in Language Disorders*, 16(2), 14–29.

Chall, J. S. (1967). *Learning to read: The great debate*. New York: McGraw-Hill.

Chall, J. S. (1983). *Stages of reading development*. New York: McGraw-Hill.

Chase, C. (1996). *Developmental dyslexia: Neural, cognitive, and genetic mechanisms.* Baltimore, MD: York Press.

Chase, C. & Jenner, A. R. (1993). Magnocellular visual deficits affect temporal processing of dyslexics. *Annals of the New York Academy of Sciences*, 682, 326–9.

Clements, S. D. & Peters, J. E. (1962). Minimal brain dysfunction in the school-aged child: Diagnosis and treatment. *Archives of General Psychiatry*, 6(3), 185–97.

Critchley, M. (1964). *Developmental dyslexia.* London: Heineman Medical Books Limited.

Dejerine, J. (1892). *Contribution à l'étude anatomo-pathologique et clinique des différents variétés de cécité verbale.* Paper presented at the Comptes Rendu des Séances. Société de Biologie et de Ses Filiales et Associées, Paris.

Demb, J., Poldrack, R. & Gabrieli, J. (1999). Functional neuroimaging of word processing in normal and dyslexic readers. In R. Klein & P. A. MacMullen (eds), *Converging methods for understanding reading and dsylexia*, 245–304. Cambridge, MA: MIT Press.

Denckla, M. B. & Rudel, R. G. (1974). "Rapid automatized naming" of pictured objects, colors, letters, and numbers by normal children. *Cortex*, 10, 186–202.

Denckla, M. B. & Rudel, R. G. (1976a). Naming of objects by dyslexic and other learning-disabled children. *Brain and Language*, 3, 1–15.

Denckla, M. B. & Rudel, R. G. (1976b). Rapid automatized naming (R.A.N.): Dyslexia differentiated from other learning disabilities. *Neuropsychologia*, 14, 471–9.

Eden, G. F. & Zeffiro, T. A. (1998). Neural systems affected in developmental dyslexia revealed by functional neuroimaging. *Neuron*, 21, 279–82.

Felton, R. H. (1993). Effects of instruction on the decoding skills of children with phonological-processing problems. *Journal of Learning Disabilities*, 26, 583–9.

Felton, R. H. & Brown, I. S. (1990). Phonological processes as predictors of specific reading skills in children at risk for reading failure. *Reading and Writing*, 2, 39–59.

Fildes, L. G. (1921). A psychological inquiry into the nature of the condition known as congenital word-blindness. *Brain*, 44, 286–307.

Foorman, B., Francis, D., Shaywitz, S., Shaywitz, B. & Fletcher, J. (1998). *The case for early reading intervention.* Mahwah, NJ: Erlbaum.

Foorman, B., Francis, D., Winikates, D., Mehta, P., Schatschneider, C. & Fletcher, J. (1997). Early intervention for children with reading disabilities. *Scientific Studies of Reading*, 1(3), 255–76.

Galaburda, A. M., Menard, M. T. & Rosen, G. D. (1994). Evidence for aberrant auditory anatomy in developmental dyslexia. *Proceedings of the National Academy of Sciences*, 91, 8010–13.

Geschwind, N. (1965). Disconnection syndrome in animals and man (Parts I, II). *Brain*, 88, 237–94, 585–644.

Geschwind, N. (1974). *Selected papers on language and the brain.* Dordrecht, Holland: D. Reidel.

Geschwind, N. (1982). Why Orton was right. *Annals of Dyslexia*, 32, 13–30.

Goswami, U. & Bryant, P. (1990). *Phonological skills and learning to read.* Hove, England: Lawrence Erlbaum.

Hanson, V. L., Liberman, I. Y. & Shankweiler, D. P. (1984). Linguistic coding by deaf children in relation to beginning reading success. *Journal of Experimental Child Psychology*, 37(2), 378–93.

Hawking, S. (1988). *A brief history of time*. Toronto: Bantam.

Heim, S. & Keil, A. (2004). Large-scale neural correlates of developmental European dyslexia. *Child & Adolescent Psychiatry*, 13, 125–40.

Hinshelwood, J. (1895). Word-blindness and visual memory. *Lancet*, 2, 1564–70.

Hinshelwood, J. (1900). Congenital word-blindness. *Lancet*, 1, 1506–508.

Hinshelwood, J. (1917). *Congenital word-blindness*. London: Lewis.

Ho, C., Tsang, S.-M. & Lee., S. H. (2002). The cognitive profile of multiple deficit hypothesis in Chinese. *Developmental Psychology*, 38, 543–53.

Huey, E. B. (1908). *The psychology and pedagogy of reading*. New York: Macmillan.

Johnson, D. J. & Myklebust, H. R. (1964). *Learning Disabilities*. New York: Grune and Stratton.

Kame'enui, E., Simmons, D., Good III, R. & Harn, B. (2001). The use of fluency-based measures in early identification and evaluation of intervention efficacy in schools. In M. Wolf (ed.), *Dyslexia, fluency, and the brain*, 307–31. Timonium, MD: York Press.

Kamhi, A. & Catts, H. (1989). *Reading disabilities: A developmental language perspective*. Austin, TX: Pro-ed.

Kirby, J., Parilla, R. & Pfeiffer, S. (2003). Naming speed and phonological awareness as predictors of reading development. *Journal of Educational Psychology*, 95(3), 453–64.

Klein, R. & McMullen, P. A. (eds) (1999). *Converging methods for understanding reading and dyslexia*. Cambridge, MA: MIT Press.

Korhonen, T. (1995). The persistence of rapid naming problems in children with reading disabilities: A nine-year follow-up. *Journal of Learning Disabilities*, 28, 232–9.

Kussmaul, A. (1877). Disturbance of speech. In H. vonZiemssen (ed.), *Encyclopedia of the practice of medicine*, 14, translated by J. A. McCreery. New York: William Wood.

Liberman, I. Y. (1971). Basic research in speech and lateralization of language: Some implications for reading disability. *Bulletin of the Orton Society*, 21, 71–87.

Liberman, I. Y., Shankweiler, D. P., Fischer, F. W. & Carter, B. (1974). Explicit syllable and phoneme segmentation in the young child. *Journal of Experimental Child Psychology*, 18(2), 201–212.

Livingstone, M. S., Rosen, G. D., Drislane, F. W. & Galaburda, A. M. (1991). Physiological and anatomical evidence for a magnocellular defect in developmental dyslexia. *Neurobiology*, 88, 7943–7.

Llinas, R. (1996). Presentation to Mind, Brain, and Behavior Subgroup on Development, Harvard University, Cambridge, MA, April, 2006.

Lovegrove, W. J. & Williams, M. C. (1993). *Visual processes in reading and reading disabilities*. Hillsdale, N.J.: Lawrence Erlbaum Associates.

Lyon, G. R. (1995). Toward a definition of dyslexia. *Annals of Dyslexia: An interdisciplinary journal*, XLV, 3–27.

McBride-Chang, C. & Manis, F. (1996). Structural invariance in the associations of naming speed, phonological awareness, and verbal reasoning in good and poor readers: A test of the double deficit hypothesis. *Reading and Writing*, 8, 323–39.

Meyer, M. S. & Felton, R. H. (1998). Evolution of fluency training: Old approaches and new directions. Paper presented at the meeting of International Dyslexia Association (to appear in *Annals of Dyslexia*).

Misra, M., Katzir, T., Wolf, M. & Poldrack, R. (2004). Neural systems for RAN in skilled readers: Unraveling the RAN-Reading relationship. *Scientific Studies of Reading*, 8, 241–56.

Morgan, W. P. (1896). A case of congenital word-blindness. *British Medical Journal*, 2, 1378.

Morris, R., Lovett, M. & Wolf, M. (1996). Treatment of developmental reading disabilities. NICHD Grant Proposal.

Morris, R., Stuebing, K., Fletcher, J., Shaywitz, S., Lyon, R., Shankweiler, D., Katz, L., Francis, D. & Shaywitz, B. (1998). Subtypes of reading disability: A phonological core with cognitive variability. *Journal of Educational Psychology*, 90, 1–27.

Myklebust, H. R., Boshes, B., Olson, D. A. & Cole, C. H. (1969). *Final Report: Minimal brain damage in children*. Washington, DC: US Department of Health, Education, and Welfare.

National Reading Panel (2000). Summary report. Bethesda, MD: NICHD.

Novoa, L. (1988). Word-retrieval processes and reading acquisition and development in bilingual and monolingual children. Unpublished doctoral dissertation, Harvard University.

Ojemann, G. A. (1983). Brain organization for language from the perspective of electrical stimulation mapping. *Behavioral Brain Science*, 6, 189–230.

Olson, R. K., Wise, B., Connors, F., Rack, J. P. & Fulker, D. (1989). Specific deficits in component reading and language skills: Genetic and environmental influences. *Journal of Learning Disabilities*, 22, 339–48.

Orton, S. T. (1928). Specific reading disability – Strephosymbolia. *Journal of the American Medical Association*, 90, 1095–1099.

Orton, S. T. (1937). *Reading, writing, and speech problems in children*. New York: W.W. Norton.

Parilla, R., Kirby, J. R. & McQuarrie, L. (2004). Articulation rate, naming speed, verbal short-term memory, and phonological awareness: Longitudinal predictors of early reading development? *Scientific Studies of Reading*, 8(1), 3–26.

Perfetti, C. A. (1985). *Reading ability*. New York: Oxford University Press.

Poldrack, R. A. (2002). Neural systems for perceptual skill learning. *Behavioral & Cognitive Neuroscience Reviews*, 1(1), 76–83.

Posner, M. I. & Raichle, M. E. (1995). *Images of mind*. New York, NY: W.H. Freeman & Company.

Rabinovitch, R. D. (1959). Reading and learning disabilities. In S. Arieti (ed.), *American handbook of psychiatry*, 1, 857–69. New York: Basic Books, Inc.

Robinson, H. M. (1946). *Why pupils fail in reading*. Chicago: University of Chicago Press.

Rosen, G., Fitch, R. H., Clark, M., Lo Turco, J. J., Sherman, G. & Galaburda, A. (2001). Animal models of developmental dyslexia. In M. Wolf (ed.), *Dyslexia, fluency, and the brain*, 129–57. Timonium, MD: York Press.

Schilder, P. (1944). Congenital alexia and its relation to optic perception. *Journal of Genetic Psychology*, 65, 67–88.

Shankweiler, D. & Liberman, I. Y. (1972). *Language by ear and by eye*. Cambridge, MA: MIT Press.

Shankweiler, D. P. & Liberman, I. Y. (eds). (1989). *Phonology and reading disability: Solving the reading puzzle*. Ann Arbor, MI: University of Michigan.

Shaywitz, S. E., Fletcher, J. M. & Shaywitz, B. A. (1996). A conceptual model and definition of dyslexia: Findings emerging from the Connecticut Longitudinal Study. In J. E. Beitchman, N. J. Cohen, M. M. Konstantaseas & R. Tannock (eds), *Language, learning, and behavior disorders: Developmental, biological and clinical perspectives*, 199–223. New York: Cambridge University Press.

Shaywitz, S., Shaywitz, B., Pugh, K., Fulbright, R., Constable, R. T., Mencl, W. E., Shankweiler, D., Liberman, A., Skudlarski, P., Fletcher, J., Katz, L., Marchione, K., Lacadie, C., Gatenby, C. & Gore, J. (1998). Functional disruption in the organization of the brain for reading in dyslexia. *Neurobiology*, 95, 2636–41.

Siegel, L. S. & Ryan, E. B. (1988). Development of grammatical sensitivity, phonological and short-term memory skills in normally achieving and learning disabled children. *Developmental Psychology*, 24(1), 28–37.

Spring, C. & Capps, C. (1974). Encoding speed, rehearsal, and probed recall of dyslexic boys. *Journal of Educational Psychology*, 66, 780–86.

Stanovich, K. E. (1986). "Matthew effects" in reading: Some consequences of individual differences in acquisition of literacy. *Reading Research Quarterly*, 4, 360–407.

Stanovich, K. E. (1990). Concepts in developmental theories of reading skill: Cognitive resources, automaticity and modularity. *Developmental Review*, 10, 72–100.

Stanovich, K. E. (1994). Are discrepancy-based definitions of dyslexia empirically defensible? In K. P. van den Bos (ed.), *Current Directions in Dyslexia Research*, 15–30. Lisse: Swets & Zeitlinger.

Torgesen, J. K., Wagner, R. K. & Rashotte, C. A. (1994). Longitudinal studies of phonological processing and reading. *Journal of Learning Disabilities*, 27(10), 276–86.

Torgesen, J., Rashotte, C. & Alexander, A. (2001). Principles of fluency instruction in reading. In M. Wolf (ed.), *Dyslexia, fluency and the brain*, 333–55. Timonium, MD: York Press.

Torgesen, J., Rashotte, C. & Wagner, R. (1998). Research on instructional interventions for children with reading disabilities. Paper presented at the Society for Scientific Study of Reading, San Diego, CA.

Tunmer, W. (1995). Intervention strategies for developing onset-rime sensitivity and analogical transfer in reading disabled children. Paper presented at the Extraordinary Brain III Conference, Kauai, Hawaii.

Tunmer, W. E. & Nesdale, A. R. (1985). Phonemic segmentation skill and beginning reading. *Journal of Educational Psychology*, 77, 417–27.

Turkeltaub, P. E., Gareau, L., Flowers, D. L., Zeffiro, T. A. & Eden, G. F. (2003). Development of neural mechanisms for reading. *Nature Neuroscience*, 6(6), 767–73.

van den Bos, K. (1998). IQ, phonological sensitivity, and continuous-naming speed related to Dutch children's performance on two word identification tests. *Dyslexia*, 4, 73–89.

Vellutino, F. R. (1979). *Dyslexia: Theory and research*. Cambridge, MA: MIT Press.

Vellutino, F. R. & Scanlon, D. (1987). Phonological coding, phonological awareness, and reading ability: Evidence from a longitudinal and experimental study. *Merrill Palmer Quarterly*, 33, 321–63.

Wagner, R. K., Torgesen, J. K. & Rashotte, C. A. (1994). The development of reading-related phonological processing abilities: New evidence of bidirectional casualty from a latent variable longitudinal study. *Developmental Psychology*, 30, 73–87.

Wimmer, H. (1993). Characteristics of developmental dyslexia in a regular writing system. *Applied Psycholinguistics*, 14, 1–34.

Wolf, M. (1979). The relationship of disorders of word-finding and reading in children and aphasics. Unpublished doctoral dissertation, Harvard University, Cambridge, MA.

Wolf, M. (ed.) (2001). *Dyslexia, fluency, and the brain*. Timonium, MD: York Press.

Wolf, M. & Bowers, P. (1999). The "Double-Deficit Hypothesis" for the developmental dyslexias. *Journal of Educational Psychology*, 91, 1–24.

Wolf, M., Bowers, P. & Biddle, K. (2000). Naming-speed processes, timing, and reading: A conceptual review. *Journal of Learning Disabilities*, 33, 387–407.

Wolf, M. & Katzir-Cohen, T. (2001). Reading fluency and its interventions. *Scientific Studies of Reading*, 5(3), 211–39.

Wolf, M., Pfeil, C., Lotz, R. & Biddle, K. (1994). Towards a more universal understanding of the developmental dyslexias: The contribution of orthographic factors. In V. E. Berninget (ed.), *The varieties of orthographic knowledge, 1: Theoretical and developmental issues. Neuropsychology and Cognition, vol. 8.* New York, NY: Kluwer Academic/Plenum Publishers.

Wolf, M., Miller, L. & Donnelly, K. (2000). Retrieval, automaticity, vocabulary, elaboration-orthography (RAVE-O): A comprehensive, fluency-based reading intervention program. *Journal of Learning Disabilities*, 33, 322–4.

Wolff, P., Michel, G. & Ovrut, M. (1990). Rate variables and automatized naming in developmental dyslexia. *Brain and Language*, 39, 556–75.

Wood, F. (1995). Naming speed deficits in dyslexia. Symposium paper presented at the Society for Research in Child Development, Indianapolis, IN.

Young, A. & Bowers, P. G. (1995). Individual differences and text difficulty determinants of reading fluency and expressiveness. *Journal of Experimental Child Psychology*, 60, 428–54.

Zurif, E. B. & Carson, G. (1970). Dyslexia in relation to cerebral dominance and temporal analysis. *Neuropsychologia*, 8, 351–61.

5    Approaches to behavioral and neurological
     research on learning disabilities: in search of a
     deeper synthesis*

*Robbie Case*

*Overview:* Progress in understanding learning disabilities requires integration of behavioral and neurological evidence across the main traditions of research on cognitive development – empiricism, rationalism,
and the sociohistorical approach. Among the key findings, researchers
in the empiricist tradition have uncovered evidence that dyslexic children have specific problems in analyzing the sounds of language and in
performing rapid processing and that these problems are reflected in particular brain activation patterns. Those in the rationalist tradition have
analyzed the structures and stages required for reading, including general
abilities, developmental pathways, and related patterns of development
of brain activity. Scholars in the sociohistorical tradition have focused on
the effects of culture and social context in the creation and consequences
of literacy, including the effects of social stratification and the effectiveness of creating an effective community of learners to support students'
literacy.                                                *The Editors*

Two themes run throughout the present volume, and the case material that
accompanies it. The first is the need to integrate clinical and research perspectives on learning disabilities. The second is the need for a theoretical framework
that comprises both the neuropsychological and the cognitive/behavioral perspectives. Volumes such as the present one are an excellent way to begin the
search for a theoretical framework with the degree of generality that is required
for these two purposes. However, as we contemplate the shape that such a framework might assume, it is important to remember that behavioral and neurological research has itself been conducted within several different traditions.
Moreover, each of these traditions has had quite a different – and sometimes

* This chapter is dedicated to the memory of Robbie Case, who died suddenly of a coronary
  aneurysm after he had written most of this chapter. Nancy Link and the editors completed the
  chapter for him. The fields of human development, cognitive science, and education have suffered
  the loss of a fundamentally important scholar and a good man.

opposing – view of the relationship between brain and behavior in general, and the neurological underpinnings of learning disabilities in particular. If we are to achieve a synthesis with the breadth and the depth to which we ultimately aspire, we need to understand the nature of these different traditions and the underlying assumptions that have guided their inquiry. Accordingly, this chapter provides a brief introduction to each tradition, and the basic research that it has generated, followed by a description of the applied research that each tradition has stimulated on the problem of learning disabilities and the way in which this research might be integrated with that done in other traditions.

Three important traditions in research on brain and behavior are empiricism, rationalism (structuralism), and the sociohistorical tradition. The three traditions have different but equally important contributions to make to the synthesis that we are seeking. Moreover, understanding the nature of the differences will help fit together the work that is reported in the rest of this volume in a more coherent fashion and provide a preliminary sense of what such a synthesis might ultimately look like. Each tradition has uncovered important discoveries about reading disabilities that need to be integrated.

### The empiricist tradition

The epistemological roots of the first tradition lie in British empiricism, as articulated by Locke (1690/1994) and Hume (1748/1955). According to the empiricist view, knowledge of the world is acquired by a process in which the sensory organs first detect stimuli in the external world, and the mind then detects the customary patterns or "conjunctions" in these stimuli. Developmental psychologists who have been influenced by this view have tended to see the goals of developmental psychology as being to describe: (1) the process by which new stimuli are discriminated and encoded (perceptual learning), (2) the way in which correlations or associations among these stimuli are detected (cognitive learning), and (3) the process by which new knowledge is accessed, tested, and/or used in other contexts (transfer). The general methodology that has been favored is drawn from experimental physics, namely: (1) make detailed empirical observations of children's learning under carefully specified conditions, (2) generate explanations for these observations that are clear and testable, and (3) conduct experiments to test these hypotheses – experiments that manipulate the variable that is hypothesized to affect performance and that rule out any possible rivals.

### *Research on behavioral development*

Under the influence of behaviorism, early work in the empiricist tradition concentrated on developing a small number of paradigms in which children's learning could be recorded in a clear fashion, and the variables that control it could be manipulated (e.g. Kendler & Kendler, 1967). After the cognitive revolution, experimenters began looking at children's learning on a broader array of tasks and developing more detailed theoretical models of the cognitive processes that underlie it, models that included such internal constructs as goals, strategies, and knowledge bases. Computer simulations of these models were also developed, using first production systems (ordered series of condition [stimulus]–action [response] commands – see Klahr & Wallace, 1976), then connectionist networks (McClelland, Rumelhart, & Hinton, 1987), and more recently a combination of the two (Siegler, 1997; Pinker, 1999).

## *Research on neurological development*

Work on the neurological substrate of children's cognition in this tradition proceeded independently from the work on children's learning but was grounded in the same foundational assumptions: (1) different types of external stimuli trigger the activation of different types of neurons or neuronal groups in the cortex, (2) lawful connections or patterns that are obtained among these stimuli are represented by biochemical associations among the corresponding neurons or neuronal groups, and (3) the biochemical processes that produce these associations are time-sensitive and incremental. Thus, every time two neuronal groups are activated at the same time, or in immediate succession, a chemical change takes place in the synapses that connect them, with the result that firing of the first element is more likely to stimulate firing of the second element on a subsequent exposure, and less likely to stimulate firing of the various alternatives (Hebb, 1949). The more general consequence is that with repeated exposure, the spatio-temporal structure of neuronal firing comes to mirror the spatio-temporal structure of events in the external world. In effect, general circuits get set up whose functioning comes to represent recurrent patterns in the external world and the responses that the growing child develops for dealing with these patterns.

The foregoing (Hebbian) conception of learning generated a number of interesting lines of empirical work. At the sensory level, the emphasis was on determining what kinds of cells are responsive to what kind of input. At higher levels, the emphasis was on mapping the higher-order areas to which these receptors project and determining which particular circuits are involved in processing which kinds of higher-order decisions and processes (e.g. Goldman-Rakic, 1987, 1994). Finally, using animal models, single cell recording, and human brain imaging, advances were made in charting the synaptic changes that take place when learning actually occurs (Greenough, Black, & Wallace, 1987; Huttenlocher, 2002). Results from all three lines of work were broadly congruent with the position of Donald Hebb, the renowned Canadian neuropsychologist.

*Behavioral research on learning disabilities*

How has the problem of learning disabilities been viewed within the empiricist tradition? Those who have been interested primarily in observed behavior have developed batteries of finely honed cognitive tasks which they have administered to reading-disabled and normal children, to see which of these tasks differentiate the two groups best. The general view that has emerged from this research is that the lion's share of the variance in early reading skill is accounted for by phonemic and letter knowledge, and that there is no qualitative difference between the problems that "reading disabled" children and other children have in acquiring this knowledge. The difference is merely one of degree (Adams, 1992; Adams, Treiman, & Pressley, 1998; Byrne, 1992; Stanovitch & Stanovitch, 1996; Taylor; Torgesen, this volume). For those who experience these difficulties in their most acute form, therefore, what is important is that their problem be identified as early as possible – which is feasible because problems of phonemic awareness are evident considerably before instruction in reading ever takes place – and that they be provided with training that is more extensive and more carefully sequenced in order to help them overcome the problem.

*Neurological research on learning disabilities*

The chapter by Wolf and Ashby (this volume) has many influences, including work in the structuralist tradition that will be summarized below. If one confines oneself simply to the research strategy that they employ, however, it is clearly empiricist in its nature, and the theoretical formulation that they propose (in which cognitive operations have to be executed in order to extract sounds from letters, assemble these sounds into recognizable words, etc.) has its roots in the information processing model that the empiricist tradition has generated. Wolf's contribution to the empiricist tradition is to suggest that there are actually two separable sources of learning deficit: a specific phonemic deficit and a broad deficit in speeded processing.

The potential implications are considerable, both for our general view of the reading process and for the remedial programs that we develop in the future. As the reader may see by viewing the protocols for the four boys (Bernstein, this volume; Appendix), children can be selected who display reasonable functioning in one of these areas but not the other – and this fact makes for the possibility of a more carefully planned and differential intervention program (Wolf, 1997, this volume).

What might the neurological basis of such problems be? Neuropsychological work in the empiricist tradition has concentrated on addressing two questions: (1) What are the circuits on which successful decoding of written material depends? (2) What possible problems might present in these neural pathways? A number of authors have devoted their attention to mapping out the specific circuitry that is involved in reading (Benes & Paré-Blagoev, this volume; Geschwind, 1974; Paré-Blagoev, this volume; Shaywitz *et al.*, 1998, 2002). Common to all these models is the notion of a circuit that connects centers for identifying visual input and for making contact with auditory input. It is in this latter regard that the work of Galaburda (this volume) becomes of such interest, for his suggestion is that a deficiency in the magnocellular pathway of the auditory cortex – one which impedes rapid processing of auditory input – may play a causal role in certain types of severe reading disability. This assertion fits well with the conclusion that has emerged from purely behavioral work. It also fits well with the remedial work by Tallal (1996) and Wolf and Katzir-Cohen (2001), who have found that for at least some children, computer-based programs that slow down certain aspects of auditory input can make an important contribution to remediating learning problems.

In sum, work in the empiricist tradition converges on the importance for early reading of making connections between particular visual stimuli and particular auditory responses. The problem of rapid phonemic identification has thus emerged as being of particular importance, and mechanisms for detecting and remediating difficulties in speeded auditory processing are under development. At the same time, the work of Wolf and others signals the possibility of other problems in speeded processing, problems of a more general nature. Some clues as to what these may be can be gleaned from the other two developmental traditions, as will be seen below.

### The rationalist (structuralist) tradition

A second theoretical tradition in which children's development has been studied is quite different from the first and has been associated with a different set of behavioral and neurological investigations. This tradition has drawn its inspiration from continental rationalism and its development by Immanuel Kant in his transcendental philosophy. Kant (1796/1961) suggested that knowledge is acquired when the human mind imposes organization on the data that the senses provide, not merely registering sensory information, as the empiricists had suggested. Concepts that play this organizational role include space, time, causality, and number. Kant argued that without some pre-existing concept in each of these categories, it would be impossible to make any sense of the data of sensory experience: to see events as taking place in space, unfolding through time, exerting a causal influence on each other, etc. He believed that these categories must exist in some a priori form rather than being induced entirely from experience.

*Research on behavioral development*

Developmental psychologists who were influenced by Kant's view tended to see the study of children's cognitive development differently from those influenced by empiricism. They presumed that one should begin by exploring the foundational concepts in each category with which children come equipped at birth and then go on to document any change that may take place in these concepts with age. The first developmental theorist to apply this approach was James Mark Baldwin (1894/1968), who proposed that children's conceptual schemata progress through a sequence of four universal stages, which he termed the stages of sensorimotor, quasi logical, logical, and hyper-logical thought. In any given stage, Baldwin believed that new experience was "assimilated" into the existing set of schemata, similar to the manner in which the body assimilates food. He saw transition from one form of thought to the next as driven by "accommodation," a process by which existing schemata are broken down and then reorganized into new and more adaptive patterns under the influence of increasing attentional capacity. Attentional capacity, in turn, was something he saw as increasing with development due to the increase in the overall connectivity of the cortex. Finally – and in this he was attempting to go beyond Kant – he saw children's conceptual understanding in each of Kant's categories as something that children construct by this process, not something that is inborn or acquired in an automatic fashion.

Using Baldwin's theory as his initial guide and evolutionary biology (not physics) as his model for empirical research, Jean Piaget (1936/1960) set out to map the full range of competencies that children develop at each major stage of their lives in each of Kant's categories. He also wanted to understand the way in which the competencies at later stages evolve out of those at earlier stages. The basic elements of his procedure were: (1) present children with a wide (indeed, a vast) range of simple problems or questions in each of Kant's categories at each of the major stages outlined by Baldwin, and interview them to determine the logic on which their responses was based; (2) hypothesize both an age-typical pattern of responding to the tasks in the domain and a logical structure that might generate this pattern; and (3) hypothesize a set of adaptive processes that would transform early logical structures into later ones, in the same way that evolutionary processes gradually transform the structure of one class of biological organisms into another.

As a result of this work, Piaget suggested a refinement of Baldwin's stages. He also suggested a refinement of the processes that lead to the transformation of one structure into the next. In addition to accommodation and the processes of differentiation and integration that were foundational to it, Piaget included "reflective abstraction" as a major developmental process. In his lexicon, reflective abstraction was a superordinate process in which the subject (person) takes his or her own internal structures as objects and abstracts a new pattern in them.

Piaget's work was criticized by empiricists as providing too monolithic a view of children's cognitive development – one that did not assign enough importance to learning and sociocultural factors. In response to these criticisms, the field went in a number of important directions (see Case, 1998, for a summary). One of the directions that is relevant to the present volume has been dubbed "neo-Piagetian." What neo-Piagetians did was to preserve Piaget's and Baldwin's emphasis on the differentiation and coordination of schemata, and to specify in detail the series of differentiations and coordinations that children had to go through in each (or at least most) of the classic Kantian categories in order to attain the conceptual understanding that is characteristic of adults. They also showed that this process could be highly influenced by learning, and that asynchronies in developmental rate could emerge across different content domains as a consequence. Like Baldwin, the general factor in development – the factor that prevented specific experience from accelerating children to adult levels in some categories while they were still at preschool levels in others – was attentional capacity, or working memory, which was in turn shown to be related to general speed of processing (Case, 1985, 1995; Demetriou, Christou, Spanoudis, & Platsidou, 2002; Fischer, 1980; Fischer & Bidell, 1998; Halford, 1982; Pascual-Leone, 1969, 1970).

*Research on neurological development*

Although structuralists never denied the possibility of learning due to Hebbian processes, they always took pains to emphasize the general context in which this learning takes place and the importance of a child's own attentional processes as mediators. Baldwin was interested in the overall connectivity of the cortex (not just certain specific circuits), and he emphasized the importance of changing attentional limits. This point was echoed by neo-Piagetian theorists with their focus on the growth of attentional capacity, working memory, and processing speed. A frequent theme in modern neuropsychological writing is that the working memory function depends on a set of circuits that are frontally localized, and that – by their projection to the posterior lobes – influence both the speed and the content with which learning takes place (Case, 1992; Fischer & Rose, 1994; Goldman-Rakic, 1987, 1994; Pascual-Leone et al., 1990).

Thatcher has developed a line of neurological research that is broadly congruent with Piagetian and neo-Piagetian theorizing, and that explicitly draws on Baldwin's notion regarding the underlying neurological basis of these stages: namely, the degree of cortical connectivity (Thatcher, 1992, 1994, 1997, this volume). Fischer and Rose have built a specific model relating this research to cognitive developmental stages or levels (Fischer & Rose, 1994; Fischer, Rose,

& Rose, this volume). Using methods that correlate one pattern of brain electrical activity (the electroencephalogram or EEG) with another (EEG coherence), Thatcher has focused on the coherence between activation in different parts of the brain under conditions where subjects have their eyes shut and are not engaged in any explicit form of mental computation. His findings indicate that there is decreasing local coherence with age – which he interprets as indicating increasing differentiation due to the formation of inhibitory connections – and for some locations increasing coherence across areas that are more widely separate, such as between frontal and posterior regions of the cortex. He interprets this long-distance coherence as indicating increasing general integration due to the formation of long-distance connections of a facilitatory sort. Of particular importance in his view are connections between the frontal and posterior lobes.

The growth of these long-distance connections and the improved synchronization that they permit appear to take place in waves, which Thatcher has suggested relate to the general stages described by Piaget, as well as the further specification of levels and substages by neo-Piagetians (Case, 1985; Fischer, 1980). Thatcher assumes, along with the empiricists, that the brain is highly responsive to experience and encodes it as a series of neural connections. However, in keeping with the structuralist tradition, Thatcher sees responsiveness to specific experience as being constrained by the general state of development of the cortex, which in turn is driven both by maturation and general (as opposed to task-specific) experience.

Thatcher's work is congruent with the structuralist tradition in one other respect. He sees higher-order regulation and reworking of experience (Piaget's reflective abstraction) as being just as important as experience itself in the process of development. In his view, development is a cyclic process. During certain phases growth is led by experience, while during other phases growth is led by the higher-order reworking of this experience. He has developed a mathematical model in which frontal and posterior growth are linked to each other, much the way the growth of predators and prey are linked in a dynamic ecosystem (Thatcher, 1997).

### Behavioral research on reading disabilities

In the classic Piagetian tradition, early work on reading focused on showing that children went through a very general progression in their understanding of language in both its spoken and written forms, and that this structural progression was similar to and governed by the same processes as children's more general cognitive development (Chall, 1982; Elkind, 1981; Sinclair, 1988). The details of children's progression in phonics was first charted by Biemiller (1970). Subsequent work by Ferreiro (1994, 1997) and others was more detailed and related the progression in phonics to classic Piagetian stages and concepts. Children with reading disabilities were thus seen as going through the same general stage progression as other children, but being delayed in the language realm (Byrne, 1992). In a longitudinal study, Rieben (1992) showed that the situation was actually more complex and that more general cognitive problems as well as specific linguistic problems might be present – a conclusion that is reminiscent of the suggestion made by Wolf and Ashby (this volume) on the basis of their recent research.

Recall that in the neo-Piagetian formulation, the emphasis on classic transition processes such as differentiation, coordination, and reflective abstraction was maintained, but the analysis of what had to be differentiated and coordinated became more particular. Knight and Fischer (1992) showed that children actually go through three different developmental sequences in their appreciation of the auditory and visual aspects of written language, and that it is the integration of the developmental strands for sound and sight that is crucial for word recognition. The advantage of this analysis of learning to read as involving a multi-strand web was that it allowed them to show that while most children integrate the branches of this web, some do not achieve this integration, and the reading problems they encounter as a result are different (Fischer, Rose, & Rose, this volume).

At the same time as Knight and Fischer were charting the specific web of differentiations and integrations that reading entails, other neo-Piagetian investigators were showing that the progression along these particular strands and their integration – regardless of which strand is the most advanced – is strongly correlated with the growth of attentional capacity and general speed of processing (Crammond, 1992; Marsh, Friedman, Welch, & Desberg, 1981). Figure 5.1 illustrates this relationship in graphic form for children in kindergarten through sixth grade performing a task of counting dots (Case, 1985, p. 361). The speed of counting correlates closely with the counting span – the number of dots that the children can remember accurately.

## Neurological research on learning disabilities

What sort of neurological problem might produce a delay in moving through the specific developmental sequences that Knight and Fischer have documented? What sort of problem might produce a more general delay in moving to an expanded attentional capacity and faster speed of processing? Work in the empiricist tradition seems directly related to the first question, in the sense that deficiencies in the magnocellular pathways of either the visual or auditory cortex may contribute. The more general problems of attentional capacity and speeded processing may be related to a delay in the frontal–posterior connections that Thatcher has focused on. As shown in Figures 5.2a and 5.2b, there is an increase in the rate of working memory growth just before the age when children

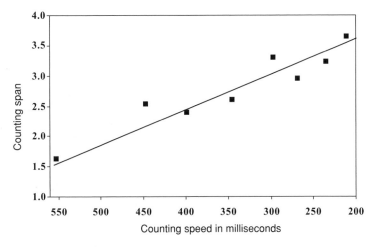

Figure 5.1   Relation of counting speed to span.
*Adapted from Case (1985), p. 361*

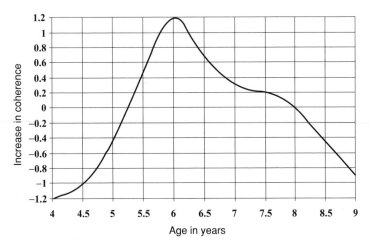

Figure 5.2a  Growth rate of EEG coherence between frontal and posterior cortex.
*Source of data:* Case (1992) and Thatcher (1992)

enter school, and it parallels the wave of growth of frontal–posterior (parietal lobe) coherence documented by Thatcher. One could therefore propose that frontal–posterior coherence in general, and frontal–temporal coherence in particular (Case, 1992; Thatcher, 1992, 1997; Fischer & Rose, 1994; Fischer, Rose, & Rose, this volume) are two critical variables that might mediate children's

Figure 5.2b  Growth rate of working memory (counting span and spatial span).
*Source of data:* Case (1992)

progress in reading, by affecting the size of working memory that they have available for integrating the results of their visual and auditory processing. (Parietal and occipital cortex, in the posterior of the head, plays a major role in hearing and vision. Temporal cortex plays a major role in language. Frontal seems to modulate these other regions, and is central to working memory.) Such a proposal, if confirmed, would fit well with Wolf's double-deficit view of reading disability and the data upon which it is based.

## The sociohistoric tradition

The third epistemological tradition has its roots in the sociohistorical inter-pretation of Hegel's (1807/1979) epistemology, as developed by Karl Marx and further expanded by modern continental philosophers (Kaufmann, 1980). According to the sociohistorical view, conceptual knowledge does not have its primary origin in the structure of the objective world (as empiricist philosophers suggested). Nor does it have its origin in the structure of the subject and his or her spontaneous cogitation (as rationalist philosophers suggested). It does not even have its primary origin in the interaction between the structure of the subject and the structure of the objective world (as both Baldwin and Piaget maintained). Instead, conceptual knowledge has its primary origin in the social and material history of the culture of which the subject is a part, and the tools, concepts, and symbol systems that the culture has developed for interacting with its environment.

*Research on behavioral development*

Developmental psychologists who were influenced by the sociohistorical perspective viewed the study of children's conceptual understanding in a different fashion from empiricists or rationalists. They believed that one should begin one's study of children's thought by analyzing the contexts in which human cultures find themselves and the social, linguistic, and material tools that they have developed over the years for coping with these contexts. One should then proceed to examine the way in which these intellectual and physical resources are passed on from one generation to the next.

The best known of the early sociohistorical theories is Vygotsky's (1934/1962). According to Vygotsky, children's thought must be seen in a context that includes both its biological and its cultural evolution, and the study of this thought must combine the sorts of ethnographic methods used by anthropologists with the experimental and observational methods used by physicists and evolutionary biologists. According to Vygotsky, three of the most important features of human beings as a species are that: (1) we have developed language, (2) we fashion our own tools, and (3) we transmit the discoveries and inventions of one generation to the next, via institutions such as schooling. From the perspective of Vygotsky's theory, the most important aspect of children's development is not their exposure to the "stimulation" that the world provides; nor is it their construction of universal logical structures for organizing that experience. Instead, it is their acquisition of language (circa 2 years of age) and their use of language (1) for internal regulatory purposes (4–7 years of age) and (2) for the purpose of acquiring the basic intellectual technology of their culture – which in our culture includes reading, writing, and arithmetic (mostly age 6 and beyond).

*Research on neurological development*

Given this view of human knowledge and its acquisition, it was natural that developmental work in the sociohistorical tradition would draw heavily on methods developed in anthropology and attempt to explore the effects of culture and social institutions, including schooling, on children's development and learning (Cole, 1996; Olson, 1994; Greenfield, 1966; Rogoff, 1990). Under the guidance of Luria, who was a close colleague of Vygotsky, an extensive series of neurological investigations was also initiated. In his early work, Luria focused on the aspect of higher-order functioning that Vygotsky had asserted was most central in children's development, namely language. In a series of classic experiments, he showed how linguistic stimuli gradually took over from visual stimuli as primary means for controlling children's behavior, during the transition from sensorimotor to pre-operational thought (Luria & Yudovitch,

1959; Luria, 1966). In his later work, he used a unique database to which he had access, which included information on all the gunshot wound patients in the Soviet Union during World War II. By combining the assessment of normal subjects with those who had experienced focused neurological insults, he was able to isolate the neurological systems that had the primary responsibility not just for the linguistic function, but for the self-regulation function that, according to Vygotsky, develops as language is internalized at around 5 to 7 years of age (Luria, 1966, 1973).

The area that Luria saw as exercising this self-regulatory or executive function was the frontal region. By the time he finished his career, Luria had proposed a view of the cortex that was differentiated along left–right, top-down, and front–back axes. In his model, the frontal lobes were specialized for planning and self-regulation, the posterior lobes for the processing of sensory information, and the limbic system for affective and emotional processing. Within the posterior lobes, the left hemisphere was seen as specialized for digital, sequential aspects of cognitive processing (which included language as well as other symbolic functions), while the right hemisphere was specialized for analogical, parallel aspects of cognitive processing.

### Behavioral research on reading disabilities

Early behavioral studies suggested that the acquisition of literacy – both within a culture and within an individual child – produces a transformation in cognitive structures that is revolutionary in its consequences and that applies to the full range of activities in which a literate individual engages. Olson (1977), while continuing to reinforce the notion that literacy is important, has suggested that its effects are a good deal more differentiated as a function of the local social, economic, and institutional context (Olson, 1994). Above all, what appears to be important is the context in which reading is learned and the purpose to which it is put (Scribner & Cole, 1981; Snow, Burns, & Griffin, 1998).

In our own culture, it has been shown that both the context and the purpose to which reading is put varies widely from one socioeconomical status level (SES) to the next (Gutierrez & Garcia, 1989). Figure 5.3 shows the level of literacy attained by young adults as a function of the years of education of their parents – which is one of the standard proxies or "indicators" of SES (Case, Griffin, & Kelly, 2001; Willms, 1997). There is an SES gradient in literacy achievement across all modern industrial cultures, but the gradient is particularly steep in the United States, being on the order of 1.5–1.75 standard deviations. With a difference this big in the means, one can expect to find a difference in the incidence of children in the lower tails of each distribution on the order of 8 times. Since falling in the lower tail of the reading distribution is precisely the criterion that is used to define reading disabilities (though the exact percentile

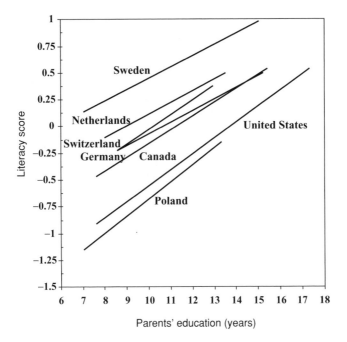

Figure 5.3    Youth literacy as a function of parents' education in seven countries.
*Source of data:* International Adult Study as reported in Case *et al.* (2001).

value varies from state to state – see Torgesen, this volume) one can expect a huge difference in the incidence of reading disabilities between extremely low and extremely high SES populations, at least in the US.

Of course, this fact makes the payoff for leveling the gradient a good deal larger than it would be in other countries as well. Two creative programs have been designed for this purpose in the sociohistorical tradition. Both programs radically alter the general social context of reading instruction, as well as the methods of teaching and the purpose of the activities within which these methods are embedded. In the first program, reading instruction takes place in neighborhood clubs, not schools (Cole, 1996). The specific context is one where children need to read instructions printed on cards in order to play computer games and to participate in the complex social activities in which these games are embedded. Communication with children in other countries via e-mail is also a feature of this program.

The second program is set in a school context, but one in which both authority relations and general social interaction are radically restructured (Brown & Campione, 1994). In a "community of learners," where both students and teachers are learning about a new topic, reading takes place as a vehicle for learning, and learning takes place for the purpose of writing group essays on topics that are selected for both their strong motivational value for the children on the one hand and their relevance for the community in which the children live, on the other. Advanced computer technology and a variety of alternative participation structures are also central features of the program. The participation structures (which include "jigsaw" grouping of students, reciprocal teaching, majoring in particular topics, and independent research) encourage all children – whether or not they have problems in reading – to take on genuine roles of intellectual leadership and to provide a context in which they can do so. The overall gains in reading scores that obtained under these conditions are extremely impressive, being on the order of several standard deviations (Brown & Campione, 1994; Campione, this volume). In effect, then, the incidence of reading disabilities is reduced to the level for students of high socioeconomic status, and the SES gradient in reading achievement is leveled.

In a well-known paper in the sociohistorical tradition, McDermott (1993) has argued with great force for the importance of not marginalizing students with reading disabilities – and letting them assume roles of genuine intellectual leadership. McDermott's point is that learning disability is a cultural category with cultural consequences, which can be deleterious for students under present conditions and which can be radically altered if teachers and principals are prepared to think imaginatively about the social context in which learning takes place. Another imaginative program that achieves this effect is the Knowledge Forum or CSILE program designed by Scardamalia & Bereiter (1999) – who also report that reading-disabled children are not distinguishable from other children in their classrooms and can assume roles of intellectual leadership.

### Neurological research on learning disabilities

One of the major objections that investigators in the sociohistorical tradition have to the empiricist view is that learning disabilities are defined as a medical syndrome, which leads to important social consequences. Consequently, one might expect little work in the sociohistorical tradition on the neurological underpinnings of reading disabilities. In fact, however, this is not the case. Interesting work has been done which has its origin in Luria's focus on the lateralization of language. Just prior to the age of formal schooling there is a rapid increase in cerebral lateralization, which appears to be due, at least in part, to the myelinization of long-distance connections across the two hemispheres through the corpus callosum (Yakovlev & Lecours, 1967). Also, evidence indicates that processing across modalities (seeing and hearing) permits more items to be held in working memory than processing within modality. Putting these two facts together, Wittelson (1983) has hypothesized that children who are delayed in lateralization will be at a disadvantage in learning to read because they are able to hold fewer phonemes and/or letters in mind simultaneously. Indeed, delays in lateralization *have* been shown to be related to certain types of reading disabilities, although the causal connection remains to be firmly established.

This hypothesis and these data relate directly to Thatcher's work. A relevant finding of Thatcher's that was not highlighted in the previous section is that at about the age of school entry children show a wave of increase in coherence that begins with the coordination of activity in the left frontal, temporal, and posterior areas and sweeps across the corpus callosum to the right hemisphere. Thatcher treats this wave as marking improvement in the capacity of the frontal lobes to orchestrate and integrate the activity of the two posterior lobes. Although the connection to reading disabilities has not been made as explicitly as in Wittelson's work, the presence of a new level of control by the frontal lobes over the language processing lobes and the concomitant increase in differentiation of linguistic and non-linguistic activity could provide the general background circuitry that is necessary for learning both reading and mathematics (Case & Mueller, 2001).

The implication, once again, is that reading disabilities need not be exclusively the result of *either* specific problems in phonemic identification (due for example to problems in the magnocellular pathways) *or* more general problems in speeded processing of any sort (due to the overall integration of the cortex). They might also be due to problems at an intermediate level, such as in the long-distance circuit under frontal control that is established during the years of transition to schooling and that links the linguistic and visual processing areas. Stated a bit differently, problems may exist not just in the auditory and visual pathways, but in the higher-order areas in the left and right posterior lobes to which they project, and in the differentiation and integration of these areas under frontal mediation.

In this regard, Wolf's measures of speeded processing are recorded in a context and on a task where interference is strong and a good deal of inhibitory control is necessary. Inhibitory control – especially in tasks with a high working-memory demand – is a particular specialty of the frontal region. The neurological underpinnings of the speed problem that she identified may involve not just speeded processing generally but the more focused speeded processing and inhibitory control that the frontal lobes control and that Thatcher's measures appear to index (see Case, 1992; Demetriou *et al.*, 1993; Pascual-Leone, 1970; Pascual-Leone *et al.*, 1990).

## Summary and conclusion

Reading is a complex act that involves the recognition and phonological decoding of visual patterns, their combination to access the meaning of individual words, and the integration of individual words into overall semantic patterns in a context where these patterns have a particular importance and purpose. Behavioral research on children's reading has been conducted within three different traditions, each emphasizing a different aspect of the reading act. The empiricist tradition has emphasized the learning of particular (stimulus–response) phonic rules. The constructivist tradition has emphasized the recognition of whole words and their cognitive integration under voluntary attentional control, in order to achieve a broader meaning. The sociohistorical tradition has emphasized the importance of linguistic communication, the social structure of the classroom in which that communication takes place, and the purpose to which reading is put. It has also emphasized the use of alternate technologies that reduce or eliminate the stigmatization that can occur when reading and writing are the only gateways through which a person can play a significant role in high-level cognitive discourse or the assembly of high-level written products.

Neurological research in the three traditions has also tended to focus on different aspects of the developing brain – and potential problems that might constitute the anatomical or functional underpinning of learning disabilities. Research in the empiricist tradition has concentrated on identifying the local circuitry that is involved in word decoding. Work in the constructivist tradition has emphasized the importance of overall cortical differentiation and integration in general (on which general speed of processing may depend), and frontal–posterior integration in particular (because attentional integration, working memory, and speeded processing under conditions of potential interference may all be frontally localized functions). Work in the sociohistorical tradition has emphasized the importance of left–right differentiation and the (frontally mediated) self-regulation that must accompany such integration in order for reading to achieve its ultimate purpose.

In principle, it seems to me, reading disabilities could be present in the behavioral capabilities that any one of the traditions has emphasized, and they could have any of the neurological underpinnings that the corresponding neurological research programs have suggested. Moreover, each potential problem could have its own preferred form of remediation. The behaviors of the four boys described by Bernstein (this volume) and in the Appendix show the potential differences between children with problems of speeded processing versus phonemic decoding, and thus suggest different ways of dealing with their reading problems. Other or more refined typologies may prove useful as further work is done and new technologies emerge. Finally, it seems to me that those of us who work in classrooms should pay particular attention to the creation of alternative, more imaginatively organized learning communities – ones in which the disability of not being able to read does not stigmatize students or prevent them from taking an active, indeed a leading, role in the intellectual life of the classrooms of which they are members (Rose, this volume; Rose & Meyer, 2002).

# REFERENCES

Adams, M. J. (1992). *Beginning to read*. Cambridge, MA: MIT Press.

Adams, M. J., Treiman, R. & Pressley, M. (1998). Reading, writing, and literacy. In I. Sigel & K. A. Renninger (eds), *Handbook of child psychology: Vol. 4: Child psychology in practice*, 5th edn, 275–355. New York: Wiley.

Baldwin, J. M. (1968). *The development of the child and of the race*. New York: Augustus M. Kelly. (Original work published 1894.)

Biemiller, A. (1970). The development of the use of graphic and contextual information as children learn to read. *Reading Research Quarterly*, 6, 75–96.

Brown, A. L. & Campione, J. C. (1994). Guided discovery in a community of learners. In K. McGilly (ed.), *Classroom lessons*, 229–72. Cambridge, MA: MIT Books.

Byrne, B. (1992). Studies in the acquisition procedure for reading: Rationale, hypotheses and data. In P. B. Gough, L. C. Ehri & R. Trieman (eds), *Reading acquisition*, 1–34. Hillsdale, NJ: Erlbaum.

Case, R. (1985). *Intellectual development: Birth to adulthood*. New York: Academic Press.

Case, R. (1992). The role of the frontal lobes in the regulation of cognitive development. *Brain and Cognition*, 20, 51–73.

Case, R. (1995). Capacity based explanations of working memory growth: A brief history and a reevaluation. In F. M. Weinert & W. Schneider (eds), *Research in memory development and competencies*, 23–44. Hillsdale, NJ: Erlbaum.

Case, R. (1998). The development of conceptual structures. In D. Kuhn & R. S. Siegler (eds), *Handbook of child psychology: Vol. 2. Cognition, perception, and language*. New York: Wiley.

Case, R., Griffin, S. & Kelly, W. M. (2001). Socioeconomic differences in children's early cognitive development and their readiness for schooling. In S. L. Golbeck (ed.), *The Rutgers invitational symposium on education series: Psychological perspectives on early childhood education: Reframing dilemmas in research and practice*, 37–63. Mahwah, NJ: Erlbaum.

Case, R. & Mueller, M. (2001). Differentiation, integration, and second order co-variance mapping as cognitive and neurological processes. In J. McClelland & R. S. Siegler (eds), *Mechanisms of cognitive development: Behavioral and neurological development*, 185–219. Mahwah, NJ: Erlbaum.

Chall, J. S. (1982). *Learning to read: The great debate* (2nd edn). New York: McGraw-Hill.

Cole, M. (1996). *Cultural psychology: A once and future discipline*. Cambridge, MA: Harvard University Press.

Crammond, J. (1992). Analyzing the basic developmental processes of children with different types of learning disability. In R. Case (ed.), *The mind's staircase: Exploring the conceptual underpinnings of children's thought and knowledge*, 285–302. Hillsdale, NJ: Erlbaum.

Demetriou, A., Christou, C., Spanoudis, G. & Platsidou, M. (2002). The development of mental processing: Efficiency, working memory, and thinking. *Monographs of the Society for Research in Child Development*, 67(1, Serial No. 173).

Demetriou, A. Efklides, A. & Platsidou, M. (1993). The architecture and dynamics of developing mind. *Monographs of the Society for Research in Child Development*, 58(5–6, Serial No 270).

Elkind, D. (1981). Stages in the development of reading. In I. E. Sigel, D. Brodzinsky, & R. M. Golinkoff (eds), *New directions in Piagetian theory and practice*, 267–79. Hillsdale, NJ: Erlbaum.

Ferreiro, E. (1994). Literacy development: Construction and reconstruction. In D. Tirosh (ed.), *Implicit and explicit knowledge: An educational approach*, 169–80. Stamford, CT: Ablex.

Ferreiro, E. (1997). Vers une théorie génétique de l'apprentissage de la lecture. *Revue Suisse de Psychologie*, 36, 109–130.

Fischer, K. W. (1980). A theory of cognitive development: The control and construction of hierarchies of skills. *Psychological Review*, 87, 477–531.

Fischer, K. W. & Bidell, T. R. (1998). Dynamic development of psychological structures in action and thought. In R. M. Lerner (ed.), *Handbook of child psychology: Vol. 1. Theoretical models of human development*, 5th edn, 467–561. New York: Wiley.

Fischer, K. W. & Rose, S. P. (1994). Dynamic development of coordination of components in brain and behavior: A framework for theory and research. In G. Dawson & K. W. Fischer (eds), *Human behavior and the developing brain*, 3–66. New York: Guilford Press.

Geschwind, N. (1974). *Selected papers on language and the brain*. Dordrecht, Holland: D. Reidel.

Goldman-Rakic, P. (1987). Development of cortical circuitry and cognitive functions. *Child Development*, 58, 642–91.

Goldman-Rakic, P. (1994). Specification of higher order cortical functions. In S. H. Broman & J. Grafmanx (eds), *Atypical cognitive deficits in developmental disorders. Implications for brain function*, 3–17. Hillsdale, NJ: Erlbaum.

Greenfield, P. M. (1966). On culture and conservation. In J. S. Bruner, R. R. Oliver & P. M. Greenfield (eds), *Studies in cognitive growth*, 225–56. New York: Wiley.

Greenough, W. T., Black, J. E. & Wallace, C. S. (1987). Experience and brain development. *Child Development*, 58, 539–59.

Gutierrez, K. D. & Garcia, E. E. (1989). Academic literacy in linguistic minority children: The connections between language, cognition and culture. *Early Child Development & Care*, 51, 109–126.

Halford, G. S. (1982). *The development of thought*. Hillsdale, NJ: Erlbaum

Hebb, D. O. (1949). *The organization of behavior*. New York: Wiley.

Hegel, G. W. F. (1807/1979). *Phenomenology of spirit* (A. V. Miller & J. N. Findlay, trans.). Oxford: Oxford University Press. (Originally published 1807.)

Hume, D. (1955). *An inquiry concerning human understanding*. New York: Bobbs Merrill. (First published in 1748.)

Huttenlocher, P. R. (2002). *Neural plasticity: The effects of environment on the development of the cerebral cortex*. Cambridge, MA: Harvard University Press.

Kant, I. (1961). *Critique of pure reason*. New York: Doubleday Anchor. (First published in 1796.)

Kaufmann, W. (1980). *Discovering the mind: Goethe, Kant and Hegel*. New York: McGraw Hill.

Kendler, T. S. & Kendler, H. H. (1967). Experimental analysis of inferential behavior in children. In L. P. Lipsitt & C. C. Spiker (eds), *Advances in children's development and behavior*, 157–90. New York: Academic Press.

Klahr, D. & Wallace, J. G. (1976). *Cognitive development: an information-processing view*. Hillsdale, NJ: Erlbaum.

Knight, C. C. & Fischer, K. W. (1992). Learning to read words: Individual differences in developmental sequences. *Journal of Applied Developmental Psychology*, 13, 377–404.

Locke, J. (1690/1994). *An essay concerning human understanding*. Essex UK: Prometheus Books.

Luria, A. R. (1966). *Higher cortical functions in man*. New York: Basic Books.

Luria, A. R. (1973) *The working brain*. London: Penguin Books.

Luria, A. R. & Yudovitch, F. J. (1959). *Speech and the development of mental processes in the child*. London: Staples Press.

Marsh, G., Friedman, M., Welch, V. & Desberg, P. (1981) A cognitive developmental theory of reading acquitistion. In T. Gary & G. E. MacKinnon (eds), *Reading research: Advances in theory and practice*. New York: Academic Press.

McClelland, J. L., Rumelhart, D. E. & Hinton, G. E. (1987). The appeal of parallel distributed processing. In D. E. Rumelhart & J. L. McClelland (eds), *Parallel distributed processing: Explorations in the microstructure of cognition: Vol 1: Foundations*, 3–44. Cambridge, MA: MIT Press.

McDermott, R. P. (1993). The acquisition of a child by a learning disability. In S. Chaikline & J. Lanes (eds), *Understanding practice: Perspectives on activity and context*, 269–305. New York: Cambridge University Press.

Olson, D. R. (1977). From utterance to text. *Harvard Educational Review*, 47, 257–81.

Olson, D. R. (1994). *The world on paper: The conceptual and cognitive implications of writing and reading*. New York: Cambridge University Press.

Pascual-Leone, J. (1969). Cognitive development and cognitive style. Unpublished doctoral dissertation, University of Geneva, Geneva.

Pascual-Leone, J. (1970). A mathematical model for the transition rule in Piaget's development stages. *Acta Psychologica*, 32, 301–45.

Pascual-Leone, J., Hamstra, N., Benson, N., Khan, I. & Englund, R. (1990). The P300 event related potential and mental capacity. Paper presented at the fourth international evoked potentials symposium, Toronto. (Available in conference proceedings.)

Piaget, J. (1960). *The psychology of intelligence*. Totowa, New Jersey: Littlefield Adams. (First published in 1936.)

Pinker, S. (1999). *How the mind works*. New York: Norton.

Rieben, L. (1992). Intelligence globale, intelligence opératoire, et apprentissage de la lecture. *Archives de Psychologie*, 60, 205–224.

Rogoff, B. (1990). *Apprenticeship in thinking. Cognitive development in social context*. New York: Oxford University Press.

Rose, D. & Meyer, A. (2002). *Teaching every student in the digital age*. Alexandria, VA: American Association for Supervision & Curriculum Development.

Scardamalia, M. & Bereiter, C. (1999). Schools as knowledge-building organizations. In D. P. Keating & C. Hertzman (eds), *Developmental health and the wealth of nations: Social, biological, and educational dynamics*, 274–89. New York: Guilford.

Scribner, S. & Cole, M. (1981). *The psychology of literacy*. Cambridge, MA: Harvard University Press.

Shaywitz, S., Shaywitz, B., Pugh, K., Fulbright, R., Constable, R. T., Mencl, W. E., Shankweiler, D., Liberman, A., Skudlarski, P., Fletcher, J., Katz, L., Marchione, K., Lacadie, C., Gatenby, C. & Gore, J. (1998). Functional disruption in the organization of the brain for reading in dyslexia. *Neurobiology*, 95, 2636–41.

Shaywitz, B. A., Shaywitz, S. E., Pugh, K. R., Mencl, W. E., Fulbright, R. K., Skudlarksi, P., Constable, R. T., Marchione, K. E., Fletcher, J. M., Lyon, G. R. & Gore, J. C. (2002). Disruption of posterior brain systems for reading in children with developmental dyslexia. *Biological Psychiatry*, 52(2), 101–10.

Siegler, R. S. (1997). *Emerging minds*. New York: Oxford University Press.

Sinclair, H. (1988). Introduction. In H. Sinclair (ed.), *La production de notations chez le jeune enfant: Language, nombre, rythmes et mélodies*, 9–15. Paris: Presses Universitaires de France.

Snow, C. E., Burns, M. S. & Griffin, P. (eds) (1998). *Preventing reading difficulties in young children*. Washington, DC: National Academy Press.

Stanovitch, K. & Stanovitch, P. (1996). Rethinking the concept of learning disabilities: The demise of the aptitude/achievement discrepancy. In D. R. Olson & N. Torrance (eds), *Handbook of human development in education: New models of learning, teaching and schooling*, 117–47. Oxford: Blackwell.

Tallal, P. (1996). Language comprehension in language-learning impaired children improved with acoustically modified speech. *Science*, 271, 81–4.

Thatcher, R. W. (1992). Cyclical cortical reorganization during early childhood. *Brain and Cognition*, 20, 24–50.

Thatcher, R. W. (1994). Cyclic cortical reorganization: Origins of human cognitive development. In G. Dawson & K. W. Fischer (eds), *Human behavior and the developing brain*, 232–66. New York: Guilford Press.

Thatcher, R. W. (1997). Human frontal lobe development: A theory of cyclical cortical reorganization. In N. A. Krasnegor, G. R. Lyon & P. S. Goldman-Rakic (eds), *Development of the prefrontal cortex: Evolution, neurobiology, and behavior*, 85–113. Baltimore, MD: Brookes Publishing Co.

Vygotsky, L. S. (1962). *Thought and language*. Cambridge, MA: MIT Press. (E. Hanfmann, G. Vaker, trans.) (Original work published in 1934.)

Willms, J. D. (1997). Family, school and community effects on children's and youth's literacy skills. Unpublished manuscript. Statistics Canada.

Wittelson, S. (1983). Bumps on the brain: Right-left anatomic asymmetry as a key to functional lateralization. In S. J. Segalowitz (ed.), *Language functions and brain organization*, 117–44. London: Academic Press.

Wolf, M. (1997). A provisional, integrative account of phonological and naming-speed deficits in dyslexia: Implications for diagnosis and intervention. In B. A. Blackman (ed.), *Foundations of reading acquisition and dyslexia: Implications for early intervention*, 67–92. Mahwah, NJ: Erlbaum.

Wolf, M. & Katzir-Cohen, T. (2001). Reading fluency and its intervention. *Scientific Studies of Reading*, 5, 211–39.

Yakovlev, P. I. & Lecours, A. R. (1967). The myelogenetic cycles of regional maturation of the brain. In A. Minkowsky (ed.), *Regional development of the brain in early life*, 3–70. Oxford: Blackwell.

# 6    Growth cycles of mind and brain: analyzing developmental pathways of learning disorders*

*Kurt W. Fischer, L. Todd Rose, and Samuel P. Rose*

*Overview:* Development is not a linear process, but a dynamic interaction between the individual's mind, brain, and social and physical environments. Considering learning disorders from this dynamic, situated perspective is especially important, because many of children's abilities to compensate for perceptual or cognitive difficulties are constructed from the properties of this interaction. For this reason, dynamic models hold great promise in helping us to understand development in learning disorders. They contribute powerful tools for assessing diverse developmental pathways in all their real-life complexity, without separating the individual's mind and brain from his or her environment. Furthermore, dynamic models enable us to conceptualize and measure development in terms of recurrent growth cycles, bringing assessment of children's developing minds and brains together under one framework. Research on electrical activity in the cortex demonstrates such growth cycles in brain growth, which seem to parallel the cognitive cycles, as discussed by Robert Thatcher in an essay for this chapter. The dynamic framework for analyzing pathways of growth provides an important conceptual and methodological advance in our ability to make connections between neurological and cognitive growth, which will have major educational implications for learning-disabled children.        *The Editors*

In recent years developmental science has been transformed – from a relatively static framework that assumes stable skills and slow, linear change to a dynamic framework that focuses on change and variation in development and activity (Fischer & Bidell, 1998; Fischer, Yan, & Stewart, 2003; Thelen & Smith, 1994; van Geert, 1998). With this dynamic framework a wide array of new tools have become available for analyzing developmental pathways of learning disorders

* Preparation of this paper was supported by grants from Frederick P. and Sandra P. Rose, the Spencer Foundation, the Harvard Children's Initiative, and the Harvard Graduate School of Education. The authors thank Thomas Bidell, Robbie Case, Robert Thatcher, and Paul van Geert for their contributions to the concepts and findings discussed in this chapter.

101

and related skills and brain processes. In this chapter, we will articulate three powerful tools that will facilitate a richer analysis of learning disorders by focusing on specific processes in individual children: (a) the analysis of constructive webs of development, (b) the construction of explicit dynamic models of growth and change, and (c) contributions from neuroscience to understanding cycles of brain and skill development. In each of these cases we will provide an introduction – a teaser if you will – to suggest how the tools can produce amazing advances in developmental science.

To provide a glimpse of how the methods can come together to relate mind, brain, and education, we will present some recent work in cognitive neuroscience describing how development of the brain, especially the cerebral cortex, relates to development of learning and thinking (Fischer & Rose, 1996; Thatcher, 1994). Biological growth generally shows recurring growth cycles, and both brain and cognitive development evidence such cycles, changing in repeating patterns that involve recurrent processes – a central characteristic of a growth cycle. Based in recent innovations in tools for brain imaging and developmental assessment, this model of growth of *mindbrain* (as we like to call the union of mind and brain) has important implications for development of learning problems and disabilities.

## The shapes of development

With any learning disorder, such as reading disability, meaningful analysis requires beginning with a framework for analyzing how multiple components contribute to a complex activity. Without a doubt, the act of reading is a phenomenally complex process that involves multiple components, each of which influences whether or not a child's effort will be successful (Knight & Fischer, 1992; LaBerge & Samuels, 1974; Snow, Burns, & Griffin, 1998). As a result, the shape of developmental pathways for reading skills must be complex. In the face of the obvious complexity of reading, a model of linear growth – such as intelligence or reading ability increasing linearly in the same way from month to month – simply makes no sense. Growth of reading is far more interesting and dynamic than many traditional linear models have assumed.

For significant progress to be made in understanding the development of learning disorders, researchers must embrace the fact that development is usually non-linear and variable, and they must adjust their methodologies accordingly. It is no longer sufficient to explain away the variability that is so pervasive in development and so evident in learning disorders! As researchers and educators, we need to recognize the complexities and variations in learning disorders and do our best to explain them. Fortunately, powerful tools are available for analyzing non-linear development and learning, providing ways of accounting for variation and diversity across groups and individuals. These tools hold

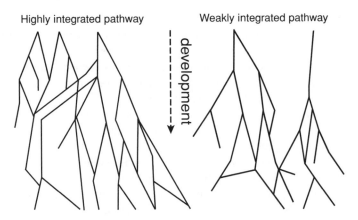

Figure 6.1 Two developmental webs showing different pathways.

enormous promise for future research and have the potential to revolutionize the science of learning disorders.

### Constructive webs of development

To progress toward a dynamic representation of development, one where non-linearity plays a central and vital role, we must first move beyond the old metaphor of development as a ladder. Children do not learn to read in a simple stage sequence, moving from one rung of a ladder to the next, but instead they develop along multiple parallel and interconnected strands, forming a web that they construct through learning and development, as illustrated in Figure 6.1 (Fischer & Bidell, 1998; Fischer, Knight & Van Parys, 1993; Snow, Burns, & Griffin, 1998). A framework built on the developmental web is a catalyst for critical reexamination of the tools and measures used in research. The shift from ladder to web helps to capture and explain the variability that is so pervasive in development.

Traditionally, cognitive development has been conceived as progression through a distinct sequence of stages, where both the start and end points are determined, and the relationship is treated as linear or monotonic. There certainly are differences in skills as a function of age, grade, and norm, but that stability needs to be understood within the framework of complex variation in developmental processes and behaviors. The methods that have come from the ladder approach, which typifies Piagetian, psychometric, and experimental traditions, have limited educators' ability to recognize developmental variability, affording only one potential pathway for development to occur. Such a static conception fails to capture the richness and complexity inherent in the dynamic phenomena of change and development. Effective teachers know intuitively that children do not all climb the same ladder, stage by stage or grade by grade, arriving at some predetermined destination. A normative approach is not optimal for most children, and it is especially problematic for children with learning disorders, where effective instruction requires understanding variation (D. Rose, this volume; Rose & Meyer, 2002).

The constructive web encompasses both stability and variability in change and development (Fischer & Bidell, 1998; Fischer, Yan, & Stewart, 2003). Instead of forcing the many processes of development into a static, restrictive ladder, the dynamic concept of a constructive web accommodates active development across many contexts, incorporating variability as an essential component rather than an unfortunate nuisance. The order and trajectory of the many strands in a constructive web are not predetermined, but instead they come from construction by a person acting in context. Both person and context (including other people) co-construct activities and skills. People construct multiple strands (domains) of their webs simultaneously, as shown in Figure 6.1, and these strands interweave as people progress toward more complex skills, such as reading.

Using the constructive web metaphor as central to a guiding dynamic framework for developmental research removes the methodological restrictions that have come from adherence to traditional static conceptions of development. One of the important implications for research on learning disorders is that people build different webs or pathways toward a skill such as reading. They do not move along a single idealized pathway. The traditional fixed, stage-based framework has left many children characterized as "developmentally delayed" merely because they do not evidence progression along some normative ladder (Fischer, Ayoub, Noam, Singh, Maraganore, & Raya, 1997). This traditional (mis)conception severely underestimates the level of complexity at which a learning-disabled child is acting, and can inadvertently misguide intervention strategies by failing to differentiate distinct pathways. Unfortunately, the traditional framework leads to seeing the child as operating at a lower level *because* the metaphor implies that there is no other possibility.

In contrast, a critical feature of the constructive web framework is that different children develop through different webs, as illustrated in Figure 6.1. Dynamic analysis in terms of webs helps educators and researchers to detect alternative pathways to reading and other important skills. The search for a comprehensive analysis of development of reading difficulties and strengths – which is a focus of this book – is greatly facilitated by a framework for analyzing multiple strands of skills in a web and their integration into the activities of the whole child. Children often construct skills that end up looking similar, as when reading is assessed with standard measures of performance; but their individual webs have different strands, different branches, and dissimilar patterns of integration. Tools from the dynamic framework can be used to detect distinctive developmental webs for different readers.

### Tools for analyzing webs

Simply changing the metaphor for development is not sufficient to produce meaningful results. To be effective, educators and researchers must be able to detect and measure alternative developmental pathways, not just pay homage to them. Within the dynamic web framework, there are powerful and straightforward methods for identifying and analyzing naturally occurring variability in developmental pathways. Although a thorough review of the methods is beyond the scope of this chapter, an essential characteristic of all of them is that they use multiple assessments of each individual child to detect naturally occurring diversity in activity and development (for more information, see Epstein, 1997; Fischer, Pipp, & Bullock, 1984; Fischer & Bidell, 1998; Singer & Willett, 2003; Thelen & Smith, 1994; van Geert, 1991). By using measures that incorporate multiple partially ordered tasks, varying assessment conditions, and different contexts, educators can begin to explain the wide range of diversity that exists in development and learning.

A study of the early development of reading single words illustrates the use of multiple tasks to assess different developmental webs (pathways) for reading (Knight & Fischer, 1992). Consistent with the guiding framework of the constructive web, a modified version of the Guttman scalogram method for testing developmental scales (Collins & Cliff, 1990; Guttman, 1944) provided an effective tool for empirically deriving potential webs, and thus detecting diversity in development. The modified method (Krus, 1977), which we call Partially Ordered Scaling of Items (POSI), follows the repeated-measures logic of the longitudinal design, which is preferable to cross-sectional designs in traditional developmental research. It also offers additional advantages that standard longitudinal designs do not, because it provides a "longitudinal" assessment every time that the tasks are administered.

An *independent task* is used to assess each step in a potential developmental pathway so that every step is assessed individually and the entire pathway is assessed in one session. The pathway is analyzed through the patterns of performance on all the tasks, providing a strong assessment of the shape of each child's developmental web with the POSI technique, or for the original Guttman scalogram a strong assessment of the ladder for each child. This design contrasts with traditional developmental assessments, which use one task, or a few unordered tasks, to infer all steps in a hypothesized developmental ladder.

The POSI technique orders performance profiles across tasks to assess not merely a linear sequence or ladder but a web with branching. Figure 6.2 shows a simple developmental web for early reading with only one point of branching

Table 6.1. *Response profiles for a Guttman scale with branch at step 2.*

| Step | Word definition | Letter identification | Rhyme recognition | Reading recognition | Rhyme production | Reading production |
|---|---|---|---|---|---|---|
| 0  | −  | −  | −  | −  | −  | −  |
| 1  | +  | −  | −  | −  | −  | −  |
| 2a | +  | +  | −  | −  | −  | −  |
| 2b | +  | −  | +  | −  | −  | −  |
| 3  | +  | +  | +  | −  | −  | −  |
| 4  | +  | +  | +  | +  | −  | −  |
| 5  | +  | +  | +  | +  | +  | −  |
| 6  | +  | +  | +  | +  | +  | +  |

Note: Pass = +; Fail = −.

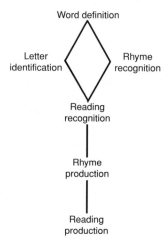

Figure 6.2 Pathway A for reading words: Developmental web with visual–graphic/auditory branching.

(Knight & Fischer, 1992). The web begins at the top with understanding the meaning of a spoken word, then branches into simple visual–graphic and auditory tasks with words (letter identification and rhyme recognition, respectively), and then as reading emerges integrates visual–graphic and auditory into skilled reading tasks. This web can be directly tested in every individual child through the reading profiles shown in Table 6.1. The profiles define the developmental orderings of six tasks for the developmental web in Figure 6.2. A linear Guttman scale, without branching, would omit the profile for Step 2b, which defines the branching of visual–graphic and auditory. A more complex web would have more branched orderings similar to Steps 2a and 2b. The use of multiple words for each child provided a set of profiles (one for each word), which allowed analysis of the web shown for each individual child.

In the study, a total of 120 children in first, second, and third grades (ages 6–8) in an Arizona public school were tested with 16 familiar words from their scholastic reading series. There were six tasks, as shown in Table 6.1 and Figure 6.2 – word definition, letter identification, rhyme recognition, rhyme production, reading recognition, and reading production – all administered for each of the 16 words. A table was created for each child to note the profiles shown for each of the 16 words. A combination of POSI and logical analysis of the patterns in the 16 profiles determined the developmental web of each child for learning to read the 16 words.

Traditional theories of reading acquisition assume that an essential precursor to skillful reading is integration of visual–graphic and sound-analysis skills (Goswami, 2002; LaBerge & Samuels, 1974; Torgesen, Wagner, & Rashotte, 1994; Wolf & Bowers, 1999; many chapters in this book). Figure 6.2 shows the developmental web in which these skills are integrated for the six tasks in Table 6.1 – Pathway A. It begins with word definition, as the child must know the word prior to actually using it effectively. Letter identification and rhyme recognition tasks are initially independent, because children in the early stages of reading development still need to integrate these skills. As the skills for sight and sound are integrated, the two branches merge to form a single strand for the remaining tasks.

For most children, the findings in the study supported this model of reading development as integration of sight and sound. In fact, Figure 6.2 was the most common pathway among the individual children, and it was associated with good reading skills. However, a number of children did not follow this proto-typical pathway, and their reading development could not be aptly described as remaining at a lower step within the web in Figure 6.2. Instead, these children followed different developmental pathways, showing two patterns distinct from that in Figure 6.2. Analysis of the patterns of task profiles for each child across the 16 words showed two alternative pathways that lacked the integration of the most common pathway, and both were associated with less skilled reading. Most of these children had some difficulty learning to read.

In Pathway B, shown in Figure 6.3a, reading and rhyming (sight and sound) remained independent in the developmental web. In this web, word definition still started development, and it then proceeded directly to letter identification. Then reading and rhyming followed two separate branches (strands), remaining independent of each other and not integrating further down the pathway. Inter-estingly, while this pathway emerged in many children who were poor readers, it was not exclusive to this group but was also evident in some effective readers, especially when they were reading words that were difficult.

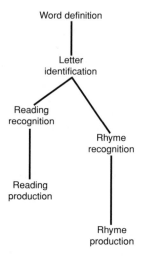

Figure 6.3a  Pathway B: Independence of reading and rhyming.

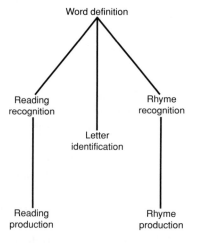

Figure 6.3b  Pathway C: Independence of reading, letter identification, and rhyming.

The third developmental web, Pathway C shown in Figure 6.3b, was found exclusively in children with serious reading difficulties. While this alternative pathway also began with word identification, it proceeded to a three-branch web, where reading, rhyming, and letter identification skills were independent of each other throughout the pathway. Even letter identification did not order with respect to reading and rhyming.

The finding of two multiple-branch, unintegrated webs for children with reading difficulties suggests that a primary difficulty of poor early reading is lack of integration of sight and sound. This finding is consonant with much other research (LaBerge & Samuels, 1974; Torgesen, Wagner, & Rashotte, 1994) as well as evidence and arguments in this book.

The POSI technique provides not only descriptions of developmental webs, such as those in Figures 6.2 and 6.3, but also measures of the distance between steps along the strands. The relative distance between any two steps on a strand is determined by the proportion of profiles that show ordering for those two tasks (Knight & Fischer, 1992). Another powerful technique for analyzing developmental scaling is Rasch (1966) analysis, which provides tools for determining developmental ordering and distance between items along a strand and is being used as well in the construction of many psychometric tests (Bond & Fox, 2001; Dawson, 2002; Dawson & Wilson, 2004). Rasch scaling has not yet been adapted, to our knowledge, for analysis of multi-branch webs, but it holds promise for tools that are even more powerful than POSI for research on pathways of learning and development.

The detection of multiple pathways in the development of reading speaks against a typical assumption, built into many standardized tests and even research methodologies – that all children learn to read in the same way. It also suggests that even when children look similar when passing or failing traditional measures of reading, their problems can be different. They are often progressing (at the same level of complexity) through distinct pathways that are dependent on the origin of their problem. These pathways can be indicative of specific learning disorders, as suggested by the distinct webs found by Knight and Fischer (1992). Rosalie Fink (1995, this book) has studied a hundred highly successful adult men and women with severe dyslexia. All of them became excellent readers and writers despite their great difficulties in integrating sight and sound (consonant with Pathways B and C). They all created their own pathways to successful reading and writing – and to eminent careers in science, education, business, and the arts.

With the constructive web framework, it is possible to use powerful tools to examine the distinctive development of individual children and adults. Analyzing these pathways provides ways to help educators, clinicians, and parents to effectively support people with learning disorders in the development of needed skills through non-normative pathways.

## Building explicit dynamic models

A second tool that is valuable for developmental analysis is construction of explicit models of the dynamics of learning and development. These models allow testing of growth processes that produce the diverse webs of development.

In the past, most developmental and educational researchers have shown an aversion to mathematical models. This resistance was probably warranted early on, as scientists were basically forcing linear mathematic models onto people's behavior. The shapes of development clearly defy this type of static analysis. Fortunately, the past decade or two have witnessed an explosion of work on the dynamical modeling of development. Because of the dedication and interest of many scientists, there now are highly effective tools for building rich non-linear models, which begin to pin down the processes described in the many theories of development and learning. This type of tool helps make explicit the many influences that shape development and thereby improves the scientific understanding of how people change, learn, and grow.

## *Experimenting with theories of development and learning*

A number of researchers, including several contributors to this book, have begun to use dynamic models to make theories explicit and to test empirically how growth produces various shapes of development and learning (Case & Okamoto, 1996; Fischer & Rose, 1994; Shultz, 2003; Thatcher, 1994; van Geert, 1991, 1998). One reason for the growing interest is the increased accessibility of these types of dynamic tools: they are widely available to any interested researcher who can use a computer. In fact, any spreadsheet program, such as Excel or Lotus 123, can be used to build non-linear, dynamic growth models because they can specify repeated-measures calculations: in development and learning, what is happening now affects what happens next (which is also a characteristic of many financial calculations, such as mortgages). In addition there are programs designed specifically for building models (such as Model Maker). Besides building a model and testing its properties, these programs provide techniques for testing how well specific data fit a model.

The ease of building and testing these dynamic models means that any well-specified theory can be put into mathematical terms to see what kinds of learning and development it produces. The models thus make it possible to *experiment* with a theory to determine whether the hypothesized processes in fact produce the predicted result. No longer must developmental analysis be restricted to regression models and analysis of variance, the tools that most researchers have been taught in graduate school. Instead, researchers and educators can now use very different types of models designed to explicate specific developmental concepts such as stage, pathway, continuity, discontinuity, learning, and even elusive transitional states. Most of these new models of development typically produce non-linear change, not traditional linear growth curves (Estes, 1956; Fischer & Bidell, 1998; Thatcher, 1998; van Geert, 1998).

This new and exciting wave of dynamic research in developmental science changes the nature of developmental theory by allowing direct experimentation with theories and models, creating what Paul van Geert (1996) calls "experimental theoretical psychology" (see also Shultz, 2003). This type of scientific research began decades ago in fields such as physics, metereology, economics, and biology as well as other kinds of science and social science (Granger & Teräsvirta, 1997; Epstein, 1997; Vallacher & Nowak, 1994). Work along these lines has been limited in developmental science and education until recently, even though the nature of development makes non-linear dynamic concepts particularly promising. The abundance of theory in developmental science provides ample sources for ideas that can be used to build models and test theories. Also, development involves many kinds of systematic change, which provide orderly phenomena to test against models. These characteristics of development provide a powerful springboard for dynamic modeling in developmental science.

Non-linear dynamic modeling has the potential to transform developmental science from a large body of rich but loosely formulated descriptions of development to very explicit dynamic models of change and transition that are rigorously grounded in empirically testable data. The tools from developmental-web and scaling analyses can greatly facilitate this endeavor as well. With its diverse and rich theoretical tradition, the field is ripe for this methodological-theoretical transition. In fact, many of the concepts of non-linear dynamics, such as attractor, self-organization, and catastrophe, have become part of the dialogue of the current developmental literature (Fischer & Bidell, 1998; Fischer & Rose, 1994; Thelen & Smith, 1994; van der Maas & Molenaar, 1992; van Geert, 1991, 1998). For dynamic modeling to realize its promise, the vague concepts and metaphors of most developmental science need to be tied down more expressly through mathematical modeling and through research on developmental webs and scales.

The process of explicating the concepts in our theories of development is a rigorous and sweeping task, and it requires reexamination of the rulers we employ to assess development. The nature of rulers for skill and knowledge is a fundamental problem that must be faced to build credible growth models. Notwithstanding numerous calls for careful research to develop effective rulers (Fischer, Pipp, & Bullock, 1984; Fischer & Rose, 1999; Flavell, 1972; McCall, 1983; van Geert, 1991; Wohlwill, 1973), many researchers have continued to use ill-defined scales to assess change. A notable exception is the progress made in the dynamic modeling of action (Bullock & Grossberg, 1988; Thelen & Smith, 1994), where researchers have profited from use of the powerful ruler provided by the Cartesian spatial-coordinate system to specify movement in space and time. Unfortunately, such precise rulers do not currently exist in areas of development where spatial movement is not relevant, although some progress is being made in building good rulers for cognitive complexity (Dawson, 2002; Dawson & Wilson, 2004; Fischer, 1980; Fischer & Bidell, 1998). Only with a

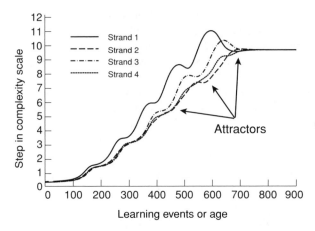

Figure 6.4 Attractor pattern of hierarchical development.

good ruler for development or learning can researchers and educators assume that measured behavior reasonably represents the phenomena represented in dynamic models.

## A model of dynamic development of hierarchical skills

A model of hierarchical skill development illustrates the usefulness of dynamic modeling, including its capacities to specify explicit developmental processes and to produce unexpected outcomes and insights. In the model, each strand grows as a series of five hierarchically connected skills (Figure 6.4), with later developing skills built upon earlier ones (Fischer & Kennedy, 1997; van Geert, 1994, 1998). Each skill is represented by a growth function, which begins with the fundamental function for living organisms – logistic growth. In its simplest form, the logistic function produces the familiar S-shaped growth curve. Figure 6.4 shows four different domains of skill that develop concurrently and influence each other.

Skills are connected hierarchically within each domain, with strong pre-requisite relations in which a later skill only begins to grow when an earlier skill reaches a certain level. For example, knowing the meaning of a word is a prerequisite for reading it in the pathways in Figures 6.2 and 6.3. Skills are also connected across domains, with relations that vary from moderate to weak to non-existent and that take several forms, including support between skills and competition (or interference). Within a domain, for instance, being skilled at rhyming the word "dog" can provide support for or interfere with rhyming another word, such as "pig." In the domain of reading a word, it can

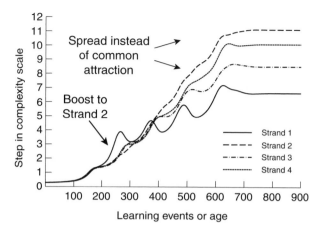

Figure 6.5  Spreading pattern of hierarchical development: The Piaget effect.

likewise support or interfere with skills such as reading "dog" and "pig." Besides connections within a person, there are also connections between people that affect growth, as when a teacher and student read jointly in a dyad or ensemble (Fischer & Granott, 1995; Fogel, 1993; van Geert, 1998).

These diverse connections affect a skill's growth function, so that development rarely shows simple S-shaped growth. Shapes vary as a function of not only different combinations of components but also different values for the same components in the same model. Shapes as diverse as S-shaped growth, stage-like change, and chaotic fluctuation all arise from the same set of equations.

A common growth pattern for the hierarchical model is stage-like growth, with clusters of spurts and drops occurring during a common interval across domains, as shown in Figure 6.4. The five stages or levels appear even though support and competition of skills across domains are weak. Across many values, the four domains (strands) show these spurts and drops as well as movement toward a common value – which is called an *attractor pattern*. It is the successive attraction toward a set of five different values (levels) that gives growth its stage-like shape, a pattern that fits many Piagetian and neo-Piagetian models of development (Case, 1991; Dawson & Wilson, 2004; Fischer, 1980; Fischer & Bidell, 1998; van der Maas & Molenaar, 1992; van Geert, 1998).

Interestingly, a slight alteration of one value within this same model – comparable to introducing a sudden growth spurt in one of the strands involved in reading words – can produce a very different growth pattern, as in Figure 6.5. A one-time boost in one strand early in the developmental pathway produces a radical switch to a spread-out pattern instead of an integrated one. We named this pattern "the Piaget effect" in honor of Jean Piaget on the 100th anniversary of his birth because the pattern illustrates his argument that unnatural perturbations in early development, such as attempts to rapidly advance young children's understanding of high-level cognitive tasks, will produce disturbances in the natural patterns of development (Fischer & Kennedy, 1997). An explicit model of development of learning disorders can produce similar discoveries of different growth patterns, perhaps helping to explain differences such as those in Figures 6.2 and 6.3.

The hierarchical skill model specifies only one of many different families of developmental shapes (Fischer & Rose, 1999). Other models include cusp-catastrophe analysis marked by empirical flags of sharply discontinuous (catastrophic) change (van der Maas & Molenaar, 1992) and predator–prey models in which components both support and compete with each other without building hierarchically, as cows and grass, cats and mice, and other predators and prey affect each other (Thatcher, 1998). Many more kinds of models will be needed to capture the diverse ways that people develop and learn.

Dynamic modeling of development is still young, but it has a remarkable potential. Biologists have had great success in building richly detailed models of interacting species in an ecosystem, and metereologists have had striking success in modeling development and change in weather systems. Similarly, developmental and educational scientists can move toward rich analysis of whole children as they learn and develop complex skills that have many components and are influenced by many factors such as attention, emotion, social support, and culture. Dynamic modeling provides the first real chance to scientifically analyze a whole child with all his or her difficulties and complexities intact – to move beyond the boxology that is so prevalent in analyses of cognitive abilities and disorders, where oversimplification and reductionism are the rules. The science and practice of learning disorders can take a giant step toward the appropriately complex models that real children require.

### Imaging and modeling mindbrain development

Most learning disorders clearly involve characteristic brain–body processes, such as dyslexics' problems with either phonological analysis or rapid perceptual processing or both, as described in Wolf and Ashby, Paré-Blagoev, and other chapters in this book. A challenge for scientists and practitioners has been to build brain models of reading problems that go beyond overly simple brain localization hypotheses. Recent advances in developmental neuroscience provide rich description of developing patterns of brain activity and anatomy as they relate to skill development, as described in the embedded essays by Thatcher, Teicher, and Caviness and in various other sources (Diamond & Hopson, 1998; Dawson & Fischer, 1994; Huttenlocher, 2002).

Brain development follows webs with independent strands, like skill development; in cognitive neuroscience they are often called parallel, distributed processes. Brain activity involves dynamically connected components that grow in several kinds of patterns, including both hierarchical organization and predator–prey relations (Fischer & Rose, 1999; Thatcher, 1998). The growth cycles for brain activity and their relations to the cycles for cognitive development illustrate the potential for rich, productive descriptions and models of brain and skill development.

We will first describe the general cycles for development of brain activity, relying especially on the work of Thatcher (1994, 1998) and Fischer and Rose (1994, 1996, 1999). Then we will explain the cycles for cognitive development and how they seem to relate to the brain cycles. The brain and cognitive cycles repeat multiple times between birth and age 30, with each recurrence producing a new capacity for learning and thinking grounded in an expanded, reorganized neural network. Each cycle also provides an opportunity for relearning skills and reshaping networks to take opportunities that were missed in earlier cycles, thus helping to explain the remarkable human capacity for plasticity, including recovery from damaging environments and neural injuries (Diamond & Hopson, 1998) and overcoming the limitations of learning disorders.

The most widely used neuroimaging technique is electroencephalography (EEG), which has existed for many years but has recently made great advances in sophistication. Other new and exciting neuroimaging techniques complement research with EEG to provide a sophisticated toolkit for analyzing development of brain functioning in real children – such as positron emission tomography (PET), magnetoencephalography (MEG), functional magnetic resonance imaging (fMRI), diffusion tensor imaging, and near-infrared spectroscopy (Dawson & Fischer, 1994; Paré-Blagoev, this volume; Thatcher, Lyon, Rumsey, & Krasnegor, 1996). Some research has used the newest techniques to analyze brain activity patterns in reading processes in normal and dyslexic children, supporting the hypothesis that many dyslexic children focus less on sound than other children in processing spoken and written language (for example, Paré-Blagoev *et al.*, 2002; Shaywitz *et al.*, 2002).

EEG and other imaging techniques can be used to investigate not only localization of functioning in skills and disorders but also connection patterns in brain networks. Research on development of connections among cortical regions illustrates the possibilities for rich analysis of patterns of brain and cognitive development.

*Cycles of growth of cortical networks*

The cortex of the brain constantly emits high-frequency electromagnetic waves, which are measured by EEG and MEG assessed with sensors on the scalp.

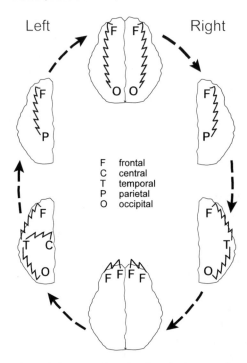

Figure 6.6  A growth cycle of cortical connections that repeat for each developmental level.
Based on Fischer & Rose (1994, 1996). View of cortex is from top of head with person facing the top of the page. Connections have been assessed by coherence EEG (of Thatcher, 1994).

These waves can be analyzed for coherence, a mathematical tool that measures connections between cortical regions through cross-correlation of wave forms (Nunez, 1981). Connections between cortical regions and other brain-wave properties show systematic growth patterns, which recur in cycles at different ages, according to research by Robert Thatcher (1994, 1998, this volume) and others (Bell & Fox, 1996; Hudspeth & Pribram, 1992; Somsen, van't Klooster, van der Molen, van Leeuwen, & Licht, 1997). The recurring cycles parallel the major levels in cognitive development that emerge at specific ages during infancy, childhood, and adolescence.

Fischer and Rose (1994, 1996, 1999) have proposed a detailed model of growth cycles of cortical activity and connectivity in relation to cognitive development, which combines Thatcher's analyses of brain development with the levels of cognitive development specified by dynamic skill theory and supported by extensive research. The hypothesized cycle for cortical connectivity is shown in Figure 6.6, which depicts how the location of peak growth

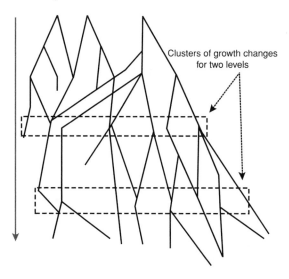

Clusters of growth changes
for two levels

Figure 6.7 Clusters of growth changes for two optimal levels across strands in a web.

of coherence moves gradually through major cortical regions. At peak times, growth continues in other cortical areas, but at a slower rate. The oscillating line between two brain regions indicates a spurt in coherence growth for those regions. Each occurrence of the cycle involves rewiring cortical networks for one cognitive-developmental level and therefore marks a new level.

In general, the frontal cortex leads most connections beginning first with long-distance links between frontal and occipital regions in both hemispheres, as shown at the top of Figure 6.6. The peak growth of coherence moves systematically first to the right hemisphere and then to the left. Within the right hemisphere, connections progress from global (frontal-occipital, frontal-parietal) to local (frontal-temporal, temporal-occipital). Then coherence spurts within the frontal lobes of both hemispheres, and next it shifts to the left hemisphere, where connections progress in the opposite pattern, from local to global. This ends one occurrence of the growth cycle and completes the emergence of a new cognitive level. Soon, the cycle begins again, and another cognitive level begins to emerge. As a result of this growth process, neural networks for each cognitive developmental level develop systematically throughout the entire cortex within a relatively short time interval (from a few months in infancy to four or five years in adolescence and early adulthood). The cycle recurs many times from birth through 25 to 30 years of age.

The growth cycle produces a wave of growth spreading through a developmental web to create approximately parallel growth spurts in separate brain regions and separate strands within a general age period. Figure 6.7 illustrates

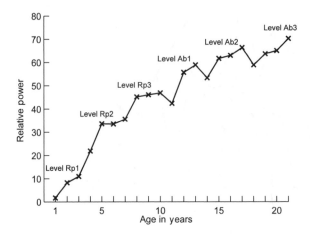

Figure 6.8 A series of spurts in development of relative energy in EEG. Relative energy was assessed for alpha frequency band in the occipital/parietal areas of the cortex. References: Matousek & Petersén, 1973; Fischer & Rose, 1994.

how separate strands can show approximately parallel, independent growth changes in multiple strands of a web, thus producing stage-like change even though the strands are mostly independent. Growth spurts in Figure 6.7 produce changes in direction of strands, branching of a strand, and joining of independent strands.

For each brain region, this wave of network growth produces a cascade of brain changes. One of the most prominent is discontinuities (spurts and drops) in the amount of energy in brain waves for that region. The first strong evidence for brain cycles was the finding of a series of spurts in energy in waves based on a Swedish study of EEG to establish medical norms by Matousek and Petersén (1973). Relative energy shows the most straightforward growth curves, as illustrated for occipital-parietal regions in Figure 6.8. Relative energy is calculated by dividing the amount of energy in a particular frequency band (the alpha band in this case) by the total amount of energy for all frequencies. At regular intervals relative energy shows a rapid increase (spurt) followed by a leveling off or plateau. For example, a spurt occurs between 1 and 2 years, a plateau at 2 to 3 years, another spurt at 3 to 5 years, another plateau at 5 to 7 years, and so forth. For each cycle of network growth (diagramed in Figure 6.6) EEG shows a spurt in relative energy in the graph.

Each spurt in Figure 6.8 (and each repetition of the cycle of coherence growth) provides the neural grounding for a new cognitive-developmental level, a capacity to build a new kind of skill. In the traditional model of development, each spurt would mark a step in the developmental ladder, but the cycle for network growth shows how development involves not merely steps but a cascade of changes across many strands in the developmental webs for brain and skill. The changes and correlations of brain volume for different cortical regions that Caviness (this volume) describes may also involve these or other growth cycles of cortical networks.

Specification of the growth cycle facilitates analysis of correspondences between sequences of brain and behavior development. For example, the cycle starts in general with more growth in the right hemisphere, moves through the regions there, and then shifts to more growth in the left hemisphere and moves through the regions there. The early predominance of the right hemisphere probably reflects the initial advantage of a global approach for learning something new, while the later predominance of the left hemisphere reflects the more differentiated approach that facilitates cumulated learning.

The general form of the cycle seems to apply not only to developmental levels, but also to development in many specific domains, such as language, music, and early reading (Bell, 1998; Coch et al., 2002; Fabbro, Brusaferro, & Bava, 1990; Gordon & Carmon, 1976; Goldberg & Costa, 1981; Immordino, 2001). Speech, music, and reading all seem to begin with more involvement of the right hemisphere, and gradually the focus shifts more to the left hemisphere. Further research can articulate the patterns in much more detail, linking particular regional connections to specific skills. For example, the emergence of crawling between 6 and 12 months of age relates closely to a spurt in coherence of frontal with occipital and parietal cortex, especially in the right hemisphere (Bell & Fox, 1996). Differences between boys and girls in coherence patterns seem to relate to sex differences in early language and motor development (Hanlon, Thatcher, & Cline, 1999).

## Cycles of cognitive development

Each cycle of network growth creates a new cognitive capacity to build a skill, according to the dynamic skill model (Fischer & Bidell, 1998; Fischer & Rose, 1994, 1996; van Geert, 1998). During childhood and adolescence, a series of seven skill levels emerge, six of which are shown in Figure 6.8. Each skill level appears with a spurt in optimal skill as well as a cycle of network growth and a spurt in EEG power. The emergence of each new optimal level thus follows a recurring cycle that shows a remarkable parallel to the growth of energy in the EEG in Figure 6.8, with spurts at similar ages for both skill level and EEG energy.

Skills are not static abilities but dynamic constructions bringing together many components in context. They are both task-specific and context-dependent, varying greatly in level and content with variations in task, context, and emotional state (Fischer, Rotenberg, Bullock, & Raya, 1993; van Geert,

1991; Young, Kulikowich, & Barab, 1997). For example, a 10-year-old girl's skill for reading and understanding a story about other children depends on her visual-graphic skills for reading written text, her phonological skills for understanding spoken language, her understanding of plots, social scripts, and social roles, her understanding of emotions and reciprocity in interactions, her memory for previous events in the story, and much more. Likewise, she has other skills for playing soccer, convincing daddy to read one more bedtime story, solving arithmetic problems, or being a supportive best friend.

Skills depend on the biological maturation of body and brain, and simultaneously on the social and emotional contexts and conditions of the particular task and activity. A skill varies in level from moment to moment as a function of these many factors, and so a person does not have a skill at a particular level but instead a skill varying across a range of levels, even for a particular domain, such as reading Roald Dahl's story *Charlie and the Chocolate Factory* (Fischer & Bidell, 1998; Yan & Fischer, 2002).

With a skilled, supportive adult priming key parts of the task, a child produces a more complex level of understanding a story than without that social support. For example, in a high-support assessment a teacher or parent can prime key parts of understanding a story that the child is reading, while in a low-support one the adult provides no direct support. Likewise, one first grade boy can sound out and suggest rhymes for words only when his teacher helps him by providing a choice of words that rhyme or by modeling the skill of sounding out (Fischer & Rose, 2001; Knight & Fischer, 1992). Well-designed artifacts such as a text, diagram, or computer program can provide similar support. Lev Vygotsky (1978), the great Russian psychologist, understood the importance of variability with social support and defined a broad variability during children's skill learning that he called the zone of proximal development.

The variation between supported and unsupported conditions is evident to people who work with children, but it has been neglected in traditional cognitive research, which often treats children as if their skill is at a single, fixed level. The *developmental range* is the zone between a child's optimal level and functional level for a domain. *Optimal level* is the best that the child can do with high support, including priming of key parts of the task. *Functional level* is the best that the child can do without support. Research shows that optimal and functional levels are both real competencies – upper limits on a child's skill in a given domain (Fischer *et al.*, 1993). In other words, a child's competence at, for example, understanding a story changes systematically depending on contextual support.

This important principle of variation in children's performance provides the solution to a major conundrum in the developmental research literature. Children sometimes show clear stage-like jumps in performance, but at other times they show smooth, continuous growth. Developmental range explains this variation: stage-like growth spurts occur only for optimal level, not for functional. When children's problem solving is analyzed according to support and its related changes in performance, the stage debate disappears. Development has strongly stage-like properties under conditions of high support, but not under conditions of low support. While functional skills typically show no stage-like growth, changing smoothly or showing inconsistent variation, optimal skills show a consistent series of spurts, drops, and qualitative changes across domains. For familiar, socialized domains such as reading and other skills taught in school, these shifts usually occur within a specific age range for each level. Across domains (strands in the web), these changes make up the large, empirically observable shifts in thinking and acting that teachers and parents see throughout childhood and adolescence, a series of levels of cognitive development.

A clear example of the difference between optimal and functional levels comes from a study of the development of abstract concepts for arithmetic operations (addition, subtraction, multiplication, and division) in 9- to 20-year-olds (Fischer & Kenny, 1986). Students performed a series of arithmetic tasks that involved explaining the relations between pairs of similar arithmetic operations (addition and subtraction, addition and multiplication, subtraction and division, and multiplication and division). First, in the low-support condition, the interviewer asked the student to explain each relation, and then in the high-support condition, the interviewer primed all the key ideas by showing the student an example of a prototypic answer. After two weeks the conditions were repeated. Correct performance required the student to produce a true abstract explanation, going beyond a concrete, problem-specific answer. Instead of the concrete explanation "Addition and subtraction relate in these problems because $8 - 3 = 5$ and $5 + 3 = 8$," they had to explain the relation in general, abstract terms and apply it to the concrete problems, such as "Addition and subtraction relate because in addition, you put together numbers, while in subtraction, you take numbers back apart. So addition and subtraction are opposites. In this problem, you are putting together the 5 and 3 to get 8 in addition, and then taking them back apart in subtraction."

Low-support performance (functional level) improved gradually with age and never climbed very high, as shown in Figure 6.9, but high-support performance (optimal level) showed a distinct spurt at age 16 that was consistent across students. Optimal performance spurted dramatically, so that no student understood more than one of the relations at age 15 and every student understood a majority of them at age 16. In the low-support, functional level condition, no such spurt occurred: only one 16-year-old understood one of the eight relations.

Similar spurts have been demonstrated across several domains for every level shown in Figure 6.8, as well as for an additional level at approximately age 25 (Level Ab4, principles integrating systems of abstractions). The series of skill

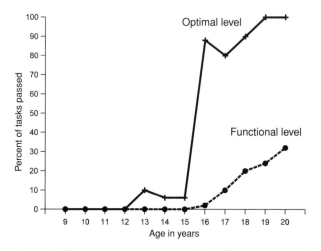

Figure 6.9 Emergence of a new optimal level for abstract mappings of arithmetic operations.
*Reference:* Fischer & Kenny (1986). Optimal level was assessed with high-support assessment, including priming of the components of a good answer as well as practice (Session 2 High Support), while functional level was assessed with low-support assessment, including spontaneous production of an answer without priming and no practice (Section 1 Low Support).

levels thus show a recurring growth cycle, with a cluster of spurts for each level, similar to the pattern for relative energy in Figure 6.8. Domains that have been studied include reflective judgment (Kitchener, Lynch, Fischer, & Wood, 1993), moral reasoning (Dawson, 2002; Dawson & Gabrielian, 2003), and self understanding (Fischer & Kennedy, 1997), as well as more traditional cognitive and school-based tasks; and the patterns of spurts obtain across countries, including the United States, China, and South Korea. The levels have been corroborated by multiple assessments of discontinuities, ranging from simple spurts like that in Figure 6.9 to gaps in developmental scales based on Rasch analysis of interview data over a wide age range (Dawson, 2002; Dawson & Wilson, 2004). These levels include Piaget's (1983) four main stages as well as additional levels. A more complete description of these discontinuities, which we call levels and tiers, is presented elsewhere (Fischer & Bidell, 1998; Fischer & Rose, 1994).

## Conclusion: dynamic development of brain and learning disorders

New tools for analysis of learning and development provide the potential to move developmental science away from the simplistic understanding of the past and toward much richer, more comprehensive understanding of learning disorders. Development moves through multi-strand, dynamic webs – not static, linear ladders; and children with learning disorders develop through distinctive webs that involve different patterns of skill differentiation and integration. Dynamic mathematical models of the processes of growth provide powerful tools for explicitly representing how multiple components work together to shape learning and development. These models make theories testable, creating experimental techniques for studying how differences in growth processes produce distinctive developmental pathways. For learning disorders, the models can be used to specify the processes underlying learning differences and to predict which kinds of interventions will be most effective.

Development of mindbrain can be illuminated by using these tools with powerful brain imaging techniques to portray development of brain activity and organization and the relation of mindbrain development to learning and learning disorders. Mindbrain development involves a recurring growth cycle of neural networks and learning, in which a child learns skills and concepts not only once, but relearns and reworks them anew at each successive optimal level. Most scholars and educators believe that the brain plays a major role in learning disorders and differences, but research and theory on brain involvement has remained overly simple, mostly involving static localization hypotheses. By using brain-imaging techniques to model differences in learning and development, including developmental webs and growth cycles for brain functioning associated with learning disorders, researchers can provide valuable insights into the nature of the disorders and derive useful information for interventions to facilitate skill development. For example, recurring growth cycles of brain and cognition may explain how early learning problems can be overcome or circumvented as a result of revisiting brain regions and skill domains, as when many children with dyslexia show a major change during early adolescence: they overcome their disability and learn to read and write skillfully (Fink, 1995, this volume). New tools for imaging and modeling brain and skill development provide ways of specifying how learning and cognitive processes relate to brain functioning and going beyond overly simple models of localized brain "deficiencies" to explain learning differences dynamically in a way that relates to real, whole human beings.

Together these three sets of tools (analyzing developmental pathways, building growth models, and imaging brain development) can revolutionize conceptualization of learning disorders and practices with children who learn differently. They can move the field a long distance toward understanding the complex nature of learning disabilities by making the tools of research and theory capable of going beyond overly simple conceptions of learning disorders to incorporate the sophisticated complexity that grounds human learning and development.

## Essay: Cycles and gradients in development of the cortex

### Robert W. Thatcher

*Connection:* The brain and cognition both develop in systematic patterns of cycles and gradients, which are evident from the very beginnings in prenatal development and continue for later developments of brain activity and behavior in childhood and adolescence. One of the most powerful tools for examining brain activity and relating it to cognitive development is the electroencephalogram (EEG), a measure of the electrical waves generated by the cortex of the brain. A valuable property of the EEG is coherence, the similarity between waves in different brain regions, which is measured by correlating wave forms through Fourier analysis. Coherence shows clear developmental cycles and gradients, which seem to relate to general patterns of cognitive development as well as individual differences.                    *The Editors*

### Gradients and cycles in prenatal development

From the moment of conception embryological development is organized in terms of spatial gradients and growth cycles. Brain development reflects these processes from its earliest origins.

#### Spatial gradients of prenatal development

Spatial gradients shape development from the beginning prenatally (Diamond, Scheibel, & Elson, 1985; Rakic, 1988). Shortly after conception, a ball of cells grows symmetrically without a clear left or right or an anterior or posterior plane. At the first differentiation, spatial polarization occurs in which a disk with an anterior and posterior end and a medial and lateral plane appears. The inner layer (i.e. the endoderm) differentiates to form the skeleton and gut, while the outer layer of the disk (i.e. the ectoderm) differentiates to form the neural plate from which the entire nervous system develops. Shortly after the formation of the neural plate (e.g. about 16 days after conception) an indentation appears along the midline which grows into a fold that becomes the neural groove. The neural groove becomes a hollow tube with the inside of the anterior end of the tube eventually becoming the forebrain ventricles and the middle and posterior end becoming the spinal canal. The neural tube begins to close to form a roof in the center of the embryonic disc. Then, like two zippers moving in opposite directions, the roofing process continues in both an anterior and posterior direction. This process represents one of the first examples of the two dominant prenatal spatial gradients; that is, the embryonic anterior-posterior and medio-lateral gradients.

Molecular biological studies have identified the regulatory genes Emx2 and Pax6 which are expressed as opposing gradients in the anterior-to-posterior and lateral-to-medial directions. These genes are believed responsible for realization of the neocortex and determination of the identity of cortical cells. Van Baal's (1997) studies and Thatcher's (1992, 1998) studies of EEG coherence development may reflect the operation of these or similar genes that may have continuing expressions during postnatal development.

*Cycles of prenatal development*

The emergence of one of the first "cyclic" processes that is embedded in the anterior-posterior and medio-lateral gradients begins at approximately 23 days after conception. The cycle is where the germinal neuroepithelia of the neural tube lies between the lumen and the outer limiting membrane. At about 23 days after conception a cyclic spatial growth process occurs in which the neuroepithelial cells alternate in activity between cell division or mitosis and synthesis of the genetic material DNA. The spatial cycle is where the neuroepithelial cell near the lumen divides → then the nucleus of each newly formed daughter cell moves laterally away from the lumen of the neural tube toward the outer limiting membrane → the nucleus then undergoes DNA synthesis or generation → then the nucleus moves medially back toward the lumen and, to repeat the cycle, the cell becomes mitotic again (Diamond, Scheibel, & Elson, 1985). The cycle time of this spatial process is approximately 4 to 24 hours per cycle.

The process continues over a period of days until a large complement of neuroepithelial cells is produced after which differentiation of the neuroepithelial cells to neuroblasts begins. The neuroblasts migrate laterally away from the lumen to form a new, outer mantle layer, which becomes the gray matter of the brain and spinal cord. As the neuroblasts differentiate into mature neurons, their axons form the marginal layer, which becomes the white matter of the brain and spinal cord. As with the earlier stages of embryogenesis, the precise timing of the development and migration of cells to different cortical regions occurs along medio-lateral and anterior-posterior spatial gradients. Detailed analyses of the operation of the anterior-posterior and medio-lateral spatial gradients have also been provided for the embryogenesis of the mouse (Smart, 1983) and rat (Bayer & Altman, 1991) brains. All mammalian species appear to exhibit dominant embryological brain development gradients along the anterior-posterior and medio-lateral spatial planes.

## Spatial gradients and cycles during postnatal development

Thatcher's (1992, 1994) studies of the development of EEG coherence demonstrated the existence of anatomical poles operating during the postnatal period that were defined by one or more of the following factors: (1) they are the dominant spatial dimensions or anatomical axes of EEG coherence development, (2) they exhibit developmental organizing properties, and (3) they exhibit spatial gradients. They appear to relate to levels and reorganizations in cognitive development (Fischer & Rose, 1996; Fischer, Rose, & Rose, this volume). The dominant patterns of the developmental trajectories of EEG coherence over the period from 1.5 years to age 16 indicate three "poles" of development from which there are gradients or organizational structure. The poles are: (a) anterior–posterior, (2) medio–lateral, and (3) left–right hemisphere (Thatcher, 1994).

### *Postnatal anterior–posterior gradients of development*

An anterior–posterior (front to back) pole of development was evident by: (1) a frontal-to-posterior dominance of cortico-cortical relations in both the left and right hemispheres (Thatcher, 1992, 1994; Thatcher *et al.*, 1987) and (2) a developmental sequence from short distance anterior–posterior connections of cortical regions (such as P3-T3 or T5-C3) to longer distance anterior–posterior electrode combinations (such as P3-F7 or P3-F1) to even longer anterior–posterior electrode combinations (such as 01-F1).

### *Postnatal medio–lateral gradients of development*

A lateral to medial (side to middle) pole of development was evident in: (1) differential rates of development of the lateral (such as F7/8 and T3/4) as opposed to the dorsal medial frontal regions (F3/4 and C3/4) and (2) a rotational sequence with a direction from lateral to medial in the left hemisphere and a direction from medial to lateral in the right hemisphere. In addition, (3) interhemispheric lateral frontal and lateral temporal regions exhibited 180° phase reversals (opposite patterns of EEG phase), whereas interhemispheric dorsal medial frontal regions did not; and (4) dorsal medial interhemispheric trajectories were mostly synchronous, whereas lateral interhemispheric trajectories were mostly asynchronous (Thatcher, 1994).

## A two-compartment model of coherence

In the last 10 years the existence of a short vs. long distance, two-compartment model of coherence of the electroencephalogram (EEG) has received considerable experimental and mathematical support (Thatcher, 1998; Thatcher *et al.*, 1986; Nunez, 1981, 1995; Pascual-Marqui, Valdes-Sosa, & Alvarez-Amador, 1988; Wright, 1997; van Baal, 1997; van Beijsterveldt & van Baal, 2002). According to the two-compartment model of EEG coherence, short- and long-distance EEG coherence reflect the operation of two distinctly different compartments: the short-distance compartment is dominated by cortico-cortical connections that reside within the gray matter and tend to exhibit a diffuse spatial dynamic (falling away exponentially with distance, described by the negative exponential), while the long-distance compartment is dominated by myelinated, long-distance cortico-cortical connections that tend to exhibit a spatial dynamic reflecting a feedback loop (with several connecting regions feeding back to each other in a dynamic network) (Nunez, 1981, 1995; Thatcher, 1992, 1994; Thatcher, Biver, Camacho, McAlaster, & Salazar, 1998; Thatcher, Krause, & Hrybyk, 1986; Wright, 1997; van Baal, 1997).

The two compartments appear to be dynamically linked and often exhibit competitive relationships in which changes in EEG coherence in the compartments are inversely related (Thatcher, 1994, 1998; Thatcher *et al.*, 1986, 1998). The competitive dynamics are mathematically modeled by assuming that neural populations can communicate with their local neighbors but that there is a trade-off for simultaneous communication with long-distance neighbors, including a dynamic oscillatory balance between the influences of the short- and long-distance systems (Thatcher, 1998). Recent identical twin studies have provided further support for the two compartments model by demonstrating possible independent inheritance for the two compartments as measured by heritability statistics (van Baal, 1997). In the van Baal longitudinal studies of twin pairs, for example, EEG coherence from short-distance connections (such as 6 to 7 cm) exhibited approximately 40% heritability, whereas EEG coherence from the long-distance connections (such as 28 cm) exhibited approximately 70% heritability (van Baal, 1997; van Beijsterveldt & van Baal, 2002).

## Conclusions

Van Baal's studies show a strong heritability for postnatal developmental changes in EEG coherence, which indicates that genetic expression of some type is operating to guide the development of synaptic connections during the postnatal period. We have hypothesized that there are spatial gradients and cycles of overproduction of synaptic connections followed by pruning of excess connections during the postnatal developmental period (Thatcher, 1992, 1994, 1998). These cycles seem to relate to cognitive-developmental levels or re-organizations, as described by Fischer and Rose (Fischer & Rose, 1996; Fischer, Rose, & Rose, this volume). Although precise molecular mechanisms have not been identified, it is reasonable to assume that genetic factors operating during the prenatal period are similar to those operating during the postnatal period (e.g. Bishop, Goudreau, & O'Leary, 2000).

REFERENCES

Bayer, S. A. & Altman, J. (1991). *Neocortical development*. New York: Raven Press.

Bell, M. A. (1998). The ontogency of the EEG during infancy and childhood: Implications for cognitive development. In B. Garreau (ed.), *Neuroimaging in child psychiatric disorders*, 97–111. Berlin: Springer-Verlag.

Bell, M. A. & Fox, N. A. (1996). Crawling experience is related to changes in cortical organization during infancy: Evidence from EEG coherence. *Developmental Psychobiology*, 29, 551–61.

Bishop, K. M., Goudreau, G. & O'Leary, D. M. (2000). Regulation of areal identity in the mammalian neocortex by Emx2 and Pax6. *Science*, 288, 344–9.

Bond, T. G. & Fox, C. M. (2001). *Applying the Rasch model: Fundamental measurement in the human sciences*. Mahwah, NJ: Erlbaum.

Bullock, D. & Grossberg, S. (1988). Neural dynamics of planned arm movements: Emergent invariants and speed-accuracy properties during trajectory formation. *Psychological Review*, 95, 49–90.

Case, R. (ed.) (1991). *The mind's staircase: Exploring the conceptual underpinnings of children's thought and knowledge*. Hillsdale: Erlbaum.

Case, R. & Okamoto, Y. (1996). The role of central conceptual structures in the development of children's thought. *Monographs of the Society for Research in Child Development*, 60 (nos. 5–6, Serial No. 246).

Coch, D., Maron, L., Wolf, M. & Holcomb, P. J. (2002). Word- and picture-processing in the human brain: An event-related potential study. *Developmental Neuropsychology*, 22, 373–406.

Collins, L. M. & Cliff, N. (1990). Using the longitudinal Guttman simplex as a basis for measuring growth. *Psychological Bulletin*, 108, 128–34.

Dawson, G. & Fischer, K. W. (eds) (1994). *Human behavior and the developing brain*. New York: Guilford Press.

Dawson, T. L. (2002). New tools, new insights: Kohlberg's moral reasoning stages revisited. *International Journal of Behavior Development*, 26, 154–66.

Dawson, T. L. & Gabrielian, S. (2003). Developing conceptions of authority and contract across the lifespan: Two perspectives. *Developmental Review*, 23, 162–218.

Dawson, T. & Wilson, M. (2004). The LAAS: A computerizable scoring system for small- and large-scale developmental assessments. *Educational Assessment*, 9, 153–91.

Diamond, M. & Hopson, J. (1998). *Magic trees of the mind: How to nurture your child's intelligence, creativity, and healthy emotions from birth through adolescence*. New York: Dutton.

Diamond, M. C., Scheibel, A. B. & Elson, L. M. (1985). *The human brain coloring book*. New York: Barnes and Noble.

Epstein, J. M. (1997). *Nonlinear dynamics, mathematical biology, and social science*. Cambridge, MA: Perseus Press.

Estes, W. K. (1956). The problem of inference from curves based on group data. *Psychological Review*, 53, 134–40.

Fabbro, F., Brusaferro, A. & Bava, A. (1990). Opposite musical-manual interference in young versus expert musicians. *Neuropsychologica*, 28, 871–87.

Fink, R. (1995). Successful dyslexics: A constructivist study of passionate interest reading. *Journal of Adolescent and Adult Literacy*, 39, 268–80.

Fischer, K. W. (1980). A theory of cognitive development: The control and construction of hierarchies of skills. *Psychological Review*, 87, 477–531.

Fischer, K. W., Ayoub, C. C., Noam, G. G., Singh, I., Maraganore, A. & Raya, P. (1997). Psychopathology as adaptive development along distinctive pathways. *Development and Psychopathology*, 9, 751–81.

Fischer, K. W. & Bidell, T. R. (1998). Dynamic development of psychological structures in action and thought. In R. M. Lerner (ed.), *Handbook of child psychology. Vol. 1: Theoretical models of human development*, 5th edn, 467–561. New York: Wiley.

Fischer, K. W. & Granott, N. (1995). Beyond one-dimensional change: Parallel, concurrent, socially distributed processes in learning and development. *Human Development*, 38, 302–14.

Fischer, K. W. & Kennedy, B. (1997). Tools for analyzing the many shapes of development: The case of self-in-relationships in Korea. In E. Amsel & K. A. Renninger (eds), *Change and development: Issues of theory, method, and application*, 117–52. Mahwah, NJ: Erlbaum.

Fischer, K. W. & Kenny, S. L. (1986). The environmental conditions for discontinuities in the development of abstractions. In R. Mines & K. Kitchener (eds), *Adult cognitive development: Methods and models*, 57–75. New York: Praeger.

Fischer, K. W., Knight, C. C. & Van Parys, M. (1993). Analyzing diversity in developmental pathways: Methods and concepts. In R. Case & W. Edelstein (eds), *The new structuralism in cognitive development: Theory and research on individual pathways*, 33–56. Basel, Switzerland: Karger.

Fischer, K. W., Pipp, S. L. & Bullock, D. (1984). Detecting discontinuities in development: Method and measurement. In R. Emde & R. Harmon (eds), *Continuities and discontinuities in development*, 95–121. New York: Plenum.

Fischer, K. W. & Rose, L. T. (2001). Webs of skill: How students learn. *Educational Leadership*, 59(3), 6–12.

Fischer, K. W. & Rose, S. P. (1994). Dynamic development of coordination of components in brain and behavior: A framework for theory and research. In G. Dawson & K. W. Fischer (eds), *Human behavior and the developing brain*, 3–66. New York: Guilford.

Fischer, K. W. & Rose, S. P. (1996). Dynamic growth cycles of brain and cognitive development. In R. Thatcher, G. R. Lyon, J. Rumsey & N. Krasnegor (eds), *Developmental neuroimaging: Mapping the development of brain and behavior*, 263–79. New York: Academic Press.

Fischer, K. W. & Rose, S. P. (1999). Rulers, clocks, and nonlinear dynamics: Measurement and method in developmental research. In G. Savelsbergh, H. van der Maas & P. van Geert (eds), *Nonlinear developmental processes*, 197–212. Amsterdam: Royal Netherlands Academy of Arts and Sciences.

Fischer, K. W., Rotenberg, E. J., Bullock, D. H. & Raya, P. (1993). The dynamics of competence: How context contributes directly to skill. In R. H. Wozniak & K. W. Fischer (eds), *Development in context: Acting and thinking in specific environments. The Jean Piaget symposium series*, 93–117. Hillsdale, NJ: Erlbaum.

Fischer, K. W., Yan, Z. & Stewart, J. (2003). Adult cognitive development: Dynamics in the developmental web. In J. Valsiner & K. Connolly (eds), *Handbook of developmental psychology*, 491–516. Thousand Oaks, CA: Sage.

Flavell, J. H. (1972). An analysis of cognitive-developmental sequences. *Genetic Psychology Monographs*, 86, 279–350.

Fogel, A. (1993). *Developing through relationships: Origins of communication, self, and culture*, Chicago: University of Chicago Press.

Goldberg, E. & Costa, L. D. (1981). Hemisphere differences in the acquisition and use of descriptive systems. *Brain and Language*, 14, 144–73.

Gordon, H. W. & Carmon, A. (1976). Transfer of dominance in speed of verbal response to visually presented stimuli from right to left hemisphere. *Perceptual and Motor Skills*, 42, 1091–100.

Goswami, U. (2002). Phonology, reading development and dyslexia: A cross-linguistic perspective. *Annals of Dyslexia*, 52, 1–23.

Granger, C. W. J. & Teräsvirta, T. (1997). *Modelling nonlinear economic relationships: Advanced texts in econometrics*. Oxford: Oxford University Press.

Guttman, L. (1944). A basis for scaling qualitative data. *American Sociological Review*, 9, 139–50.

Hanlon, H. W., Thatcher, R. W. & Cline, M. J. (1999). Gender differences in the development of EEG coherence in normal children. *Developmental Neuropsychology*, 16, 479–506.

Hudspeth, W. J. & Pribram, K. H. (1992). Psychophysiological indices of cerebral maturation. *International Journal of Psychophysiology*, 12, 19–29.

Huttenlocher, P. R. (2002). *Neural plasticity: The effects of environment on the development of the cerebral cortex*, Cambridge, MA: Harvard University Press.

Immordino, M. H. (2001). Working memory for music and language: Do we develop analogous systems based on similar symbolic experience? Qualifying Paper, Harvard Graduate School of Education, Cambridge, MA.

Kitchener, K. S., Lynch, C. L., Fischer, K. W. & Wood, P. K. (1993). Developmental range of reflective judgment: The effect of contextual support and practice on developmental stage. *Developmental Psychology*, 29, 893–906.

Knight, C. C. & Fischer, K. W. (1992). Learning to read words: Individual differences in developmental sequences. *Journal of Applied Developmental Psychology*, 13, 377–404.

Krus, D. J. (1977). Order analysis: An inferential model of dimensional analysis and scaling. *Educational and Psychological Measurement*, 37, 587–601.

LaBerge, D. & Samuels, S. J. (1974). Toward a theory of automatic information processing in reading. *Cognitive Psychology*, 6, 293–323.

Matousek, M. & Petersén, I. (1973). Frequency analysis of the EEG in normal children and adolescents. In P. Kellaway & I. Petersén (eds), *Automation of clinical electroencephalography*, 75–102. New York: Raven Press.

McCall, R. B. (1983). Exploring developmental transitions in mental performance. In K. W. Fischer (ed.), *Levels and transitions in children's development* (Vol. 21, pp. 65–80). San Francisco: Jossey-Bass.

Nunez, P. (1981). *Electric fields of the brain: The neurophysics of EEG*, New York: Oxford University Press.

Nunez, P. (1995). *Neocortical dynamics and human EEG rhythms*, New York: Oxford University Press.

Paré-Blagoev, E. J., Cestnick, L., Rose, T., Clark, J., Misra, M., Katzir-Cohen, T. & Poldrack, R. (2002). The neural basis of phonological awareness in normal-reading children examined using functional magnetic resonance imaging. *Journal Of Cognitive Neuroscience*, F53(Suppl S April).

Pascual-Marqui, R. D., Valdes-Sosa, P. A. & Alvarez-Amador, A. (1988). A parametric model for multichannel EEG spectra. *International Journal of Neuroscience*, 40, 89–99.

Piaget, J. (1983). Piaget's theory. In W. Kessen (ed.), *Handbook of child psychology: Vol. 1. History, theory, and methods*, 103–26. New York: Wiley.

Rakic, P. (1988). Specification of cerebral cortical areas. *Science*, 241, 170–76.

Rasch, G. (1966). An item analysis which takes individual differences into account. *British Journal of Mathematical and Statistical Psychology*, 19, 49–57.

Rose, D. & Meyer, A. (2002). *Teaching every student in the digital age*. Alexandria, VA: American Association for Supervision & Curriculum Development.

Shaywitz, B. A., Shaywitz, S. E., Pugh, K. R., Mencl, W. E., Fulbright, R. K., Skudlarksi, P., Constable, R. T., Marchione, K. E., Fletcher, J. M., Lyon, G. R. & Gore, J. C. (2002). Disruption of posterior brain systems for reading in children with developmental dyslexia. *Biological Psychiatry*, 52(2), 101–10.

Shultz, T. R. (2003). *Computational developmental psychology*. Cambridge, MA: MIT Press.

Singer, J. D. & Willett, J. B. (2003). *Applied longitudinal data analysis: Modeling change and event occurrence*. New York: Oxford University Press.

Smart, I. H. M. (1983). Three dimensional growth of the mouse isocortex. *Journal of Anatomy*, 137, 683–94.

Snow, C. E., Burns, M. S. & Griffin, P. (eds) (1998). *Preventing reading difficulties in young children*. Washington, DC: National Academy Press.

Somsen, R. J. M., van't Klooster, B. J., van der Molen, M. W., van Leeuwen, H. M. P. & Licht, R. (1997). Growth spurts in brain maturation during middle childhood as indexed by EEG power spectra. *Biological Psychology*, 44, 187–209.

Thatcher, R. W. (1992). Cyclic cortical reorganization during early childhood development. *Brain and Cognition*, 20, 24–50.

Thatcher, R. W. (1994). Cyclic cortical reorganization: Origins of human cognitive development. In G. Dawson & K. W. Fischer (eds), *Human behavior and the developing brain*, 232–66. New York: Guilford Press.

Thatcher, R. W. (1998). A predator-prey model of human cerebral development. In K. Newell & P. Molenaar (eds), *Applications of nonlinear dynamics to developmental process modeling*, 87–128. Mahwah, NJ: Erlbaum.

Thatcher, R. W., Biver, C., Camacho, M., McAlaster, R. & Salazar, A. M. (1998). Biophysical linkage between MRI and EEG coherence in closed head injury. *NeuroImage*, 7, 352–67.

Thatcher, R. W., Krause, P. & Hrybyk, M. (1986). Corticocortical associations and EEG coherence: a two compartmental model. *Electroencephalography and Clinical Neurophysiology*, 64, 123–43.

Thatcher, R., Lyon, G. R., Rumsey, J. & Krasnegor, N. (eds) (1996). *Developmental neuroimaging: Mapping the development of brain and behavior*. New York: Academic Press.

Thatcher, R. W., Walker, R. A. & Guidice, S. (1987). Human cerebral hemispheres develop at different rates and ages. *Science*, 236, 1110–13.

Thelen, E. & Smith, L. B. (1994). *A dynamic systems approach to the development of cognition and action*. Cambridge, MA: MIT Press.

Torgesen, J., Wagner, R. & Rashotte, C. (1994). Longitudinal studies of phonological processes of reading. *Journal of Learning Disabilities*, 27, 276–86.

Vallacher, R. & Nowak, A. (1994). *Dynamical systems in social psychology*. New York: Academic Press.

van Baal, C. (1997). A genetic perspective on the developing brain. Dissertation, Vrije University, Netherlands Organization for Scientific Research (NWO), ISBN: 90-9010363-5.

van Beijsterveldt, C. & van Baal, G. (2002). Twin and family studies of the human electroencephalogram: A review and a meta-analysis. *Biological Psychology*, 61, 111–38.

van der Maas, H. L. J. & Molenaar, P. (1992). A catastrophe-theoretical approach to cognitive development. *Psychological Review*, 99, 395–417.

van Geert, P. (1991). A dynamic systems model of cognitive and language growth. *Psychological Review*, 98, 3–53.

van Geert, P. (1994). *Dynamic systems of development: Change between complexity and chaos*. London: Harvester Wheatsheaf.

van Geert, P. (1996). The dynamics of Father Brown: Essay review of book *A dynamic systems approach to the development of action and thought* by E. Thelen & B. Smith. *Human Development*, 39, 57–66.

van Geert, P. (1998). A dynamic systems model of basic developmental mechanisms: Piaget, Vygotsky, and beyond. *Psychological Review*, 105, 634–77.

Vygotsky, L. (1978). *Mind in society: The development of higher psychological processes* (M. Cole, V. John-Steiner, S. Scribner & E. Souberman, trans.). Cambridge MA: Harvard University Press.

Wohlwill, J. F. (1973). *The study of behavioral development*. New York: Academic Press.

Wolf, M. & Bowers, P. (1999). The "double-deficit hypothesis" for the developmental dyslexias. *Journal of Educational Psychology*, 91, 1–24.

Wright, J. J. (1997). EEG simulation: Variation of spectral envelope, pulse synchrony, and 40 Hz oscillation. *Biological Cybernetics*, 76, 181–94.

Yan, Z. & Fischer, K. W. (2002). Always under construction: Dynamic variations in adult cognitive development. *Human Development*, 45, 141–60.

Young, M., Kulikowich, J. & Barab, S. (1997). The unit of analysis in situated assessment. *Instructional Science*, 25, 133–50.

# 7    Brain bases of reading disabilities

*Francine Benes and Juliana Paré-Blagoev*

*Overview:* For a century and a half, brain–behavior correlates in language were studied via the lesion approach, in which functional deficits after localized neurological damage are used to deduce the brain's organization. While much of the basic information gleaned from this research tradition still holds and new lesion-based discoveries continue to be made, modern advances with in vivo imaging techniques reveal that language processing in fact recruits many brain areas. In particular, different aspects of spoken and written language, such as orthography and semantics, require different kinds of neuropsychological processing. Given the complex distribution of language-related skills in the brain, the heterogeneity of dyslexic profiles is not surprising. In the end, it is likely that this very heterogeneity will prove key not just to unlocking the true nature of dyslexia but to understanding better the spoken and written language systems themselves.                                          *The Editors*

Since the late 1800s, scientists have known that there are specialized brain areas crucially involved in language reception and production, including understanding and producing written language. Reading impairments associated with a condition termed 'visual word blindness' were independently reported at the end of the nineteenth century by Scottish ophthalmologist James Hinshelwood and British physician Pringle Morgan (Hinshelwood 1895; Morgan 1896). These are generally considered the first behavioral accounts of the syndrome now called dyslexia. In the 1890s, based on lesion data collected by Monsieur Dejerine in adults, the left inferior parieto-occipital region along with the posterior section of the corpus callosum, called the splenium, were implicated as brain regions playing a special role in this disorder. At the beginning of the twenty-first century, it was confirmed that these areas, in conjunction with numerous others, play a role in language-related tasks. A number of excellent studies and reviews have been published of specific findings regarding brain morphology and function associated with dyslexia (Habib 2000). The nature of the interactions between these regions and the bi-directional effects of disruptions on brain and reading deficits remains only partially explored.

In this chapter, we describe studies across wide ranging perspectives about language and brain. The studies reviewed used a variety of techniques to explore a range of questions related to the identification of brain areas and cytoarchitecture involved in the encoding of language and its expression either as the spoken or written "word." A promising new technique called diffusion tensor imaging now permits the study of white-matter tracts in vivo and may be capable of proving to be a particularly important window into the connectivity of the brain. Taken together, the studies provide insight into the complexity of language and reading, and the massive interconnections between brain regions that are required for linguistic processing. Whatever else may be true regarding the occurrence of dyslexia, it seems likely that alternations in the functional connectivity between key brain regions must be involved.

## Historical overview: brain bases of language production

We begin with a historical overview of early findings showing the left temporal lobe to be critically involved in different aspects of language production. Spoken language calls upon capacities related to and partially overlapping with those required in reading. An inquiry into reading disorders reasonably includes an inquiry into spoken language for this reason and also because dyslexics often show deficits in oral language articulation (Korhonen 1995; Heilman, Voeller *et al.* 1996). At the 1861 meeting of the Anthropological Society of Paris, a French neurologist named Ernest Aubertin presented the case of a man who had unsuccessfully attempted suicide through a gunshot to the head. After the attempt, he was left alive but with a severe wound: the frontal bones of his head were blown off and his frontal lobes were left exposed. Aubertin took the opportunity to experiment with direct cortical stimulation. Using a spatula, he discovered that if he discretely stimulated portions of the frontal lobe, particularly on the left side and particularly in the inferior frontal convolution, the speech of the unfortunate patient could be predictably disrupted. In his presentation to the Anthropological Society in Paris, Aubertin hypothesized that speech was localized in the frontal lobes, particularly on the left side.

This single case provided a fascinating story, but not compelling enough proof that the left frontal lobe is crucially involved in language. Twenty years before Aubertin conducted his inquiry, another French neurologist, Paul Broca, had been introduced to a patient who was suffering from epilepsy. The sufferer, Monsieur Labone, had lost the ability to speak, with the exception of a few words. One word he could still form was "tann" and he was known as Tann to his friends and family. Just six days after Aubertin presented his case study, Tann passed away and Broca performed an autopsy. This revealed a discrete focal lesion in the left inferior frontal area. Broca did not himself recognize and identify the link between the location of the damage and Tann's language loss.

However, over the next 10 to 15 years, some of his colleagues did appreciate this link, and in time the relationship between what is now called Broca's area and the ability to produce language. Current research suggests that in children with specific language impairment, Broca's area is significantly smaller than in controls. Further, unusual morphology in this and other language areas correlates with depressed language ability (Gauger, Lombardin, et al., 1997).

As the introduction and the examples of Broca and Aubertin suggest, the late 1800s were an important time for breakthroughs in our identification of gross brain areas critically important to different aspects of language use. In 1874, at the age of 26, Karl Wernicke published ten famous cases describing different variations of aphasia. These studies took us beyond identification of isolated brain regions to a consideration of interconnections between specific regions. His work was largely speculative and in many instances only scant empirical evidence supported his conclusions. Still, he had a tremendous impact on our understanding of the brain and the way in which the brain handles language. He recognized accurately that there are networks of systems rather than single areas involved with different aspects of language. He speculated that a disruption of the connections between the elements of these networks might result in a *conduction aphasia*. With this condition, one would be able to speak and understand language, but not be able to connect the two.

In honor of their contributions, two language areas of the brain have been named for Broca and Wernicke. In the inferior frontal lobe of the dominant hemisphere (usually the left), there is an expressive area named for Broca. More posteriorly, including the superior temporal gyrus and the supramarginal gyrus, is an area named for Wernicke. Wernicke's area seems to have a more central role in encoding logical grammatical relations. Just as current studies have shown correlations between depressed language ability and abnormal function or structure in Broca's area, similar findings exist for Wernicke's area (Galaburda & Sherman, this volume; Galaburda, Mednard, et al., 1994).

The approach taken by Broca and Wernicke looking at the effects of naturally occurring lesions on previously normal functions is a time-honored one and has yielded many important results. In modern times, however, and particularly in the last decade, the development and refinement of non-invasive neuroimaging techniques have expanded the range of questions that can be addressed with lesion studies. This progress has also increased our ability to ethically study brain and behavior correlates in healthy or moderately impaired individuals. The following section begins with a review of two studies that use neuroimaging techniques to investigate language function in the deaf and also in dyslexics. This discussion is intended to highlight the variations in brain activation possible when the brain is processing language in an unusual manner. In the case of the deaf, the initial processing difference is immediately obvious: they process language through visual not auditory modalities. In the case of dyslexics, the differences in language processing are more subtle. However, a basic principle is likely shared between these two groups. That is, since the inputs underlying language processing are different from normal, the subsequent neurological processing will be likewise different and will, therefore, follow different developmental trajectories.

### Contributions from brain imaging studies

One of the advantages of the new neuroimaging techniques is that they do not rely on postmortem studies. Instead, their non-invasive nature allows the study of the brains of lesioned, impaired individuals as well as completely healthy ones while they are still living. Two of these non-invasive techniques (structural and functional magnetic resonance imaging; MRI and fMRI respectively) can be used in conjunction with one another to provide information about how the living brain functions on a specified task of interest.

One way to study language is to use a modality other than hearing, as for example in users of sign language. This strategy is related to the lesion approach in that it relies on information about abnormal function to obtain insights into normal function. In many cases, hearing impaired individuals are deaf not because of neuronal damage, but because of damage to the external auditory system (i.e. within the ears or peripheral nerve damage). In the latter case, the lack of normal inputs to the central auditory system implies that the auditory cortex might be be recruited for alternative uses. In that sense, the hearing impaired represent a group whose brains are likely to be organized differently than individuals without such an impairment. Broadly speaking, this is a "lesion" approach through which a better understanding of brain function can be derived through comparing abnormal brains with "normal" brains. In this case, speakers of sign language do not rely on or use auditory processing to communicate language. Instead, by generating symbols with their fingers and hands, also called "signing," visual processing may substitute for hearing. Since individuals with normal auditory function utilize hearing as the dominant modality for learning language, functional imaging studies of sign-language speakers can teach us about the brain regions that are important for language.

Neville and colleagues used fMRI to compare cerebral activation patterns among hearing subjects, deaf subjects who use ASL, and hearing subjects who were native in both ASL and spoken English (Neville, Bavelier, *et al.*, 1998). When viewing a video of a deaf native ASL speaker producing sentences in ASL, bilateral activation was observed in the deaf ASL speakers *and* the native hearing ASL speakers. Activation in the left hemisphere was observed in the inferior frontal gyrus (Broca's area), the superior temporal gyrus (including Wernicke's area), and the left prefrontal cortex. In the right hemisphere, equivalent areas were activated during the same task. Hearing English speakers without knowledge of ASL showed no increased activation during presentation of the ASL video when compared to a control period.

The surprising finding in this study was the largely symmetric activation in speakers of ASL during ASL language processing. Typically, language function is considered primarily to be the responsibility of the left hemisphere in right-handed individuals. This study suggests the idea that language function, in its fullest expression, works collaboratively with both sides of the brain and for some language-related tasks may use areas that otherwise are not usually implicated in language function. In an interesting and complicating twist, hearing or deaf ASL users with aphasias induced by strokes or other lesions of the brain have generally incurred damage to the *left* side of the brain. This might indicate that although their ability to respond to ASL normally shows a bilateral distribution, the basic encoding of language in these individuals is still confined largely to the dominant left hemisphere.

Some researchers suspect that subtle problems in auditory processing, sequencing, or timing underlie some forms of dyslexia (Tallal, Miller, *et al.*, 1993; Wolf & Ashby, this volume). Importantly, when there is a disorder in some aspect of brain processing the brain adapts, and generally some amount of rerouting occurs so that additional brain areas are recruited to compensate. An obvious implication is that this rerouting will manifest itself in measurable changes across a range of behaviors including, but not limited to, those typically associated with the originally damaged or disordered brain region(s). In the case of some dyslexics, whether there is a disorder of auditory or phonological processing, it is important to identify those brain regions that are recruited to compensate for the unusual inputs being received and/or for the aberrant processing of normal inputs. One promising direction along these lines is followed by the Shaywitzes at the Haskins Laboratory at Yale University.

The Shaywitzes and colleagues argue that among other discoveries, the beginning reader must become aware that spoken words consist of combined sounds referred to as phonemes (Shaywitz, Shaywitz, *et al.*, 1996; Shaywitz *et al.*, 2002). This requires phonological, orthographic, and semantic encoding skills. Recognizing the phoneme as a basic building block of all language, whether spoken or written, is the key to making progress with reading skills. In written language, these phonemes must be recognized as having written symbolic counterparts. For example, in "bat" there are three phonemes /b/, /æ/, /t/ and each has a corresponding orthographic representation: b, a, t. Reading requires the ability to understand both orthographic and phonological encoding. In addition, semantic encoding, i.e. recognizing that the spoken word "bat" and the written word "bat" both refer to the same furry creature with leathery wings, is also crucial.

Using fMRI and an experimental paradigm designed to isolate the brain function associated with each the three major processes involved in reading (i.e. phonological, orthographic, and semantic encoding), the Shaywitzes and colleagues found interesting patterns of brain activations in normal readers. For example, activation during orthographic encoding was observed in extra striate areas that are posterior and close to the primary visual cortex. In contrast, for phonological encoding, the activation observed was primarily in the inferior frontal gyrus. For semantic encoding, however, the pattern was more complex, with activation occurring in the inferior aspects of both the middle and superior temporal gyri of both hemispheres; in women, there were more anterior prefrontal sites also activated. This study is important for two reasons. First, it provides a picture of brain regions important for perceiving, processing, and representing different reading-related language tasks. With this information, it is possible to begin investigating the activation patterns of individuals with dyslexia in order to better understand how the brain may be processing language in a way that results in a reading disorder. Second, this study shows the range of interconnected regions that are likely to be involved in dyslexia.

Another imaging study of language, conducted by Hanna Damasio and colleagues, provides an indication of another complicating facet of language encoding and retrieval, and one which implicates multiple regions outside of the classic language areas (Damasio, Grabowski, *et al.*, 1996). In addition to the three functional processes of semantic, phonological, and orthographic encoding described in the Shaywitz study, this Damasio study suggests additional complexities, within the categorization of semantic meanings, involving an interaction between two functional systems mediated by a third. One system is responsible for the reconstruction and explicit phonemic representation of words. A second supports the encoding of conceptual knowledge. The third, a mediating system, provides a way to link these first two systems. A cohort of individuals who had suffered focal brain injuries resulting in problems with naming in specific categories was studied. In some cases, their naming difficulties were restricted to naming persons, in others to naming animals, and in yet others to naming tools. In some individuals, the naming deficits involved two or all of the categories. Damasio *et al.* interpret their findings to suggest that the identified brain regions (described below) are critically involved in the third mediating system.

Using data collected from structural MRI scans, three-dimensional reconstructions were prepared and the sites of the focalized lesions were precisely identified. The localizations of different lesions were correlated with the different naming deficits. For individuals with difficulty naming persons, lesions tended to be in the anterior tip of the temporal lobe, while lesions for those with difficulty naming animals tended to occur in the inferior temporal gyrus in an anterior and medial location. Finally, for those with tool-naming deficits, the lesions were most pronounced in areas of the inferior frontal gyrus in relatively more posterior and lateral locations.

To further investigate their findings, Damasio and colleagues utilized another functional brain imaging technique, positron emission tomography (PET), to identify those regions used by healthy individuals while naming persons, animals, or tools. Their findings suggest that the inferior temporal lobe is likely to play a role in categorical naming. For the normal, non-lesioned subjects in this PET study, the task of naming persons elicited activation in the anterior portion of the temporal pole. This was both like and unlike the findings in the lesion study. Both studies implicated the anterior portion of the temporal pole, but in the lesion study, the lesions were found in the left hemisphere predominantly, whereas the PET study revealed bilateral activation. This difference suggests that bilateral areas are necessary for normal function and that disruption of only one of the areas interferes significantly with task performance. This finding underscores the importance of recognizing that connectivity between brain regions contributes to normal naming of objects. Identification of abnormal brain regions correlated with abnormal behavior can be interpreted to indicate that the lesioned area is involved in, but not necessarily responsible for, the disrupted behavior.

This cautionary message is supported as well by the PET study findings for the naming of animals and tools. As in the structural study of lesioned individuals, activation patterns in healthy subjects during the naming of animals and tools implicated the inferior temporal region. And again, as with the lesion and PET study data for the person-naming task, the regions activated showed overlapping but not entirely congruent brain regions compared to the lesion data.

In a descriptive and analytical review of the Damasio work, Caramazza provided the following graphical schematic representing the interaction between the phonological segments and the semantic features of the Damasio *et al.* findings (Caramazza, 1996; see Figure 7.1). The semantic features associated with a person, animal, or tool might overlap to some extent. Similarly, phonological segments appropriate for a given person, animal, or tool will overlap as well. The figure shows how the coordinated and selective activation of certain phonemes and certain semantic features could, over time, give rise to the functional categorization of words as persons, animals, or tools.

These imaging studies leave us with important questions. Do imaging studies such as those conducted by the Shaywitzes suggest that *all* orthographic encoding occurs in the extra striate portions of the brain and that all phonological encoding occurs in the inferior frontal gyrus? Alternatively, do these studies indicate that activated areas are neural substrates for encoding these aspects of language, but ones that are not necessarily critical for these tasks? Regarding the Damasio study, how can we begin to understand the neurophysiological substrates underlying the connectivity implied by their framework? Generally, PET neuroimaging allow us to get a gross picture of brain function. But, are there cellular level differences that might be even more important in identifying

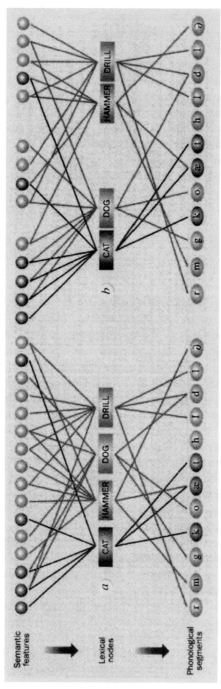

Figure 7.1 (a) The three levels of representation of word knowledge necessary for speech production. Semantic features (carnivorous, furry, domesticated, pet) activate lexical nodes (the word CAT) which, in turn, activate their corresponding phonological features (k, æ, t). (b) Organization of the three levels in the form proposed by Damasio et al. (1996). The neural system for conceptual information consists of a distributed network involving structures in both the left and right hemispheres. These networks are connected to lexical representations in the left temporal lobe which are organized by semantic category – animals in the inferior temporal (IT) lobe; tools in the posterior regions of the IT lobe and the occipito-temporo-parietal junction. The selected lexical representation in turn activates its associated phonological features for speech production (from Caramazza 1996).

the underlying neural substrates of language and language disorders such as dyslexia? And, what neural circuits, not just neural regions, might be important for language function? In the next section, relevant studies of such questions are addressed.

## Language processing at the cellular and circuitry level

Using the lesion-based approach, examination of brains during postmortem studies is crucially important to understanding and interpreting the abnormal and normal behavior exhibited by subjects while alive. Postmortem studies of normal brains are important because they can provide important information at the cytoarchitectural level of and within the individual neurons, although this is at best only cross-sectional in nature. Animal studies are also important because they can provide ongoing information regarding the function of individual neurons. For example, the technique of single-cell recording allows the study of electrical activity at the level of both neurons and circuits. In two of the studies reviewed in this section, postmortem studies of normal brains were conducted, while in a third study, animal studies were used to record from small clusters of neurons. In both cases, hypotheses have been generated as to how language skills may be supported at the cellular level.

Hutsler and Gazzaniga obtained autopsy information from normal individuals specifically regarding regions of the brain implicated in the processing of language functions (Hutsler & Gazzaniga 1997). The regions included the superior temporal gyrus, the supramarginal gyrus, the inferior frontal gyrus and others. They were particularly interested in the size of pyramidal neurons in these brain regions. Pyramidal neurons are the principal projection cells of the cortex and are believed to be responsible for triggering behavioral events including those involving language. In most right-handed people with normal language function, the left hemisphere is the dominant hemisphere for language processing and production. Hutsler and Gazzaniga compared the pyramidal cells in target brain regions of the left and right hemispheres. They found that the left hemisphere almost consistently showed a tendency to have larger pyramidal cells, particularly in the upper ranges of size.

Functionally, this is an important observation because larger neurons generally receive a greater number of inputs through their dendritic trees and also send a proportionately larger number of axonal outputs to other regions of the brain. This observation suggests that in language-related areas of the dominant hemisphere, there are particularly large pyramidal cells that are perhaps well poised to subsume a particularly important role in the mediation of language function. This study, as with all postmortem studies, leaves open the question of whether the pyramidal cells in the language-related areas were larger before ever being used for language or if the cumulative experience of a lifetime of using language stimulates those neurons to increase the size of their somata, dendritic trees, and axonal projections.

Another important question at the neuronal level is the relation of cortical circuitry to normal function. Drawing from the work of Sir John Eccles in the latter half of the twentieth century, we understand that the pyramidal cells described by Hutsler and Gazzaniga are organized into large arrays with a diameter of approximately one-third of a millimeter. These arrays, termed macro-columns, are considered to be the smallest functional unit of the cortex. Knowledge about macro-columns comes in part from animal studies and specifically from studies of the somatosensory cortex of mice. It has been found that single whiskers on the face of a mouse could activate a single macro-column in the somatosensory cortex (Woolsey & Van der Loos, 1970). In the human visual cortex, similar arrays of neurons have also been observed, and it is generally accepted that the macro-column is the smallest unit of organization for behavior.

Pyramidal neurons form macro-columnar arrays that send projections to many brain regions both in the same hemisphere and to those on the opposite side of the brain. Three different types of projections seem to exert the primary influence on the activity of these macro-columns. One is from the thalamus, while another comes from other cortical areas, the so-called associative fibers traveling distances as great as seven to eight millimeters. The third input is the collateral branch of pyramidal neurons within the same macro-columns; these cover relatively shorter distances. Overall, macro-columns can convey information along long or short distances.

Macro-columns can be considered as a possible pathway of communication for the multiple encoding functions described in the Shaywitz research above (Shaywitz, Shaywitz, *et al.*, 1996; Shaywitz, *et al.*, 2002). For example, macro-columnar arrays may be responsible for connectivity between the supramarginal gyrus, Wernicke's area, or in the inferior frontal gyrus. The serial activation of macro-columns responsible for encoding "b," "a," and "t" may be responsible for the phonological, orthographic, and semantic processing that generates what we experience as the word "bat" with the specific semantic context of either an animal or a tool. When there are problems with the development of reading ability as there is in dyslexia, the problem could lie in the communication that occurs among such macro-columns and could involve subtle aspects of their structural or functional connectivity.

Other research, conducted by Rizzolatti, Arbib, and colleagues using single-cell recording of monkey neurons, has suggested a possible role for a special class of neurons in language function (Kohler, *et al.*, 2002; Rizzolatti & Arbib, 1998). These investigators have identified what they have called "mirror" neurons in the premotor cortex of monkeys. The monkeys were trained to watch an experimenter perform various hand movements, such as grasping and reaching.

Reliably, certain neurons in the F5 area of the cortex fired both when the movement was observed and also later when the monkey mimicked the movement. These neurons were termed mirror neurons. Other neurons in F5 fired only when the monkey performed the movements, but not when the movements were simply observed.

Rizzolatti and Arbib observed that transcranial magnetic stimulation (TMS) and positron emission tomography (PET) studies support the hypothesis that, in humans, Broca's area seems to have mirror neurons similar to those found in the monkey F5 region. Again, these mirror neurons seem to fire during viewing or performing communicative hand gestures. As they review, cytoarchitectonic and connectivity studies also suggest that the monkey F5 and human Broca's area are homologous brain regions. Rizzolatti and Arbib propose that these mirror systems for gesture recognition, coupled with a developed system for consciously controlling a widening repertoire of possible vocalizations, may provide a basis for the development of language in humans. For subhuman primates lacking the ability to control discrete muscle groups such as those of the larynx may be a limiting factor for non-human vocal communication.

Presumably, in the human brain, the ontogenetic development of language function could similarly rely upon mirror neuron activity. The mirror neurons identified by Rizzolatti and Arbib must receive an input from the vision system, because the motor movements must be perceived in order to drive mirror neuron firing. The firing of these latter cells may facilitate the formation of a visual representation of the motor movement and at the same time may drive the production of a similar motor movement. Thus, mirror neurons may provide a means for linking perceptive sensory inputs with productive motor outputs via a single internal representation. It is intriguing to consider whether similar mirror neurons might also integrate motor movements perceived through a non-visual modality, such as audition. This question is relevant for understanding how the brain might process the spoken "word." Overall, Rizzolatti and Arbib's study has suggested a fruitful line of research that could eventually shed light on the complex question of how language is read, heard, and translated into a spoken or written response.

This study raises some very important questions. For example, are there mirror neurons for the motor movements required to produce phonemes that are activated when phonemes are heard? Do putative phoneme mirror neurons and canonical phoneme production neurons control the muscles of the larynx, pharynx, tongue, and lips in formulating a representation of a phoneme? Are there some forms of dyslexia that may be attributable to a problem with this mirror neuron system? Currently, the techniques necessary to address questions of this type regarding mirror neurons in the human brain are not available; however, in the future, it may be possible to conduct some experimentation in vivo as functional brain imaging technology continues to advance.

## Considering dyslexia more specifically

Any survey of the dyslexia literature, no matter how brief, will reveal that there is a great deal of controversy regarding the specific behavioral characteristics that may be present in individuals with this disorder. Within the population of those with developmental dyslexia, there is great heterogeneity. This is reflected in the definition of dyslexia:

Dyslexia is one of several distinct learning disabilities. It is a specific language-based disorder of constitutional origin characterized by difficulties in single word decoding, usually reflecting insufficient phonological processing abilities. These difficulties in single word decoding are often unexpected in relation to age and other cognitive and academic abilities; they are not the result of generalized developmental delay or sensory impairment. Dyslexia is manifest by variable difficulty with different forms of language, often including, in addition to reading problems, a conspicuous problem with acquiring proficiency in writing and spelling. (Operational definition of the Orton Dyslexia Society Research Committee, New York, April 18, 1994)

Given the complexity of the brain and behavioral components of language identified in the discussion above, the heterogeneity of the developmental dyslexic profile is not surprising (see Wolf & Ashby, this volume). As reviewed by Stein and Walsh, although there are several compelling models attempting to explain developmental dyslexia, none are yet sufficient to address the myriad characteristics and deficits observed clinically (Stein & Walsh, 1997). For example, discrete disturbances, such as a reversal of letters, a blurring or distortion of letters, and a complete overlap of phrases, fit a model in which temporal (i.e. timing) processes may be disrupted. However, this model does not help to explain other deficits noted in dyslexia. In Figure 7.2, a drawing by a child with dyslexia is reproduced. In this drawing, a clock is depicted with all the numbers clustered on one side, while on the opposite side, there are no numbers at all. Similar drawings are produced by patients with focal damage in the supramarginal gyrus of the right hemisphere. In such a patient, this deficit is referred to as a *constructional dyspraxia*. Stein and Walsh suggest that such disturbances, although identified in only a subset of dyslexic individuals, go unidentified in the larger dyslexic population because this type of testing is not typically done.

The existence of such a deficit implicates brain regions not typically associated with language function. Specifically, Stein and Walsh emphasize the posterior parietal cortex, including areas that are understood to play a role in spatial localization and orientation. Again, these areas rely heavily on functional connectivity in order to produce intact behaviors. A behavioral deficit of this sort then might implicate a relatively widespread disturbance in connectivity

Figure 7.2 Left neglect in a dyslexic child of 7 years 11 months. The child had a reading age that was retarded by 20 months. The child's I.Q. was 92 (reprinted from Stein & Walsh, 1997).

that manifests most apparently in reading difficulties, but which can be accompanied by a range of other characteristics and deficits as well.

As the Stein and Walsh example of blurred and/or overlapping letters suggests, and as common sense confirms, reading involves visual processes. As described in more detail by Galaburda and Sherman in this volume, the visual processing deficits associated with dyslexia may be related to parallel deficits in the magnocellular system of the lateral geniculate nucleus.

Adding to the list of brain regions apparently involved in and affected by reading and reading disorders (Shaywitz, Shaywitz, et al., 1996; Shaywitz et al., 2002), orthographic processing involves extra striate areas within the visual area. Importantly, these areas project extensively into the pulvinar which is phylogenetically most developed in the human brain. The thalamus is known as the way-station of the brain and nearly all brain regions are connected through it. Massive projections from the pulvinar extend upwards to the inferior parietal lobule which includes the supramarginal gyrus, a key part of Wernicke's area.

The picture that emerges here regarding language circuitry is one of a large network of massively interconnected regions. The implication for understanding developmental dyslexics is that they are enormously heterogeneous. Future studies of dyslexia and language function must deal with these factors and strive to be more precise in identifying specific brain regions involved in language and related tasks. The neuroscientific tools now available to study brain functioning in intact, functioning humans are not adequate for clearly defining the neuronal circuits that ultimately will hold at least part of the answer to the question of what causes dyslexia. Over time, however, new forms of technology will be developed. Promising work utilizing the recently introduced technique of diffusion tensor imaging is already being applied to the study of dyslexia. With this approach, it will be possible to map some aspects of cortical connectivity. And, although few studies applying this technique to the study of dyslexia have been undertaken, one has already identified microstructural differences of the white-matter tracts between normal controls and language/reading impaired adults (Klingberg, Hedehus, et al., 2000).

Together, the studies reviewed here cover a wide range in terms of the brain and behavior. Certainly, there are specific theories regarding the brain bases of dyslexia. However, the final story has yet to be told. When it is, numerous brain regions and mechanisms are likely to be involved and variations in clinical manifestations may be found to depend on various aspects of network interconnections that encode language and reading skills.

## REFERENCES

Caramazza, A. (1996). The brain's dictionary. *Nature* 380, 485–6.

Damasio, H., T. Grabowski, D. Tranel, R. D. Hichwa, & A. R. Damasio (1996). A neural basis for lexical retrieval. *Nature* 380, 499–505.

Galaburda, A. M., M. T. Menard, & G. D. Rosen (1994). Evidence for aberrant auditory anatomy in developmental dyslexia. *Proceedings of the National Academy of Sciences USA*, 9, 8010–13.

Gauger, L. M., L. J. Lombardin, *et al.* (1997). Brain morphology in children with specific language impairment. *Journal of Speech Language and Hearing Research* 40, 1272–84.

Habib, M. (2000). The neurological basis of developmental dyslexia: An overview and working hypothesis. *Brain* 123, 2373–99.

Heilman, K., K. Voeller & A. W. Alexander (1996). Developmental dyslexia: a motor-articulatory feedback hypothesis. *Annals of Neurology* 39, 407–12.

Hinshelwood, J. (1895). Word blindness and visual memories. *Lancet* 2, 1566–70.

Hutsler, J. J. & M. A. Gazzaniga (1997). The organization of human language cortex: Special adaptation of common cortical design? *The Neuroscientist* 3(1), 61–72.

Klingberg, T., M. Hedehus, *et al.* (2000). Microstructure of temporo-parietal white matter as a basis for reading ability: Evidence from diffusion tensor magnetic resonance imaging. *Neuron* 25, 495–500.

Kohler, E., Keysers, C., Umilta, M. A., Fogassi, L., Gallese, V. & Rizzolatti, G. (2002). Hearing sounds, understanding actions: Action representation in mirror neurons. *Science* 297, 846–8.

Korhonen, T. (1995). The persistence of rapid naming problems in children with reading disabilities: A nine-year follow-up. *Journal of Learning Disabilities* 28(4), 232–9.

Morgan, W. (1896). A case of congenital word blindness. *British Medicine* 1, 1378.

Neville, H., D. Bavelier, D. Corina, J. Rauschecker, A. Kasri, A. Lalwani, A. Braun, V. Clark, P. Jezzard, & R. Turner (1998). Cerebral organization for language in deaf and hearing subjects: Biological constraints and effects of experience. *Proceedings of the National Academy of Sciences* 95(3), 922–9.

Rizzolatti, G. & M. Arbib (1998). Language within our grasp. *Trends in Neuroscience* 21(5), 188–94.

Shaywitz, B. A., Shaywitz, S. E., Pugh, K. R., Skudlarksi, P., Fulbright, R. K., Constable, R. T., Fletcher, J. M., Liberman, A. M., Shankweiler, D. P., Katz, L., Bronen, R. A., Marhcione, K. E., Lacadie, C., & Gore, J. C. (1996). The functional organization of brain for reading and reading disability (dyslexia). *The Neuroscientist* 2(4), 245–55.

Shaywitz, B. A., Shaywitz, S. E., Pugh, K. R., Mencl, W. E., Fulbright, R. K., Skudlarksi, P., Constable, R. T., Marchione, K. E., Fletcher, J. M., Lyon, G. R. & Gore,

J. C. (2002). Disruption of posterior brain systems for reading in children with developmental dyslexia. *Biological Psychiatry*, 52(2), 101–10.

Stein, J. & V. Walsh (1997). To see but not to read; the magnocellular theory of dyslexia. *Trends in Neuroscience* 20(4), 147–52.

Tallal, P., S. Miller & R. Fitch (1993). Neurobiological basis of speech: a case of the preeminence of temporal processing. *Annals of the New York Academy of Sciences* 682, 27–47.

Woolsey, T. A. & H. Van der Loos (1970). The structural organization of layer IV in the somatosensory region (SI) of mouse cerebral cortex: The description of a cortical field composed of discrete cytoarchitectonic units. *Brain Research* 17(2).

# 8 The neural correlates of reading disorder: functional magnetic resonance imaging

*Juliana Paré-Blagoev*

*Overview:* Functional magnetic resonance imaging (fMRI) provides a powerful tool for analyzing brain correlates of reading problems, although conclusions must be qualified by methodological confounds that researchers need to examine. Theoretical analyses of diverse patterns of dyslexia suggest three different impairments in phonological, visual, or auditory skills. Recent research with fMRI indicates that distinct brain regions most likely show reduced activation for each of these problems. For children with phonological problems, reduction is in left temporo-parietal regions, which are involved in speech. For those with visual problems, reduction is in the magnocellular system, which is involved in vision. For those with temporal processing problems, reduction seems to include the frontal and left temporal areas. *The Editors*

Ever since Dejerine's work implicated the left angular gyrus as playing a special role in impairments of reading and writing, neuroscientists have recognized the importance of understanding the neural underpinnings of dyslexia (Dejerine, 1891). The invention in the 1990s of functional magnetic resonance imaging (fMRI), a non-invasive neuroimaging technique, allows unprecedented access to the human brain at work at spatial resolutions of millimeters and temporal resolutions of seconds. (Some analysis techniques push this resolution even lower.) Findings have mirrored differences found in morphological studies with prior techniques, and gone beyond them: on the order of a dozen different brain regions have been shown to have different blood flow patterns during reading-related tasks in dyslexics as compared to normal readers. Further refinement of specific differences between dyslexic and normal brain structure and function continues to be the subject of research.

However, this search can be hampered by a lack of theory to guide investigation. One challenge facing fMRI researchers is to use this tool to do more than localize functions to structures. Fortunately, researchers studying dyslexia have articulated several competing theories about the nature and interaction of the deficits underlying dyslexia. Three are especially relevant for this review of fMRI studies of dyslexia. The first focuses on the role of phonological disorders, the second on visual system abnormalities, and the third on deficits in temporal rate processing. Each theory carries implications for appropriate interventions, implications that increase the importance of determining when or if each might apply to dyslexics in general or different subgroups of dyslexics. One valuable role for fMRI is to help test and refine these theories: fMRI data can help analysis of complex interactions among key factors, including neuronal deficits, targeted interventions, neuronal reorganization subsequent to interventions, and always, the associated development of changing reading skills.

In this chapter, I briefly review important characteristics of the dyslexic population in terms of the three theories for explaining important deficits in dyslexia. The basics of fMRI as a technology and as a research method for studying dyslexia are introduced, including a discussion of important potential confounds relevant to dyslexia research. Building on this background, results from fMRI studies of dyslexia are analyzed in terms of the question: what underlies the heterogeneous set of characteristics that can all be a part of dyslexia?

## Characteristics of the dyslexic population in reference to three theoretical explanations

Children with developmental dyslexia show an unexpected reading failure or deficit that is not explained by low intelligence quotient or environmental factors (Wolf & Ashby, this volume). It is estimated that in the US anywhere from 4% (DSM-IV) to 17–20% of children are dyslexic or at risk for developing reading problems (Shaywitz, Shaywitz, Fletcher, & Escobar, 1990) and the disorder appears in all languages, not only English. A diagnosis of developmental dyslexia requires specific problems with reading and does not require associated deficits in related domains such as oral language acquisition, writing abilities, mathematical abilities, or motor coordination; but the co-occurrence of multiple deficits in a variety of combinations is not uncommon. Cognitive neuroscientists hypothesize that the differing patterns of skill deficits and cognitive strategies in different subgroups of dyslexics correspond with differing neural activation patterns (Benes & Paré-Blagoev; Galaburda & Sherman, this volume).

### Phonological skills

Phonological impairments are generally considered the most common mechanism leading to reading disorders, with numerous studies showing a causal link between sensitivity to phonological structures of words and progress in learning to read (Bradley & Bryant, 1983; Goswami, 2002; Hatcher, Hulme, & Ellis, 1994; Lundberg, Frost, & Petersen, 1988; Lundberg, Olofsson, & Wall, 1980). Frequently these impairments are manifested initially in problems in oral language and speech acquisition. However, many dyslexics do not initially show oral language impairments, and there are individuals with severe dysphasia in oral language who learn to read normally. This complex pattern follows the general rule that there are no absolutes in dyslexia. Instead, there is a tremendous heterogeneity of deficits in the dyslexic population.

Within this diverse range, the most common core deficit according to much research is the ability to manipulate the sound constituents of oral language in an abstract form – that is, phonological awareness. For example, well before they learn to read, children who will not become dyslexic demonstrate the ability to segment words into smaller units, whereas future dyslexic children are unable to perform this task not only before they read but even after several months of reading and writing (Bradley & Bryant, 1983; Liberman, 1973). These phonological deficits persist through childhood and even into adulthood (Bruck, 1992; Fink, this volume; Manis, Custodio, & Szeszulski, 1993; Masterson, Hazan, & Wijayatilake, 1995; Torgesen, this volume; Wagner, Torgesen, & Rashotte, 1994).

Another important indicator of the role of phonological awareness skills in reading development is the demonstration that improving the skills can lead to improvement in reading skills. Lundberg and colleagues, for example, demonstrated that children receiving training in phonological awareness tasks involving word segmentation showed improved reading abilities (Lundberg *et al.*, 1988). Importantly, however, the scope of deficit in phonological awareness for dyslexics varies greatly among children. Results from some studies seem to indicate two subgroups of dyslexics, phonological (or deep) dyslexics and non-phonological (or surface) dyslexics (Boder, 1973; Castles & Coltheart, 1993; Manis, Seidenberg, Doi, McBride-Chang & Peterson, 1996; Mitterer, 1982; Murphy & Pollatsek, 1994; Seymour & MacGregor, 1984; see Wolf & Ashby, this volume).

*Visual and auditory skills*

Theories of dyslexia focusing on phonological awareness cannot easily account for the sensory deficits that many dyslexics show in both visual and auditory processing. A long line of research suggests that dyslexics show subtle deficits in visual processing. Boder's (1973) classification of dyslexic types characterized the "dyseidetic" dyslexic as having a visual deficit as the origin of their disorder. Many dyslexic children, up to 75%, show ophthalmological problems represented by disturbances in binocular vision, ocular tracking, or motion perception. However, this evidence alone is difficult to interpret because each of those abilities can be influenced by experience in reading.

More compelling evidence combines visual psychophysics experiments with in-depth analysis of the human visual system, which together have produced the magnocellular deficit hypothesis in dyslexia: the hypothesis is that many dyslexics have a disturbance of the magnocellur (transient) component of the visual system, as evidenced by studies showing visual contrast sensitivity deficits (Cornelissen, Hansen, Hutton, Evangelinou & Stein, 1998; Eden, VanMeter, Rumsey, Maisog, Woods & Zeffiro, 1996; Eden, VanMeter, Rumsey, & Zeffiro, 1996; Galaburda & Sherman, this volume; Lovegrove, Bowling, Badcock, & Blackwood, 1980; Lovegrove, Heddle, & Slaghuis, 1980; Lovegrove, Martin, Bowling, Blackwood, Badcock & Paxton, 1982). This system mediates visual perception of global form, movement, and temporal resolution. There is also evidence from fMRI that dyslexics' visual processing shows deficit-related differences compared to normals, which will be reviewed below. At the same time, a larger number of studies show no contrast sensitivity deficit in dyslexics than show a deficit (Skottun, 2000). As argued by Eden and Zeffiro (1998) such conflicting results may reflect that some dyslexics do have visual behavioral deficits associated with abnormal processing of magnocellular/transient stimuli, but it is not clear that these deficits have any causal link with reading abnormalities.

Another body of evidence regarding sensory deficits contributing to dyslexia focuses on a temporal rate-processing deficit, primarily in the auditory domain, although some evidence suggests this deficit may also exist in the visual system and may be related to the proposed visual magnocellular deficit described above (Galaburda & Sherman, this volume; Tallal, Stark, & Mellits, 1985; Wolf & Ashby, this volume; Wolf & Katzir-Cohen, 2001). In 1973, Tallal and Piercy showed that children with a deficit related to but different from dyslexia, Language Learning Impairment (LLI), showed a deficit in processing auditory stimuli that change very rapidly (Tallal & Piercy, 1973). This deficit was most pronounced when the stimulus changes occurred in the range of tens of milliseconds, which is the characteristic range for the acoustics of speech. In follow-up studies to their 1973 work, Tallal and Piercy (1974, 1975) showed that children with LLI showed impaired performance relative to controls with normally presented syllables but could make the discriminations competently when the acoustics of syllables were artificially expanded.

Reflective of the attractiveness of brain-based explanations and interventions for dyslexia, a remediation program (Fast ForWord) developed by Tallal and colleagues and ostensibly based on their research results was made commercially available and has received considerable popular and scientific attention. Studies conducted by this group of investigators demonstrating the effectiveness of this temporally based remedial method (Merzenich, Jenkins, Johnston, Schreiner, Miller, & Tallal, 1996; Tallal et al., 1996) are promising and have been replicated in some instances (DeMartino, Espesser, Rey, & Habib, 2000; Habib, Espesser, Reg, Giraud, Bruas, & Gres, 1999) but not replicated in others (Hook, Macaruso, & Jones, 2001; McAnally, Hansen, Cornelissen, & Stein, 1997). A recent, different, promising technique also aimed at temporal processing issues is currently being evaluated to determine its effectiveness (Wolf & Ashby, this volume; Wolf & Katzir-Cohen, 2001; Wolf, Miller, & Donnelly, 2000).

In addition to the inconsistencies in studies of this temporal processing intervention, there is also unresolved controversy regarding the basic theory itself. Mody and colleagues have challenged the initial findings of Tallal and Piercy (1975) on the basis of an apparent confusion between the concepts of time duration and sequential processing (Mody, Studdert-Kennedy, & Brady, 1997). In a critique of this challenge, Denenberg argues that Mody and her colleagues inappropriately selected "poor readers" as subjects and that the statistical power reached in their study was insufficient to challenge existing evidence (Denenberg, 1999). Farmer and Klein (1995) reviewed temporal processing studies and concluded that many developmental dyslexics manifest temporal processing deficits and that further research is needed to elucidate the likely role that such a deficit may play in dyslexia.

It is reflective of the tremendous heterogeneity in the dyslexic population that there is so much controversy and so many apparently inconsistent results in neuropsychological, behavioral, and psychophysical studies of dyslexia. A similar combination of sometimes conflicting and sometimes corroborating results can be expected in neuroimaging studies of dyslexia.

## Basic experimental approaches and goals of fMRI research

Functional neuroimaging studies are based on the rationale that task performance inherently places specific information processing demands on the brain. These demands are reflected in changes in local blood flow produced by changes in neural activity (Casey, Davidson, & Rosen, 2002; Logothetis, Paulis, Augath, Trinath, & Oeltermann, 2001). With appropriate design, different tasks can elicit elemental cognitive and sensory operations in different and separable combinations. Depending on the paradigm, comparisons can be made between subjects on the same tasks as well as within subjects on differing tasks. These kinds of comparisons can be done using either a blocked analysis, in which conditions are blocked together and the responses to individual items are not recoverable, or an event-related analysis, in which fMRI signal changes associated with individual items can be measured and analyzed.

One common approach to experimental design uses subtraction of signals: the signals recorded during different conditions or items are subtracted from each other to determine which brain regions are more or less active during conditions of interest in relation to comparison conditions. For example, one study using block design and subtraction of signals focused on the role of the angular gyrus in developmental dyslexia (Pugh *et al.*, 2000). Another approach is to correlate task difficulty and performance to changes in activation patterns and strengths, as in a study that employs both subtraction and correlation approaches (Shaywitz *et al.*, 2002). An approach conceptually similar to the correlation measures used in fMRI has been used in morphological studies as well. For example, Larsen and colleagues demonstrated that a subgroup of dyslexics with impaired performance on a non-word reading task had symmetrical planum temporales in contrast to control children and dyslexics with impaired word recognition but not non-word, both of whom showed an asymmetry in that region (Larsen, Hoien, Lundeberg, & Odegaard, 1990).

Regardless of the experimental paradigm used, the basic goals of neuroimaging studies of fMRI of dyslexia are: (1) identifying brain regions active during tasks that elicit the subprocesses underlying reading; and (2) assessing whether these regions differ between dyslexic and normal readers (see Benes & Paré-Blagoev, this volume). In conjunction with these goals, interpretation of an appropriately designed fMRI study can also directly contribute to the testing and refinement of theories of the neuronal functioning associated with core deficits of dyslexia.

As a first step, fMRI studies can be used to localize relevant functions to neuronal structures. These studies can both test and extend the results found in morphological studies. Moving forward from the important but sometimes atheoretical studies using fMRI to localize functions, researchers can draw more explicitly and precisely from neuropsychological models of the deficits underlying dyslexia attempting to explore their validity and develop them further. Given the lack of agreement on the presence of morphological deviations in even the most widely studied regions such as the planum temporale (Shapleske, Rossell, Woodruss, & David, 1999), it is wise not to restrict investigations to only previously identified regions. The range of skill deficits already identified in dyslexics and the numerous behavioral tools developed to probe the deficits represent a ready and extensive pool for paradigm development. To be most immediately and directly relevant to the extensive research on dyslexia, fMRI researchers can dip into that pool rather than only developing new paradigms. Of course, the logistic demands of fMRI will usually require some modifications of existing paradigms, but the use of paradigms with a long history provides significant benefits in generalizability and leveraging of new results with old.

### Methodological confounds

There are numerous difficulties associated with the interpretation of imaging studies of developmental language disorders. The difficulties can be compounded in comparisons of results across multiple studies, particularly when trying to assess the relevance of adult results to children. Most of the difficulties are methodological, including differing criteria for subject selection and lack of consensus about definitional criteria for regions of interest, including how to measure them and whether to include gray vs. white matter (Leonard,

1996). Differences and similarities between adults and children in activation patterns associated with spatial working memory, response inhibition, and fluency point to the need for fMRI studies of children and the potential problems associated with using adult data to explore theoretical questions about developmental dyslexia. For example, Gaillard and colleagues looked at letter and word fluency tasks, comparing adults and children. Children showed significantly greater activation (more pixels) (Gaillard, Hertz-Pannier, Mott, Barnett, LeBihan & Theodore, 2000). Rubia and colleagues also found different patterns of activation between young adolescents and young adults during tasks of motor inhibition (Rubia *et al.*, 2000).

In addition to variations in the source and variation of imaging signals between adults and children, another frequently occurring problem is subject selection criteria in studies of dyslexia in adults. In his review of 13 studies of brain functional imaging (magnetoencephalogram, functional magnetic resonance imaging, position emission tomography, and Xenon inhalation) Habib (2000) found little systematic effort to retrospectively ascertain the type and intensity of the disorder in the adult subjects. In other words, the studies failed to deal with the heterogeneity of dyslexia and potentially combined cases with different pathophysiological mechanisms.

Another issue that is both a potential confound and an important area of study in its own right is the potential effect of training on both morphological and functional characteristics. For example, it has been shown that training in the auditory modality can modify the degree of asymmetry in the posterior auditory region (Schlaug, Jancke, Huang, & Steinmets, 1995). Studies of the role of the angular gyrus in reading and reading disorders suggest it plays a key role (Pugh *et al.*, 2000; Rumsey, Horwitz, Donohue, Nace, Maisog, & Andreason, 1999). In an fMRI study of the effect of rehabilitative measures for a stroke patient with acquired dyslexia, brain activation patterns shifted from the left angular gyrus prior to therapy to the left lingual gyrus after therapy (Small, Flores, & Noll, 1998). This shift in activation pattern was accompanied by a shift in reading strategy from a lexical, whole-word reading approach to a sub-lexical, decomposition strategy. In other cases, the pattern change may be attributable less to a strategy shift and more to improved competence or automaticity. These effects point to the importance of understanding and documenting the strategies and skill characteristics of fMRI subjects in relevant domains.

Related to these confounds is the issue of neural plasticity (Huttenlocher, 2002; Immordino-Yang & Deacon, this volume). In imaging findings with adults and even older children with dyslexia, who have extensive experience with reading, neuronal patterns may result from either developmental neuronal abnormalities giving rise to dyslexia or compensatory strategies developed over years of training. As methodological and technical challenges continue to be met, it is becoming more feasible to use fMRI with younger children (Poldrack,

Paré-Blagoev, & Grant, 2002). Imaging younger children, prior to their exposure to reading instruction, increases the likelihood of detecting activation abnormalities before compensatory processing effects become established.

### Patterns of brain activity

Building on the decades — in some senses centuries — of morphological studies relevant to dyslexia, fMRI studies have most often contributed to understanding the neuroanatomical locations of reading-related processes and the differences in these regions between dyslexics and normals. Evidence indicates that as many as a dozen regions show some differential activation (Grigorenko, 2001). These tend to be clustered so that they appear primarily, but not exclusively, in one of several areas: inferior frontal gyrus, superior temporal gyrus, posterior brain regions including the left angular gyrus and surrounding cortex, regions of visual cortex including the locations designated as MT/V5, corpus callosum, and the cerebellum.

Tables 8.1 to 8.3 describe fMRI studies of reading and reading disorders in terms of their relevance to the three theories of phonological, visual, and temporal processes in dyslexia. In reading these tables, it is important to keep several issues in mind. First, one consequence of the theoretical organization is that all activation sites found in any given study are not listed in the tables. Also, there are a number of factors across studies that complicate direct comparisons. For example, studies often used task paradigms that are related but different. Furthermore, different studies use different reporting conventions for brain regions. Studies vary widely also in the extent to which activation patterns are interpreted for their implications rather than simply reported. An important issue is that the ages of subjects vary across studies, which is particularly relevant for a developmental disorder of a learned process. Because there is no reliable model relating neuronal patterns associated with reading and learning to age and reading proficiency, collapsing results across different age groups can be problematic.

### *Phonological processing studies*

A consistent finding across multiple studies, striking in part because of many other inconsistent findings, is that during tasks requiring phonological processing, dyslexics show reduced activity compared to normals in left temporoparietal regions, as summarized in Table 8.1 (Pugh *et al.*, 2001; Pugh *et al.*, 2000; Shaywitz *et al.*, 2002; Shaywitz *et al.*, 1998; Temple *et al.*, 2001). This finding is stable across studies using different paradigms and analysis techniques and has been demonstrated in both children and adults. There are also some results suggesting that for dyslexics the homologous right hemisphere

Table 8.1. *fMRI studies of phonological processing in dyslexic and normal readers.*

| Task paradigm | Subjects | Results | Study |
|---|---|---|---|
| Subjects made same/different judgments for two items in five conditions designed to make progressively greater demands on phonologic assembly skills. Stimuli were presented visually. | 61 right-handed adult subjects 29 dyslexics, 14 men, 15 women, 16–54 years 32 non-impaired readers, 16 men, 16 women, ages 18–63 years. | As tasks become progressively more difficult, controls, not dyslexics increase activation across the posterior cortical system including Wernicke's area, the angular gyrus and extrastriate and striate cortex. As tasks become more difficult, dyslexic readers show a pattern of overactivation, compared to controls, in anterior regions, notably the inferior frontal gyrus including the pars operculum and pars triangularis. Results support claims of a phonological processing impairment in dyslexics. | (Shaywitz *et al.*, 1998) |
| Subjects made same/different judgments for two items in five conditions designed to make progressively greater demands on phonologic assembly skills. Stimuli were presented visually. | 144 right-handed children 70 dyslexics, 21 girls, 49 boys, 7–18 years 74 non-impaired readers, 31 girls, 43 boys, ages 7–17 years. | Compared to controls, older dyslexics, not younger dyslexics, showed overactivation of left and right inferior frontal gyrus during the most phonologically demanding task. Nonimpaired readers showed greater activation across multiple left hemisphere sites compared to dyslexics. This supports claims that dyslexic children manifest an organic dysfunction in left hemisphere posterior reading circuits not ascribable to experience as poor readers. | (Shaywitz *et al.*, 2002) |
| Subjects made same/different judgments for two items in five conditions designed to make progressively greater demands on phonologic assembly skills. Stimuli were presented visually. | 61 right-handed adult subjects 29 dyslexics, 14 men, 15 women, 16–54 years 32 non-impaired readers, 16 men, 16 women, ages 18–63 years. | Regression analyses were performed to assess differences in functional connectivity between angular gyrus and posterior site in left and right hemispheres. In phonologically demanding tasks, non-impaired readers, not dyslexics, had strong functional connectivity. Both groups showed left hemisphere connectivity for tasks placing low demand on phonological assembly skills. Dyslexics showed functional connectivity at right-hemisphere homologues for high-demand phonological assembly tasks. Results suggest intact functional connectivity between angular gyrus and posterior site in the left hemisphere is key for phonological assembly skills that are important for normal reading development. | (Pugh *et al.*, 2000) |

| Phonological and orthographic tasks: rhyming and matching visually presented letter pairs. | Compared to non-impaired readers, dyslexics showed reduced activation in the left-hemisphere temporo-parietal regions during the phonological task. On the same task, dyslexics showed greater inferior frontal gyrus activation than did controls, with the control children's activation somewhat more posterior relative to controls. Results suggest inferior frontal regions may be recruited in dyslexics as compensatory areas for left-hemisphere temporo-parietal regions which are not functioning normally during phonological tasks. | 24 dyslexic children, 19 boys, 5 girls, ages 8–12 years 15 non-impaired readers, 12 boys, 3 girls, ages 8–12 years. | (Temple et al., 2001) |
| Phonological rhyme judgment task on visually present pseudowords compared to a letter-case judgment. (Note: additional tasks assessing temporal processing issues are reported in Table 8.3.) | Compared to the baseline task, the phonological judgment task activated regions in the posterior section of the left inferior frontal gyrus including the pars triangularis and pars opercularis. Of these two, only the pars triangularis was activated also during presentation of acoustically modified speech, which is relevant for the temporal processing model of dyslexia. | No dyslexic subjects, normal readers only. 8 right-handed adults, 4 male, 4 female, ages 20–29. | (Poldrack et al., 2001) |

Note: Results reported here focus on regional activation patterns interpreted by the authors in terms of this neurobiological model of dyslexia. Invariably, additional brain regions not included in this table were also reported for each of the studies reviewed.

Table 8.2. *fMRI studies of visual pathways in dyslexic and normal readers.*

| Task paradigm | Results | Subjects | Study |
|---|---|---|---|
| Moving sine wave gratings were presented at a control speed of 20.8°/sec. Test condition speed varied, but was always greater than the control speed. Subjects were asked to indicate which stimuli appeared to move faster. Stimulus contrast and duration were randomized. | Compared to controls, dyslexics showed reduced brain activity in primary visual cortex and area MT and adjacent motion-sensitive areas (MT+), which are understood to be part of the magnocellular visual system. A greater V1 and MT+ response correlated with accurate task performance and faster reading times in behavioral assessments. Results support theory that there are visual motion processing differences in dyslexics and controls and that the degree of difference in activation patterns correlates with reading speed. | 5 dyslexic adults, 2 females, 3 males, average age 22.2 years. 5 non-impaired readers, adults, 2 females, 3 males, average age 26.8 years. | (Demb et al., 1998) |
| Subjects viewed patterns of dots that were either moving or stationary. | For all dyslexics, in contrast to the pattern seen in normal readers, moving stimuli failed to produce activation in area V5/MT, which is part of the magnocellular visual system. Stationary dot patterns were associated with equivalent patterns of activation in dyslexics and normal readers. Results support theory that there are visual motion processing differences in dyslexics, and they also control for visual tasks associated with the magnocellular system. | 6 dyslexics, adult males. 8 non-impaired readers, adult males. | (Eden, VanMeter, Rumsey, Maisog et al., 1996) |

*Note:* Results reported here focus on regional activation patterns interpreted by the authors in terms of this neurobiological model of dyslexia. Invariably, additional brain regions not included in this table were also reported for each of the studies reviewed.

Table 8.3. *fMRI studies of temporal processing in dyslexic and normal readers.*

| Task paradigm | Results | Subjects | Study |
|---|---|---|---|
| Comprehension of sentences presented aurally at four different levels of compression which maintained spectral features but manipulated rate of acoustic change. (Note: additional task assessing phonological processing is reported in Table 8.1.) | Left inferior frontal gyrus (specifically the pars triangularis region), superior temporal regions (specifically Broca's and Wernicke's areas), and right inferior frontal cortex showed increased activation as compression increased but speech was still comprehensible. As speech became incomprehensible, activation decreased. Linear increases in activation with increasing compression were seen bilaterally in the middle frontal gyri. Bilaterally, auditory cortex showed compression related decreases when stimuli became incomprehensible. Results demonstrate that the pars triangularis is involved in phonological processing and is sensitive to transient acoustic features of comprehensible speech as well. | No dyslexic subjects, normal readers only. 8 right-handed adults, 4 male, 4 female, ages 20–29. | (Poldrack *et al.*, 2001) |
| Subjects were presented with either high pitched or low pitched non-linguistic auditory stimuli and indicated when they heard the high-pitched ones. Stimuli were further modified so as to mimic spectro-temporal acoustic changes known to characterize consonant-vowel-consonant syllables; changes could be either rapid or slow non-speech analogues. 2 dyslexic subjects completed a training program intended to improve processing of speech stimuli, including those mimicked with presented stimuli. Pre and post scans were done. | For non-impaired readers, regions in the left prefrontal cortex along the middle and superior frontal gyri showed greater activation correlated with increased accuracy processing rapidly changing stimuli. Also, the same regions were sensitive to the rapidly changing stimuli compared to the slowly changing stimuli. In contrast in the dyslexics, this sensitivity was essentially absent. For the two subjects who completed a training program, activation patterns post-training became more similar to non-impaired readers in the left prefrontal cortex, and behavioral assessments of different reading related tasks indicated improvement. Results support a temporal rate processing model specifying that adults with dyslexia show disruption in neural processing associated with processing rapidly transient acoustic stimuli and suggesting that this disruption can be influenced by appropriate training. | 8 dyslexic adults, with mean age of 28, 7 male, 1 female. 10 non-impaired readers, with mean age of 32, 9 male, 1 female. | (Temple *et al.*, 2000) |

(cont.)

Table 8.3. (*cont.*)

| Task paradigm | Results | Subjects | Study |
|---|---|---|---|
| Subjects were presented with pairs of naturally spoken syllables which were either constant ("ma ma") or variable ("ma na"). Stimuli were presented at normal or slow speech rates. 42% of pairs had a second syllable presented at a lower pitch and subjects were asked to indicate when they heard the lower pitch. | For non-impaired readers, during normal rate speech but not slowed speech, a network including Broca's area and the left supramarginal gyrus showed activation. For the same comparison, dyslexics showed no activation. Dyslexics showed greater activation in Broca's area during the slowed speech compared to controls. Results support the hypothesis of a perceptual deficit for rapid stimuli in dyslexia and suggest that the neural basis for improvement in performance from training could involve enhanced activity in Broca's area, as seen for the dyslexics during processing of slowed speech. | 6 dyslexic adults, average age 30.<br><br>11 non-impaired readers, average age 28, French speaking. | (Ruff *et al.*, 2002) |

*Note*: Results reported here focus on regional activation patterns interpreted by the authors in terms of this neurobiological model of dyslexia. Invariably, additional brain regions not included in this table were also reported for each of the studies reviewed.

temporo-parietal region acts as a compensatory area for phonological assembly tasks (Pugh *et al.*, 2000).

Some study results suggest that dyslexics show a greater extent and/or degree of activation in the left inferior frontal gyrus compared to controls during phonologic tasks (Brunswick, McCrory, Price, Frith, & Frith, 1999; Helenius, A, Cornelissen, Hansen, & Salmelin, 1999; Shaywitz *et al.*, 2002; Shaywitz *et al.*, 1998; Temple *et al.*, 2001). Others fail to replicate this finding (Georgiewa, 1999, Corina *et al.*, 2001; Grossglenn *et al.*, 1991; Paulesu *et al.*, 1996; Rumsey, Nace, Donohue, Wise, Maisog, & Andreason, 1997).

### Visual processing deficit

There are relatively few fMRI studies of the visual processing deficit, but those few do represent positive evidence for a visual processing impairment in dyslexic populations. One study using simple stimuli of either moving or stationary dots demonstrated that for dyslexics there are visual processing abnormalities associated with the moving stimuli but not other stimuli. Dyslexics in comparison to normals showed a lack of functional activation during the moving dot condition in parts of the magnocellular visual subsystem (Eden, VanMeter, Rumsey, Maisog, *et al.*, 1996). Demb and colleagues (Demb, Boynton & Heeger, 1998) also found magnocellular deficits in dyslexics' processing of visual stimuli using fMRI. They further reported a three-way correlation between brain activity, speed discrimination thresholds for the visual task, and speed of reading. There was a positive correlation between reading speed, better performance on the visual task, and increased activation in regions that are part of the magnocellular pathway (areas named V1 and MT+). Although, as reviewed above, the psychophysical evidence for a visual processing deficit in dyslexia is rife with conflicting findings, these two studies suggest an organic basis for the positive findings.

Taken together, the behavioral and neuroimaging findings suggest that future neuroimaging studies might usefully focus on comparing dyslexic groups with and without manifestations of impairments in visual processing behavior. A combination of fMRI and magnetoencephalography (MEG) on the same subject group would be fruitful, with MEG bringing much greater temporal resolution than fMRI, on the order of milliseconds. The MEG literature on dyslexia provides evidence for subtle visual processing differences, reflected in longer latencies for dyslexics compared to control subjects during processing of apparent-motion stimuli (Simos *et al.*, 2000).

### Temporal rate processing deficit

As for the visual motion processing theory, there is only a small fMRI literature relevant to the temporal rate processing theory for dyslexia. Results suggest a neural basis for the temporal rate processing deficits in dyslexia found in behavioral studies. In a study of normal readers, Poldrack and colleagues (Poldrack *et al.*, 2001) demonstrated that the inferior frontal cortex, specifically the pars triangularis, is both active during phonological assembly tasks and sensitive to transient acoustic features of speech. Studies would be useful that, like this one, use acoustically manipulated stimuli matching those in behavioral studies of temporal rate processing deficits. Such methods would make it possible to tease out the neural relation between a possible temporal processing deficit and impaired phoneme discrimination.

Temple and colleagues (Temple, 2002) and Ruff and colleagues (Ruff, Cardebat, Marie, & Demonet, 2002) both found positive fMRI evidence for temporal rate processing differences between dyslexics and non-impaired readers. The Temple study suggests that adults with dyslexia show a disruption in neural processing of rapidly transient acoustic stimuli in middle and superior frontal gyri. Their findings also suggest that this disruption can be influenced by appropriate training. The Ruff study found enhanced activity in Broca's area for dyslexics during the processing of slowed speech. This suggests that training programs based on manipulating the temporal dynamics of stimuli and gradually increasing the speed of presentation as performance improves (Tallal *et al.*, 1996; Wolf *et al.*, 2000) could work through neural plasticity in Broca's area. As with research on visual processing deficits, joint utilization of MEG and fMRI for the study of temporal rate processing could be most promising (Nagarajan, Mahncke, Salz, Tallal, Roberts, & Merzenich, 1999).

## Conclusion: neural bases of types of reading impairment

fMRI is a relatively new tool in neuroscience and there are high hopes that it can be brought fruitfully to bear on the long-standing problem of understanding reading disorders. To date, there has been no neural map of dyslexia or more broadly of the many processes associated with reading and learning to read. Most relevant fMRI studies to date have contributed to knowledge of the structure/function correlates in reading processes. Along the way, they have confirmed that there is likely a neural basis to each of the three processes specified by the theories of reading impairment reviewed here. Beyond contributing to understanding which brain regions underlie which functions and which show differences between dyslexics and normals, fMRI and other neuroimaging techniques represent a valuable tool to investigate and refine existing theories of dyslexia and increase the precision of models of the main types of deficits. Before fMRI can fully live up to expectations, however, progress must be made to overcome some of the methodological confounds described above. Some of these are primarily in the hands of the neuroimaging community — for example, moving toward more consistent criteria for identifying and reporting neural regions. Similarly, both behavioral and neuroimaging studies of dyslexia would be well served by adoption of more consistent criteria for identifying and categorizing dyslexics according to their performance on standardized tests. Fundamentally, developmental dyslexia is a disorder in which behavioral characteristics change over time, presumably in response to both maturation and experience. fMRI, ideally in combination with other neuroscience techniques, can add to the analysis and understanding of development and remediation of the complicated phenomena of dyslexia.

## REFERENCES

Boder, E. (1973). Developmental dyslexia: A diagnostic approach based on three atypical reading-spelling patterns. *Developmental Medicine and Child Neurology*, 15, 663–87.

Bradley, L. & Bryant, P. (1983). Categorizing sounds and learning to read – a causal connection. *Nature*, 301, 419–21.

Bruck, M. (1992). Persistence of dyslexics' phonological awareness deficits. *Developmental Psychology*, 28, 874–86.

Brunswick, N., McCrory, E., Price, C., Frith, C. & Frith, U. (1999). Explicit and implicit processing of words and pseudowords by adult developmental dyslexics – A search for Wernicke's Wortschatz? *Brain*, 122(10), 1901–917.

Casey, B., Davidson, M. & Rosen, B. (2002). Functional magnetic resonance imaging: Basic principles of and application to developmental science. *Developmental Science*, 5(3), 301–9.

Castles, A. & Coltheart, M. (1993). Varieties of developmental dyslexia. *Cognition*, 47, 149–80.

Cornelissen, P. L., Hansen, P. C., Hutton, J. L., Evangelinou, V. & Stein, J. (1998). Magnocellular visual function and children's single word reading. *Vision Research*, 38, 471–82.

Cornia, D., Richards, T., Serafini, S., Richards, A., Steury, K., Abbott, R., Echelard, D. R., Marvaliaa, K. R., & Berninger, V. W. (2001). fMRI auditory language differences between dyslexic and able reading children. *Neuroreport*, 12(6), 1195–201.

Dejerine, J. (1891). Sur un cas de cécité verbale avec agraphie, suivi d'autopsie. *Mémoires Société Biologique*, 3, 197–201.

DeMartino, S., Espesser, R., Rey, V. & Habib, M. (2000). The 'temporal processing deficit' hypothesis of dyslexia: new experimental evidence. *Brain and Cognition*, 46(1–2), 104–108.

Demb, J., Boynton, G. & Heeger, D. (1998). Functional magnetic resonance imaging of early visual pathways in dyslexia. *Journal of Neuroscience*, 18(17), 6939–51.

Denenberg, V. (1999). A critique of Mody, Studdert-Kennedy and Brady's 'Speech perception deficits in poor readers: auditory processing or phonological coding?' *Journal of Learning Disabilities*, 32, 379–83.

Eden, G. F., VanMeter, J. W., Rumsey, J. M., Maisog, J. M., Woods, R. & Zeffiro, T. A. (1996). Abnormal processing of visual motion in dyslexia revealed by functional brain imaging. *Nature*, 382, 66–9.

Eden, G. F., VanMeter, J. W., Rumsey, J. M. & Zeffiro, T. A. (1996). The visual deficit theory of developmental dyslexia. [Review]. *Neuroimage*, 4, S108–17.

Eden, G. F. & Zeffiro, T. (1998). Neural systems affected in developmental dyslexia revealed by functional neuroimaging. *Neuron*, 21, 279–82.

Farmer, M. & Klein, R. (1995). The evidence for a temporal processing deficit linked to dyslexia: A review. *Psychonomic Bulletin & Review*, 2(4), 460–93.

Gaillard, W., Hertz-Pannier, L., Mott, S., Barnett, A., LeBihan, D. & Theodore, W. (2000). Functional anatomy of cognitive development. fMRI of verbal fluency in children and adults. *Neurology*, 54(1), 180–86.

Georgiewa, P., Rzanny, R., Hopf, J., Knab, R., Glauche, V., Kaiser, W. & Blanz, B. (1999). fMRI during word processing in dyslexic and normal reading children. *Neuroreport*, 10, 3459–65.

Goswami, U. (2002). Phonology, reading development and dyslexia: A cross-linguistic perspective. *Annals of Dyslexia*, 52, 1–23.

Grigorenko, E. (2001). Developmental dyslexia: An update on genes, brain, and environments. *Journal of Child Psychology and Psychiatry*, 42(1), 91–125.

Grossglenn, K., Duara, R., Barker, W., Loewenstein, D., Chang, J., YoshiI, F., Apicella, A., Pascal, S., Boothe, T., Sevush, S., Jallad, B., Novoa, L. & Lubs, H. (1991). Positron emission tomographic studies during serial word-reading by normal and dyslexics adults. *Journal of Clinical and Experimental Neuropsychology*, 13(4), 531–44.

Habib, M. (2000). The neurological basis of developmental dyslexia: An overview and working hypothesis. *Brain*, 123, 2373–99.

Habib, M., Espesser, R., Rey, V., Giraud, K., Bruas, P. & Gres, C. (1999). Training dyslexics with acoustically modified speech: Evidence of improved phonological performance. *Brain and Cognition*, 40(1), 143–6.

Hatcher, P., Hulme, C. & Ellis, A. (1994). Ameliorating early reading failure by integrating the teaching of reading and phonological skills: The phonological linkage hypothesis. *Child Development*, 65, 41–57.

Helenius, P., A, T., Cornelissen, P. L., Hansen, P. C. & Salmelin, R. (1999). Dissociation of normal feature analysis and deficient processing of letter-strings in dyslexic adults. *Cerebral Cortex*, 9, 476–83.

Hook, P., Macaruso, P. & Jones, S. (2001). Efficacy of Fast ForWord training on facilitation acquisition of reading skills by children with reading difficulties – A longitudinal study. *Annals of Dyslexia*, 51, 75–96.

Huttenlocher, P. R. (2002). *Neural plasticity: The effects of environment on the development of the cerebral cortex*. Cambridge, MA: Harvard University Press.

Larsen, F., Hoien, T., Lundeberg, I. & Odegaard, H. (1990). MRI evaluation of the size and symmetry of the planum temporale in adolescents with developmental dyslexia. *Brain and Language*, 39, 289–301.

Leonard, C. (1996). Structural variation in the developing and mature cerebral cortex: Noise or signal? In R. Thatcher, G. Lyon, J. Rumsey & N. Krasnegor (eds), *Developmental Neuroimaging*, 207–31. Orlando: Academic Press.

Liberman, I. (1973). Segmentation of the spoken word and reading acquisition. *Bulletin of the Orton Society*, 23, 65–77.

Logothetis, N., Paulis, J., Augath, M., Trinath, T. & Oeltermann, A. (2001). Neurophysiological investigation of the basis of the fMRI signal. *Nature*, 412, 150–57.

Lovegrove, W., Bowling, A., Badcock, D. & Blackwood, M. (1980). Specific reading disability: differences in contrast sensitivity as a function of spatial frequency. *Science*, 210, 439–40.

Lovegrove, W., Heddle, M. & Slaghuis, W. (1980). Reading disability: spatial frequency specific deficits in visual information store. *Neuropsychologia*, 18, 111–15.

Lovegrove, W., Martin, F., Bowling, A., Blackwood, M., Badcock, D. & Paxton, S. (1982). Contrast sensitivity functions and specific reading disability. *Neuropsychologia*, 20, 309–15.

Lundberg, I., Frost, J. & Petersen, O. (1988). Effects of an extensive program for stimulating phonological awareness in preschool children. *Journal of Experimental Child Psychology*, 18, 201–12.

Lundberg, I., Olofsson, A. & Wall, S. (1980). Reading and spelling skills in the first school years predicted from phonemic awareness skills in kindergarten. *Scandinavian Journal of Psychology*, 21, 159–73.

Manis, F., Custodio, R. & Szeszulski, P. (1993). Development of phonological and orthographic skill: A 2-year longitudinal study of dyslexic children. *Journal of Experimental Child Psychology*, 56, 64–86.

Manis, F., Seidenberg, M., Doi, L., McBride-Chang, C. & Peterson, A. (1996). On the bases of two subtypes of developmental dyslexia. *Cognition*, 58, 157–95.

Masterson, J., Hazan, V. & Wijayatilake, L. (1995). Phonemic processing problems in developmental phonological dyslexia. *Cognitive Neuropsychology*, 12, 233–59.

McAnally, D., Hansen, P., Cornelissen, P. & Stein, F. (1997). Effect of time and frequency manipulation on syllable perception in developmental dyslexics. *Journal of Speech, Language and Hearing Research*, 40, 912–24.

Merzenich, M., Jenkins, W., Johnston, P., Schreiner, C., Miller, S. & Tallal, P. (1996). Temporal processing deficits of language-learning impaired children ameliorated by training. *Science*, 271, 77–81.

Mitterer, J. (1982). There are at least two kinds of poor readers: Whole word poor readers and recoding poor readers. *Canadian Journal of Psychology*, 36, 445–61.

Mody, M., Studdert-Kennedy, M. & Brady, S. (1997). Speech perception deficits in poor readers: Auditory processing or phonological coding. *Journal of Experimental Child Psychology*, 64, 199–231.

Murphy, L. & Pollatsek, A. (1994). Developmental dyslexia: Heterogeneity without discrete subgroups. *Annals of Dyslexia*, 44, 120–46.

Nagarajan, S., Mahncke, H., Salz, T., Tallal, P., Roberts, T. & Merzenich, M. (1999). Cortical auditory signal processing in poor readers. *Proceedings of National Academy of Science, USA*, 96, 6483–88.

Paulesu, E., Frith, U., Snowling, M., Gallagher, A., Morton, J., Frackowiak, R. & Frith, C. (1996). Is developmental dyslexia a disconnection syndrome? Evidence from PET scanninng. *Brain*, 119, 143–57.

Poldrack, R., Paré-Blagoev, E. & Grant, P. (2002). Pediatric fMRI: Progress and challenges. *Topics in Magnetic Resonance Imaging*, 13, 61–70.

Poldrack, R., Temple, E., Protopapas, A., Nagarajan, S., Tallal, P., Merzenich, M. & Gabrieli, J. (2001). Relations between the neural bases of dynamic auditory processing and phonological processing: Evidence from fMRI. *Journal of Cognitive Neuroscience*, 13(5), 687–97.

Pugh, K., Mencl, W., Jenner, A., Katz, L., Frost, S., Lee, J., Shaywitz, S. & Shaywitz, B. (2001). Neurobiological studies of reading and reading disability. *Journal of Communication Disorders*, 34, 479–92.

Pugh, K., Mencl, W., Shaywitz, B., Shaywitz, S., Fulbright, R., Constable, R., Skudlarski, P., Marchione, K., Jenner, A., Fletcher, J., Liberman, A., Shankweiler, D., Katz,

L., Lacadie, C. & Gore, J. (2000). The angular gyrus in developmental dyslexia: Task-specific differences in functional connectivity within posterior cortex. *Psychological Science,* 11(1), 51–6.

Rubia, K., Overmeyer, S., Taylor, E., Brammer, M., Williams, S., Simmons, A., Andrew, C. & Bullmore, E. (2000). Functional frontalisation with age: Mapping neurodevelopmental trajectories with fMRI. *Neuroscience and Biobehavioral Reviews,* 24(1), 9–13.

Ruff, S., Cardebat, D., Marie, N. & Demonet, J. (2002). Enhanced response of the left frontal cortex to slowed down speech in dyslexia: an fMRI study. *Neuroreport,* 13(10), 1285–9.

Rumsey, J., Horwitz, B., Donohue, B., Nace, K., Maisog, J. & Andreason, P. (1999). A functional lesion in developmental dyslexia: Left angular gyral blood flow predicts severity. *Brain and Language,* 70, 187–204.

Rumsey, J. M., Nace, K., Donohue, B., Wise, D., Maisog, J. M. & Andreason, P. (1997). A positron emission tomographic study of impaired word recognition and phonological processing in dyslexic men. *Archives of Neurology,* 54(5), 562–73.

Schlaug, G., Jancke, L., Huang, Y. & Steinmets, H. (1995). In vivo evidence of structural brain asymmetry in musicians. *Science,* 267, 699–701.

Seymour, P. & MacGregor, C. (1984). Developmental dyslexia: A cogntivie experimental analysis of phonological, morphemic, and visual impairments. *Cognitive Neuropsychology,* 1, 43–83.

Shapleske, J., Rossell, S., Woodruss, P. & David, A. (1999). The planum temporale: a systematic, quantitative review of its structural, functional and clinical significance. *Brain Research Reviews,* 29, 26–49.

Shaywitz, B., Shaywitz, S., Pugh, K., Mencl, W., Fulbright, R., Skudlarski, P., Constable, R., Marchione, K., Fletcher, J., Lyon, G. & Gore, J. (2002). Disruption of posterior brain systems for reading in children with developmental dyslexia. *Biological Psychiatry,* 52(2), 101–10.

Shaywitz, S., Shaywitz, B., Fletcher, J. & Escobar, M. (1990). Prevalence of reading disability in boys and girls. *Journal of American Medical Association,* 264, 998–1002.

Shaywitz, S., Shaywitz, B., Pugh, K., Fulbright, R., Constable, R., Mencl, W., Shankweiler, D., Liberman, A., Skudlarski, P., Fletcher, J., Katz, L., Marchione, K., Lacadie, C., Gatenby, C. & Gore, J. (1998). Functional disruption in the organization of the brain for reading in dyslexia. *Proceedings of National Academy of Science, USA,* 95, 2636–41.

Simos, P., Breier, J., Fletcher, J., Foorman, B., Bergman, E., Fishbeck, K. & Papanicolaou, A. (2000). Brain activation profiles in dyslexic children during non-work reading: a magnetic source imaging study. *Neuroscience Letters,* 290, 61–5.

Skottun, B. (2000). The magnocellular deficit theory of dyslexia: The evidence from contrast sensitivity. *Vision Research,* 40, 111–27.

Small, S., Flores, D. & Noll, D. (1998). Different neural circuits subserve reading before and after therapy for acquired dyslexia. *Brain and Language,* 62, 298–308.

Tallal, P., Miller, S., Bedi, G., Byma, G., Wang, X., Nagarajan, S., Schreiner, C., Jenkins, W. & Merzenich, M. (1996). Language comprehension in language-learning impaired children improved with acoustically modified speech. *Science,* 271(5), 81–4.

Tallal, P. & Piercy, M. (1973). Defects of non-verbal auditory perception in children with developmental aphasia. *Nature,* 241, 468–9.

Tallal, P. & Piercy, M. (1974). Developmental aphasia: Rate of auditory processing and selective impairment of consonant perception. *Neuropsychologia*, 12, 83–93.

Tallal, P. & Piercy, M. (1975). Developmental aphasia: The perception of brief vowels and extended stop consonants. *Neuropsychologia*, 13, 69–74.

Tallal, P., Stark, R. & Mellits, E. (1985). Identification of language-impaired children on the basis of rapid perception and production skills. *Brain and Language*, 25, 314–22.

Temple, E. (2002). The developmental cognitive neuroscience approach to the study of developmental disorders. *Behavioral and Brain Sciences*, 25(6), 771.

Temple, E., Poldrack, R. A., Protopapas, A., Nagarajan, S., Salz, T., Tallal, P., Merzenich, M. M. & Gabrieli, J. D. (2000). Disruption of the neural response to rapid acoustic stimuli in dyslexia: Evidence from functional MRI. *Proceedings of the National Academy of Sciences* 97(25), 13907–912.

Temple, E., Poldrack, R. A., Salidis, J., Deutsch, G. K., Tallal, P., Merzenich, M. M. & Gabrieli, J. D. (2001). Disrupted neural responses to phonological and orthographic processing in dyslexic children: An fMRI study. *Neuroreport*, 12(2), 299–307.

Wagner, R., Torgesen, J. & Rashotte, C. (1994). Development of reading-related phonological processing abilities: New evidence of bi-directional causality from a latent variable longitudinal study. *Developmental Psychology*, 30, 73–87.

Wolf, M. & Katzir-Cohen, T. (2001). Reading fluency and its intervention. *Scientific Studies of Reading*, 5, 211–39.

Wolf, M., Miller, L. & Donnelly, K. (2000). Retrieval, automaticity vocabulary, elaboration-orthography (RAVE-O): A comprehensive, fluency-based reading intervention program. *Journal of Learning Disabilities*, 33, 322–4.

# 9     Patterns of cortical connection in children with learning problems

*Frank H. Duffy*

*Overview:* Behavior is based on brain functioning, and measures of brain activity such as the electroencephalogram (EEG) provide powerful tools for analyzing the relation between brain and behavior, including learning and development. In a study of brain activity in children with learning disorders, which included two of the boys who are a focus of this book (Andrew and Brian), EEG coherence was used to measure connectivity among cortical regions. Learning problems were associated with reduced connectivity of the left mid-temporal region with a cluster of central, frontal, and parietal locations: weaker connections seemed to relate to learning problems. Limited connectivity among brain regions also appears to characterize many victims of child abuse, as discussed in an essay for this chapter by Martin Teicher. At the same time, caution is required because of methodological issues about interpretation of brain activity measures, which are still in their infancy.

*The Editors*

The neurological perspective on behavior is based on the assumption that all behavior derives from the brain, a position based on lesion studies and aphasia. Having had the privilege of working with people such as Derek Denny-Brown, Ray Adams, and Norman Geschwind, all of whom contributed enormously to the understanding of brain–behavior relationships based on studies of brain lesions, I find this position difficult to resist. Indeed, it is amazing what complex patterns of behavior can be produced by very simple lesions that simply unhook key portions of a neural network that is otherwise functional.

This approach guides the work of the Learning Disabilities Research Center (LDRC) at Boston Children's Hospital. We assume that knowledge of the physiology of the brain is a necessary, though not sufficient, prerequisite for understanding a child. Our focus is on the spectrum of children who are referred for learning problems, not just reading-disabled children, although reading disability is well represented in the population that we work with.

## Relating brain systems to behavior and learning disorder

The behavioral tasks used with the four boys in this book have been selected to examine what are hypothesized to be fundamental elements of behavior. The goal is to explore the degree to which performance on lower-level tasks predicts higher-level dysfunction. This philosophical stance carries through into neurophysiology as well, translating in our current work into a paradigm of stressing the functioning of both the parvocellular and the magnocellular visual processing systems (Galaburda & Sherman, this volume; Livingstone, Rosen, Drislane, & Galaburda, 1991; Paré-Blagoev, this volume; Wolf & Ashby, this volume). To do this, we are looking at speed of neural processing with evoked cortical potentials, evaluating how the brain handles single, double, and triple stimuli, and at the coherence between electrical activity in cortical areas, which presumably reflects transmission of information between areas.

### Methodological challenge of research on cortical activity

The biggest current challenge in this work is methodological (Duffy, 1994; Duffy, McAnulty, & Albert, 1996; Duffy, Valencia, McAnulty, & Waber, 2001; Paré-Blagoev, this volume). A large part of the problem stems from the enormous amount of data created by assessments of brain activity and the need to choose an appropriate focus. The problem is especially severe for assessments like coherence of the electroencephalogram (EEG), which involves comparisons among electrodes.

The basic concept of *coherence* is as follows: if two different regions have the same spectral content – the same patterns of brain waves – as time passes, then they must be connected. For example, if my colleague Peter Wolff and I would both sing "Mary had a little lamb" together, we would most likely have similar spectral content and very high coherence: we are singing the same song and we are singing together. If a partition is put between us so that our ability to sing together is reduced or even eliminated, our coherence would drop – maybe even to zero – although the spectral content (the song elements) would remain more or less the same. We think of coherence as assessing connectivity – in the example, being able to see and hear each other singing – but note that coherence will go down if Peter does not want to sing or cannot sing or chooses not to respond, even though I see him and can hear him and am connected to him. Similarly, I could be listening to Vivaldi through headphones or have other things to do, and I could pay only partial attention to what he is singing: then coherence will go down. When we are singing together, however, coherence assesses our connection or coordination.

Effective research with coherence requires dealing with an enormous quantity of data, which means that even more than with other methods, researchers must make good a priori choices of what to measure. EEG is commonly measured with 24 electrodes, any 2 of which might be singing together. With 24 electrodes paired against each other over 64 frequencies, the result is 17,664 variables per study per subject and per state. An a priori reduction of spectral bands reduces the number to 4,416 variables, which is still a daunting number for analysis and interpretation.

## Cortical correlates of learning problems

We used data reduction techniques to deal with the large quantity of data – principal components and factor analysis. Using the singular value decomposition algorithm, which works in a stable manner, we were able to factor an asymmetrical matrix, that is, one with many more variables than cases. We examined the top 20 factors and their input data for the population of children referred for learning problems and the comparison group of children without learning problems. With about 4,000 variables, 40 to 50 percent of the variance was accounted for in the first 20 factors, a good condensation (Duffy, McAnulty, & Waber, 1999; Duffy *et al.*, 2001; Waber *et al.*, 2000). The factors are not typically simple or obvious, such as left versus right hemisphere, front to back, or local to long distance. They tend to involve complex patterns such as connections between the mid-temporal region and the central area of the cortex.

When we compared a learning-impaired group to a non-learning-impaired group, one factor stood out – factor 16. This factor was dramatically different between the two groups, as shown in Figure 9.1, and was highly correlated with their tapping scores and their reading scores, although it did not by any means explain all the variance. The factor represents coherence in the slow beta, fast alpha, 10 to 14 Hz range, between the left mid-temporal region to the large central area, including portions of the motor and motor association cortices and the mid-medial frontal and anterior parietal areas, as shown in Figure 9.2.

The EEG data included the standard resting-eyes open state and the memory portion of the tapping tasks. The latter, which were similar to the tapping tasks used for the four boys in this book, assessed a child's ability to maintain the rhythm provided by a metronome once the metronome had been switched off. The EEG of the learning-impaired group seemed more different at rest than during the task, although the differences were subtle.

How do we interpret this pattern? We suspect that the learning-impaired children showed reduced connectivity between the left mid-temporal region and these areas. This pattern implicates the motor system, including the ability to access the working memory of the original rhythm that the child is trying to tap to. A reduction in connectivity could reasonably be a factor in reducing the ability to tap appropriately. Most likely, the thalamus is involved in facilitating or

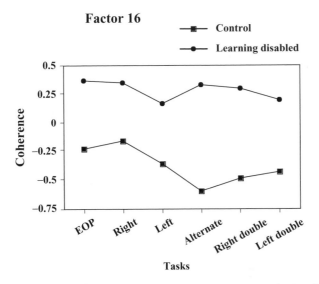

Figure 9.1 Coherence values for factor 16 in diverse tasks for learning disabled and control children.
*Key:* EOP eyes open. Other tasks involve various finger-tapping conditions.

regulating this coupling of cortical regions, and the increase in synchronization (coherence) begins before the start of the action.

### *Two boys*

Two of the children discussed in this book, Andrew and Brian, were members of the group referred for learning problems to the Learning Disabilities Research Center. In relation to the group findings for factor 16, Andrew's protocol showed a reduction of coherence. From the perspective of a practicing pediatric neurologist, Andrew struck me as one of the more impaired children, with real neurological issues and sensorimotor difficulties. Watching him made me want to have him run and do stressed gait maneuvers. I itched to grab a reflex hammer and look for motor overflow. Hearing him talk initially, I thought that he was both dysarthric and dysphasic, but then I was surprised at how much better he did at reading single words in sequence than he did in spontaneous speech. He is the sort of child who might have an underlying neurological issue, leading to questions about his early birth history and his medical background. He also showed some long pauses, suggesting that abnormal brain electrical activity may be contributing to his behavior. My impression was that problems in motor performance or initiation of action were more likely than actual seizures. Review of the EEGs obtained as part of the research studies

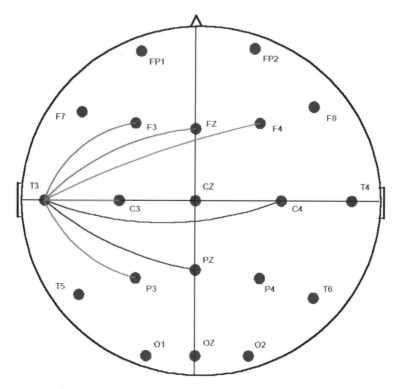

Figure 9.2 Pattern of cortical connection based on coherence (factor 16) associated with learning disorders.
*Key:* FP prefrontal, F frontal, C central, T temporal, P parietal, O occipital, Z midline.

indicates that Andrew did not have seizure discharges. However, his EEG pattern did implicate the parasaggital regions, the vascular watershed zone, which is often affected by mild hypoxic ischemic injury. There is thus some evidence for neurological problems.

What about the reduced coherence in factor 16 of his EEG? Importantly, the reduction occurred not only during tapping but also in the resting, eyes-open state. Brian gave some evidence of this reduction as well. Brian looks to me like a serial producer and thinker, very constrained. Whereas William, for example, moves around, Brian always grasps his hands or closes his arms, apparently as a strategy to handle anxiety. As a clinician, I would ask about emotional problems in the family, any depression. Beyond the specifics of Andrew and Brian, it appears that reduction in connectivity may be an integral part of these children's neurophysiological make-up.

Why should children who have reading problems have tapping (or other) problems? One can hypothesize that this reduction in coherence from the left temporal lobe is indicative of a more global problem affecting other functions dependent on the integrity of left hemisphere mechanisms. Perhaps an hypothesized underlying problem such as a reduction in connectivity can explain some part of the difficulty associated with the motor system and also some of the difficulty in transferring language information, both in and out.

**Interpreting coherence**

As this study illustrates, analysis of spectral coherence is important and promising because of its potential for analyzing neural connections and networks to illuminate learning and development (see also Als *et al.*, 2004; Fischer, Rose, & Rose, this volume; Thatcher, this volume). However, conclusions based on coherence need to be drawn with care because of the limitations of the measure. Coherence requires synchrony in the time domain and is measured by the relation between electrical activity in two different parts of the brain, as indexed by the activity under two electrodes in the EEG.

The first consideration is the meaning of higher or lower coherence. The assumption is often that if coherence is high, that is a good thing, indicating connection between two brain regions, while low coherence is a bad thing, indicating disconnection. Note, however, that for optimal neurobehavioral functioning, it is not desirable to have all the regions of the brain talking to each other all of the time. In sleep, for example, mid brain and the brain stem are driving cortical activity, which produces higher coherence as a person becomes drowsy. Falling asleep thus produces higher coherence, but it is clearly not a sign of functioning at a higher cognitive level. It would seem that a sign of maturity would be for a child to manage coherence during an activity so that when he or she acts in some way, the regions activated to support the behavior move into higher coherence, with coherence possibly becoming lower in other regions.

A second major issue with coherence is how to interpret it developmentally. The physical changes with growth of the head and skull have poorly understood implications for measurement of coherence. For example, detection of an epileptic spike from the scalp of an adult requires that about 6 square centimeters of brain be active. In a newborn, in contrast, such a spike can be detected from only 1 to 1.5 square centimeters. The newborn skull is thinner and thus less of a "smearing lens" than that of an adult. To date, there are no well controlled studies on the effect of changes in the skull on measurement.

In addition, the scale of reference necessarily changes for a given array of electrodes as the head and brain grow, and these changes are important in interpreting EEG patterns. Effectively nature changes the scale of reference by changing the skull as a child grows. If a dense array of electrodes is laid directly on the cortical surface, regions of high coherence are seen to be highly linear: the pattern of high coherence runs right along the cortical gyrus. How does lengthening of the gyrus with growth affect coherence, and how do such changes affect measurement of coherence as children grow? The standard measuring instrument involves the "same" electrode system at different ages without compensation for any changes in the scale of reference. This problem may not be severe in cross-sectional research on children in one age group, but it is probably significant in longitudinal studies in which variability introduced by growth of the skull needs to be taken into account.

A third important issue is the interpretation of region of coherence (see Thatcher, Krause, & Hrybyk, 1986). Measurement is typically categorized as left to right hemisphere, forward to back within a hemisphere, or local. Local generally means a time scale of about half a lobe, which is in fact a relatively large cortical region. For example, posterior temporal lobe to mid temporal lobe is considered a local coherence, whereas frontal lobe to occipital lobe is a long-distance coherence. At this scale, subtleties within a lobe are invisible, yet they are most likely important, especially for questions such as the cortical effect of learning to tap a finger. For this type of question, which is most likely important for analyzing learning and learning disorders, we lack tools that are fine enough to assess meaningful coherence changes.

The conclusion? Spectral coherence of the EEG is a great measure for examining learning and development, but it is a tough one, one of the toughest measures in electrophysiology. A lot of methodological challenges will have to be addressed before coherence can be confidently interpreted in longitudinal designs and reach its full potential for interpreting questions of learning and learning disorder.

### Conclusion: diversity of learning disorders

Is it possible to predict if someone is a poor reader on the basis of just their coherence data or other electrophysiological data? Not yet. The field may get to that point, but there is a major issue beside the methodological ones that I have raised. The issue is that reading or other learning disorders are sufficiently diverse in their origins and forms that coherence or any other brain-activity measure will likely reflect this variation as well. Once the fundamental properties to measure in EEG are established, the next step will be to search for patterns or clusters that relate to clinical or educational difficulties. The existence of large variability is clear, but its meaning for clinical work and education is not yet clear.

The idea of looking for fundamental physiological building blocks of behavior has had an uneven history. With due care, I believe that it is possible to create high-quality, multi-variable prediction of behavioral outcomes based on a series of EEG measures, including coherence and evoked potential latency. Neurophysiological indices of factors such as the speed of neural processing, the ability to inhibit responses in order to handle rapidly occurring stimuli or pairs of stimuli, and the connectivity among cortical regions hold great promise for contributing to a better understanding of the neural substrates of both learning and learning disorders.

## Essay: The role of experience in brain development: adverse effects of childhood maltreatment

### Martin H. Teicher

*Connection:* One of the most important generalizations in developmental neuroscience is that the brain shows remarkable plasticity in its development, with the plasticity typically greatest at early ages (Diamond & Hopson, 1998; Huttenlocher, 2002). One aspect of plasticity is change in the connectivity of different brain regions. Both biological factors and vivid experiences can powerfully shape brain connectivity and other aspects of brain development. Just as learning disorders may involve reduced connectivity of specific cortical regions, so maltreatment seems to reduce cortical connections, both within the left hemisphere and between hemispheres. Also it affects the functioning of other brain regions, especially in the left hemisphere. Thus the evidence suggests that early experience of maltreatment strongly shapes brain functioning. This essay thus indicates both: (a) that maltreatment can shape brain development and organization, including possibly the development of reading – a topic that is worthy of future research; and (b) that problems in connections between brain regions may be important in various kinds of behavior disorders. This essay also serves as a reminder that children's social histories have implications for their neuropsychological development. *The Editors*

Childhood maltreatment has adverse effects on children's functioning and shapes their neural development (Teicher, 2000, 2002). Over the last several years we have been studying the effects of sexual abuse, physical abuse, and psychological trauma on development of the central nervous system (CNS) in children and adults. We have found that there are a number of vulnerable targets.

First, the left hemisphere seems to be disproportionately affected. There is a marked increase in the incidence of left-sided but not right-sided clinically significant abnormalities in the electroencephalogram (EEG) (Ito, Teicher, Glod, Harper, Magnus, & Gelbard, 1993). There is also an increased ratio of left-sided vs. right-sided neuropsychiatric abnormalities (Ito *et al.*, 1993). EEG coherence, which provides an index of cortical differentiation and development, indicates that the left hemisphere is less developed in children with a documented history of sexual abuse relative to healthy controls, and relative to their own right hemispheres (Teicher, Ito, Glod, Andersen, Dumont, & Ackerman, 1997; Ito, Teicher, Glod, & Ackerman, 1998). Also the left hippocampus, but not the right, seems to be smaller in adult patients with a history of childhood sexual abuse and adult symptoms of post-traumatic stress disorder (PTSD) (Stein, Koverola, Hanna, Torchia, & McClarty, 1997; Bremner et al., 1997).

We also found evidence for diminished left/right hemisphere integration during memory recall (Schiffer, Teicher, & Papanicolaou, 1995). Adults with a history of trauma seemed to strongly activate their left hemisphere during recall of neutral memories, and they activated right hemisphere during recall of unpleasant childhood memories. Healthy controls appeared to activate both hemispheres to a much more equal extent during both tasks. MRI examination of the corpus callosum showed that it was decreased by about 30 percent in children with a history of abuse, indicating an apparent decrease in connectivity between the two hemispheres (Teicher et al., 1997). De Bellis et al. (1999) have confirmed this finding and shown that boys are more affected than girls. Further analysis of our data indicates that neglect is the form of maltreatment with greatest impact on boys, whereas girls seem to be most strongly affected by sexual abuse.

Another region that appears to be quite vulnerable to the effects of early maltreatment is the cerebellar vermis. This brain region has a protracted developmental course, and it has the highest density of glucocorticoid receptors during development, which may render it particularly sensitive to effects of stress hormones. This region shows evidence of diminished flow of blood in young adults with a history of repeated sexual abuse. In addition to its roles in posture, balance, and locomotion, the vermis appears to play a role in emotional balance, arousal, timing, and sequencing.

These results indicate pervasive effects of child maltreatment on brain development and organization. The brain changes presumably provide part of the basis for learning differences in children with histories of trauma (Teicher, 2000, 2002).

REFERENCES

Als, H., Duffy, F. H., McAnulty, G. B., Rivkin, M. J., Vajapeyam, S., Mulkern, R. V., Warfield, S. K., Huppi, P. S., Butler, S. C., Conneman, N., Fischer, C. & Eichenwald, E. C. (2004). Early experience alters brain function and structure. Pediatrics, 113, 846–57.

Bremner, J. D., Randall, P., Vermetten, E., Staib, L., Bronen, R. A., Mazure, C., Capelli, S., McCarthy, G., Innis, R. B. & Charney, D. S. (1997). Magnetic resonance imaging-based measurement of hippocampal volume in posttraumatic stress disorder related to childhood physical and sexual abuse – a preliminary report. Biological Psychiatry, 41, 23–32.

De Bellis, M. D., Keshavan, M. S., Clark, D. B., Casey, B. J., Giedd, J. N., Boring, A. M., Frustaci, K. & Ryan, N. D. (1999). A. E. Bennett Research Award. Developmental traumatology. Part II: Brain development. Biological Psychiatry, 451, 271–84.

Diamond, M. & Hopson, J. (1998). *Magic trees of the mind: How to nurture your child's intelligence, creativity, and healthy emotions from birth through adolescence*. New York: Dutton.

Duffy, F. H. (1994). The role of quantified electroencephalography in psychological research. In G. Dawson & K. W. Fischer (eds), *Human behavior and the developing brain*, 93–133. New York: Guilford.

Duffy, F. H., McAnulty, G. B. & Albert, M. S. (1996). Effects of age upon interhemispheric EEG coherence in normal adults. *Neurobiology of Aging*, 17, 587–99.

Duffy, F. H., McAnulty, G. B. & Waber, D. P. (1999). Auditory evoked responses to single tones and closely spaced tone pairs in children grouped by reading or matrices abilities. *Clinical Electroencephalography*, 30, 84–93.

Duffy, F. H., Valencia, I., McAnulty, G. B. & Waber, D. P. (2001). Auditory evoked response data reduction by PCA: Development of variables sensitive to reading disability. *Clinical Electroencephalography*, 32, 168–78.

Huttenlocher, P. R. (2002). *Neural plasticity: The effects of environment on the development of the cerebral cortex*. Cambridge, MA: Harvard University Press.

Ito, Y., Teicher, M. H., Glod, C. A. & Ackerman, E. (1998). Preliminary evidence for aberrant cortical development in abused children: A quantitative EEG study. *Journal of Neuropsychiatry and Clinical Neurosciences*, 10, 298–307.

Ito, Y., Teicher, M. H., Glod, C. A., Harper, D., Magnus, E. & Gelbard, H. A. (1993). Increased prevalence of electrophysiological abnormalities in children with psychological, physical, and sexual abuse. *Journal of Neuropsychiatry and Clinical Neurosciences*, 5, 401–8.

Livingstone, M., Rosen, G., Drislane, F. & Galaburda, A. M. (1991). Physiological and anatomical evidence for a magnocellular defect in developmental dyslexia. *Proceedings of the National Academy of Sciences USA*, 88, 7943–7.

Schiffer, F., Teicher, M. H. & Papanicolaou, A. C. (1995). Evoked potential evidence for right brain activity during recall of traumatic memories. *Journal of Neuropsychiatry and Clinical Neurosciences*, 7, 169–75.

Stein, M. B., Koverola, C., Hanna, C., Torchia, M. G. & McClarty, B. (1997). Hippocampal volume in women victimized by childhood sexual abuse. *Psychological Medicine*, 27, 951–9.

Teicher, M. (2000). Wounds that time won't heal: The neurobiology of child abuse. *Cerebrum*, 2(4), 50–67.

Teicher, M. H. (2002). Scars that won't heal: The neurobiology of child abuse. *Scientific American*, 286 (March), 68–75.

Teicher, M. H., Ito, Y. N., Glod, C. A., Andersen, S. L., Dumont, N. & Ackerman, E. (1997). Preliminary evidence for abnormal cortical development in physically and sexually abused children using EEG coherence and MRI. *Annals of the New York Academy of Science*, 821, 160–75.

Thatcher, R. W., Krause, P. J. & Hrybyk, M. (1986). Cortico-cortical associations and EEG coherence: A two-compartmental model. *Electroencephalography and Clinical Neurophysiology*, 64, 123–43.

Waber, D. P., Weiler, M. D., Bellinge, D. C., Marcus, D. J., Forbes, P. W., Wypij, D. & Wolff, P. H. (2000). Diminished motor timing control in children referred for diagnosis of learning problems. *Developmental Neuropsychology*, 17, 181–97.

# Part III

# Watching Children Read

# 10 Finding common ground to promote dialogue and collaboration: using case material to jointly observe children's behavior

*Jane Holmes Bernstein*

*Overview:* The new era of learning disorders research and practice is marked by cross-disciplinary discussion and collaborative thinking about children's development across mind, brain, and education. A major issue in this effort is the practical question of where to begin discussion, so that researchers from psychology, neuroscience, cognitive science, and education can communicate across their perspectives and settings, ranging across the experimental laboratory, the hospital, the special-needs classroom, and many others. Bernstein suggests that a fruitful approach to collaboration is to step back from disciplinary perspectives and reframe the discussion in terms of the whole child in a real context who is actively working to adapt to the world with his or her skills and limitations. A helpful tool for promoting collaborative insight is to share and interpret common observations, as with the chapters in this section: each author addresses the behaviors of four boys performing various activities related to reading. In her own observations, Bernstein asserts that understanding each child's performance requires analyzing not just the child as observed (looking at the child) but the child as an interactive partner in context (being with the child). Each child acts in a social relationship with the interviewer or teacher and responds cognitively and emotionally to the activities, the physical surroundings, and the emotional climate of the situation, adapting his or her skills and limitations to cope.

*The Editors*

What is a good way to promote dialogue among researchers and practitioners from different perspectives in order to improve understanding of learning disorders, especially with respect to their brain bases? Work on learning disorders requires input from multiple disciplines, but despite this need, interdisciplinary cooperation on learning disorders and their brain bases has not been notably successful until relatively recently.

In the United States, the learning disorder that has provoked the most research effort – as well as great acrimony among research groups – is reading disability. Understanding the nature of both reading and reading breakdown poses

181

challenging questions for professionals in the disciplines of education, psychology, and the neurosciences. A number of the problems of dyslexia and other learning disorders can be solved only by bringing together in a collaborative effort professionals from this range of disciplines.

The challenge of bringing together different groups of professionals to engage in productive dialogue is not trivial, however. It is difficult for most professionals to "hear" points of view that are different from their own because of their commitment to a particular framework or theory. The problem of interdisciplinary dialogue is central: how can we facilitate mutual engagement of professionals in areas as potentially disparate as developmental psychology, school and educational psychology, neuropsychology (both research and clinical), pediatric neurology, behavioral neurology, psychiatry, education, public health, social policy, and administration? How can we bring together mind, brain, and education in research and practice?

To address the challenge of interdisciplinary dialogue, we realized, requires some mechanism by which each participant can start from the same place – that is, a mechanism that establishes a common ground as the basis for shared discussion among a wide range of professionals from neuroscientists to teachers to policy makers. At the conference that led to this book, we wanted the experts in research and practice to go beyond reporting their own work; rather, we wanted them to engage in thinking together about dyslexia, sharing the fruits of their expertise in the field. A good way to begin together from the same place was to go "back to basics" and start the discussion from a firm foundation of shared observations.

All the participants directly observed children actually reading, and thus everyone started with the same core data for discussion and analysis, in a format similar to the "grand rounds" traditionally used in medicine. The way we created this experience at the conference was to show the actual behavior of different children reading and doing other relevant tasks on videotape. Direct observations of the boys' behavior provided the grounding for our arguments and analyses of those behaviors. In this book, the boys' performances on the various tasks are presented as a transcript in the Appendix.

### Using case studies to promote dialogue

The film format was chosen as a means of providing participants in the conference with a common framework from which to develop their discussion of the brain bases of behavior – with the specific behavioral context being, in this instance, reading. The format was highly successful, provoking spirited and fruitful discussion, both formal and informal, across disciplines over the day and a half of the conference. The nature of the discussions provided important information about observing and interpreting case material and promoting collaborative interaction. In the chapters in this section of the book the authors each analyze the four boys' actions as viewed on the film.

One of the most salient observations of participants was the large individual differences among the boys. In the literature, the phrase *individual differences* often refers to smaller groups within a larger group of interest, such as good readers and poor readers. Different researchers have argued for exploring individual differences among readers by comparing poor readers with normal readers, by analyzing the reading performance of poor readers versus normal readers versus good readers, or by comparing dyslexic individuals (specifically defined – usually with reference to a gap between reading skill and IQ) with "garden-variety poor readers" (Stanovich, 1988). Similarly, in the mathematics domain, the analysis of mathematics skills by comparing the performances of poor versus normal "math-ers" has been extended to comparisons of poor versus good versus "perfectionistic" math-ers (Siegler, 1988).

The four boys discussed in this book, however, showed real *individual* differences. Three of the boys had presented with the same manifest symptom of difficulty acquiring beginning reading skills; one had had no difficulty learning to read. They all did the same tasks, some that directly tapped the index domain of reading, others that were selected to illustrate correlates of reading behavior that have been discussed in the relevant literature. What proved to be very striking were, indeed, the differences between the boys. Even though the *level* of performance on specific tasks was often very similar, the *quality* of performance – the way in which each boy tackled the tasks – was typically quite different. This difference was as salient for the youngster who had not had difficulty learning to read as it was for the boys with the histories of reading difficulty.

These differences showed how easily an understanding of the *brain bases* of a given skill (what the brain is actually doing when reading – or doing any other skill) can be obscured and even lost completely if a research endeavor focuses on only the behavioral end-products. In the words of one participant in the conference, "I resolved that I probably could learn some things if I spent more time actually out watching the kids read and interact with their teachers . . . although I do look at videotapes . . . from time to time."

### Making the videotape of the boys

The film was made (by JHB) at the Children's Hospital, Boston. One of the boys was recruited from Maryanne Wolf's Reading Intervention Study at Tufts University (Wolf & Ashby, this volume; Wolf & Katzir-Cohen, 2001). Two boys were recruited from the Learning Disabilities Research Center at the Children's Hospital (Waber *et al.*, 2001). The fourth boy who had not experienced any difficulty learning to read was distantly related to a colleague who in the course of informal conversation about the project spontaneously suggested that the child was of the right age and might enjoy participating. The boys with a history of reading difficulty were selected on the basis of their performance on reading measures obtained in the course of the respective research investigations.

Maryanne Wolf and Jane Bernstein contacted the parents of the boys, explained the nature and purpose of the film, and answered questions in full. The parents were enthusiastic about the project and gave consent for the boys to participate, and the boys agreed to do so. All of the boys appeared to enjoy the experience and the attention – and had detailed plans for their stipends!

For the filming the boys were asked to complete a variety of tasks that either involved reading or have been shown to be related to the reading process. The boys were filmed as they completed each of the tasks in their entirety, and they were also interviewed initially and debriefed at the end of the session. The final videotape comprised selected excerpts from the tasks, the interviews, and the debriefing session. The Appendix provides summaries of these performances, as well as copies of the children's products. The interview and debriefing excerpts were chosen to give a sense of the personality and language style of each of the boys.

The excerpts were chosen by a standard procedure designed to select the most informative material for observers. On the *rapid naming* tasks (Denckla & Rudel, 1976), the film segment was limited to the first three lines. On the *timed and untimed word and non-word reading* tasks (Torgesen & Mathes, 2000; Wagner, Torgesen, & Rachotte, 1999), the film segment showed only those items that presented maximum difficulty. For the *paragraph reading* task (Gray Oral Reading Test, 3rd edition: Wiederholt & Bryant, 1992), one paragraph was presented. Only the first boy was shown actually drawing the *Rey-Osterrieth Complex Figure* (Osterrieth, 1944; Rey, 1941) and only in one of the three conditions (the copy condition; the other two conditions were immediate recall and delayed recall). The final drawings for all three conditions for each boy were shown one by one with voice-over commentary by JHB. For the *motor tapping* task (Wolff, Michel, Ovrut, & Drake, 1990), the film segment showed the boys completing one alternating (left-right-left-right) hand condition and one asynchronous (both-right-one-right) hand condition. The handwriting samples shown were the completed products.

On the film each task was completed by each of the boys with both the boys and the tasks being presented in the same order each time. The sequence of tasks in the final film was as follows: Part I: initial interview, rapid naming of colors, letters, objects, numbers, timed reading of words, timed reading of non-words, untimed reading of words, untimed reading of non-words; Part II: paragraph reading, complex figure, motor tapping, handwriting sample, debriefing session. The full transcript of the film can be found in the Appendix.

Authors in this section each viewed the film before the conference, commented at the conference, and then revised their comments to form the chapters that follow. Although each reviewer received the complete film (in two parts), she or he was asked to consider either Part I (which focused on reading tasks) or Part II (which focused on other tasks) but not both.

### *Looking at* versus *being with*: different modes of clinical analysis

The individual differences among the boys with respect to their performance on specific tasks were not the only important differences illustrated by the film format. Participants' reactions to the film highlighted differences in observation and interpretation of behavioral data, which are reflected in the chapters in this book. In both research and the clinical settings these observational differences are a major issue, having theoretical, methodological, and practical implications for explanation of brain–behavior relations and intervention with children.

These differences derive in part from the different viewing conditions of different participants. The way that a professional interprets a behavior from looking at a child is often not the same way that she or he interprets the same behavior when interacting with the child. Indeed, which stance one takes – examining what one is *looking at* versus analyzing the experience of *being with* a child – reflects a fundamental difference in beliefs and assumptions about the role of the brain with respect to behavior.

In response to the film, most observers talked about the boys and their behavior on the tests from a perspective of viewing the boys as "cases," objects to be analyzed, "out there." They talked primarily about the boys and what they were doing. On the basis of their discussion they appeared to frame their analyses of brain–behavior relations from the same perspective: their working model of brain–behavior relations was primarily one in which *brain acts on world* – or, in Bakker's (1984) terms, brain-as-independent-variable. During the main discussions, there were very few (two or three only) observations of the behavior of the adults working with the boys on the film. Consequently, participants did not integrate into their analyses data that reflected the role of the brain-as-dependent-variable: *world acts on brain*. Given a brain-acts-on-world perspective, participants essentially saw the boys – and their brains – as the source of the learning problems.

Our approach to the understanding of behavior resists this perspective (Bernstein, 2000; Holmes-Bernstein & Waber, 1990; Sorensen, Forbes, Bernstein, Weiler, Mitchell, & Waber, 2003). Brains develop in individuals shaped by their ecological niches, environments, and contexts (see chapters by Benes & Paré-Blagoev; Duffy; Fischer, Rose, & Rose; Galaburda & Sherman; Paré-Blagoev; Teicher, this volume). A proper analysis of problems in acquiring expected behavior (that is, learning problems) requires that the contextual and environmental demands that elicit behavior from that child/brain on a moment-by-moment basis be incorporated into the analysis. It also requires consideration of development as reflected in both the changing competencies of the brain and its multiple systems and the emerging functional capacities that it supports. The theoretical matrix guiding the analysis of behavior, clinically and in the research setting, is one of a *brain–context–development* interaction. All behaviors must be scrutinized within this matrix.

In this framework, a learning disorder is conceived as a *failure to adapt successfully* to the environment (Holmes-Bernstein & Waber, 1990). A comparable position has been argued by Wakefield (1992), who conceptualizes "mental disorder" as the outcome of a "harmful dysfunction." That is, the problem for which clinical attention is sought involves a dysfunctional mechanism that is, necessarily, also experienced as harmful by its owner (or its owner's mother and father!). A dysfunctional mechanism need not be particularly maladaptive; if it does not create a problem for its owner, then there is no "disorder." The role of the environment or context, both physical and social, is crucial to the diagnosis of learning (or mental) disorder, which is taken to be not a property of the child (or brain), but rather of the *child–world system* created by the interaction (Bernstein, 2000; Fischer, Ayoub, Noam, Singh, Maraganore, & Raya, 1997; Holmes-Bernstein & Waber, 1990). This distinction is, of course, not only one of diagnosis, but also defines the design of the entire clinical assessment process. Furthermore, it entails a view of brain function that includes not only how brains work in and of themselves, but also – and critically – how brains work in response to situational demands.

The *brain-context-development* framework is the basis for a *whole child* approach to assessment. A full description of brain–behavior relations cannot be achieved by focusing on behavioral end-products under highly constrained conditions, as implied by the standard usage of psychometric tests (see Matarazzo, 1990; Vanderploeg, 1994). A full description must incorporate knowledge of how brains actually develop and work in real world contexts, not in highly structured settings that tap into only limited aspects of the organism's functioning at any one time. Knowing the brain's workings in this way requires examining as broad a range as possible of the behavior of the brain's owner – that is, the child.

The whole child approach has, then, three important assumptions. One, the analysis of behavior has to incorporate the full range of skills that the brain has to learn, not just those needed for goal-oriented problem-solving, but also those basic to self-regulation. Learning to manage themselves on an independent basis in order to explore and solve problems to the highest level is as important a developmental challenge for young brains/children as is problem-solving itself. Two, how the brain supports behavior is critically dependent on context and cannot be understood without analyzing contextual variables (Buller &

Hardcastle, 2000; Fischer, Rotenberg, Bullock & Raya, 1993; Fischer, Rose, & Rose, this volume; Quartz & Sejnowski, 1997). Indeed, brains are dependent for their very development on experience with the world "out there" (see chapters in Parts I and II of this volume). Three, it is not enough to understand what skill (or parts thereof) a person does or does not have. It is equally important to know how the skill is used. As noted above, dysfunction need not lead to disorder – in which case it does not need managing. For example, one's vulnerability to making more or less subtle paraphasic errors in language or to retrieving specific words rather slowly (both of which may be picked up on well-designed language tests) may be completely irrelevant to one's ability to tell a good story or make a good verbal presentation. Here, the goal is the message, and minor perturbations of the medium go totally unnoticed by listeners who are likely, after all, to be users of the language themselves and thus easily able to decode the message under all sorts of deficiencies in the signal-to-noise ratio of the incoming linguistic signals. These assumptions influenced the way in which we observed and interpreted the behavior of the boys shown on the film as we interacted with the four youngsters.

### Looking at and being with the boys

The distinction between brain as independent versus dependent variable typically appears in discrepancies between observations by people *looking at* a client's or student's behavior, as with the boys in this book, and those by an examiner in a relationship of *being with* the boys, that is, actually working with them. Maryanne Wolf conducted the initial interview session with William, whom she knows well. I interviewed the other three youngsters. I also administered the different tasks to all the boys and completed the debriefing session with them, using the *brain–context–development* perspective in my observation, analysis, and interpretation of the interactions.

#### William

The *looking-at/being-with* distinction in perspective was manifest in interactions with all the boys. It was well highlighted in the case of William. He was characterized by more than one participant in very positive terms ("Mr Cheerful" as some participants called him). Indeed, William is a youngster of considerable personal charm who exudes a real sense of *joie de vivre*. He has wide interests and a developed musical talent (he sings in a children's opera group) that he patently enjoys. He is able to "read" others and laugh at himself. Nonetheless, the struggle to learn to read text has been a hard one for him. In the not too distant past, his reading skills were seriously limited and his demoralization profound. He has benefited tremendously from his participation in the reading intervention study led by Maryanne Wolf (Wolf & Ashby, this volume; Wolf & Katzir-Cohen, 2001) and at the time of filming was doing well in reading basics. However, although his skills have improved, his emotional comfort level with things academic still has some way to go! (The dissociation between self-esteem with respect to academics and self-esteem in other areas of life, as exemplified by William, has been well documented by Susan Harter, 2000.)

*Looking at* William on the film reveals the cheerful, upbeat charm of this engaging boy. Careful attention to the *being with* of the examiner with William tells a somewhat different story, however. Observation of the behavior of the adults working with William (both Wolf and myself) reveals that he elicits from the adult working with him maximum support, reassurance, and nurturance. Maryanne Wolf's voice in talking with him is measured and soothing, full of encouraging and validating remarks. I felt the same pull to provide support and encouragement as he tackled the various tasks presented, and I noted the behaviors William used to support himself: gripping with both hands the editor's desk holding the stimuli, taking deep breaths to help him engage with a difficult challenge, anxiously waiting for a hard task to end. In the context of these tasks (which were chosen expressly to challenge the different processing capacities considered important for reading), William came over as decidedly fragile. Independent validation of this observation came also from his tutor from the Reading Intervention Project, who was a member of the audience: she vehemently nodded her head in agreement at the observation of fragility when I described my experience in working with him. In William's case, the *looking at* stance focused attention on the evident charm and personality of this young man. Analysis of the *being with* interaction highlighted the support he still needs when faced with the (for him) challenging reading activities.

### Brian

Brian elicited a similar discrepancy in viewpoint. On film he came over as anxious, sitting up oddly straight and using language, both spontaneously and on specific tasks, in a highly dysfluent fashion, apparently gulping breaths word by word. He did not, however, "feel anxious" to me as I worked with him. There was no sense of strain or lack of involvement on his part. Instead, he appeared stiff and awkward with lack of fluency of motor movements of all types – to the point that he seemed dyspraxic. His speech was marked by a lack of synchrony of breath pulses and phrase boundaries, lending his speech pattern a breathy and staccato quality. The back-and-forth of conversation was also dysfluent: Brian answered tag questions and rhetorical questions, repeated the form of questions, and failed to overlap his utterances with those of the person he was speaking to.

In the *brain–context* analysis, taking note of the ongoing behavior of both members of the interacting pair clearly revealed that the person feeling the strain was not Brian but me, the examiner, as I tried to encourage language that did not come easily, to offer choices to facilitate conversation, and so forth. The balance of utterances between me and Brian was significantly weighted toward me, not typical of the usual expectations of an 9-year-old boy in such a situation. The fact that I was carrying the greater load of language behavior in the interaction was strongly suggestive of an underlying problem in language production in this young man (see below). However, to me (trying to keep the interaction going reasonably fluently), Brian presented not just as an individual with language output problems, but as the ultimate "dysfluent kid" with the lack of behavioral fluency going from bottom to top, so to speak – not only involving academic skill development but also rendering atypical his deployment of motor skills, his management of voice and breath, and his comfort in interacting socially. In Brian's case, observations of the same behaviors led to different conclusions by participants coming from different stances: *looking at* him suggested anxiety; analysis of the *being with* interaction with him, in contrast, raised questions of the efficiency of his overall motor system.

*Andrew*

Andrew could be characterized as having a multi-modal language disorder underlying his struggle with written language. As observed, for example, by Kytja Voeller at the conference: ". . . he clearly has difficulty initiating articulatory patterns. He may know what he wants to say – [although] we don't know this for sure – but he probably understands . . . The problem he has formulating the sounds and getting them out into the motor speech system is really very extreme . . . In the course of that little snippet about Captain Cat . . . he has a severe anomia as well . . . It's very hard for him to formulate sentences, he drops the conversational ball, he makes assumptions about what the listener knows . . . Not only are his syntactic and morphemic abilities questionable, but his pragmatics aren't very good either." On the film, Andrew's lack of a sense of where he is in the world was also apparent: he appeared somewhat awkward physically, contrasting notably with Jonathan, the reader of the group and self-declared sportsman whose personal spatial sense is evidently well developed.

Based on observations of his overall presentation on the film, Andrew was described as very stressed, very anxious, somewhat dysphoric. Again, however, this was not how I experienced him in the *being with* of the interaction: he felt comfortable with himself, and I experienced the interaction as comfortable also. This experience was supported by the additional clinical data that had been collected for the children who participated in the research studies at Children's Hospital. As a participant, Andrew's parents and teacher had been given the *Behavior Assessment System for Children* (BASC: Reynolds & Kamphaus, 1992). On this measure, there was remarkable consensus between mother and father (responding individually) as well as the classroom teacher. Responses revealed some concerns about attentional skills that varied somewhat by person responding. But what was notable was the consensus on Andrew's self-reliance, adaptability, and social skills. He is actually considered quite a leader. It appears that his clearly evident neurobehavioral insecurities do not – at least not at this point in his career – interfere with peer interactions and relationships; indeed, other children are reported to like him. His parents are also very involved and supportive. Andrew clearly has a lot going for him as he faces the continuing academic struggle. The strong contrast between *looking at* and *being with* was between a potentially psychologically stressed youngster seen from the former perspective and a quite comfortable fellow in spite of manifest neuropsychological differences from the latter perspective.

### Jonathan

Not surprisingly perhaps, Jonathan, who has not had a history of struggle with reading skills, presented as very relaxed in this setting. His affect was bright, and he was animated, even mischievous, in his interaction with me. Indeed, he was a socially aware, sophisticated young fellow who knew that his last remark in the interview (about breaking his teeth in sports!) would not be expected: he waited for its effect! Jonathan used conversational language fluently, taking turns smoothly with appropriate cross-cutting of his and my remarks. He leaned forward with his arms on the table, comfortably participating in the conversational space. He gazed upwards when thinking or formulating remarks, and then focused appropriately on me when making his point. Intonation was within normal limits, varying appropriately with the content of conversation. Altogether Jonathan was comfortable with himself, enjoying the one-on-one adult attention. Although he had no history of difficulty in acquiring reading skills and performed well on reading-related tasks, more than one observer noted that he revealed more or less subtle discontinuities in fine and graphomotor performance. The *looking at/being with* distinction, however, was not particularly salient in considering him.

### Learning disorder as adaptation by a whole child

In the clinical analysis of behavior as in the research investigation, both what one *sees* and how one *interprets* what one sees are – importantly – a function of the theory guiding the assessment process. In our theoretical approach (Bernstein, 2000; Holmes-Bernstein & Waber, 1990), behavior is interpreted within an evolutionary framework, as an adaptation to the demands of a specific ecological niche (see Immordino-Yang & Deacon, this volume). Thus, our definition of learning disability (or, as we prefer, "learning disorder" – to capture the full range of things that the brain must learn that could go wrong!) is framed as a "failure to adapt . . . to the environment," which, in our case, can be understood within the context of developmental neuropsychological theory. This focus on adaptation to specific circumstances comes from a view of the child as the primary unit of analysis in the assessment process.

The child is viewed as a whole organism, rather than as a package, so to speak, of neuropsychological functions. The *whole child* – including his or her brain – is understood to be participating in transactions with the environment that result in continuous "behaving." This theoretical stance has important implications for the nature of the assessment process or strategy employed to evaluate neuro-behavioral function in the child. It determines the design of the *experiment with the N of 1* that is the clinical assessment. It is also important with respect to the methodology employed. The *whole child* stance necessarily extends the range of what has traditionally been seen as relevant for psychological assessment. The neurobehavioral "portrait" of the child (Matarazzo, 1990) that is the goal of clinical analysis cannot be achieved solely (or primarily) by means of the quantitative data provided by psychological tests, but requires analysis of the transactions between the child and the various contextual demands of his or her environment. Environment includes both people (from the societal to the individual) and the physical world (at both "macro" and "micro" levels).

In the assessment context, this type of analysis has three important requirements. First, transactional and contextual information must not only be gathered as part of the evaluation, but must also contribute directly to the diagnostic formulation, rather than serving only as moderator variables that may influence the interpretation of other data. Second, the clinician must collect data relevant to the child's functioning in the natural environment. This requirement necessitates not only the use of behavioral rating scales and targeted questionnaires completed by people who interact with the child on an everyday basis; it also requires the development of "analytic-dynamic interviewing" skills by which the clinician actively analyzes, within the framework of the *brain–context–development* model and on a moment-to-moment basis, the information acquired during a face-to-face or telephone interview. Third, the clinician must incorporate in the evaluative and diagnostic decision-making an appreciation of his or her role as an active agent (rather than a more passive observer) in the collection of data required for the formulation of a diagnostic portrait. This latter requirement was highlighted by the differences between the *looking at* and *being with* views of the boys and their behavior. (See Bernstein, 2000 and Bernstein and Weiler, 2000, for extended discussion of the requirements of a clinical assessment in the developmental neuropsychological context.)

### The role of the clinician

Scrutinizing the roles of the various participants in an interaction is of particular importance to clinicians whose job is to evaluate and interpret behavior. The following discussion is framed in the context of a clinical assessment. The points to be made, however, are not restricted to that setting: given a view of brain functioning in which interaction with context is fundamental, an appreciation for the parameters of behavioral interaction will be critical for understanding brain–behavior relations in both research and clinical settings. In an important sense, all human interactions can be called "clinical." Clinicians are merely human beings with behavioral observation skills that are highly developed with respect to the data needed for their particular discipline.

Perhaps the most important point to make with respect to the role of the clinician – or of any participant in an interaction – is that this role is not a neutral one. In observing the transactions between the adults and the boys on this film from the *being with* perspective, it was clear, for example, that different boys' behavior elicited and shaped different aspects of the adults' behavior. Indeed, in any (humane) interaction between human beings, it is impossible for the participants to be uninfluenced by each other. This reflects the so-called "uncertainty principle" of Bohr and Heisenberg brought into the behavioral domain: the observer (observing instrument) is integral – indeed, inseparable – from what is observed. The point was made for psychiatry by Globus (1973): " . . . there is no single reality, as reality cannot be conceived of independent of the perspective by means of which 'reality' is assessed . . ." It has been elegantly addressed with respect to the assessment of children by Ginsburg (1997) in his analysis of "standardized" versus "clinical" assessment: the core assumption of standardized testing, that all children will be treated equally, is untenable in the normal interaction between child and adult. The requirement to establish *rapport* that is mandated of clinicians in all test manuals is actually antithetical to the basic assumptions of the standardization of the tests!

The influence of transactions on the participants in the transaction occurs for individuals of all ages. The influence is greater, however, in adult–child transactions to the extent that the child's brain – and behavioral output – is being shaped by the more competent brain of the adult in the ongoing socialization of the child. Adults naturally support and scaffold children's behavior as youngsters develop their skills. In evaluating behavior in the developmental context, this natural adult–child interaction is honed and polished by the clinician.

For the clinician working in an adaptational framework, these transactions provide another tool to aid in the fuller understanding of the child's behavior. Clinicians do not primarily administer and interpret tests. They are expected to observe and interpret both test and non-test behaviors as the basis for their diagnostic decisions. Furthermore, they are expected to recognize their inherent role as agents for eliciting behavioral data and to observe and interpret the elicited behavior rigorously. What does this mean? Consider the following examples:

I am sitting in my office – I have been in this office for the last, say, ten years – it is MY office. I have been in my office for ten minutes with a child I have just met – and I start to feel that my personal space has been invaded. My interpretation: THE CHILD has a social problem!

I have been in my office for ten minutes with another child and I find myself speaking in my best, English (in my case), clipped, consonants, talking slowly and distinctly, repeating and rephrasing as I go. THE CHILD has a language problem!

Note that I may need to use a variety of targeted psychological tests in order to determine the specific *nature* of the social problem or the language problem. The *fact* of the social or language problem is, however, clearly signaled in the change in *my* behavior. In response to reduced input from the child to the ongoing behavioral transaction, I am essentially "pulled" from my behavioral baseline to fill in what is required to keep the interaction going as efficiently as possible. (See the example of this in the description of Brian above.) The clinician's analysis of ongoing behavioral change in him- or herself thus becomes a critical tool in the clinical armamentarium – and requires, as do all the tools of clinical analysis, rigor in behavioral analysis and interpretation. For example, the observation (written in the report) that "language addressed to X needs to be slowed, simplified, repeated, and rephrased" is an important datum in the "diagnostic behavioral cluster" (Bernstein, 2000; Holmes-Bernstein & Waber, 1990) that frames the child's difficulties and forms the basis for management and intervention.

## Conclusion: observing differences in children and observers

A person's stance in interpreting a child's behavior has powerful effects on what he or she observes and interprets for the same behaviors by the child. Such differences have clear implications for clinical assessment, where one's theoretical stance determines which behaviors are observed in the first place and which are then deemed relevant for diagnosis and management. The differences are also important in furthering our understanding of how the brain works to support behavior. The *looking at/being with* distinction is an important one, reflecting different neurobehavioral theories with different explanatory goals and different questions for future research in developmental behavioral neuroscience. Is the brain an independent actor on the world whose workings can be reduced to a range of isolatable functions that interact to achieve specific goals? Or is the brain an integral part of its world, both responsive to and dependent upon it? When the task is to examine behavior, what you think is what you see, shaped by the environment! Both views have their own validity, and both need to be considered in clinical assessment and research.

Distinguishing such differences in the observation and interpretation of data is critical for ongoing theory development and thus for the progress of any field. It is particularly important to counter the problem highlighted by Siegler (1996), by which ". . . existing assumptions, methods and theories [act] in a mutually supportive way to make what we typically do seem essential . . . and to make doing otherwise . . . seem impossible."

The chapters that follow in this section by Brady, Blachman, Taylor, and Torgesen represent several distinct perspectives on analyzing the behaviors of the four boys. Other chapters in the book bring still more diverse perspectives to bear – not only *looking at* and *being with* but also perspectives from neuroscience, genetics, developmental science, and educational practice.

REFERENCES

Bakker, D. (1984). The brain as a dependent variable. *Journal of Clinical Neuropsychology*, 6, 1–16.
Bernstein, J. H. (2000). Developmental neuropsychological assessment. In K. O. Yeates, M. D. Ris & H. G. Taylor (eds), *Pediatric neuropsychology: Theory, research and practice*. New York: Guilford.
Bernstein, J. H. & Weiler, M. D. (2000). "Pediatric neuropsychological assessment" examined. In G. Goldstein & M. Hersen (eds), *Handbook of psychological assessment* 3rd edn. New York: Pergamon.
Buller, D. J. & Hardcastle, V. G. (2000). Evolutionary psychology, meet developmental neurobiology: Against promiscuous modularity. *Brain and Mind*, 1, 307–25.
Denckla, M. B. & Rudel, R. G. (1976). Rapid automatized naming (R. A. N.): Dyslexia differentiated from other learning disabilities. *Neuropsychologia*, 14, 471–9.
Fischer, K. W., Ayoub, C. C., Noam, G. G., Singh, I., Maraganore, A. & Raya, P. (1997). Psychopathology as adaptive development along distinctive pathways. *Development and Psychopathology*, 9, 751–81.
Fischer, K. W., Rotenberg, E. J., Bullock, D. H. & Raya, P. (1993). The dynamics of competence: How context contributes directly to skill. In R. H. Wozniak & K. W. Fischer (eds). *Development in context: Acting and thinking in specific environments*, 93–117. Hillsdale, NJ: Erlbaum.
Ginsburg, H. P. (1997). *Entering the child's mind: The clinical interview in psychological research and practice*. New York: Cambridge University Press.
Globus, G. G. (1973). Consciousness and brain, I. The identity thesis. *Archives of General Psychiatry*, 29, 153–60.
Harter, S. (2000). *The construction of the self: A developmental perspective*. New York: Guilford.
Holmes Bernstein, J. & Waber, D. P. (1990). Developmental neuropsychological assessment: The systemic approach. In A. A. Boulton, G. B. Baker & M. Hiscock (eds), *Neuromethods: Volume 17, Neuropsychology*. Clifton, NJ: Humana Press.
Matarazzo, J. D. (1990). Psychological assessment versus psychological testing. *American Psychologist*, 45, 999–1017.

Quartz, S. R. & Sejnowski, T. J. (1997). The neural basis of cognitive development: A constructivist manifesto. *Behavioral and Brain Sciences*, 20, 537–96.

Osterrieth, P. A. (1944). Le test de copie d'une figure complexe. *Archives de Psychologie*, 30, 206–356.

Rey, A. (1941). L'examen psychologique dans le cas d'encéphalopathie traumatique. *Archives de Psychologie*, 28, 286–340.

Reynolds, C. R. & Kamphaus, R. W. (1992). *Behavior assessment system for children.* Circle Pines, MN: American Guidance Service.

Siegler, R. S. (1988). Strategy choice procedures and the development of multiplication skill, *Journal of Experimental Psychology: General*, 117, 258–75.

Siegler, R. S. (1996). *Emerging minds.* New York: Oxford University Press.

Sorensen, L. G., Forbes, P. W., Bernstein, J. H., Weiler, M. D., Mitchell, W. M. & Waber, D. P. (2003). Psychosocial adjustment over a two-year period in children referred for learning problems: Risk, resilience, and adaptation. *Learning Disabilities Research and Practice*, 18(1), 10–24.

Stanovich, K. E. (1988). Explaining the differences between the dyslexic and garden-variety poor reader: the phonological-core variable-difference model. *Journal of Learning Disabilities*, 21, 590–612.

Torgesen, J. K. & Mathes, P. (2000). *A basic guide to understanding, assessing, and teaching phonological awareness.* Austin, TX: PRO-ED Publishing, Inc.

Vanderploeg, R. D. (1994). Interview and testing: the data-collection phase of neuropsychological evaluations. In R. D. Vanderploeg (ed.) *Clinician's guide to neuropsychological assessment.* Hillsdale, NJ: Lawrence Erlbaum Associates.

Waber, D. P., Wolff, P. H., Weiler, M. D., Bellinger, D., Marcus, D. H., Forbes, P. & Wypij, D. (2001). Processing of rapid auditory stimuli in school-age children referred for evaluation of learning disorder. *Child Development*, 72, 37–49.

Wagner, R. K., Torgesen, J. K. & Rashotte, C. A. (1999). *Comprehensive test of phonological processes.* Austin, TX: PRO-ED Publishing, Inc.

Wakefield, J. C. (1992). The concept of mental disorder: On the boundary between biological facts and social values. *American Psychologist*, 47, 373–88.

Weiderholt, J. L. & Bryant, B. R. (1992). *Gray oral reading tests*, 3rd edn. Austin, TX: PRO-ED.

Wolf, M. & Katzir-Cohen, T. (2001). Reading fluency and its intervention. *Scientific Studies of Reading*, 5, 211–39.

Wolff, P. H., Michel, G. F., Ovrut, M. & Drake, C. (1990). Rate and timing precision of motor coordination in developmental dyslexia. *Developmental Psychology*, 26, 349–59.

# 11    Analyzing the reading abilities of four boys: educational implications*

*Susan Brady*

*Overview:* In order for neuropsychological research on dyslexia to be useful to educators and learning-disabled children, its educational implications must be laid out explicitly, and the working definitions and categories framing the neuropsychological research must be tested against the demonstrated needs of dyslexic children. The goal is to assure a good fit between the questions guiding the neuropsychological research and the questions asked by educators about their students. Brady translates the neuropsychological work, such as research on rapid serial naming, into recommendations for educational practice and indicates where neuropsychological research categories seem incongruent with the educational evidence. For example, research indicating that dyslexic children have phonological processing problems often has unclear implications, because several relevant skills, such as phonemic awareness and grapheme decoding, are unjustifiably lumped together. Progress on understanding dyslexia requires better analysis of the relations between written and oral language processing, including component reading skills.

*The Editors*

As Jane Holmes Bernstein describes in Chapter 10 (this volume), four boys varying in reading ability were filmed and given a battery of tests to provide a framework for discussion about current views on reading acquisition and reading difficulties. The boys are presented in three contexts. First, each is introduced and portions of his individual conversations with the tester are included, providing a brief window on each boy's language skills and personality. Next, samples of each child's performance on three of the rapid naming tasks are shown: color naming, letter naming, and object naming. Third, footage is included of the children as they are taking portions of two timed tasks of word and non-word reading from the Test of Word Reading Fluency (Torgesen & Mathes, 2000;

* This paper was supported in part by grant HD-01994 from the National Institutes of Health to Haskins Laboratories. The author thanks Hollis Scarborough for her helpful comments on an earlier draft.

Torgesen, Wagner, & Rashotte, 1999; Wagner, Torgesen, & Rashotte, 1999) and portions of two untimed reading tasks from the Woodcock-Johnson Psycho-educational Battery, Revised (Woodcock & Johnson, 1990) (i.e. the Letter-Word Identification subtest and the Word Attack subtest). Using this sample of information from the film and the summary data in the Appendix, I will comment on the educational implications concerning the boys' reading development and on whether the data presented support or challenge my theoretical perspective.

In commenting on this film, I will primarily analyze the reading errors the boys are making, focusing on what can be surmised about each boy's phoneme awareness and decoding abilities. The pattern of difficulties in each of these areas for the three boys who are less skilled readers fits well with the phonological account of reading acquisition and reading disability (e.g. Shankweiler, 1999). This analysis also identifies the need for additional information that would serve as an important backdrop for interpreting what one is seeing, and that would allow testing of hypotheses about the boys' sources of difficulties. In addition to evaluating their progress in reading, I will comment on the rapid naming measures, noting some recent research that helps address the basis of the association of rapid naming performance and reading impairment. Throughout the discussion, issues will be raised regarding treatment of the boys' reading difficulties.

To begin, let me offer my general impressions from the snippets of conversation in the introductory section where the boys were being interviewed. First, Jonathan, a normal reader, came across as capable, affable, bright, and reasonably articulate. The second child, William, was notably cheerful and responsive. From this sample, and knowing he has some reading problems, one might guess that he may be a classic dyslexic, having reading difficulties while being intelligent and having other strengths. If the phonological problems that we will see later were addressed, it seems likely that comprehension would not be a problem for him. At the same time, the cheerfulness carried a bit of anxiety, suggesting he may have concerns about his reading difficulties and about performing well.

Looking at the next two boys, Brian and Andrew, raised additional questions for me, particularly about Andrew. Brian was somewhat reluctant to reply, and his utterances seemed rather forced and brief. When he was asked about being a twin, his response was a little disjointed and dispassionate, possibly because this is a routine question for him. However, this style may also signal some difficulties organizing his thoughts and responding in a coordinated fashion with what was asked. Later on the other measures he had a notably staccato speaking style, producing words in a much more isolated, non-fluent style than is usual. These behaviors indicate that a more thorough investigation of his cognitive and oral language abilities would be necessary if one were aiming for a complete diagnostic evaluation.

Andrew more strikingly appears to have oral language problems. He has an odd voice quality: it is not uncommon to see intonation abnormalities in children who have broader cognitive and linguistic impairments. I was also curious about the fact that for a language sample for him on the tape, what was selected was a section in which he was telling the story of "Captain Cat." Was it difficult to get him to talk about other things? Was he thus asked to talk about something that was highly familiar to him? If so, that brings with it the possibility that his speaking about it might have been very practiced and may not have been the best indication of his use of sentence structure and vocabulary when it is not practiced. Yet even with this familiar content, errors were apparent, such as leaving off appropriate grammatical endings and making vocabulary substitutions (i.e. "Blond Hair . . . er! . . . army person" instead of "a blond-haired [army] sergeant").

For assessment purposes one would want a broader evaluation of language abilities and of listening comprehension for the boys with apparent difficulties. Such an evaluation might include the retelling of a novel experience to get away from canned, practiced responses that may limit sentence structure and word choice, as well as to reveal working memory performance. Also relevant are information about IQ, vocabulary knowledge, listening comprehension, and attention performance to determine if the problems are restricted to reading or seem to imply the need for a more extensive remedial program.

## Reviewing reading performance: general patterns

Regardless of whether other disabilities are present, an evaluation of reading achievement should include analysis of where a child is in the process of developing fully explicit phoneme awareness and mastery of the decoding/spelling system, and, if germane, evaluation of reading comprehension. Such analyses set the stage for timely and effective instructional recommendations. To gain this information, in addition to the pseudoword and real word reading measures on the film, one would want to assess phoneme awareness, spelling and writing skills, text fluency, and reading comprehension. (See Siegel, 1999, for a sensible discussion of how to evaluate whether a child has a reading disability and Stanovich, 1999 for a critique of the shortcomings of the IQ-achievement discrepancy score as grounds for assigning remedial services.)

From the sample of reading on the word attack and word identification reading measures, I will offer an interpretation of the errors that occurred. Confirmation of this interpretation could be gained by tests designed to target particular phoneme awareness, spelling, and decoding skills (e.g. Phonological Awareness Test, Robertson & Salter, 1997; Developmental Spelling Analysis, Ganske, 2000; Decoding Skills Test, Richardson & DiBenedetto, 1985). Evaluation of accuracy and rate of text reading could be assessed with the Gray Oral Test of

Table 11.1. *Reading performance (number correct/number presented on film).*

| Measures | Jonathan | William | Brian | Andrew |
|---|---|---|---|---|
| Real words – untimed | 17/18 | 17/18 | 12/18 | 8/18 |
| Real words – timed | 56/57 | 45/52 | 37/43 | 24/33 |
| Non-words-untimed | 14/18 | 10/18 | 4/18 | 5/18 |
| Non-words-timed | 27/30 | 21/29 | 13/17 | 11/14 |

Untimed tasks were from the Woodcock-Johnson Psycho-Educational Battery – Revised (Word Attack and Letter/Word Identification) (Woodcock & Johnson, 1990); Timed tasks were from the Test of Word Reading Efficiency (Torgesen, Wagner, & Rashotte, 1999). On the timed tasks, scores are the number read in 45 seconds.

Reading (Wiederholt & Bryant, 1992). (Note: in a portion of the film each boy read a paragraph at a third grade level, but performance on the passage and on the test as a whole was not formally scored.)

Given this framework, my first step will be to look at the information available for the four boys. For an overview, Table 11.1 presents the scores for the boys on the measures of reading real words and nonsense words in both timed (Torgesen *et al.*, 1999) and untimed (Woodcock & Johnson, 1990) versions. Because information was not available about performance on the entire set of tasks, particularly for the two untimed Woodcock measures, the numbers listed are a rough measure based on the number correct out of the number of items for each boy that was included in the video. (Recall that the video included only samples of each child's performance on the different tasks, and that the samples were selected to include portions difficult for the individual children and hence tended to differ for the four boys.) A further point to keep in mind when looking at their performance is that the Woodcock-Johnson tasks and the *Test of Word Reading Efficiency* did not, of course, have the same stimuli. Consequently, comparisons of the timed and untimed measures have to be made with some qualifications, and even within the two test batteries the measures of word and non-word reading were not designed to have parallel stimuli in terms of phonemic structure.

Nonetheless, a consistent pattern is evident across the real-word and nonsense-word tasks and in the speeded and unspeeded versions. To forecast my interpretation, all of the children would benefit from code-based instruction, though to different degrees, and the three weaker readers also need additional help to develop adequate sight word vocabularies and fluency.

In Table 11.1, Jonathan is performing the best on all of the measures. His accuracy is lower for non-words than for real words on both of the reading tests, and on the timed measures the number of items read in 45 seconds is much lower for non-words. William scored as well as Jonathan on the untimed real words, but began to slip in comparison on the timed measure of real words, suggesting differences between the boys in automaticity of sight word recognition. On the untimed non-word task, it becomes evident that William is a little weaker at the code: when presented with new words that he has not seen before, he is less accurate at pronouncing them than Jonathan, even when there is no time pressure. On the timed task, both boys got through a greater number of items, but the magnitude of differences between them was roughly comparable to the untimed task. William's performance on the non-word measures points to the need for further work on decoding concepts, and suggests that decoding weaknesses may be a factor in his less rapid reading of real words. In the same table, Brian and Andrew are progressively less accurate and are able to read fewer words. Both read more real words than non-words, though, as noted above, comparisons are qualified somewhat by the fact that the tasks did not appear to have exactly parallel stimuli in terms of word and non-word items.

These results are corroborated by the normative data provided in Table A.4 in the Appendix for the untimed reading scores as assessed by the Woodcock-Johnson Psychoeducational Battery (1990). Jonathan was at the 83rd percentile on word reading, but dropped to the 57th percentile for word attack skills. It is not uncommon to see word attack lower for a capable child who has not had direct instruction. With that pattern, one would anticipate that he would be lower on spelling accuracy as well. Jonathan stumbled a bit on some of the longer multi-syllabic words in the measure. I will hazard a guess that we are seeing shades of a whole language classroom, that this is an average-to-good reader with a good sight word vocabulary who is not as strong as he could be at decoding. With some instruction on how to tackle multi-syllabic words (i.e. learning about the main types of syllables) and some practice of awareness of phonemes in clusters, he would do better at reading new regular words or non-words such as those on this test that he missed (e.g. personality, experiment, meest). He could also use reinforcement of vowel rules: Jonathan misread "stip" as "step" and "plin" as "pline." For the other three boys, deficits in word reading correspond with poor skills at non-word reading: William, word reading – 37th percentile, non-word reading – 26th percentile; Brian, word reading – 18th percentile, non-word reading – 21st percentile; Andrew, word reading – 10th percentile, non-word reading – 22nd percentile.

From the nature of some of their responses on the tape, I speculate that at least William and Andrew have had remedial efforts, and that Brian perhaps has not had the benefit of as much remedial instruction. Research by Byrne, Fielding-Barnsley, & Ashley (2000) is telling in this regard. In their study, a group of children were put in a phonological awareness intervention program during their kindergarten year. By the end of kindergarten, all had attained a

Table 11.2. *Sample of William's word and non-word reading errors.*

| Target item | → | Response |
|---|---|---|
| overt | → | over |
| glide | → | guild |
| hardly | → | harleyed, hardy |
| flint | → | finelin |
| extent | → | excitin |
| snirk | → | snirink |
| sluke | → | snunk |
| skree | → | streak |
| frip | → | flip |

From performance on the film of portions of the Woodcock-Johnson Psycho-Educational Battery – Revised (Woodcock & Johnson,1990) (i.e. the Word Identification and Word Attack subtests) and from the Test of Word Reading Efficiency (Torgesen *et al.*, 1999).

specified level of awareness, though there were individual differences in the time course of reaching that level: for some it was relatively quick, for others it was a protracted endeavor that spanned much of the year. Interestingly, how long it took to attain the phoneme awareness concepts accounted for additional variance in subsequent reading achievement in addition to that accounted for by the actual level of phoneme awareness attained. Thus, when children are assessed for phoneme awareness and reading prowess, one needs to know the quality and extent of support provided up to that point in order to interpret better the child's current level and future prognosis. Likewise, interpreting patterns among variables such as phoneme awareness and rapid serial naming would be informed by knowledge of individuals' prior training and progress.

### Reviewing reading performance: analyzing errors

To gain further insight into the levels of reading ability for these participants I compiled the errors for each boy and reviewed each set of errors for patterns of difficulty: almost all fell into the categories of errors described here. Jonathan, as noted above, revealed some problems with decoding both novel and familiar multi-syllabic items.

William's errors are listed in Table 11.2. The majority of his errors consist of words or non-words that have clusters with either an /r/ or an /l/ in conjunction with a stop consonant or another phoneme such as /n/. For example, he struggled on "hardly," trying a couple of versions. In the second reading, he

Table 11.3. *Sample of Brian's word and non-word reading errors listed by error type (target → response).*

| Cluster/Sequence | Vowel | Grapheme/Phoneme |
|---|---|---|
| crowd → coward | baf → bafe | jox → jok |
| plot → people | lat → late | |
| shoulder → shouder | fet → fate | |
| sluke → skluk | nup → nape | |
| snirk → skit | yosh → us | |
| | tayed → towel | |
| | loast → lost | |
| Focus on initial syllable | | |
| correctly → crocodile | | |
| personality → persil | | |
| experimental → expertmental | | |

From perfomance on the film of portions of the Woodcock-Johnson Psycho-Eductional Battery – Revised (Woodcock & Johnson, 1990) (i.e. the Word Identification and Work Attack subtests) and the Test of Word Reading Efficiency (Torgesen *et al.*, 1999).

dropped the /l/, producing "hardy." On "flint" he again separated the /l/ as a way to handle the cluster (saying "finelin"). I would surmise that if one gave him a phoneme awareness test with words with clusters, weaknesses in awareness would be detected, or if one assessed his spelling, that similar misrepresentations of clusters might appear. The parallels between phoneme awareness, spelling, and reading are now supported widely in research and need to be appreciated more in clinical application (see Ehri, 2000, and Moats, 1995, for discussion). As mentioned earlier, William's listening comprehension score may well be normal, given his general level of responses during the testing, but this would require verification. If so, his limiting difficulties with reading are shortcomings with phoneme awareness, decoding, and fluency. These could be addressed in parallel, but it would be important to carefully select text to correspond with his decoding skills and to target awareness and decoding skills for clusters and /r/–/l/ distinctions. Experts on fluency recommend that text levels should be selected to correspond with a 95% accuracy rate for the words. (See Meyer & Felton (1999), the *National Reading Panel Progress Report* (2000), and Wolf and Katzir-Cohen (2001) for reviews of techniques to increase fluency.)

Brian also had some difficulties with clusters, as illustrated in the leftmost column in Table 11.3. At the same time, Brian is having more basic problems. In the second column he is misreading the vowels: in a simple consonant–vowel–consonant (CVC) setting (e.g. baf), he is not pronouncing even short vowels correctly. This looks to be about a first to second grade level of decoding, and it calls for instruction on foundation skills. Likewise, the fact that he did somewhat better on real words than non-words suggests that he has memorized a core of sight words, but that he has yet to acquire the decoding skills necessary for even these beginning word patterns. In addition, letter–sound correspondence should be checked for gaps in knowledge. Brian read "jox" as "jok," perhaps showing lack of understanding that the grapheme "x" represents the two phonemes /ks/, and he misread the "y" in "yosh." Brian, too, likely would benefit (in tandem with decoding instruction) from phoneme awareness activities with vowels in words with simple CVC stimuli, and once those are reliably identified by him, from moving on to items with clusters in initial position (CCVC) and then to final clusters (CVCC). Without a solid grasp of which phonemes are occurring in all positions of such spoken words, he will be impeded in his ability to master decoding concepts and to read words encountered for the first time.

It should be recognized that the occurrence of "first-time-seen" words is an ongoing challenge, not merely a hurdle in the early elementary years. Nagy and Anderson (1984) estimate that approximately 10,000 such words are encountered in print per year in the mid-upper elementary grades as the content of text expands. The long words presented in the reading sample are clearly beyond Brian's level of reading achievement. He overloads on long words, either bailing out and guessing after the first syllable or attempting to sound out the letters in an erratic fashion. Of course, without prior grasp of vowel patterns in simple open and closed syllables, among other syllable types, tackling such words will be a frustrating and difficult endeavor. Along with instruction on the basic skills, Brian should be reading for meaning with books selected to reinforce decoding concepts and to increase fluency.

Finally, I will analyze Andrew's performance. Andrew had a spotty pattern leading me to guess that he has had some assistance and despite difficulty retaining what he has been taught, has some islands of decoding knowledge (e.g. reading the "ed" at the end of "fixed" correctly). In Table 11.4, one can see a widespread vowel problem with short vowels, long vowels, and more complex vowel patterns both for real words and for non-words. In contrast to Brian, Andrew does not appear to be as strong at retaining orthographic knowledge of grapheme patterns and words (e.g. not knowing the "ight" pattern in his response to "dright" and confusing "g" with "ng" and "ht" for "th"; not recognizing words he probably has seen numerous times (e.g. work, dear, kind). Andrew also struggles with clusters in words. The first error listed (kind → kid) raises questions about his awareness of nasal consonants following a vowel, particularly when there is a final cluster. This is an extremely common occurrence for beginning readers in the early grades or for disabled readers. A phoneme awareness difficulty with nasalized vowels could be explored and overcome with systematic use of an exercise such as the Say-It-and Move-It procedure of

Table 11.4. *Sample of Andrew's word and non-word reading errors listed by error type (target → response).*

| Cluster/Sequence | Vowel | Grapheme/Phoneme |
|---|---|---|
| kind → kid | fixed → fexed | whole → wol |
| since → sine | since → sine | dright → bringth |
| gusp → goots | gusp → goots | |
| work → worm | pate → pet | |
| fine → find | loast → lost | |
| | sluke → sluk | |
| | din → bine | |
| Focus on Initial Syllable/Phoneme | | Syllabification |
| correctly → cried | | able → ab-el |
| experimental → eraser | | |

From performance on the film of portions of the Woodcock-Johnson Psycho-Educational Battery – Revised (Woodcock & Johnson, 1990) (i.e. the Word Identification and Word Attack subtests) and from the Test of Word Reading Efficiency (Torgesen *et al.*, 1999).

Blachman, Ball, Black, & Tangel (2000; Blachman, this volume). (See Adams, Foorman, Lundberg, & Beeler, 1998, for lists of words that facilitate discovery on listening tasks of the nasal consonant in such words, e.g. proceeding in Say-It-and-Move-It from "pay" to "pain" to "paint.") Such treatment is far more expeditious and more likely to generalize than would be telling a child how to spell individual words of this type.

Andrew also demonstrated some shakiness with "d" and "b" recognition (e.g. saying "bine" for "din," but getting the "b" in "able"), another pattern typical of children at beginning reading levels. (See Liberman, Shankweiler, Orlando, Harris, & Bell-Berti, 1971, and Wolff & Melngailis, 1996, for evidence that reversal errors are not the hallmark of poor readers but may be linked to the phonological similarity of these phonemes, and see Ehri and McCormack, 1998, for a mnemonic that helps children remember the proper orientation of "b" and "d.") Andrew is still learning monosyllabic word patterns and is not able to read multi-syllabic words accurately. With the word "able," he did not recognize the consonant-le syllable pattern preceded by a long vowel, and instead treated "ab" as a closed syllable. With longer words he appears to analyze only the beginning of the word and to rely on guessing. Andrew would be helped by introduction to syllable patterns, learning closed and open syllables first as he masters short and long vowels.

In sum, these four boys portray a continuum of acquisition of the English writing system. They range in the extent of phoneme awareness and decoding knowledge acquired, and their errors reveal much about what concepts they have learned and which require clear, systematic instruction. One can see that as decoding and sight recognition abilities increase, so does reading speed on isolated words. In a formal test of text fluency, a similar pattern would probably be observed, though text fluency places some additional reading demands. The progression of skills observed here aligns with current understanding of the development of word recognition (e.g. Ehri & McCormack, 1998), phoneme awareness (e.g. Goswami, 2002; Torgesen, this volume; Torgesen & Mathes, 1998, 2000), and spelling abilities (e.g. Moats, 1995). In my opinion, the order-liness of their error patterns underscores the value of this kind of error analysis for determining instructional levels both for normal and reading-disabled children. Research by Morris, Blanton, Blanton, Nowacek, and Perney (1995) has shown, for example, that spelling instruction is most effective if provided at the child's level of spelling development (see Moats, 1995, for discussion). Like-wise, as summarized in the report of the National Reading Panel (2000), much research supports the superiority of systematic decoding instruction over inci-dental decoding lessons or predominantly meaning-based approaches. Regard-less of the presence of other potential problems for some of these boys or whether additional areas require treatment, analysis of their reading errors informs us about where each is in the process of learning to read and where each would profit from further instruction. The pattern of development in the four children conforms with the findings of the past thirty years: learning the phonological structure of the writing system, both in terms of awareness of the phonemic composition of spoken words and in terms of acquisition of the code mapping phonemes to print, is central to reading success.

## Review of rapid serial naming performance

The final area to be discussed concerns the rapid serial naming performance of the four boys. Before commenting on the patterns observed, I want to take a moment to address research and terminology issues that are relevant. In rapid serial naming tasks, large arrays of highly familiar stimuli are presented, and the child is asked to name the items in the array as rapidly as possible. For example, in the Denckla and Rudel (1976) naming measures, each 5 × 10 matrix con-tains ten occurrences, in random order, of five items (pictured objects, colored patches, letters, or digits). The focus in research has been on individual differ-ences in the speed with which children name the set of stimuli. Over the past two decades a large body of evidence has shown that speed of naming famil-iar visual symbols is often associated with reading development (e.g. Badian, 1993; Blachman, 1984, this volume; Bowers, 1995; Denckla & Rudel, 1976; Wolf, Bally, & Morris, 1986; Wolf & Ashby, this volume). Although rapid serial naming is a fairly good early predictor of reading achievement in kindergarten to second grade, it appears to be even more useful and important for identifying which poor readers are likely to make the slowest progress over subsequent years, even with appropriate educational intervention (e.g. Korhonen, 1991; Levy, Bourassa, & Horn, 1999; Lovett, Steinbach, & Frijters, 2000; Meyer, Wood, Hart, & Felton, 1998; Scarborough, 1998).

A further question regarding rapid serial naming has been whether slow naming reflects a cognitive weakness common to or separate from that responsible for deficits in phonological awareness and decoding. Some researchers have proposed that naming speed is associated with phonological awareness and reading skill because all depend on phonological coding (e.g. Baddeley, 1986; Elbro, 1996; Shankweiler, 1999; Share, 1995; Wagner & Torgesen, 1987). An alternative view is that rapid naming taps other non-phonological processes that are important in reading development, such as speed of processing or sensitivity to temporally ordered information (e.g. Wolf, 1997; Wolf & Ashby, this volume; Wolf, Bowers, & Biddle, 2000; Wolf & Katzir-Cohen, 2001). Full discussion of the evidence on rapid serial naming goes beyond the scope of this paper. (For several relevant articles, see the *Journal of Learning Disabilities*, July/August 2000, and Manis, Seidenberg, & Doi, 1999.) However, in future work on this topic it will be important for researchers to define constructs carefully and consistently.

### *Defining phonological processing*

Within the field, one term in particular – phonological processing – has been used to mean many different things (Brady, 2004; Scarborough & Brady, 2002). Because this construct is central to the debate about the basis of rapid serial naming deficits, I want to briefly differentiate between the different current uses of the term, identifying three cognitive domains. One domain pertains to *reading* itself: knowledge of grapheme–phoneme correspondences, decoding accuracy, decoding speed, text fluency, and comprehension. The term phonological processing has been applied to the first three listed – those reading tasks more narrowly tapping knowledge of the code. A second domain concerns *metaphonological* processes, the ability to reflect on the phonological structures in *spoken* words including phonological sensitivity to larger and more salient phonological entities such as rhyme and alliteration and more fine-grained phonemic awareness (i.e. complete awareness of the individual phonemes in spoken words). In this domain, "phonological processing" has been used to describe the cognitive demands of both phonological sensitivity and/or phonemic awareness. The third domain refers to hypothesized processing *below conscious awareness* entailing *use of a phonological code*. Perception of the phonemes in words, maintenance of phonological patterns in verbal working memory, motor planning for speaking, and lexical storage and retrieval of the phonological details of words are some of the instances when such "phonological processes" occur. This level, at the heart of language use, serves both reading and phonological awareness tasks, but those domains have additional and unique processing components. At the level of underlying phonological processing, researchers have also examined the extent of shared variance among tasks hypothesized to tap this level. Mixed findings have been obtained, as well as shifts in the patterns observed as reading progresses (e.g. Wagner, Torgesen, Laughon, Simmons, & Rashotte, 1993; Wagner, Torgesen, & Rashotte, 1994). The interactions between the three broad areas is a further issue: for example, reciprocal relations between phonological awareness and reading have been documented (e.g. Perfetti, Beck, Bell, & Hughes, 1987), and interactions between phoneme awareness and speech perception have also been studied (see Brady, 1997, for discussion).

Important distinctions between these three levels are obscured either by lumping levels (e.g. labeling phoneme awareness and decoding measures jointly as "phonological processes") or by using the term "phonological processing" to refer variably to any of the three domains. I would argue that the term "phonological process" most aptly fits the third arena, underlying processing involving a phonological code. In any case, without agreement in the field about how the term should be used, it is often difficult in individual studies or published reports to determine what is being described and assumed about phonological processing. This problem has particularly complicated discussion of two issues about rapid serial naming: (1) whether rapid naming, a task involving underlying phonological processes, taps shared and/or unique variance with phoneme awareness and decoding measures; and (2) whether deficits in rapid serial naming stem from weaknesses related to the phonological or non-phonological requirements of the task.

### Double deficit hypothesis

These concerns apply to the double deficit theory of reading difficulties, a proposal that two deficits, one in phoneme awareness and decoding and one in rapid naming speed, are independent and may occur singly or in combination (e.g. Wolf et al., 2000; Wolf & Ashby, this volume; Wolf & Katzir-Cohen, 2001). When both deficits are present, i.e. the double deficit, numerous studies report worse reading performance (e.g. Lovett et al., 2000; Wolf & Bowers, 1999), although recent scrutiny of the consequences of grouping children based on dual deficits indicates that the greater severity of reading impairment found in children with impairments in both could be due in part to a statistical artifact (Schatschneider, Carlson, Francis, Foorman, & Fletcher, 2002). Maryanne Wolf and her co-authors, major proponents of the double deficit theory, have suggested that the difficulties evident on rapid naming tasks arise from non-phonological factors associated with speed of processing (Wolf, 1997; Wolf et al., 2000). While it is true that rapid serial naming correlates strongly with speeded reading tasks (e.g. Bowers, 1993, 1995; Bowers & Swanson, 1991) and with measures of orthographic knowledge (Manis *et al.*, 1999; Manis, Doi, & Bhadha, 2000), this may reflect the similarities in the verbal and orthographic demands of the tasks rather than implicating non-phonological components per se.

One study by Scarborough and Domgaard (1998) that was designed to explore the relationship between reading and rapid serial naming (RSN) speaks to this issue. With a sample of 56 third graders, numerous naming matrices and other measures were administered to test a host of hypotheses about the bases of reading group differences in RSN. Pertinent to this discussion, four of the hypotheses tested were that reading group effects in RSN stem from differences in domain-general processing speed, in visual scanning, in visual item identification, or in speech production. Of these four, only the last hypothesis was supported. Low, non-significant correlations were obtained between rapid serial naming performance with letter or digit arrays and measures thought to tap domain-general processing speed (i.e the Wechsler Intelligence Scale for Children Coding and Doehring (1968) Underlining tasks). Also, when comparing across the various rapid serial naming arrays, reading group differences were comparable regardless of whether participants were asked to scan an array forwards or backwards (testing visual scanning), or whether the items were faint and visually similar or presented clearly with a visually distinct letter set (testing visual identification). In contrast, when arrays differed in speech production demands, reading group differences were notably absent for those in which the speech production demands were minimal (i.e. when "yes/no" responses were given in arrays asking about each item. "Is it an H?" or "Is it lower case?") and were present for those requiring spoken naming of the items. Thus, when the need to formulate and produce the phonological strings constituting the names of the items was eliminated, reading-group effects disappeared. This study suggests that at least three non-phonological accounts (general processing speed, visual scanning, and visual identification) are not the basis for poor rapid serial naming. Instead, the results link reading group differences in rapid serial naming with speech production, which is intrinsically phonological in nature.

Given results such as those obtained by Scarborough and Domgaard (1998), I am concerned that the use of "phonological processes" by Wolf and her colleagues to refer jointly to phoneme awareness and/or decoding, but not to rapid serial naming, is potentially misleading. This usage may contribute to the likelihood in the field that the labels will be interpreted as explanations, and it fails to preserve distinctions between the metaphonological and reading domains. It would be preferable in my opinion to refer to phoneme awareness and decoding measures as such rather than as "phonological processes," and to pursue further research to explore the basis of the interesting and significant naming speed deficits in some poor readers.

## The four boys

With respect to the four boys studied in the present context, a summary of their rapid serial naming performance is presented in the Appendix. Jonathan, William, and Brian are all at least slightly below the mean for their age in speed of rapid serial naming, though Jonathan and Brian are within one standard deviation of the mean on most of the naming tasks. Because RSN performance is not strongly linked with reading performance for good readers, as noted above, the fact that Jonathan was not above average on this measure was not particularly surprising. By double-deficit categorization, neither Jonathan nor Brian would be labeled as having a naming speed deficit. William was somewhat slower, particularly on the color-naming and number-naming measures that were two standard deviations below the mean for this age group. Andrew, a clear outlier, was markedly slow on all of the RSN tasks, though his slowest time was for object naming (127 seconds to name 50 items) and his fastest was for letter naming (67 seconds to name 50 items).

With this sample of four cases, it is difficult to surmise the role of rapid naming deficits in their reading difficulties, or, for the boys with reading problems, their remedial outlook. Compatible with prior studies of reading-disabled children, Andrew, the most impaired reader with the poorest prognosis, is also the child with striking difficulties in naming. Yet, whether this characteristic is tied strictly to his reading deficits or to broader language difficulties remains a question. There has been research reporting slower rapid naming times for language-impaired children (e.g. Katz, Curtiss, & Tallal, 1992), as well as for reading-disabled children. Also, the Scarborough and Domgaard (1998) study described earlier found a correlation between object naming and IQ-related variables (i.e. vocabulary knowledge and decision speed), while letter naming corresponded more closely with phonological variables such as articulatory speed. Given that Andrew's object naming score was most impaired, this again may indicate broader deficits that will impede his progress.

William's weaknesses in naming may suggest that he will need relatively greater amounts of practice and instruction to build his reading skills than would children at his level of reading development who do better at naming. While he is a stronger reader at this time than is Brian, William may also have had more remedial assistance, as mentioned earlier. The lack of naming problems for Brian may mean that were he given the reading instruction he needs, he would respond well.

### Cycle of learning in reading acquisition

In considering these questions, I want to address a dichotomy emerging in the literature between accuracy of phoneme awareness/decoding and speed/fluency of reading. While it is possible to find cases for whom one difficulty or the other is prominent, building accuracy and automaticity applies to each step in learning to read, as Barbara Wise (2001) has articulated. That is, rather than viewing automaticity in reading as an endpoint in reading development, Wise conceptualizes building automaticity for each aspect of learning to read. Accordingly, she recommends a cycle of learning for teachers and children: "The cycle begins with efficiently guided discovery of principles, then practice using the principles to read and spell items to competence and to fluent mastery (with accuracy and smoothness), and only then to do three steps aimed specifically at transfer: 1) speeded practice of mastered skills until times no longer decrease, 2) application of all skills in contextualized reading and writing, and 3) encouragement and monitoring of independent transfer of the skills to new material beyond the teaching situation." This cycle of acquiring a concept, becoming reliably accurate at it, and then attaining proficiency through practice is applied by Wise to every component of reading acquisition. (For analysis of its applicability to other kinds of learning, see Fischer, 1980; Fischer, Yan, & Stewart, 2003.) Thus a child in the beginning stages of learning to read must become facile at recognizing phonemes in spoken words, at knowing letter names and sounds, at reading monosyllabic words that are closed syllables, and so forth. By this view, lack of "fluency" will not be evident simply in the later stages of reading development, but may occur all along for a child experiencing difficulty learning to read.

In the Byrne *et al.* (2000) study discussed earlier, the children who were slower to acquire phoneme awareness in kindergarten were also slower at learning to read in the elementary years. Though assessment of phoneme awareness is not measured by speed of responding, the duration of time required to achieve "fluent mastery with accuracy and smoothness" of phoneme awareness was predictive of later reading proficiency. This type of analysis opens a new and exciting way to study the extent of overlap between acquisition of accurate knowledge of phonemic and orthographic concepts and the progressive development of automatic and fluent reading abilities.

The connection between the development of accuracy and of rate skills in reading also is evident in remediation studies. When Lovett *et al.* (2000) classified children with reading difficulties into the three subgroups of the double deficit framework, they found that children in all three groups were significantly impaired on all dimensions of reading, spelling, and comprehension skill, as well as in basic letter–sound knowledge. Correspondingly, children in all three groups benefited from either of two approaches to remedial instruction that targeted word reading accuracy (working on either phoneme awareness and decoding skills or word identification strategies). Similarly, Levy *et al.* (1999) reported that a group of children with rapid serial naming speed and a group with slow naming speed both made the best gains with reading instruction that focused at the level of the phoneme. Though more research is needed to explore the basis and consequences of slow serial naming, at this point the need for explicit instruction in phonics concepts is supported for all struggling readers, apparently regardless of their status of having a single or double deficit.

## Closing remarks

Examination of the reading abilities of the four boys revealed a range of reading acquisition from very early levels to successful mastery of grade-appropriate material. A general correspondence was observed between speed and accuracy measures of reading and between word and non-word reading skills. The latter outcome conforms with the large body of evidence finding that the extent of decoding skills demonstrated on non-word tasks is highly correlated with ability to read real-word stimuli, including exception words (e.g. Gough & Walsh, 1991; Tunmer & Chapman, 1998). Analysis of the boys' errors in terms of decoding knowledge showed a predictable progression from the need for basic concepts in the poorest reader to more advanced decoding concepts in the best reader. Both the hints of particular problems in phoneme awareness (e.g. difficulty identifying vowels or isolating the phonemes in clusters) and the indications of deficits in decoding (e.g. difficulties with the code for vowels, lack of understanding of syllabification rules) provide clear markers for what focus of instruction is needed for the four boys. It would be optimal to incorporate Wise's (2001) cycle of learning to assist each child in mastering not only accurate but fast application of skills as they advance their reading abilities. From an educational perspective, the informal analyses of the boys' reading errors in the film were among the most informative, and point out the value of using such information to determine individual interventions for all students encountering reading difficulties. Assessment measures specifically designed to identify which specific skills have been mastered and those in need of further instruction are particularly helpful for guiding instruction (e.g. Bear, Invernizzi, Templeton, & Johnston, 2004; Ganske, 2000, Richardson & DiBenedetto, 1985).

The additional information on rapid serial naming gives evidence most clearly for Andrew of significant difficulties with naming. In combination with his weaknesses in word identification, his limited decoding skills, and some indications of more extensive deficits in language and cognition, this child has the poorest prognosis. Yet, as Andrew illustrated, the interpretation of test data and student performance is hampered unless one knows about the educational history of a child and his/her broader profile of strengths and weaknesses.

Early proponents of phonological accounts of reading development and of reading difficulties hypothesized that deficits for poor readers are not limited to phoneme awareness and to decoding, but that they are related to more fundamental functions of the underlying phonological system (e.g. Liberman &

Shankweiler, 1985; Liberman *et al.*, 1971). Current findings such as those by Scarborough and Domgaard (1998) continue to support this position. (For a sample of the literature on phonological factors in reading, also see Blachman, 1997; Brady, 1997; Brady & Shankweiler, 1991; Catts, Fey, Zhang, & Tomblin, 1999; Elbro, 1996; Tunmer & Hoover, 1992; and Vellutino, Scanlon, Small, & Tanzman, 1991.) Nonetheless, the challenge remains to fully understand the extent to which weaknesses in rapid serial naming evidence derive from weaknesses in the phonological system or from other factors. To move forward in unveiling the sources of individual differences in reading abilities, it will be important to define constructs clearly and to test the validity of those constructs carefully. A close collaboration among experts in education, psychology, and neuroscience will help ensure that these conditions are met and will facilitate discovery of the brain bases of learning disorders.

## REFERENCES

Adams, M. J., Foorman, B. R., Lundberg, I. & Beeler, T. (1998). *Phoneme awareness in young children.* Baltimore, MD: Paul H. Brookes.
Baddeley, A. (1986). *Working memory.* New York: Oxford University Press.
Badian, N. (1993). Phonemic awareness, naming, visual symbol processing, and reading. *Reading and Writing: An Inter-disciplinary Journal,* 5, 87–100.
Bear, D. R., Invernizzi, M., Templeton, S. & Johnston, F. (2004). *Words their way: Word study for phonics, vocabulary and spelling instruction.* Upper Saddle River, NJ: Pearson/Merrill Prentice Hall.
Blachman, B. A. (1984). Relationship of rapid naming ability and language analysis skills to kindergarten and first-grade reading achievement. *Journal of Educational Psychology,* 76, 610–22.
Blachman, B. A. (ed.) (1997). *Foundations of reading acquisition and dyslexia: Implications for early intervention.* Mahwah, NJ: Lawrence Erlbaum Associates.
Blachman, B. A., Ball, E. W., Black, R. & Tangel, D. M. (2000). *Road to the code: A phonological awareness program for young children.* Baltimore, MD: Paul H. Brookes.
Bowers, P. G. (1993). Text reading rereading: Predictors of fluency beyond word recognition. *Journal of Reading Behavior,* 25, 133–53.
Bowers, P. G. (1995). Tracing symbol naming speed's unique contributions to reading disabilities over time. *Reading and Writing: An Interdisciplinary Journal,* 7, 189–216.
Bowers, P. G. & Swanson, L. B. (1991). Naming speed deficits in reading disability: Multiple measures of a singular process. *Journal of Experimental Child Psychology,* 51, 195–219.
Brady, S. (1997). Ability to encode phonological representations: An underlying problem for poor readers. In B. Blachman (ed.), *Foundations of reading acquisition and dyslexia: Implications for early intervention.* Mahwah, NJ: Lawrence Erlbaum Associates.

Brady, S. (2004). Terminology matters: Sorting out the 'Phon' words in dyslexia. In M. Joshi (ed.), *Myths, misconceptions, and some practical applications*. Baltimore, MD: International Dyslexia Association.

Brady, S. & Shankweiler, D. (eds) (1991). *Phonological processes in literacy: A tribute to Isabelle Y. Liberman*. Hillsdale, NJ: Lawrence Erlbaum Associates.

Byrne, B., Fielding-Barnsley, R. & Ashley, L. (2000). Effects of pre-school phoneme identity training after six years: Average benefits but no vaccination effects. *Journal of Educational Psychology*, 92, 659–67.

Catts, H., Fey, M., Zhang, X. & Tomblin, J. B. (1999). Language basis of reading and reading disabilities: Evidence from a longitudinal investigation. *Scientific Studies of Reading*, 3(4), 331–61.

Denckla, M. & Rudel, R. G. (1976). Rapid "automatized" naming (RAN): Dyslexia differentiated from other learning disabilities. *Neuropsychologia*, 14, 471–9.

Doehring, D. (1968). *Patterns of impairment in specific reading disability*. Bloomington IN: Indiana University Press.

Ehri, L. (2000). Learning to read and learning to spell: Two sides of a coin. *Topics in Language Disorders*, 20(3), 19–36.

Ehri, L. & McCormick, S. (1998). Phases of word learning: Implications for instruction with delayed and disabled readers. *Reading and Writing Quarterly: Overcoming Learning Difficulties*, 14, 135–63.

Elbro, C. (1996). Early linguistic abilities and reading development: A review and a hypothesis about underlying differences in distinctness of phonological representations of lexical items. *Reading and Writing: An Interdisciplinary Journal*, 8, 453–85.

Fischer, K. W. (1980). Learning and problem solving as the development of organized behavior. *Journal of Structural Learning*, 6, 253–67.

Fischer, K. W., Yan, Z. & Stewart, J. (2003). Adult cognitive development: Dynamics in the developmental web. In J. Valsiner & K. Connolly (eds), *Handbook of developmental psychology*, 491–516. Thousand Oaks, CA: Sage.

Ganske, K. (2000). *Word journeys: Assessment-guided phonics, spelling, and vocabulary instruction*. New York: The Guilford Press.

Goswami, U. (2002). Phonology, reading development and dyslexia: A cross-linguistic perspective. *Annals of Dyslexia*, 52, 1–23.

Gough, P. B. & Walsh, M. A. (1991). Chinese, Phoenicians, and the orthographic cipher of English. In Brady, S. A. and D. P. Shankweiler (eds), *Phonological processes in literacy: A tribute to Isabelle Y. Liberman*, 199–210. Mahwah, NJ: Lawrence Erlbaum Associates.

Katz, W., Curtiss, S. & Tallal, P. (1992). Rapid automatized naming and gesture by normal and language-impaired children. *Brain and Language*, 43, 623–41.

Korhonen, T. T. (1991). Neuropsychological stability and prognosis of subgroups of children with learning disabilities. *Journal of Learning Disabilities*, 24, 48–57.

Levy, B. A., Bourassa, D. C. & Horn, C. (1999). Fast and slow namers: Benefits of segmentation and whole word training. *Journal of Experimental Child Psychology*, 71, 45–61.

Liberman I. Y. & Shankweiler, D. P. (1985). Phonology and the problems of learning to read and write. *Remedial and Special Education*, 6, 8–17.

Liberman, I. Y., Shankweiler, D. P., Orlando, C., Harris, K. & Bell-Berti, F. (1971). Letter confusions and reversals of sequence in the beginning reader: Implications for Orton's theory of developmental dyslexia. *Cortex*, 7, 127–42.

Lovett, M. W., Steinbach, K. A. & Frijters, J. C. (2000). Remediating the core deficits of developmental reading disbility: A double-deficit perspective. *Journal of Learning Disabilities*, 33, 334–58.

Manis, F. F., Doi, L. M. & Bhadha, B. (2000). Naming speed, phonological awareness, and orthographic knowledge in second graders. *Journal of Learning Disabilities*, 33, 325–33.

Manis, F. R., Seidenberg, M. S. & Doi, L. M. (1999). See Dick RAN: Rapid naming and the longitudinal predication of reading subskills in first and second graders. *Scientific Studies of Reading*, 3(2), 129–57.

Meyer, M. & Felton, R. H. (1999). Repeated reading to enhance fluency: Old aproaches and new directions. *Annals of Dyslexia*, 49, 283–307.

Meyer, M., Wood, F. B., Hart, L. A. & Felton, R. H. (1998). The selective predictive values in rapid automatized naming within poor readers. *Journal of Learning Disabilities*, 31, 106–117.

Moats, L. (1995). *Spelling development, disability, and instruction*. Baltimore: York Press.

Morris, D., Blanton, L., Blanton, W. E., Nowacek, J. & Perney, J. (1995). Teaching low-spellers at their "instructional level." *The Elementary School Journal*, 96, 163–77.

Nagy, W. E. & Anderson, R. C. (1984). How many words are there in printed school English? *Reading Research Quarterly*, 19, 304–330.

*National Reading Panel Progress Report* (2000). www.nationalreadingpanel.org.

Perfetti, C. A., Beck, L., Bell, L. & Hughes, C. (1987). Phonemic knowledge and learning to read are reciprocal: A longitudinal study of first grade children. *Merrill Palmer Quarterly*, 33, 283–319.

Richardson, E. & DiBenedetto, B. (1985). *Decoding Skills Test*. Los Angeles: Western Psychological Services.

Robertson, C. & Salter, W. (1997). *The Phonological Awareness Test*. East Moline, IL: LinguiSystems, Inc.

Scarborough, H. S. (1998). Predicting the future achievement of second graders with reading disabilities: Contributions of phonemic awareness, verbal memory, rapid naming, and IQ. *Annals of Dyslexia*, 48, 115–36.

Scarborough, H. S. & Brady, S. A. (2002). Toward a common terminology for talking about speech and reading: A glossary of the "Phon" words and some related terms. *Journal of Literacy Resarch*, 34, 299–334.

Scarborough, H. S. & Domgaard, R. M. (1998). An exploration of the relationship between reading and rapid serial naming speed. A presentation at the annual conference for the Society for the Scientific Study of Reading, San Diego, CA, April, 1988.

Schatschneider, C., Carlson, C., Francis, D., Foorman, B. & Fletcher, J. (2002). Relationship of rapid automatized naming and phonological awareness in early reading development: Implications for the double-deficit hypothesis. *Journal of Learning Disabilities*, 35, 245–56.

Shankweiler, D. (1999). Words to meanings. *Scientific Studies of Reading*, 3(2), 113–27.

Share, D. L. (1995). Phonological recoding and self-teaching: Sine qua non of reading acquisition. *Cognition*, 55, 151–218.

Siegel, L. S. (1999). Issues in the definition and diagnosis of learning disabilities: A perspective on Guckenberger v. Boston University. *Journal of Learning Disabilities*, 32, 304–319.

Stanovich, K. E. (1999). The sociopsychometrics of learning disabilities. *Journal of Learning Disabilities*, 32, 350–61.

Torgesen, J. K. & Mathes, P. (1998). What every teacher should know about phonological awareness. *Reading research anthology: The Why? of reading instruction*. Novato, CA: Arena Press.

Torgesen, J. K. & Mathes, P. (2000). *A basic guide to understanding, assessing, and teaching phonological awareness*. Austin, TX: PRO-ED Publishing, Inc.

Torgesen, J. K., Wagner, R. K. & Rashotte, C. A. (1999). *Test of Word Reading Efficiency*. Austin, TX: PRO-ED Publishing, Inc.

Tunmer, W. E. & Chapman, J. W. (1998). Language prediction skill, phonological reading ability, and beginning reading. In C. Hulme & R. M. Joshi (eds), *Reading and spelling: Development and disorders*, 33–67. Mahwah, NJ: Lawrence Erlbaum Associates.

Tunmer, W. E. & Hoover, W. A. (1992). Cognitive and linguistic factors in learning to read. In P. Gough, L. Ehri & R. Treiman (eds), *Reading Acquisition*, 175–214. Hillsdale, NJ: Lawrence Erlbaum Associates.

Vellutino, F. R., Scanlon, D. M., Small, S. G. & Tanzman, M. S. (1991). The linguistic bases of reading ability: Converting written to oral language. *Text*, 11, 99–133.

Wagner, R. K. & Torgesen, J. (1987). The nature of phonological processing and its causal role in the acquisition of reading skills. *Psychological Bulletin*, 101, 192–212.

Wagner, R. K., Torgesen, J. K., Laughon, P., Simmons, K. & Rashotte, C. A. (1993). Development of young readers' phonological processing abilities. *Journal of Educational Psychology*, 85, 83–103.

Wagner, R. K., Torgesen, J. K. & Rashotte, C. A. (1994). Development of reading-related phonological processing abilities: New evidence of bi-directional causality from a latent variable longitudinal study. *Developmental Psychology*, 30, 73–87.

Wagner, R. K., Torgesen, J. K. & Rashotte, C. A. (1999). *Comprehensive Test of Phonological Processes*. Austin, TX: PRO-ED Publishing, Inc.

Wiederholt, J. L. & Bryant, B. R. (1992). *Gray Oral Reading Test – Third Edition*. Austin, TX: Pro-ed.

Wise, B. (2001). The indomitable dinosaur builder (and how she overcame her phonological deficit and learned to read instructions and other things). *Journal of Special Education*, 35(3), 134–44.

Wolf, M. (1997). A provisional, integrative account of phonological and naming-speed deficits in dyslexia: Implications for diagnosis and intervention. In B. Blachman (ed.), *Foundations of reading acquisition and dyslexia: Implications for early intervention*. Mahwah, NJ: Erlbaum Associates.

Wolf, M., Bally, H. & Morris, R. (1986). Automaticity, retrieval processes and reading: A longitudinal study in average and impaired readers. *Child Development*, 57, 988–1000.

Wolf, M. & Bowers, P. G. (1999). The "double-deficit hypothesis" for the developmental dyslexias. *Journal of Educational Psychology*, 91, 1–24.

Wolf, M., Bowers, P. G. & Biddle, K. (2000). Naming-speed processes, timing, and reading: A conceptual review. *Journal of Learning Disabilities*, 33, 387–407.

Wolf, M. & Katzir-Cohen, T. (2001). Reading fluency and its intervention. *Scientific Studies of Reading*, 5, 211–39.

Wolff, P. H. & Melngailis, I. (1996). Reversing letters and reading transformed text in dyslexia: A reassessment. *Reading and Writing: An Interdisciplinary Journal*, 8, 341–55.

Woodcock, R. W. & Johnson, M. B. (1990). *Woodcock-Johnson Psycho-Educational Battery – Revised*. Allen, TX: DLM.

# 12    First impressions: What four readers can teach us

*Benita A. Blachman*

*Overview:* Watching real children read reminds us what we do and do not yet understand about the reading process, especially how little is known about the underlying processing deficits that cause dyslexic behavioral patterns. To ground this point, Blachman compares the three dyslexic readers to Jonathan, an effective reader, and stresses the relation between accuracy and fluency in the production of functional reading. While much neuropsychological research focuses on the processes underlying reading accuracy, methods to remediate poor fluency need attention in research and practice (see Wolf and Ashby, this volume). From an educational perspective, children must combine accuracy and fluency in order to improve their comprehension and their comfort with reading.     *The Editors*

What do you see when you watch four young boys read? To prepare for the conference on which this volume is based, speakers were asked, essentially, to reflect on this question. We were asked to view a videotape of four 9-year-old boys, one typical reader and three poor readers, and use the profiles of these children as the centerpiece for our remarks. The videotape was divided into two sections, each showing the children engaged in a series of diagnostic tests, and speakers were asked to respond to one section or the other. I was asked to respond to the section that included measures of rapid naming (Denckla & Rudel, 1976) and measures of isolated word reading (reading words and non-words from lists) (*Test of Word Reading Efficiency*, Torgesen, Wagner, & Rashotte, 1999; *The Woodcock-Johnson Psycho-Educational Battery–Revised*, Woodcock & Johnson, 1989). As the reader will soon find out, I often cheated and included observations from the paragraph-reading measure (*Gray Oral Reading Tests*, Wiederholt & Bryant, 1992) that was not part of my assignment.

Despite the fact that I, like many of the conference participants, have had extensive experience with reading-disabled children exactly the age of the children in the videotapes, I was initially uncomfortable with the task at hand. Part of the challenge came from not having all the data one might have liked on these four boys. For example, although William, Brian, and Andrew, the three struggling readers, all exhibited difficulty decoding non-words, a behavior indicative

217

of their difficulty dealing with the phonology (e.g. Rack, Snowling, & Olson, 1992), there were no spelling or purely phonological processing measures (such as a phoneme deletion task) to help unpack this core difficulty (for reviews of the role of phonological processing in reading see, for example, Blachman, 1997, 2000; Brady & Shankweiler, 1991; Brady, this volume; Goswami, 2002; Liberman & Shankweiler, 1985, 1991; Shankweiler, 1999; Stanovich, 1988; Wagner & Torgesen, 1987, this volume; Wagner *et al.*, 1997). As I got further into the task of writing about these boys, I realized that my discomfort came as much from the realization of how much we still have to learn to help children like Andrew, the most disabled of the three poor readers, as it did from the data I wanted but didn't have access to. What we were shown on the videotape forced us to confront the painful reality that children with reading disabilities experience on a daily basis.

I will proceed first with a few remarks based on an initial viewing of the videotape, and then I will go into more detail about the four boys, each in turn. Although my observations overlapped with others at the conference, I think by sharing our points of agreement and disagreement the real complexity of the reading problem emerges. The videotape starts with an introductory dialogue between Dr Jane Bernstein and each of the boys, followed by diagnostic assessments of the children's language, reading, and visuomotor skills. What struck me during the introductory dialogue with the boys – before I heard them name the first object or read the first word – was that for Jonathan, a child without a reading disability, and for William, a child who has had some difficulty in reading, words roll off the tongue. The ease with which Jonathan and William could articulate their strengths and the pleasure that accompanied the telling was in striking contrast to Brian, who appeared reticent and seemed at a loss for words, and Andrew, whose lack of fluency and odd intonation were evident even in his brief retelling of a story at the beginning of the videotape.

## The boys

### Jonathan

I appreciated having the profile of a typical reader, Jonathan, as an anchor in this exercise. It is very easy when working with children with disabilities to focus on the disability and lose sight of where a child's behavior falls within the framework of typical development. Watching Jonathan and other average readers should serve as a reminder of the relative ease with which many children learn to read. This ease is apparent not only when watching them read real words that may have been seen before in print, but also when watching them read non-words, or words that we know children have never been exposed to – a point I will revisit shortly.

The diagnostic battery presented on the videotape begins for each child with the rapid automatized naming tasks (RAN) (Denckla & Rudel, 1976). For each of the RAN tasks (color, letter, and object conditions are shown in the videotape), children are shown a chart that consists of 50 stimuli (either colors, letters, or objects) made up of 5 different items displayed in random order over 5 rows of 10 items per row. Children are asked to name the items on the chart as rapidly as possible. Children with reading disabilities, as a group, are often slower at naming items on such tasks (for a review see Wolf, 1991; and also Brady, this volume; and Wolf & Ashby, this volume). Performance on the RAN tasks appeared relatively effortless for Jonathan, however, just as one might expect.

The next four tasks in the battery include reading lists of real words and lists of non-words in untimed (Woodcock & Johnson, 1989) and timed conditions (Torgesen, Wagner, & Rashotte, 1999). Jonathan's reading of real words, both untimed and timed, was comfortable, deliberate, but steady. He started to falter slightly only when confronted with a less familiar multi-syllable word, such as "experiment," which although decoded accurately, was pronounced with a pause between the first two syllables. When reading non-words, Jonathan could decode words never seen before, such as "thrept," and faltered rarely in his attempts at pronunciation. I was particularly interested in one slip of the tongue that Jonathan made during *timed* reading of non-words, specifically when Jonathan read the word "plin" as "pline." This error was of special interest because around the time I viewed the videotape I had just reviewed the protocols of third grade boys with reading disabilities for a research project I was working on (Blachman *et al.*, 2004) and had been struck by the frequency with which they made such errors on even *untimed* tests of real word reading (e.g. reading "hat" as "hate"). I was interested to see what it would take to get a typical reader like Jonathan to make even one such error. It took the most stressful word reading condition, timed reading of non-words, to get Jonathan to make this error, despite the fact that the list included 13 opportunities to do so. Jonathan is a good example of a typical reader, one who has most likely had no instruction reading non-words, yet who demonstrates a propensity for, as Linnea Ehri (1997) put it, using spellings as "phonemic maps that lay out the pronunciations of words visually" (p. 171).

When listening to Jonathan carefully enunciating each sound as he reads the word "thrept," one is reminded of the advantage Jonathan will have in his reading by being able to read words never seen before in print. Although some in the reading community have suggested that "skill in reading involves not greater precision, but more accurate first guesses" (Goodman, 1976, p. 504, as reported in Share & Stanovich, 1995), Jonathan's fluency with non-words calls these observations into question, as do virtually all scientific studies that have addressed the value of using context to guess the pronunciation of unknown words (e.g. Nicholson, 1991; Perfetti, 1985; Rayner, 1997; Share & Stanovich,

1995; Stanovich, 1994). Jonathan will have little need to guess. In contrast to many poor readers, Jonathan will be less likely to hesitate in the absence of pictures, or even in the absence of background knowledge on a given topic, because he can rely on the print to access the phonology of the word. It is the poor readers, unfortunately, who are forced to guess. For Jonathan, the self-teaching hypothesis outlined by Share & Stanovich (1995) appears to be working:

> According to the self-teaching hypothesis, each successful decoding encounter with an unfamiliar word provides an opportunity to acquire the word-specific orthographic information that is the foundation of skilled word recognition and spelling. In this way, phonological recoding [measured, for example, by reading non-words] acts as a self-teaching mechanism or built-in teacher enabling a child to independently develop knowledge of specific word spellings and more general knowledge of orthographic conventions. . . . Phonological recoding may be the principal means by which the learner attains word recognition proficiency. (p. 18)

As I indicated at the beginning of this essay, I cheated a bit by watching the section of the videotape that showed each boy reading a paragraph. I thought it was essential to developing reasonable hypotheses about each child to get a glimpse of how each child was trying to put it all together in text-based reading. Although Jonathan was a bit monotone – perhaps not showing the interest in the passage a more engaging storyline might have elicited – when he got to direct quotations, he started to read with expression. He tried to make the print come alive, and in so doing allowed us to see that he understood the purpose of this endeavor – namely, to get meaning from the text.

### William

The next child seen on the tape was William. William is an engaging youngster who brings a smile to your face with his infectious laugh. Although I noticed initially that William was slower than our typical reader on his first RAN task – naming colors – that observation was short-lived. During the next RAN tasks, William settled into a rhythm that was not much slower than our typical reader. As I watched William read real words, both untimed and timed, he struck me as a child who has had some success remembering words as whole units and who has acquired a substantial sight vocabulary, as evidenced by his accurate reading of words such as "shoulder" and "island." With regard to non-words, on both tests, untimed and timed, he made a variety of errors such as misreading vowels, but often he would guess from visual features, turning non-words into words – for example, reading "snirk" as "shrink" and "skree" as "streak." While reading a passage orally, William showed evidence of self-monitoring. For example, when what he was reading did not make sense or when he realized he was repeating something already read, he went back without prompting and read it again – always a good sign and one that bodes well for maintaining good comprehension (Dole, Duffy, Roehler, & Pearson, 1991).

William appeared to get by to a great extent on his facility for memorizing words – compiling a considerable sight vocabulary along the way. I wondered, however, about William's spelling. Spelling would give us a clearer picture of what William and all the boys understand about the phonological structure of words (Ehri, 1989; Stage & Wagner, 1992; Tangel & Blachman, 1992, 1995; Treiman, 1993, 1997). William's spelling and reading of multi-syllable words may suffer over time unless he learns more about how phonological and morpho-phonological structure are represented in the orthography.

### Brian

The next child shown on the videotape was Brian. Brian's style on the rapid naming tasks was striking. He bore down on each item with intense concentration and laser-like focus, spitting out each item's name before going on to the next. Although rate was not a problem on the RAN, his performance lacked fluidity. I mention his RAN performance because it was so like the way he approached each reading task. When reading real words, he was deliberate and focused; but once he started to fail, he guessed from partial letter cues, for example, reading "shoulder" as "shouted" and "correctly" as "crocodile." His reading of nonsense words provides some insight into why he relied so heavily on guessing from partial letter clues – his decoding skills are limited. It appears that Brian has had some instruction in this area because he was able to read several closed syllables made up of two- and three-phoneme items, such as "ig," "om," and "wum." There was also some evidence that he has been introduced to another syllable pattern taught early in most instructional sequences – the silent "e" syllable. Although Brian correctly identified "pate," he also overgeneralized and added a silent "e" to many words that do not follow the pattern, for example, reading "lat" as "late," "fet" as "fate," and "nup" as "nape." It is not uncommon for children who have been taught the vowel sounds common to a particular syllable pattern to confuse them as new syllable types are introduced. So, although Brian read the non-word "wum" correctly, when confronted with "nup," his apparent knowledge of the sound of $/\Lambda/$ in a closed syllable was lost as he turned "nup" into "nape." There was also a perseverative quality to his errors, especially when reading timed non-words. Once he turned the first closed syllable into a silent "e" syllable (i.e. reading "lat" as "late"), this error pattern continued for several words running.

I was most struck by Brian's robot-like quality when reading text. Similar to his performance on the RAN tasks, he also spit out each word on the passage he was asked to read as though each word was on a list and not part of a meaningful paragraph. When he misread a critical word, substituting a word that made no sense in the sentence, there was no evidence that he was attending to meaning. For example, a paragraph about children who were getting ready for school included the predictable phrase "ready at last." Brian read it as "reading at last" and made no attempt to correct his error. Brian's lack of automaticity and fluency provides an example of what can happen when, as Stanovich (1986) suggests, "slow, capacity-draining word-recognition processes require cognitive resources that should be allocated to higher-level processes of text integration and comprehension" (p. 364). Brian is an excellent example of how accuracy *without* fluency does not bring about functional reading. As Brian continues to work on improving his decoding skills, he also needs to learn to read in thought units and to integrate all the pieces of this complex behavior. There is a sense with Brian, more so than William, that many aspects of reading will need direct, systematic instruction. That is, not only will decoding require explicit instruction, but so will fluency and strategies for self-monitoring of comprehension.

### Andrew

Finally we come to Andrew, the most impaired of the three struggling readers. Watching Andrew on the videotape while he was naming objects, then colors, and finally letters, is painful. Andrew grips the table and gives the task intense concentration in an effort to get through it. But when he misspeaks on the rapid naming of colors task and starts to say "blue" when he should have said "green," he throws up his arms in frustration, as though surprised by what is coming out of his mouth. On the letters task, when confronted with the letter "o," Andrew stops dead in his tracks. It is as though he has never seen an "o" before, given the length of time it takes him to recall the letter's name. By the third line of letters, when he is confronted with the letter "a" and can't get access to its name, Andrew tries to "run at the letter again," starting the line over, much as you might go back to the stairs on the high diving board and walk out a second time in hopes of getting a better start. Nothing that he tries helps.

Andrew is then shown on the videotape reading a list of real words. He uses first letters to guess when the words stretch the limits of what he can read comfortably, so "correctly" became "cried" and "experiment" became "eraser." When asked to read non-words, he uses what decoding skills he has. There is a pattern to what he can read correctly – closed syllable non-words without blends (e.g. "pim," "baf," "fet"). Perhaps he has not yet had instruction in other syllable patterns. Watching him attempt the oral reading was as painful as watching him on the naming tasks, perhaps because a third grade passage is simply beyond his reach. An even more likely explanation is that, for Andrew, reading a passage is a continuous naming task of the worst sort. His struggle to keep his place, starting first with a pen in his right hand and then moving it to the left hand when his right hand was covering up the words, is one of the most elaborate procedures I have ever witnessed. Andrew's problems are obviously more pervasive in every domain – and it is unlikely that reading is the only problem he confronts in school or in life.

I think Andrew describes Andrew best when he says at the end of the tape "my mind is like, uh, scrambling up words." I was struck by the many un-answered questions raised by Andrew's naming errors and slow naming speed. Do Andrew's naming errors reflect, as suggested by Katz and Shankweiler (1985), "deficiencies in processing phonological information stored at specific lexical addresses and possibly also . . . deficiencies in the quality or complete-ness of the phonological specification" (p. 624)? There has been intense interest in how phonological representations change over time in young children (e.g. becoming more segmental) and how the phonological representations of good and poor readers might differ in quality and specificity (Brady, 1997, this vol-ume; Elbro, 1996; Elbro, Borstrøm, & Petersen, 1998; Fowler, 1991; Metsala & Walley, 1998). There are also questions about the extent to which performance on measures of naming speed, like the RAN, for example, reflect phonological processing and to what extent other underlying mechanisms (such as processing speed) are implicated (for a detailed review see Wolf & Bowers, 1999; Wolf & Katzir-Cohen, 2001; and Wolf & Ashby, this volume). The chapters in this book represent many different perspectives about what Andrew's performance illustrates and what questions we should be asking to better understand it.

### Final thoughts

The picture that emerges of these four boys, although incomplete, reinforces much of what we have learned over the last thirty years about the role of phonological processing in learning to read. For each of the three struggling readers, their difficulty reading non-words suggests they do not yet understand how the phonology, or sound structure of the language, is represented in print. This greatly constrains the boys' ability to take advantage of the economy inherent in an alphabetic writing system. To many struggling readers who miss the point of an alphabetic system, each word still looks like something that must be memorized in its entirety. For a struggling reader like William, who appears to have considerable capacity for memorizing words, the breakdown in reading looks less dramatic than it does when a child seems to lack *both* the facility for memorizing large numbers of words *and* the knowledge needed to use the alphabet effectively to read unknown words. The intense concentration and effort Brian exerts to read each word demonstrates clearly how draining it is and how it impedes comprehension when decoding skills are not automatic. Andrew's difficulty gaining access to the names of things adds yet another layer to the reading problem. Although we have instructional models that have been shown to increase accuracy, increasing fluency is still somewhat of a mystery. Andrew exemplifies an important challenge for reading research – how to insure that children reach high levels of accuracy *and* fluency. Watching four boys read can teach us a great deal. It reinforces what we know and shows us where we have to go next.

## REFERENCES

Blachman, B. A. (ed.). (1997). *Foundations of reading acquisition and dyslexia: Implications for early intervention.* Mahwah, NJ: Lawrence Erlbaum Associates.

Blachman, B. A. (2000). Phonological awareness. In M. L. Kamil, P. B. Mosenthal, P. D. Pearson & R. Barr (eds), *Handbook of reading research* (Vol. III), 483–502. Mahwah, NJ: Lawrence Erlbaum Associates.

Blachman, B. A., Schatschneider, C., Fletcher, J. M., Francis, D. J., Clonan, S. M., Shaywitz, B. A. & Shaywitz, S. E. (2004). Effects of intensive reading remediation for second and third graders and a 1-year follow-up. *Journal of Educational Psychology*, 96, 444–61.

Brady, S. (1997). Ability to encode phonological representations: An underlying difficulty of poor readers. In B. A. Blachman (ed.), *Foundations of reading acquisition and dyslexia: Implications for early intervention*, 21–47. Mahwah, NJ: Lawrence Erlbaum Associates.

Brady, S. & Shankweiler, D. (eds). (1991). *Phonological processes in literacy: A tribute to Isabelle Y. Liberman.* Hillsdale, NJ: Lawrence Erlbaum Associates.

Denckla, M. B. & Rudel, R. G. (1976). Rapid "automatized" naming (R.A.N.): Dyslexia differentiated from other learning disabilities. *Neuropsychologia*, 14, 471–9.

Dole, J. A., Duffy, G. G., Roehler, L. R. & Pearson, P. D. (1991). Moving from the old to the new: Research on reading comprehension instruction. *Review of Educational Research*, 61, 239–64.

Ehri, L. C. (1989). Development of spelling knowledge and its role in reading acquisition and reading disabilities. *Journal of Learning Disabilities*, 22, 356–65.

Ehri, L. C. (1997). Sight word learning in normal readers and dyslexics. In B. Blachman (ed.), *Foundations of reading acquisition and dyslexia: Implications for early intervention*, 163–89. Mahwah, NJ: Lawrence Erlbaum Associates.

Elbro, C. (1996). Early linguistic abilities and reading development: A review and a hypothesis about distinctness of phonological representations. *Reading and Writing: An Interdisciplinary Journal*, 8, 453–85.

Elbro, C., Borstrøm, I. & Petersen, D. K. (1998). Predicting dyslexia from kindergarten: The importance of distinctness of phonological representations of lexical items. *Reading Research Quarterly*, 33(1), 36–60.

Fowler, A. E. (1991). How early phonological development might set the stage for phoneme awareness. In S. A. Brady & D. P. Shankweiler (eds), *Phonological processes in literacy: A tribute to Isabelle Y. Liberman*, 97–117. Hillsdale, NJ: Lawrence Erlbaum Associates.

Goodman, K. S. (1976). Reading: A psycholinguistic guessing game. In H. Singer & R. B. Rudell (eds), *Theoretical models and processes of reading*, 497–508. Newark, Delaware: International Reading Association.

Goswami, U. (2002). Phonology, reading development and dyslexia: A cross-linguistic perspective. *Annals of Dyslexia*, 52, 1–23.

Katz, R. B. & Shankweiler, D. (1985). Repetitive naming and the detection of word retrieval deficits in the beginning reader. *Cortex*, 21, 617–25.

Liberman, I. Y. & Shankweiler, D. (1985). Phonology and the problems of learning to read and write. *Remedial and Special Education*, 6, 8–17.

Liberman, I. Y. & Shankweiler, D. (1991). Phonology and beginning reading: A tutorial. In L. Rieben & C. A. Perfetti (eds), *Learning to read: Basic research and its implications*, 3–17. Hillsdale, NJ: Lawrence Erlbaum Associates.

Metsala, J. L. & Walley, A. C. (1998). Spoken vocabulary growth and the segmental restructuring of lexical representations: Precursors to phonemic awareness and early reading ability. In J. L. Metsala & L. C. Ehri (eds), *Word recognition in beginning literacy*, 89–120. Mahwah, NJ: Lawrence Erlbaum Associates.

Nicholson, T. (1991). Do children read words better in context or in lists? A classic study revisited. *Journal of Educational Psychology*, 83, 444–50.

Perfetti, C. A. (1985). *Reading ability*. New York: Oxford University Press.

Rack, J. P., Snowling, M. J. & Olson, R. K. (1992). The nonword reading deficit in developmental dyslexia: A review. *Reading Research Quarterly*, 27, 29–53.

Rayner, K. (1997). Understanding eye movements in reading. *Scientific Studies of Reading*, 1, 317–39.

Shankweiler, D. (1999). Words to meanings. *Scientific Studies of Reading*, 3, 113–28.

Share, D. L. & Stanovich, K. E. (1995). Cognitive processes in early reading development: Accommodating individual differences into a model of acquisition. *Issues in Education*, 1, 1–57.

Stage, S. & Wagner, R. (1992). Development of young children's phonological and orthographic knowledge as revealed by their spellings. *Developmental Psychology*, 28, 287–96.

Stanovich, K. E. (1986). Matthew effects in reading: Some consequences of individual differences in the acquisition of literacy. *Reading Research Quarterly*, 21, 360–407.

Stanovich, K. E. (1988). Explaining the differences between the dyslexic and the garden-variety poor reader: The phonological-core variable-difference model. *Journal of Learning Disabilities*, 21, 590–612.

Stanovich, K. E. (1994). Romance and reality. *The Reading Teacher*, 47, 280–91.

Tangel, D. & Blachman, B. A. (1992). Effect of phoneme awareness instruction on kindergarten children's invented spelling. *Journal of Reading Behavior*, 24, 233–61.

Tangel, D. & Blachman, B. A. (1995). Effect of phoneme awareness instruction on the invented spelling of first grade children: A one year follow-up. *Journal of Reading Behavior*, 27, 153–85.

Torgesen, J. K., Wagner, R. K. & Rashotte, C. (1999). *Test of Word Reading Efficiency*. Austin, TX: Pro-Ed.

Treiman, R. (1993). *Beginning to spell*. New York: Oxford University Press.

Treiman, R. (1997). Spelling in normal children and dyslexics. In B. A. Blachman (ed.), *Foundations of reading acquisition and dyslexia: Implications for early intervention*, 191–218. Mahwah, NJ: Lawrence Erlbaum Associates.

Wagner, R. K. & Torgesen, J. K. (1987). The nature of phonological processing and its causal role in the acquisition of reading skills. *Psychological Bulletin*, 101, 192–212.

226     *Benita A. Blachman*

Wagner, R. K., Torgesen, J. K., Rashotte, C. A., Hecht, S. A., Barker, T. A., Burgess, S. R., Donahue, J. & Garon, T. (1997). Changing relations between phonological processing abilities and word-level reading as children develop from beginning to skilled readers: A 5-year longitudinal study. *Developmental Psychology, 33*, 468–79.

Wiederholt, J. L. & Bryant, B. R. (1992). *Gray Oral Reading Tests, Third Edition*. Austin, TX: PRO-ED.

Wolf, M. (1991). Naming speed and reading: The contribution of the cognitive neurosciences. *Reading Research Quarterly, 26*, 123–41.

Wolf, M. & Bowers, P. (1999). The "double-deficit hypothesis" for the developmental dyslexias. *Journal of Educational Psychology, 91*, 415–38.

Wolf, M. & Katzir-Cohen, T. (2001). Reading fluency and its intervention. *Scientific Studies of Reading, 5*, 211–39.

Woodcock, R. W. & Johnson, M. B. (1989). *Woodcock-Johnson Psycho-Educational Battery–Revised*. Chicago, IL: The Riverside Publishing Co.

# 13 Analysis of reading disorders from a neuropsychological perspective

## H. Gerry Taylor

*Overview:* Uncovering the true nature of dyslexia requires more research on the relation between environmental and neurological influences on the development of reading. One factor that complicates diagnosis of core deficits is children's use of compensatory strategies to deal with task demands. To get around this problem, Taylor suggests focusing on basic cognitive abilities, making connections between children's cognitive weaknesses and their possible neurological deficits. For example, he suggests that the child William's difficulties with copying the Rey-Osterrieth Complex Figure and with sequencing items may stem from problems with executive function and deficits in frontal lobe processing. This approach hones in on deficits and the separation of children's primary neurological problems from the complex effects of environmental influence and individual compensation.                    *The Editors*

The snapshots of behavior and task performance seen in the videotape segments document wide-ranging differences between children with normal learning abilities, such as Jonathan, and students with learning problems. These segments also demonstrate the variability in learning problems and associated cognitive and behavioral traits present within even a small sample of children with reading disabilities. The divide between normal and disabled is by no means unidimensional.

However, children with reading disorders also have characteristics in common. One of our assumptions about the boys with reading disabilities is that they have had chronic and relatively intractable problems in learning to read. A second assumption is that their reading problems have emerged in spite of opportunities to learn and lack of more obvious explanations for their learning failure, such as mental retardation, severe emotional disturbance, or sensory deficits. Although these boys may differ from each other and from Jonathan in global cognitive function, the between-child variations in reading skills are not likely to be explained in terms of IQ or other indices of global mental ability (Francis, Fletcher, Shaywitz, Shaywitz, & Rourke, 1996; Lyon, Fletcher, & Barnes, 2003). In this sense, the reading problems of Andrew, Brian, and

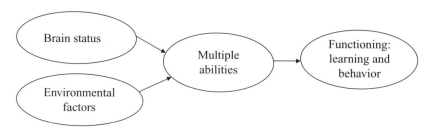

Figure 13.1  A conceptual framework for neuropsychological assessment.

William are "unexpected." A final assumption is that the boys' performances on the tasks shown in the videotape segments are representative of their competencies. The assumption that the tasks tell us something relevant about the boys' academic and cognitive competencies is supported by the impression that they are highly motivated and cooperative. The uniqueness of their patterns of strengths and weaknesses suggests that the videotape segments provide us with important clues as to the nature of their reading problems.

As a neuropsychologist, I have a special interest in cases like the ones presented in these segments. The role of neuropsychological assessments in analysis of children's problems is illustrated by the schema presented in Figure 13.1. Emphasis is placed by the neuropsychologist on the study of cognitive abilities as determinants of children's learning competence and behavior. Study of cognitive abilities is a means for understanding the basis of difficulties in learning and behavior, as well as for elucidating the contribution of brain status and social factors to these functions. By virtue of the effects of biological and social variables on well-defined cognitive constructs, brain–behavior relationships can be clarified and the consequences of neurological insult or abnormality isolated from environmental influences. Neuropsychological assessment, in other words, is useful both in developing a psychological account for problems and in identifying underlying neural mechanisms (Taylor & Fletcher, 1990). Cognitive constructs, although central to neuropsychological analysis of children's problems, do not imply a disinterest in other influences on learning. Personality characteristics and children's psychosocial and educational histories are other relevant considerations. The premises of child neuropsychological assessment are summarized in Table 13.1.

In reviewing and interpreting the performances shown in Part II of the videotape segments, I first describe and contrast the ability profiles of the three children with reading disorders. Emphasizing parallels between these profiles and recognized subtypes of reading disorders, I speculate about the nature and possible etiology of each child's reading disorder and note some of the difficulties I had in interpreting test performance. I then consider the need for further developmental and neuroscience research on reading disorders. I conclude by

Table 13.1. *Premises of child neuropsychological assessment.*

1. Multiple levels of analysis of learning problems (biological, cognitive, functional).
2. Different types of learning disorders corresponding to different underlying processes.
3. Factors besides processing deficits need to be taken into account (e.g. psychosocial problems, family issues, child's medical, developmental, educational history).

highlighting some common misunderstandings about reading disabilities and the types of policy changes that are needed if we are to lessen the impact of these disorders and optimize psychoeducational outcomes.

## Case analysis and interpretation

### Andrew

Andrew is clearly the most disabled reader in the group. He also performs more poorly than the other children on the cognitive tests. In Part II of the videotape segments, Andrew is a slow and disfluent reader. He makes many uncorrected errors and struggles in his attempts to decode individual words. He is unable to tap in time with the tones, even on the simple alternating tapping task. His copy of the Rey-Osterrieth Complex Figure (ROCF) is distorted and he has poor recall of individual elements of the design relative to the other children and to his own direct copy of the design. Andrew shows little dominant hand advantage in sentence writing and he has difficulty expressing himself in the debriefing session. Similar expressive language problems are observed in his slow and labored retrieval of names and in his answers to open-ended questions in Part I of the videotape segments. For example, he calls soldiers "army person" and refers to potato peeling as "scraping the potatoes." Andrew's overall pattern of performance, therefore, is characterized by pervasive problems across multiple skill areas and by the absence of a right–left asymmetry in writing. Table 13.2 summarizes impressions of Andrew's skills in comparison with those of the other two boys with reading disabilities.

Andrew appears to have a severe form of specific reading disability, and one associated with deficits in a wide array of language processing skills. Further testing would likely reveal deficits in phonological awareness and verbal short-term memory, in addition to the deficiencies in speeded naming evident in Part I of the videotape. According to recent research on subtypes of reading disorders (Morris *et al.*, 1998), children with this pattern of cognitive impairment tend to have extreme difficulties learning to read, as well as positive family histories of reading disability. Andrew's deficits in mental organization and sequencing, as demonstrated on the drawing and motor tasks, also suggest weaknesses in attention and executive function. The comorbidity of reading and attention deficits is

Table 13.2. *Case analysis of boys with reading disorders.*

|  | Andrew | Brian | William |
|---|---|---|---|
| Oral reading | − | − | + |
| Single word decoding | − | − | + |
| Expressing speech | − | − | + |
| Naming speed | − | + | − |
| Motor tapping | − | + | − |
| Drawing | − | + | − |
| L-R difference in sentence writing | Right = Left | Right = Left | Right = Left |
| General Impression | Phonological & rate disorder | Phonological disorder | Rate disorder |

Deficits are indicated by "−" and strengths by "+."

well established (Shaywitz & Shaywitz, 1994), and several studies have found evidence for weaknesses in executive function, non-verbal skills, and speed of processing in children with reading disabilities (Catts, Gillispie, Leonard, Kail, & Miller, 2002; Denckla, 1989; Horn & Packard, 1985; Kelly, Best, & Kirk, 1989; Light, Pennington, Gilger, & DeFries, 1995; Satz, Buka, Lipsett, & Seidman, 1998; Taylor, Anselmo, Foreman, Schatschneider, & Angelopoulos, 2000).

Other interesting aspects of Andrew's performances include the absence of clear right-hand dominance in sentence writing and his poor recall of the ROCF. Andrew's lack of right-hand superiority in sentence writing raises the possibility of atypical lateralization of function and is consistent with findings showing an absence of normal anatomical asymmetries and anomalies in left-hemisphere development among children with dyslexia (Filipek, 1995; Galaburda, 1989; Galaburda & Sherman, this volume; Rumsey, 1996). Andrew's inability to remember elements of the ROCF may reflect problems in the initial coding of the information due to organizational deficits, or difficulties retrieving and integrating elements of the figure when drawing it from memory. Although the physiological basis of Andrew's deficit on the ROCF is unclear, this deficit may signal more diffuse neuropathology, possibly implicating right-hemisphere and frontal systems (Rumsey, 1996).

One of the challenges presented by this case is reconciling Andrew's severe difficulties in single-word decoding with his somewhat better performance in oral reading. Andrew's good effort in oral reading suggests that some aspects of his language development, such as vocabulary or verbal reasoning abilities, may be relatively intact. The observation that oral reading fluency is better than one would expect based on his ability to decode words in isolation may also be accounted for by a history of intensive remedial reading instruction. The manner in which Andrew meticulously breaks down words in an effort to sound them out is consistent with this possibility. Andrew's persistence on the tasks provides further testimony to appropriate interventions.

### Brian

Brian's reading, like Andrew's, is extremely disfluent. Judging from the decoding weaknesses evident in Part I of the videotape segments, both boys have deficits in phonological processing. The two boys also show the same lack of clear right-hand dominance in sentence writing and expressive difficulties in answering open-ended questions in conversation. In contrast to both Andrew and William, however, Brian displays relative strengths in naming, motor tapping, and drawing. Furthermore, while Brian takes a part-oriented rather than configurational approach to the ROCF, his reproduction of the elements of this design from memory is age appropriate. As summarized in Table 13.2, Brian seems to have the same core deficit in phonological processing as Andrew, but in the context of more intact skills in other language and non-verbal functions.

Brian's reading disorder represents a subtype in which deficits in phonological processing are present in relative isolation (Morris et al., 1998). His pattern of cognitive impairment is thus consistent with the phonological-core variable-difference model proposed by Stanovich (1988). According to this model, deficient phonological processing is the primary factor responsible for reading disorders, with weaknesses in other language and cognitive skills contributing to variability in the severity and expression of these problems. Brian's pattern of performance suggests a relatively pure "phonological core" type of disability, which contrasts with the more mixed disability shown by Andrew.

Brian's more limited language impairment may be one reason why he reads better than Andrew. Other explanations are that Brian has a less severe form of phonological deficit, or an ability to use his language strengths to compensate for weaknesses in phonological skill. The manner in which Brian calls out words in almost robotic fashion, evident in both the naming and reading tasks, suggests that he may be putting his naming skills to use to increase his reading speed. Unfortunately, the potential advantage of this compensatory strategy may be offset to some extent by an overfocus on individual words and an accompanying failure to attend to the higher-level linguistic processes involved in reading, such as speech prosody and sentence meaning. An analogous circumstance is observed in young children who are not able to decode words but who are proficient in visual memory. Whereas children who read in this way might seem to be mastering the reading process at lower grade levels, their reading problems become readily apparent over time and with increases in reading vocabulary and the need for rapid decoding of unfamiliar words. The ability of these children to compensate for their decoding problems has the unfortunate effect of obscuring early manifestations of their reading disability and thus delaying appropriate interventions.

The neural mechanisms responsible for Brian's reading problems may be similar to those underlying Andrew's reading disorder. One can only speculate as to the neural basis of Brian's relative strengths in naming and sequencing. Variable anomalies of brain maturation might explain these differences. Findings linking reading disabilities to quantitative trait loci could also account for these phenotypic variations, with variability in the expression of reading problems depending on the type and number of contributing genes (Pennington, 1995, 2002).

## William

William's reading disability is easily distinguished from the other two boys' disorders. Despite some difficulty decoding non-words under time pressure, William reads connected text with good fluency and he is reasonably accurate in decoding words and non-words. Despite these strengths, William has difficulty in the naming and motor tapping tasks. His copy of the ROCF is poorly organized, and his reproduction of the design from memory is not well structured. In contrast to Brian, William has greater difficulties in sequencing tasks than in oral reading or single word decoding. In sum, William's ability profile, depicted in the third column of Table 13.2, is the mirror image of Brian's.

William would most likely be classified as "rate-disabled" according to the subtyping scheme of Morris *et al.* (1998). This profile has been associated with motor weaknesses, as well as with problems in reading comprehension (Lovett, Borden, DeLuca, Laceerenza, Benson, & Branckstone, 1994; Wolf, Pfeil, Lotz, & Biddle, 1994). In William's case, difficulties in sequencing skills are suggested by his errors on the rapid naming and oral reading tasks and his inability to maintain a steady tapping pattern in the motor tasks. He points to keep his place in naming, makes mistakes when rushing in timed naming of non-words, skips a line in reading, and is unable to maintain the temporal pattern on the tapping tasks.

In view of what appears to be normal dominance in sentence writing, the neurological basis for William's problems may be different from that responsible for the reading disorders of Andrew and Brian. The problems in executive function suggested by William's low scores on the ROCF, together with his weaknesses in sequencing, suggest involvement of frontal lobes or circuits connecting the frontal lobes to other areas of the brain, including the basal ganglia. Findings consistent with this possibility include evidence for hypoactivation of the frontal regions of persons with reading disabilities during reading tasks (Rumsey, 1996) and data suggesting that attention is impaired by damage to frontal-subcortical circuits (Lou, 1996).

One aspect of William's reading disorder about which there is some uncertainty is his ability to decode words. Although William's difficulties in timed reading of nonsense words may reflect inefficient retrieval or a tendency to rush, these problems may also signal weaknesses in rapid or automatic word decoding. William's reading disorder may thus represent a higher-level manifestation of the same type of problem that characterizes the reading disabilities of Andrew and Brian. Observation of students with similar problems indicates that these children read rapidly but with many decoding errors and little awareness of their comprehension failures. Deficiencies in organizational and study skills are also characteristic of these children. William's problems thus may be due to both lack of automatization of decoding skills and weaknesses in executive function. In the latter respect, William may have some of the same cognitive deficits as Andrew.

William's poor performance on the motor tasks is also subject to alternative interpretations. He performs well on the first motor task when guided by the tone, but he has difficulty when the tone is not present or when a more complex tapping pattern is required. Although test results suggest weaknesses in motor sequencing, William's inability to modulate his attention and remain on task may be hampering his tapping performance. William's accuracy in tapping with the guidance of the tone may be due to an ability to coordinate movement so long as an internal representation of the temporal pattern is not required. Alternatively, the tone may simply have helped William to remain focused on the task. The dependence of William's motor performances on specific task demands illustrates the importance of taking task parameters into account in test interpretation. As noted earlier, the strategy that children use to compensate for deficits can sometimes obscure the nature of their academic or cognitive problems. To further illustrate this point, if William had slowed down in an effort to read more accurately, his difficulties in oral reading may have appeared to be more related to decoding problems than to inattention. The effects of variations in task demands on performance are frequently useful in entertaining alternative explanations for learning difficulties or low test scores.

### Research directions

*Studies of psychological development*

Numerous studies indicate that phonological processing skills are fundamental in acquiring reading skill, and that impairment in this area is a necessary and sufficient condition for reading disability (Shaywitz, 1998). Other correlates of reading disabilities include deficits in rapid serial naming, lexical and vocabulary skills, working memory ability, and morphological awareness, although the relationship of these skills to reading disabilities is as yet unclear

(Fletcher, Foorman, Shaywitz, & Shaywitz, 1999). Some of the latter abilities predict reading competence, even after phonological processing skills have been taken into account – a finding that raises the possibility of multiple primary determinants of reading disorders.

It is unlikely, however, that all of the cognitive correlates of reading failure are causally related to children's reading problems. A given cognitive deficit may be a consequence of a more primary cognitive impairment, or secondary to the reading disorder itself (Taylor, 1988b). Stanovich and his colleagues, for example, have demonstrated that the restrictive reading experience of children with reading disorders leads to diminished vocabulary and declarative knowledge over time (Stanovich, 1986; Stanovich, West, & Harrison, 1995). Failure to read as frequently as one's peers also jeopardizes the further development of phonological skills and negatively impacts continued acquisition of word decoding and spelling abilities (Snowling, Goulandris, & Defty, 1996).

Other cognitive and behavioral correlates of reading disorders may be neither primary determinants nor direct consequences of the reading disorder, but may relate instead to the reading disability in less direct ways (Taylor, 1988b). A given cognitive deficit, for example, may moderate the influence of a more primary impairment on reading acquisition. Cognitive deficits accompanying reading disabilities also may be associated with a comorbid condition that is causally independent of the reading problem, or they may be manifestations of a broader biological vulnerability. The disorder in temporal processing proposed by Wolff (1993; Wolf & Ashby, this volume), as illustrated by the asynchronous tapping performances of William and Andrew, may be an instance of the latter type of deficit.

Further research is needed to explore the cognitive correlates of reading disabilities and the relationships of these correlates to each other and to children's reading skills. We know relatively little, for example, about the psychological processes that underlie inefficient serial naming (Fletcher et al., 1999; Neuhaus, Foorman, Francis, & Carlson, 2001) or deficiencies in drawing of complex designs such as the ROCF. In view of evidence linking reading disabilities with deficits in executive functions and in visual processing skills, continued investigation of these constructs is also warranted (Fletcher et al., 1999; Horn & Packard, 1985). Theoretical formulations of reading-related processes should prove useful in generating hypotheses about the nature of cognitive constructs and their relationship to reading (Fletcher et al., 1999; Foorman, 1994).

An equally important research goal is to better understand the developmental "pathways" that children take in learning to read, or in failing to do so, and the influences of environmental factors on reading acquisition (Rutter, 1994). The presence of early reading difficulties frequently leads to a chain of adverse experiences, including disinterest in reading, limited exposure to print, and negative teacher and parent interactions. Each of these experiences, in turn, makes it more difficult for children to catch up with their peers in reading skill. According to this view, reading disorders are not entirely predetermined by the child's neurological status. Constitutional factors, instead, are seen as biological susceptibilities or predispositions to environmental influence (Galaburda, 1989; Galaburda & Sherman, this volume; Pennington, 1995, 2002; Plomin & Rutter, 1998).

More information on the developmental antecedents and consequences of reading disorders is needed if we are to find ways to break these causal chains. Although delays in language development presage reading difficulties (Scarborough, 1991), it would be helpful to know more about how phonological processing skills evolve in early childhood and about the potential environmental influences on these skills. A better understanding of the impact of instructional methods and psychosocial adjustment on reading acquisition would also be useful. Research findings confirm the utility of code-based methods of early reading instruction in improving early reading skills (Foorman, Francis, Beeler, Winikates, & Fletcher, 1997; Goswami, 2002; Torgesen, 1997, this volume; Torgesen *et al.*, 2001; Vellutino *et al.* 1996). But little is known about how environmental or psychosocial factors contribute to the persistence of these problems over time. Advances in knowledge will require longitudinal follow-up and an expanded scope of inquiry, including investigation of children's learning abilities and adaptational styles and of school and family influences on reading acquisition (Ceci, 1991; Taylor, 1988a; Wachs, 1992).

*Neural mechanisms*

Research on the neuropathologic correlates of dyslexia, a term used to refer to persons with specific reading disabilities, confirms the existence of an anatomic-physiologic basis for reading problems (Galaburda, 1989; Galaburda & Sherman, this volume; Rumsey, 1996). Evidence for constitutional determinants includes demonstration of specific effects of brain lesions on reading, anomalies in the anatomical organization of the brains of dyslexic individuals, and differences between persons with reading disabilities and normal readers in patterns of brain activation in response to behavioral tasks.

Research findings indicate that certain brain regions are of particular importance in mediating reading skills, but that widely distributed neural networks are additionally involved (Breier *et al.*, 2003; Rumsey, 1996). A study showing hypoactivation in the region of the left angular gyrus in persons with reading disabilities during reading-related tasks suggests that anomalies in the structure or function of this area may be closely linked to reading disorders (Shaywitz *et al.*, 1998). Studies of persons with reading disorders have also revealed abnormalities in frontal and subcortical regions (Filipek, 1995; Rumsey, 1996), as well as evidence for genetic influences (Galaburda, 1989; Galaburda &

Sherman, this volume; Pennington, 1995, 2002). Changes in brain activation patterns in response to reading intervention provide even more direct evidence for neural correlates of skilled reading (Simos *et al.*, 2002).

In undertaking research along these lines, it will be important to identify anatomic and physiologic correlates of different subtypes of reading disorder. The implications of different forms of early brain insult for reading acquisition also deserve investigation (Barnes, Faulkner, & Dennis, 2001). We may discover that patterns of cortical activation vary across different subtypes of reading disorder, and that reading problems related to genetically programmed disturbances in brain maturation may differ from disorders that are secondary to unfavorable pre- or perinatal conditions. A further possibility is that neural mechanisms that account for population variation in reading-related skills differ from those responsible for atypical forms of reading disability (Pennington, 1995). In light of the diverse cognitive weaknesses associated with reading problems, underlying anatomic and physiologic anomalies may prove to be part of dynamic brain networks subserving a number of functions in addition to reading (Pennington, 1997, 2002).

To illustrate the cross-fertilization of the behavioral and neurological sciences, findings showing that children with reading disabilities are deficient in multiple skills raise the possibility of diffuse abnormalities in brain function. Conversely, observations of activation differences between normal and disabled readers in subcortical and frontal brain regions encourage investigation of the relationships of deficits in attention and executive function to reading disability. Efforts to relate brain status to behavior have a long and prosperous history in the fields of neuropsychology and cognitive neuroscience (Fletcher & Taylor, 1984; Geschwind, 1981; Sarter, Berntson, & Cacioppo, 1996). A better appreciation of the neural mechanisms underlying faulty acquisition of reading skills will likely follow from continued studies of brain–behavior relationships. These studies may involve investigations of the ways in which brain processes are altered by learning, or of the manner in which behavior maps onto indices of brain development or maldevelopment (Dawson & Fischer, 1994; Nelson & Bloom, 1997).

## Child needs and educational policy

### *Correcting misconceptions about reading disabilities*

The boys in the videotape segments appear well adjusted and highly motivated; they have positive attitudes and have made obvious progress in learning how to read. Unfortunately, many of the vast numbers of children who experience reading problems early in their school careers fare far less well than these boys (Satz *et al.*, 1998). The high frequency of poor academic and behavioral outcomes may be related in part to several prevailing misconceptions about reading disorders. Because these misconceptions may lead to provision of inappropriate or inadequate services to children with reading difficulties, it is important that they be dispelled.

One frequent misconception is the tendency to view reading disorders as distinct from normal variation in reading skill, and to define these disorders in terms of discrepancies between global cognitive ability and reading achievement. In fact, data from a probability-sampling-based population study by Shaywitz and associates (Shaywitz, Escobar, Shaywitz, Fletcher, & Makuch, 1992) suggest a continuous distribution of reading skill in elementary school children. These investigators failed to find evidence for the type of bimodal distribution of reading ability that would be predicted if specific reading disorders were a distinct subset of the broader continuum of reading skill. In light of the variable nature of reading disabilities and the failure of IQ-achievement discrepancy formula to identify children with unique types of reading problems (Fletcher *et al.*, 1994; Francis *et al.*, 1996), there is no scientific basis for restricting special education services to children who meet these criteria. The types of deficits illustrated in the videotape segments are observed in many students who fail to qualify for special education, yet who might benefit from special instructional techniques (Lovett, Steinbach, & Frijters, 2000; Shaywitz, Fletcher, & Shaywitz, 1996).

Another misconception is that one needs to wait until the child has been in school several years before identifying a reading problem (Fletcher & Foorman, 1994). Delays in identification stem in large part from the use of IQ-achievement discrepancy criteria, which fail to detect reading problems in younger children. Early detection of reading problems would likely be enhanced by screening procedures that capitalized on teacher observations and included evaluations of the academic and cognitive correlates of reading disabilities (Taylor *et al.*, 2000). Given the availability of research-validated methods of beginning reading instruction, early detection may well lead to amelioration or even prevention of reading failure in many children (Foorman *et al.*, 1997; Torgesen, 1997, this volume; Torgesen *et al.*, 2001; Vellutino *et al.*, 1996).

A final misconception is that reading problems are unidimensional. Although impaired phonological processing may be a fundamental determinant of reading disabilities, reading problems are frequently accompanied by multiple cognitive deficits. The nature of these deficiencies, together with motivational and family factors, need to be considered in formulating intervention plans for individual children (Taylor, 1989). Psychosocial factors may help to account, at least partially, for the lack of responsiveness shown by a small subset of children to otherwise effective interventions (Vellutino *et al.*, 1996). The shortcomings of recent research-validated reading programs, including limited evidence of generalization of skills and continued difficulties in achieving reading fluency (Fletcher & Lyon, 1998), may also be explained in this manner.

*Policy implications*

Appropriate treatment of children with reading problems requires that we implement programs that are consistent with our current knowledge base. Efforts must be made to identify reading-related weaknesses early in development and to employ effective instructional techniques. Further intervention studies will be required to refine these techniques and to develop methods for working with preschoolers and with children who are having difficulty acquiring more advanced levels of reading skills (Fletcher & Lyon, 1998).

Expansion of services is likewise necessary. Special assistance needs to be made available to a larger segment of the student population. The spectrum of resources required to meet this goal ranges from intensive individual remediation of basic skills to accommodation of the child within the regular classroom, enhancement of student motivation, development of study skills and learning strategies, provision of alternative methods for acquiring knowledge and for assisting students in taking on academic challenges, and help in making transitions between grades and from secondary school to higher education or employment (Adelman, 1989; Hennessy, Rosenberg, & Tramaglini, 1998; Meltzer, Roditi, & Stein, 1998; Zigmond, 1995). The success of these strategies will depend on the availability of research-validated methods of intervention, teacher training, and positive involvement of children and parents in the learning process. Undertaking these initiatives will also demand an understanding of the biological and cognitive underpinnings of reading disorders, a willingness to adapt instruction to individual differences, and advocacy for policy changes that promote reading skills while avoiding the adverse consequences of initial difficulties in learning to read.

REFERENCES

Adelman, H. S. (1989). Beyond the learning mystique: An interactional perspective on learning disabilities. *Journal of Learning Disabilities*, 22, 301–4, 328.
Barnes, M. A., Faulkner, H. & Dennis, M. (2001). Poor reading comprehension despite fast word decoding in children with hydrocephalus. *Brain and Language*, 76, 35–44.
Breier, J. I., Simos, P. G., Fletcher, J. M., Castillo, E. M., Zhang, W. & Papanicolaou, A. C. (2003). Abnormal activation of temporoparietal language areas during phonetic analysis in children with dyslexia. *Neuropsycyhology*, 17, 610–21.
Catts, H. W., Gillispie, M., Leonard, L. B., Kail, R. V. & Miller, C. A. (2002). The role of speed of processing, rapid naming, and phonological awareness in reading achievement. *Journal of Learning Disabilities*, 35, 509–24.
Ceci, S. J. (1991). How much does schooling influence general intelligence and its cognitive components? A reassessment of the evidence. *Developmental Psychology*, 27, 703–22.
Dawson, G. & Fischer, K. W. (eds) (1994). *Human behavior and the developing brain*. New York: Guilford.

Denckla, M. B. (1989). Executive function, the overlap zone between attention deficit hyperactivity disorder and learning disabilities. *International Pediatrics*, 4, 155–60.

Filipek, P. A. (1995). Neurobiologic correlates of developmental dyslexia: How do dyslexics' brains differ from those of normal readers? *Journal of Child Neurology*, 10, S62–S69.

Fletcher, J. M. & Foorman, B. R. (1994). Issues in definition and measurement of learning disabilities: The need for early intervention. In G. R. Lyon (ed.), *Frames of references for the assessment of learning disabilities: New views on measurement issues*,184–200. Baltimore, MD: Paul H. Brookes.

Fletcher, J. M., Foorman, B. R., Shaywitz, S. E. & Shaywitz, B. A. (1999). Conceptual and methodological issues in dyslexia research: A lesson for developmental disorders. In H.Tager-Flusberg (ed.), *Neurodevelopmental disorders. Developmental cognitive neuroscience*, 271–305. Cambridge, MA: MIT Press.

Fletcher, J. M. & Lyon, G. R. (1998). Reading: A research-based approach. Unpublished manuscript, Department of Pediatrics, University of Texas-Houston Medical School, Houston, TX.

Fletcher, J. M., Shaywitz, S. E., Shankweiler, D. P., Katz, L., Liberman, I. Y., Fowler, A., Francis, D. J., Stuebing, K. K. & Shaywitz, B. A. (1994). Cognitive profiles of reading disability: Comparisons of discrepancy and low achievement definitions. *Journal of Educational Psychology*, 85, 1–18.

Fletcher, J. M. & Taylor, H. G. (1984). Neuropsychological approaches to children: Towards a developmental neuropsychology. *Journal of Clinical Neuropsychology*, 6, 24–37.

Foorman, B. R. (1994). The relevance of a connectionistic model of reading for "The Great Debate." *Educational Psychology Review*, 6, 25–47.

Foorman, B. R., Francis, D. J., Beeler, T., Winikates, D. & Fletcher, J. M. (1997). Early interventions for children with reading problems: Study designs and preliminary findings. *Learning Disabilities: A Multidisciplinary Journal*, 8, 63–71.

Francis, D. J., Fletcher, J. M., Shaywitz, B. A., Shaywitz, S. E. & Rourke, B. P. (1996). Defining learning and language disabilities: Conceptual and psychometric issues with the use of IQ tests. *Language, Speech, and Hearing Services in Schools*, 27, 132–43.

Galaburda, A. M. (1989). Learning disability: Biological, societal, or both? A response to Gerald Coles. *Journal of Learning Disabilities*, 22, 278–82, 286.

Geschwind, N. (1981). Neurological knowledge and complex behaviors. In D. A. Norman (ed.), *Perspectives on cognitive science*, 27–35. Norwood, NJ: Lawrence Erlbaum.

Goswami, U. (2002). Phonology, reading development and dyslexia: A cross-linguistic perspective. *Annals of Dyslexia*, 52, 1–23.

Hennessy, N., Rosenberg, D. & Tramaglini, S. (1998). A high school model for students with dyslexia: Remediation to accommodation. *Perspectives: The International Dyslexia Association*, 24, 22–4.

Horn, W. F. & Packard, T. (1985). Early identification of learning problems: A meta-analysis. *Journal of Educational Psychology*, 77, 597–607.

Kelly, M. S., Best, C. T. & Kirk, U. (1989). Cognitive processing deficits in reading disabilities: A prefrontal cortical hypothesis. *Brain and cognition*, 11, 275–93.

Light, J. G., Pennington, B. F., Gilger, J. W. & DeFries, J. C. (1995). Reading disability and hyperactivity disorder: Evidence for a common genetic etiology. *Developmental Neuropsychology*, 11, 323–35.

Lou, H. C. (1996). Etiology and pathogenesis of Attention-Deficit Hyperactivity Disorder (ADHD): Significance of prematurity and perinatal hypoxic-haemodynamic encephalopathy. *Acta Paediatrica*, 85, 1266–71.

Lovett, M. W., Borden, S., DeLuca, T., Laceerenza, L., Benson, N. & Branckstone, D. (1994). Treating the core deficits of developmental dyslexia: Evidence of transfer of learning after phonologically- and strategy-based reading training programs. *Developmental Psychology*, 30, 805–22.

Lovett, M. W., Steinbach, K. A. & Frijters, J. C. (2000). Remediating the core deficits of developmental reading disability: A double-deficit perspective. *Journal of Learning Disabilities*, 33, 334–58.

Lyon, G. R., Fletcher, J. M. & Barnes, M. A. (2003). Learning disabilities. In E. J. Mash & R. A.Barkley (eds), *Child psychopathology*, 2nd edn, 520–86. New York: Guilford.

Meltzer, L., Roditi, B. & Stein, J. (1998). Strategy instruction: The heartbeat of successful inclusion. *Perspectives: The International Dyslexia Association*, 24, 10–13.

Morris, R. D., Stuebing, K. K., Fletcher, J. M., Shaywitz, S. E., Lyon, G. R., Shankweiler, D. P., Katz, L., Francis, D. J. & Shaywitz, B. A. (1998). Subtypes of reading disability: Variability around a phonological core. *Journal of Educational Psychology*, 90, 347–73.

Nelson, C. A. & Bloom, F. E. (1997). Child development and neuroscience. *Child Development*, 68, 970–87.

Neuhaus, G., Foorman, B. R., Francis, D. J. & Carlson, C. D. (2001). Measures of information processing in rapid automatized naming (RAN) and their relation to reading. *Journal of Experimental Child Psychology*, 78, 359–73.

Pennington, B. F. (1995). Genetics of learning disabilities. *Journal of Child Neurology*, 10, S69–S77.

Pennington, B. F. (1997). Using genetics to dissect cognition. *American Journal of Human Genetics*, 60, 13–16.

Pennington, B. F. (2002). *The development of psychopathology: Nature and nurture*. New York: Guilford Press.

Plomin, R. & Rutter, M. (1998). Child development, molecular genetics, and what to do with genes once they are found. *Child Development*, 69, 1223–42.

Rumsey, J. M. (1996). Developmental dyslexia: Anatomic and functional neuroimaging. *Mental Retardation and Developmental Disabilities Research Reviews*, 2, 28–38.

Rutter, M. (1994). Beyond longitudinal data: Causes, consequences, changes, and continuity. *Journal of Consulting and Clinical Psychology*, 62, 928–40.

Sarter, M., Berntson, G. G. & Cacioppo, J. T. (1996). Brain imaging and cognitive neuroscience: Toward strong inference in attributing function to structure. *American Psychologist*, 51, 13–21.

Satz, P., Buka, S., Lipsett, L. & Seidman, L. (1998). The long-term prognosis of learning disabled children: A review of studies (1954–1993). In B. K. Shapiro, A. Capute & P. J. Accardo (eds), *Specific reading disabilities: A view of the spectrum*, 223–50. Parkton, MD: York Press.

Scarborough, H. S. (1991). Early syntactic development of dyslexic children. *Annals of Dyslexia*, 41, 207–20.

Shaywitz, B. A. & Shaywitz, S. E. (1994). Learning disabilities and attention disorders. In K. Swaiman (ed.), *Principles of pediatric neurology*, 1119–51. St. Louis, MO: C. V. Mosby.

Shaywitz, S. E. (1998). Dyslexia. *New England Journal of Medicine*, 338, 307–12.

Shaywitz, S. E., Escobar, M. D., Shaywitz, B. A., Fletcher, J. M. & Makuch, R. (1992). Distribution and temporal stability of dyslexia in an epidemiological sample of 414 children followed longitudinally. *New England Journal of Medicine*, 326, 145–50.

Shaywitz, S. E., Fletcher, J. M. & Shaywitz, B. A. (1996). A conceptual model and definition of dyslexia: Findings emerging from the Connecticut Longitudinal Study. In J. H. Beitchman, N. J. Cohen, M. M. Konstantareas & R.Tannock (eds), *Language, learning, and behavior disorders: Developmental, biological, and clinical perspectives*, 199–223. New York, NY: Cambridge University Press.

Shaywitz, S. E., Shaywitz, B. A., Pugh, K. R., Fulbright, R. K., Constable, R. T., Mencl, W. E., Shankweiler, D. P., Liberman, A. M., Skudlarski, P., Fletcher, J. M., Datz, L., Marchione, K. E., Lacadie, C., Gatenby, C. & Gore, J. C. (1998). Functional disruption in the organization of the brain for reading in dyslexia. *Proceedings of the National Academy of Science*, 95, 2636–41.

Simos, P. G., Fletcher, J. M., Bergman, E., Breier, J. I., Foorman, B. R., Castillo, E. M., Davis, R. N., Fitzgerald, M. & Papanicolaou, A. C. (2002). Dyslexia-specific brain activation profile becomes normal following successful remedial training. *Neurology*, 58, 1202–13.

Snowling, M. J., Goulandris, N. & Defty, N. (1996). A longitudinal study of reading development in dyslexic children. *Journal of Educational Psychology*, 88, 653–99.

Stanovich, K. E. (1986). Matthew effects in reading: Some consequences of individual differences in the acquisition of literacy. *Reading Research Quarterly*, 21, 360–407.

Stanovich, K. E. (1988). Explaining the differences between the dyslexic and the garden-variety poor reader: The phonological-core variable-difference model. *Journal of Learning Disabilities*, 21, 590–604.

Stanovich, K. E., West, R. F. & Harrison, M. R. (1995). Knowledge growth and maintenance across the life span: The role of print exposure. *Developmental Psychology*, 31, 811–26.

Taylor, H. G. (1988a). Learning disabilities. In E. Mash & L. Terdal (eds), *Behavioral assessment of childhood disorders*, 2nd edn, 402–50. New York, NY: Guilford.

Taylor, H. G. (1988b). Neuropsychological testing: Relevance for assessing children's learning disabilities. *Journal of Consulting and Clinical Psychology*, 56, 795–800.

Taylor, H. G. (1989). Learning disabilities. In E. Mash & R. A. Barkley (eds), *Treatment of childhood disorders*, 347–80. New York, NY: Guilford.

Taylor, H. G., Anselmo, M., Foreman, A, Schatschneider, C. & Angelopoulos, J. (2000). Utility of kindergarten teacher judgements in identifying early learning problems. *Journal of Learning Disabilities*, 33, 200–10.

Taylor, H. G. & Fletcher, J. M. (1990). Neuropsychological assessment of children. In M. Hersen & G. Goldstein (eds), *Handbook of psychological assessment*, 2nd edn, 228–55. New York, NY: Plenum.

Torgesen, J. K. (1997). The prevention and remediation of reading disabilities: Evaluating what we know from research. *Journal of Academic Language Therapy*, 1, 11–47.

Torgesen, J. K., Alexander, A. W., Wagner, R. K., Rashotte, C. A., Voeller, K., Conway, T. & Rose, E. (2001). Intensive remedial instruction for children with severe reading disabilities: Immediate and long-term outcomes from two instructional approaches. *Journal of Learning Disabilities*, 34, 33–58.

Vellutino, F. R., Scanlon, D. M., Sipay, E. R., Small, S. G., Pratt, A., Chen, R. & Denckla, M. B. (1996). Cognitive profiles of difficult-to-remediate and readily remediated poor readers: Early intervention as a vehicle for distinguishing between cognitive and experiential deficits as basic causes of specific reading disability. *Journal of Educational Psychology*, 88, 601–38.

Wachs, T. D. (1992). *The nature of nurture*. Newbury Park, CA: Sage.

Wolf, M., Pfeil, C., Lotz, R. & Biddle, K. (1994). Towards a more universal understanding of the developmental dyslexias: The contribution of orthographic factors. In V. W. Berninger (ed.), *The varieties of orthographic knowledge*, Vol. 1, 137–71. Dordrecht, The Netherlands: Kluwer Academic Publishers.

Wolff, P. H. (1993). Impaired temporal resolution in developmental dyslexia. *Annals of the New York Academy of Sciences*, 683, 87–103.

Zigmond, N. (1995). Models for delivery of special education services to students with learning disabilities in public schools. *Journal of Child Neurology*, 10, S86–S92.

# 14 An educational/psychological perspective on the behaviors of three children with reading disabilities

## Joseph K. Torgesen

*Overview:* From an educational perspective, deriving meaning from text is paramount, and all other reading processes subserve this goal. Torgesen suggests that dyslexia be described at two levels that reflect this fact – the primary level of cognitive and neurophysiological deficits and the secondary level of behavioral and comprehension deficits that are associated with, but not necessarily caused by, neurological conditions. He shows how these two levels work with the four boys whom he was asked to analyze. In the end, while primary deficits will manifest in timed measures, phonological problems, and other reading-related subskills, secondary deficits seem to matter more in educational contexts. Children often build skills that work around their primary deficits so that they have virtually no secondary deficits. Analyzing brain–behavior correlations and their relations to educational functioning requires distinguishing these two levels of reading disorder. *The Editors*

In this essay, I will discuss the behaviors of four children performing several reading and non-reading tasks from an educational/psychological perspective. I would like to begin with the simple observation that it is easy for researchers like myself to lose sight of the full individuality of children with reading disabilities when we spend most of our time thinking about the children only in terms of patterns of scores on a narrowly selected set of tests. Although William, Brian, and Andrew were all similar because they had experienced difficulties in learning to read to varying degrees, they each have complex personalities and response styles that are uniquely their own. Watching them deal with the requirements of several different kinds of tasks reminds us that their reading difficulties are only one small part of their overall intellectual and social individuality. Although it can be confusing and may undermine to some extent the nice generalizations that are the stuff of systematic empirical research, the experience of watching these videotapes reminds me that my own efforts to understand reading difficulties should include a bit more time directly interacting with children and observing them and a bit less time sifting through test data.

There are two general points to make about these children before I address the specific task of commenting on the behaviors observed in Part II of the tape. First, three of these children have had reading difficulties of one degree or another, but none of them has what I would consider a *severe* reading disability. Andrew comes the closest, although with word reading skills at the 10th percentile and phonemic decoding skills at the 22 percentile, he is a much more capable reader then most of the older children that we, and others, work with in our remedial research (Lovett, Lacerenza, Borden, Frijters, Seteinbach, & DePalma, 2000; Wise, Ring, & Olson, 1999; Torgesen *et al.*, 2001; Torgesen, in press). The children we study perform on average about the 2nd percentile on these same reading tests. Additionally, since criteria for the identification of learning disabilities in most states are designed to identify the 5% of children with the most difficult learning problems, they also would not qualify in many communities for learning disabilities support services.

I also found it interesting that the children showed considerable variability in their ability to read real words both in and out of context, but that their untimed phonemic decoding skills did not differ very much. They appeared to differ more strongly in the *fluency* of their phonemic decoding skills, and the fluency of their decoding skills was more strongly related to overall reading outcomes than was their phonemic decoding accuracy. I was drawn to this general observation because it is similar to a pattern in the data from one of our studies with older children with reading problems (Torgesen, Wagner, & Rashotte, 1999), in which we found speed of phonemic decoding to be more strongly related to accuracy of word reading in paragraphs and to passage comprehension than were untimed measures of accuracy. Theoretically, this makes sense if we assume that fluency of phonemic decoding reflects to some degree the ease with which these processes take place. If they are easier to apply, they will be more likely to be applied during the complex mental activities that are required for text processing.

### Observations about paragraph reading skills

Now to observations about the behaviors on Part II of the video. As I am offering an educational perspective on this part of the children's behavior, I will start with the paragraph reading task. I found it useful as a way of thinking systematically about the differences among children on this task to first examine their performance quantitatively. Some dimensions of their performance on the third grade paragraph are reported in Table 14.1.

As was obvious from the tapes, two of the children, Brian and Andrew, have clear problems with reading rate, while Andrew is obviously different from the other children in terms of the number of errors he made. Although half of Andrew's error total was contributed by the words in one line that he completely

Table 14.1. *Descriptive aspects of paragraph reading performance in four children.*

| Aspect of performance | Jonathan | William | Brian | Andrew |
|---|---|---|---|---|
| Rate of reading | 129 wpm. | 125 wpm. | 72 wpm | 39 wpm. |
| Errors | 0 | 4 | 4 | 18 |
| % self-correction | – | 50% | 25% | 18% |
| Expressive/correct phrasing | yes | yes | no | no |

failed to read, even if that is only counted as one error, he still made twice as many errors as the other two children with reading difficulties.

The errors the children made were of somewhat different types, but they all showed some evidence of self-correction of errors. For example, most of William's errors appeared to be caused by anticipation of meaning (*brown* for *blue*, *at* for *for*, and insertion of *their*), but two of the substitutions were corrected when the word that was spoken did not match the print. So William is doing a good job of thinking about meaning as he is reading, while at the same time attending to the fact that the words he reads need to match the print. William's phrasing suggested that he was actively constructing the meaning of the story as he went along. Although William may not be reading as strongly as some of his other abilities suggest he should be, he is clearly reading at the third grade level within the average range. He shows good coordination of different sources of information about the words in text (Ehri, 1998), and he appears to be attending well to the meaning of what he is reading.

Brian's reading sounded more like list reading than story reading, and there was little evidence in his phrasing that he was actively thinking about the meaning of the passage as he read it. Two of his four errors were inconsistent with the context (substituting *in* for *and*, and *reading* for *ready*) and they remained uncorrected. Although we have available an extremely small error sample here, one can speculate that Brian's lack of connection to the meaning of the passage allowed him to leave uncorrected these errors that violated both the syntactic and semantic constraints of the story. Executing word level reading processes (both sight word recognition and phonemic decoding) is more effortful for Brian than William, and that is one explanation for Brian's lack of fluency in text reading (Torgesen, Rashotte, & Alexander, 2001), but it may not be the whole story. For example, Brian reads text only 58% as fast as William, but he reads words out of context (in a list) 82% as fast as William. His ability to read words in lists is much more similar to William's than is his fluency in reading words in text. William appears to obtain some advantage from the context of a passage that Brian does not. Brian appears "stuck" in a word-by-word reading strategy, and could likely profit from guided experiences in reading text that include both modeling of fluent reading processes and instruction in comprehension strategies (Meyer & Felton, 1999). Such instruction might assist him to discover what William has learned about using context to assist in fluent text processing. In other words, in contrast to Andrew who is at an earlier period in the development of his word reading skills, Brian appears more able at this point to make the transition to fluent text processing and good reading comprehension.

Andrew's reading sounded a lot like Brian's, and he also did not appear to be actively processing the meaning of the passage as he identified the words. As is suggested by his weaker skills on the list reading tasks, he also made more errors than Brian while reading text. Like Brian, he had a number of uncorrected errors that were inconsistent with either the syntactic or semantic structure of the passage (i.e. reading *on children* for *one child*, reading *inside* for *instead*, and leaving out one whole line toward the end of the story). His errors never deviated dramatically from the graphic information in the text (except for the missing line), which suggests that he has received good instruction in attending to the print while reading text. Andrew is clearly much further away from becoming a fluent and accurate reader than Brian. He needs continued strong support in basic word reading processes, but could also likely profit from extended opportunities for guided practice in reading text with an emphasis on fluency and comprehension efforts. His fluency and comprehension work should begin with reading materials lower than the third grade passage used in the video.

### The copying and finger tapping tasks

Since I'm offering an educator's perspective on the behaviors observed in Part II, I will simply state that I did not find the behaviors observed on the copying and finger tapping tasks particularly helpful in understanding these children's reading problems. However, the psychologist part of my professional identity suggested that we might understand which of the non-reading tasks tap cognitive processing skills most relevant to the differences in reading skill among our children by looking at the degree to which individual differences in performance are consistent across tasks. In Table 14.2, I have summarized my estimate of the children's rank order for performance on each of the tasks. The number 1 stands for the strongest performance, and 4 the weakest. Contrasts that I would assert with confidence are in bold; those about which I have less certainty are in regular typeface.

On the paragraph reading task, the order of skill among the children was relatively clear: Jonathan performed best, then William, then Brian, and then Andrew. This was also the order of performance on the non-word fluency measure and on all the measures of real word reading. I thought the task from Set II that produced the most similar ordering of the children was the finger tapping

Table 14.2. *Relative performance of children on four tasks.*

| Task | Child | | | |
| --- | --- | --- | --- | --- |
| | Jonathan | William | Brian | Andrew |
| Reading paragraphs | 1 | 2 | 3 | 4 |
| Finger tapping | 1 | 3 | 2 | 4 |
| Rey-Osterrieth copying | | | | |
| Organization | 1 | 4 | 2 | 3 |
| Accuracy of recall | 3 | 1 | 2 | 4 |
| Handwriting | 2 | 4 | 3 | 1 |

task, although the order of performance between William and Brian might have been different from the paragraph reading task. Clearly, however, Jonathan performed most effectively on this task, and Andrew was the least skilled. This order of performance contrasts sharply with that for the handwriting task, on which Andrew appeared to be the most efficient, followed by Jonathan, and Brian and William.

The ordering of performance on the copying task appeared to vary depending upon the aspect of performance that was being evaluated. If the organization of the copying is evaluated, then Jonathan was strongest and William was weakest. However, if accuracy of delayed recall was considered, then William was the strongest and Andrew was the weakest. From my perspective, it is difficult to see much connection between performance on the copying task, in either its immediate or delayed recall forms, and the difficulties the children showed on the reading tasks.

This analysis suggests the finger tapping task showed the closest correspondence in its assessment of individual differences among children to the paragraph reading task. However, I also take this analysis with a large grain of salt, as I am not an expert in evaluating performance on any of the tasks except paragraph reading. However, if this relationship were to be borne out in large, multivariate studies (i.e. Fletcher *et al.*, 1994) it would present an interesting theoretical/explanatory challenge. It might even suggest that individuals such as Maryanne Wolf, and others (Wolf & Ashby, this volume; Wolf & Bowers, 1999; Wolf & Katzir-Cohen, 2001) are right to focus our attention on timing, rate, timing/control, and fluency functions in the brain as one part of an explanation for some of the difficulties children experience in acquiring fluent reading skills.

**Comments during the debriefing**

In listening to the debriefing of the children, I was struck by the fact that the examiner extracted from William and Andrew an explanation of their difficulties on the rapid naming tasks that involved word-finding difficulties. After the idea was suggested by the examiner, both children agreed that they sometimes had difficulty "remembering the name" of the colors or objects. This suggests that significant variability on the rapid naming tasks might be accounted for in terms of word-finding difficulties. However, in watching the children perform the naming tasks, I was also struck by the fact that the poorest performer (Andrew) was not consistently slow in his naming rate, but rather that he showed an erratic naming rate. He had many more long pauses between items than the other children. This may have been due to problems finding names for specific items, but it is also a pattern that we have observed on other tasks that involve rapid execution of simple responses that do not involve naming.

A number of years ago a student of mine (Wenger, 1980) did a study of factors responsible for individual differences on the Coding Subtest of the *Wechsler Intelligence Scale for Children: Revised* (Wechsler, 1974). This task requires that children write in the marks associated with digits from 1 to 9 on a coding form. While performing the task, they can examine a key that tells them which mark goes with which digit. The score is the number of marks filled in within a time limit. We examined whether manual dexterity, memory for the coded relationships, pattern of eye movements between the answer sheet and the key, or consistency of response rate were most important in accounting for individual differences on the task within a given age or whether they accounted for developmental differences across ages. We found that younger children had much more variable response rates (time elapsed between making each response) than older children, and that poorer performance within an age group was also associated with high variability in response rate. We interpreted variability in response rate to reflect difficulties in maintaining focus on the task, or in maintaining the proper task set when the individual operations are still challenging for children to perform. I offer this example only to suggest that a number of different explanations for the naming-rate differences among the four children observed in this sample deserve our consideration.

### Concluding comments

If one of the goals of this conference is to explore issues related to the development of a theory of reading disabilities that provides coherent links between the behaviors observed by educators and the brain mechanisms studied by neurologists and neurophysiologists, the three cases we have observed amply document the difficulties of this enterprise. For example, systematic research in this area has discovered that there is one large group of children with reading disabilities whose primary difficulty in becoming good readers involves problems acquiring accurate and fluent word identification skills (Adams & Bruck, 1993; Perfetti,

1985; Stanovich, 1988). Further, a large segment of these children with word reading difficulties appear to have problems from the earliest stages of instruction when they are expected to acquire facility in the use of grapheme–phoneme correspondences to help identify unknown words in text (Share & Stanovich, 1995; Siegel, 1989). These observations have given rise to the theory of phonologically based reading disabilities, which is currently the most complete and coherent (across levels of explanation from reading behavior to neurology) theory in this area (Goswami, 2002; Share & Stanovich, 1995; Torgesen, 1999). The primary impetus for the development of this coherent theory was the observation that one relatively narrow kind of reading difficulty (problems acquiring phonemic decoding skills) could account for failure to learn to read in many children.

In contrast to the relative simplicity of the dominant theory of reading disabilities just outlined, the three children with reading disabilities we observed at this conference showed sufficient diversity of reading behaviors to defy explanation by one theory. Only one of the children, Andrew, appeared to have serious difficulties with accuracy of word level processes. Brian showed reasonably accurate word level processes, but these processes were not implemented fluently in his oral reading, and he did not appear to be actively engaged in constructing the meaning of what he read. William showed very little in the way of obvious reading difficulties. Of course, at the conference we were not presented with information on the developmental history of these children, nor did we understand the specific types of reading instruction they had received. It is possible, for example, that William may have shown reading behaviors similar to Andrew several years ago, but subsequently received much more effective and intensive remedial instruction than Andrew. It is also possible that both Brian's dysfluent style and apparent lack of focus on meaning are the consequences of an earlier primary difficulty in acquiring accurate and dependable phonemic decoding skills. A full theoretical treatment of reading disabilities will need to include explanations for both the initial, or *primary* difficulties in learning to read, and the *secondary* characteristics of these children that arise as an adaptation to the initial difficulties in learning to read (Torgesen, 1993). There is no requirement within the overall conceptual framework of reading disabilities that these secondary characteristics have any coherent links to primary problems in neurophysiological function.

At the very least, the diversity in the current reading behavior of the three children studied at this conference suggests the need for careful longitudinal specification of reading outcome behaviors as a starting place for the development of multi-level theories (Torgesen *et al.*, 2001). Unless we are both clear and very specific in our selection of the behavioral outcomes to be explained, reliable brain–behavior connections in this area will remain exceedingly difficult to establish.

## REFERENCES

Adams, M. J. & Bruck, M. (1993). Word recognition: The interface of educational policies and scientific research. *Reading and Writing: An Interdisciplinary Journal,* 5, 113–39.

Ehri, L. C. (1998). Grapheme-phoneme knowledge is essential for learning to read words in English. In J. Metsala & L. Ehri (eds). *Word recognition in beginning reading,* 3–40. Hillsdale, NJ: Lawrence Erlbaum Assoc.

Fletcher, J. M., Shaywitz, S. E., Shankweiler, D. P., Katz, L., Liberman, I. Y., Stuebing, K. K., Francis, D. J., Fowler, A. E. & Shaywitz, B. A. (1994). Cognitive profiles of reading disability: Comparisons of discrepancy and low acheivment definitions. *Journal of Educational Psychology,* 86, 6–23.

Goswami, U. (2002). Phonology, reading development and dyslexia: A cross-linguistic perspective. *Annals of Dyslexia,* 52, 1–23.

Lovett, M. W., Lacerenza, L., Borden, S. L., Frijters, J. C., Seteinbach, K. A. & DePalma, M. (2000). Components of effective remediation for developmental reading disabilities: Combining phonological and strategy-based instruction to improve outcomes. *Journal of Educational Psychology,* 92, 263–83.

Meyer, M. S. & Felton, R. H. (1999). Repeated reading to enhance fluency: Old approaches and new directions. *Annals of Dyslexia,* 49, 283–306.

Perfetti, C. A. (1985). *Reading ability.* New York: Oxford University Press.

Share, D. L. & Stanovich, K. E. (1995). Cognitive processes in early reading development: A model of acquisition and individual differences. *Issues in Education: Contributions from Educational Psychology,* 1, 1–57.

Siegel, L. S. (1989). IQ is irrelevant to the definition of learning disabilities. *Journal of Learning Disabilities,* 22, 469–79.

Stanovich, K. E. (1988) Explaining the differences between the dyslexic and the garden-variety poor reader: The phonological-core variable-difference model. *Journal of Learning Disabilities,* 21, 590–604.

Torgesen, J. K. (1993). Variations on theory in learning disabilities. In R. Lyon, D. Gray, N. Krasnegor, and J. Kavenagh (eds), *Better understanding learning disabilities: Perspectives on classification, identification, and assessment and their implications for education and policy.* Baltimore: Brookes Publishing.

Torgesen, J. K. (1999). Phonologically based reading disabilities: Toward a coherent theory of one kind of learning disability. In R. J. Sternberg & L. Spear-Swerling (eds), *Perspectives on learning disabilities,* 231–62. Hillsdale, NJ: Lawrence Erlbaum Assoc.

Torgesen, J. K. (2005). Recent discoveries on remedial interventions for children with dyslexia. In M. J. Snowling & C. Hulme (eds), *The science of reading: A handbook.* Oxford UK: Blackwell.

Torgesen, J. K., Alexander, A. W., Wagner, R. K., Rashotte, C. A., Voeller, K., Conway, T. & Rose, E. (2001). Intensive remedial instruction for children with severe reading disabilities: Immediate and long-term outcomes from two instructional approaches. *Journal of Learning Disabilities,* 34, 33–58

Torgesen, J. K., Rashotte, C. A. & Alexander, A. (2001). Principles of fluency instruction in reading: Relationships with established empirical outcomes. In M. Wolf (ed.), *Dyslexia, fluency, and the brain.* Parkton, MD: York Press.

Torgesen, J. K., Wagner, R. K. & Rashotte, C. A. (1999). *Test of Word Reading Efficiency.* Austin, TX: PRO-ED Publishing, Inc.

Wechsler, D. (1974). *Wechsler Intelligence Scale for Children: Revised.* New York: The Psychological Corporation.

Wenger, J. (1980). Behaviors involved in the performance of the coding subtest of the WISC-R. Unpublished Master's Thesis, Florida State University, Tallahassee, Florida.

Wise, B. W., Ring, J. & Olson, R. K. (1999). Training phonological awareness with and without explicit attention to articulation. *Journal of Experimental Child Psychology*, 72, 271–304.

Wolf, M. & Bowers, P. (1999). The "Double-Deficit Hypothesis" for the developmental dyslexias. *Journal of Educational Psychology*, 91, 1–24.

Wolf, M. & Katzir-Cohen, T. (2001). Reading fluency and its intervention. *Scientific Studies of Reading*, 5, 211–39.

.

*Part IV*

Reading Skills in the Long Term

# 15    The importance of comprehension in reading problems and instruction

*Joseph C. Campione*

*Overview:* In many American schools, reading and learning skills of most students are comparable to or worse than those of diagnosed dyslexics, particularly with regard to reading comprehension. This high incidence of reading problems does not lessen the importance of clearly defining and understanding "true" dyslexia as a neuropsychological phenomenon, but it highlights the importance of translating knowledge about remediation for dyslexics into practices for use with children whose poor academic skills do not involve neuropsychological causes. In an essay for this chapter Sandra Priest Rose describes the deep needs of schools for tools to help diverse students learn to read and write more effectively. We suggest that research should focus on similarities and differences between dyslexics' poor reading and the reading of other disadvantaged children, with the goal of determining useful connections for improving learning of reading skills in both populations.        *The Editors*

I am neither a neuroscientist nor an expert on reading differences. I am a psychologist who is interested in children's learning and who has turned his attention to how to design classroom-based learning environments that accommodate children who show strong individual differences in learning in schools. The goal is to foster ways in which all children can be stimulated to achieve high levels of literacy.

## A broad view of reading, with a focus on comprehension

Ann Brown and I have worked with a team of researchers and educators in inner Oakland and Alameda in California, collaborating with specific groups, entire classrooms, and sometimes a whole school. The population with which we have worked is comprised of urban children, including up to 98 percent minority (something of an oxymoron) students in a class. Students in these schools tend to be notably underachieving with mean percentile ranks in mathematics and reading somewhere between the 5th and 15th percentile.

These are students who have different kinds of learning problems and certainly different kinds of reading problems from the four cases that we have focused on in this book. Not many are labeled as learning disabled, although we have dealt with some who have been classified as dyslexic. One reason that many are not labeled is that there simply are not enough slots in the school district to accommodate the children who would qualify for special services based on skill levels if there were no financial restrictions. The majority of students perform poorly in school, and most of them have a variety of reading problems distinct from specific dyslexia.

To begin addressing my concerns, I will make some contrasts among different approaches to evaluation. An important focus is instructional practices that follow from distinct characterizations of reading differences. The literacy work that has been described in most of this book, painted with broad strokes, focuses on basic skills underlying reading. This focus makes a great deal of sense when talking about dyslexia, where a child's problem really is breaking the code and being able to read smoothly and efficiently. A consequence of this approach, however, is that it tends to shape evaluation strategies: the behaviors and characteristics evaluated, the manner of evaluation, and the tests used focus on phonological acquisitions, word attack, and word identification skills. This emphasis was reflected to a large extent in the film of the four boys. What I did not see is a focus on comprehension, which is fundamentally important not only for reading but for education more broadly (Snow, Burns, & Griffin, 1998; Fink, this volume; Immordino-Yang & Deacon, this volume; Wolf & Katzir-Cohen, 2001).

Of course, nobody is going to deny the importance of comprehension, but there was little in the cases that examined the ways in which children understand input or the abilities required to understand it. For example, there could be tasks in which the children made use of information in texts that they read. For children who have severe difficulties with reading, comprehension skills can be evaluated by examining other forms of input, such as listening to someone reading a text or viewing a film. For example, students hear stories or view different kinds of vignettes, and then talk about them and answer questions. A child's comprehension skills are an essential part of the full picture of his or her reading, or more broadly academic learning, skills.

(As an aside, let me note that Ann Brown herself was a classic dyslexic, indeed one of the subjects of some of Rosalie Fink's research. She did not learn to read until she was twelve years old. Early in her school career, she was simply regarded as "slow" and not a candidate for instruction in higher-order thinking skills. Then, a nun noted that when texts were read aloud, Ann's comments and questions were the best and most impressive in the class. This led to a re-evaluation of her "abilities" and a concerted effort to teach her to read and catch up on the learning opportunities that had been denied her earlier. The rest, as they say, is history, and by age 23 Ann had a PhD in psychology. The point, of course, is that when the evaluation criteria changed from simply reading to understanding, the picture of her changed, instruction changed, opportunities changed, and success followed. Without the comprehension component added to the evaluation, who knows what would have happened?)

I live in different environments and different cultures from the one assumed in the dominant approach to dyslexia in most of this book. Most of the frameworks being used stem from medical models, which assume that difficulties and differences are not only associated with children but are an inherent part of the individual (but see Bernstein; Case; D. Rose, this volume). Many of the other groups with which I interact are more socioculturally oriented. For them, differences in performance are explained through the context and settings in which people behave rather than necessarily reflecting the mental apparatus that people bring to bear on particular kinds of tasks. This perspective has specific implications for the ways in which educators orchestrate instruction and assessment (Brown & Campione, 1996, 1998; Bereiter & Scardamalia, 2004; Scardamalia & Bereiter, 1999).

The focus on basic skills and particular kinds of behaviors has two major implications that are potentially problematic. First, such a narrow focus tends to create a system of instruction that is driven by a specific, limited characterization of the individual and a description of differences at a specific level of analysis. In our work we have called this the "leap to instruction" (Brown & Campione, 1986). For example, characterizing a student who has a severe reading difficulty as having a problem with a specific behavior leads to a tendency to key instruction to that behavior – even when that is not the actual source of the difficulty (D. Rose, this volume; Snow *et al.*, 1998). Focusing narrowly on a specific behavior then runs the risk of producing teaching that is focused only on what has been identified in one or another assessment battery rather than on the student and his or her actual learning style and potential.

My other concern is with the long-term outcome for education in reading. Starting with a system where assessment and teaching emphasize, for example, differences in phonological processes, efficiency, and word identification skills, the likelihood is that many children will end up learning to read but will not understand what they are reading. Or as Jeanne Chall (1996) would phrase it, children learn to read but are unable to read to learn.

The focus on phonological analysis, word attack skills, and related basic skills emphasized in most of the reading research and curricula in this book transmits an inappropriate – or at least seriously incomplete – view of what reading is, particularly for the children themselves. Reading can all too easily be seen as a process of identifying words and engaging in oral reading, but not as what it really is – an act of problem solving, a comprehension-seeking process that is essential for learning from reading.

In summary, providing a better characterization of individuals or groups of individuals requires focusing on their comprehension skills and the extent to which they learn from what they read and use that information in meaningful ways. Instructional programs are required that teach comprehension skills, problem-solving skills, and executive functioning or metacognition. Let me also note that such instruction can take place outside the "normal" realm of reading, that is, in listening or viewing contexts. This emphasis is what I will focus on, presenting some of our data.

## Intervention programs in schools

Our work actually started many years ago, with children who had learned to decode, who could read orally at an appropriate and acceptable rate, but who lagged significantly behind in their ability to understand the text that they read. There are a significant number of such children. Palinscar and Brown (1984) developed Reciprocal Teaching, a method for teaching children a set of comprehension-fostering and comprehension-monitoring skills. Briefly, the students and their teacher took turns leading a discussion about a text segment, a discussion requiring the discussion leader to *pose questions* about the text's meaning, attempt to *clarify* any misunderstandings, *predict* the content of future text segments, and *summarize* what had just been read and discussed. Through this intervention, they were able to bring children up at least to grade level. We have subsequently tried to expand our investigations to address a number of other questions about reading and to expand the program to incorporate other forms of literacy (Brown & Campione, 1996; Campione, Shapiro, & Brown, 1995).

One of the things we want to do is seduce children, if you will, into reading a great deal. The seduction involves making selections of texts and topic areas that are interesting and motivating for them to read. What Rosalie Fink (1995, this volume) learned from her successful dyslexic group is what should happen in the classroom – introducing texts that are challenging, that accumulate over time, that push toward higher-order comprehension skills, and that enable teachers to model and teach higher-order comprehension skills. In order to accomplish these goals, teachers need appropriate texts and support materials to enlist the interest of students.

To further support this approach, some data indicate that including comprehension components in a reading program also has the effect of increasing word identification and word attack skills (Snow *et al.*, 1998). A common assumption is that if teaching can improve word identification and fluency, then comprehension will most likely follow. However, the effect also appears to occur reciprocally: good comprehension in a situation where children do a significant amount of reading will itself help to increase their willingness to engage in reading and their ability to read.

We have some evidence to support this pattern from a few case studies with dyslexic students who did not do well at the beginning of our school program, but became more willing to engage in reading – and became much more proficient in terms of oral reading – as the program progressed. Not only did they become immersed in reading about material that was interesting to them, but they also taught what they learned to other students, thereby engaging in practice of oral and presentation skills.

My last point relates to our interest in preventive studies and to the effects of incorporating comprehension instruction in pre-readers. I will describe a pair of such studies, for one of which we have data primarily from our school collaborators, and for the other we have stronger quantitative data.

Regarding the first project, a number of years ago, we had access to all the first grade children who were labeled "at risk" in Springfield, Illinois. These students were identified as at risk for a variety of reasons. We did a study in which half the children participated in an experimental program and half in the control program. The experimental program was focused on listening skills, with the goal of teaching being the development of listening comprehension. The general procedure was the same as in the reading case: input of a segment of text followed by students and their teacher taking turns adopting the role of discussion leader. The difference was that, as non-readers were the focus, the teacher read the target text segment aloud. Half the students experienced this program, while the control group had their regular (often remedial) reading program. The outcome measure was the occurrence of reading problems in third grade, that is, the number of students with reading problems sufficient to prompt referral for evaluation and placement in special education classes or remedial reading programs. The bottom line is that the experimental group – those students who were engaged in active comprehension instruction from first grade on – had a lower incidence of reading problems than did the control group.

The second study (Palincsar, Brown, & Campione, 1993) also involved first grade non-readers. They were exposed to a series of texts that were thematically related, focused on a number of biological themes. The idea, of course, was to provide them texts that could support cumulative learning over time, as the themes reappeared in different contexts and different guises. The experimental group experienced the listening version of reciprocal teaching for 20 sessions, whereas the control group simply listened to the same texts and answered questions about them. Assessment consisted of having the students answer questions about listened-to texts and engage in card-sorting tasks to evaluate understanding of the biological themes. Briefly, (1) the experimental and control groups did not differ on baseline measures; (2) the experimental group outperformed the control group in terms of their ability to answer questions about novel texts, 70% correct vs. 40% on sessons 11–20; (3) the difference was particularly dramatic when questions were addressed to the gist of the texts, rather than more clearly text-related questions, 64% vs. 11% for the same sessions; (4) even more dramatic when the students were asked to solve a novel problem by analogy to a just listened-to text, 77% vs. 17%; and (5) the experimental group's sorting of exemplars was primarily based on thematic principles, 54% of the time, while the control group sorted primarily on surface features, showing thematic sorts only 14% of the time. Thus, although the students were non-readers, the instructional program did succeed in instilling comprehension strategies and skills identical to the ones underlying effective reading comprehension, along with an ability to use text in the service of learning. Comprehension instruction can be introduced successfully early in students' school lives, and even in the case of non-readers.

Finally, an important effect of active teaching of comprehension appears to be the carry-over to decoding and word identification skills. The lesson is that comprehension is not just a downstream element in the sequence of mastering reading skills – decoding to fluency to comprehension. It is an integral part of the dynamics between learning to read and reading to learn, and it needs to be encouraged and supported from the beginning, especially for students who are poor readers for reasons other than dyslexia.

# Essay: Bring reading research to the trenches

## Sandra Priest Rose

*Connection:* This short essay is an emotional plea from an urban educator to translate research into a form that is usable in schools. Research on reading and writing skills needs to move out of the laboratory and into the schools, which have a pressing need for answers about effective practice, especially for disadvantaged or learning-disabled students, but also for many "normal" and able students. Research on learning problems is not just a theoretical exercise! Thousands of children, together with their parents and teachers, look to researchers and educators for guidance in helping students who have difficulties with reading and other important skills. Fortunately several chapters in this book reflect exactly this kind of effort – to create knowledge about reading problems and instruction that can positively affect school practice and improve instruction for children with diverse kinds of reading problems.                    *The Editors*

I am a teacher and reading consultant. My colleague Esther Sands and I work in the classrooms of New York City inner-city areas. We work for an organization called Reading Reform Foundation of New York, which was founded by *teachers* to train teachers in the classroom.

Our organization sends trainers, when invited by principals or district superintendents, into sixty public school classrooms twice a week all year long to help teachers apply what they have learned from us in courses taken the previous summer in the teaching of reading, writing, and spelling. It is one of the most intensive programs I know of; in fact, I do not know of any other like it. Although the children make dramatic gains, the most important contribution we make is that we leave the classroom teacher with training in approaches to teaching reading that he or she can use for the rest of his or her teaching life.

It is fascinating to learn about cognitive science and brain development in relation to reading problems, as in this book, but I would like to make an urgent request that relates to my worm's eye view from the trenches. I am pleading with researchers and educators to use your fascinating studies by applying them to the regular classroom. It is essential that what researchers learn from studying learning-disabled and other children, be used to teach us about ordinary children, as Joseph Campione also argues in his chapter.

We need you. We need your unified voices to add to the massive unequivocal evidence about phonetic methods that use multisensory techniques by which to learn. These methods work with children who have problems, as well as those who do not have problems. Huge federal studies support the use of direct, phonetic instruction first and fast in the early grades (Snow, Burns, & Griffin, 1998; Report of the National Reading Panel, 2000) and new evidence about other tools is also encouraging (Fink, this volume; Wolf & Katzir-Cohen, 2001).

Jeanne Chall's work exemplified fine research that was closely linked to actual students in her Harvard Reading Laboratory and in the classrooms to which she applied her findings. Her final book (*The Academic Achievement Challenge: What Really Works in the Classroom* 2000), stresses her findings that teacher-centered approaches result in higher achievement overall. Her studies showed that systematic teaching and learning of academic skills, facts, and information produced better results.

To give you an idea of the immensity of the New York City school population, we have 1,200,000 students in the schools, 65,000 teachers, 800 elementary schools, and over 100 high schools. A small elementary school has 900 students; average-size elementary schools have 1,500 children. Public school classrooms contain children with a range of learning and skill problems from mild to severe, and inclusion of such students in regular classrooms is not a theory; it is practice by default.

Although these problems are serious in New York City because of size, I can also say that they exist in privileged suburbs as well. I have estimated informally that somewhere between 33% and 50% of the children in privileged areas receive private tutoring, with most of the schools and the parents neglecting to admit that this is happening. I also receive calls all the time from parents of children in the most prestigious private schools whose children need private tutoring in reading. What I am saying is that we are failing children in privileged schools as well as inner-city schools.

Can brain and cognitive studies be done under conditions of using actual training methods that can be employed in schools? Can brain and cognitive studies be done with children who have been taught in different ways to compare the efficacy of different methods? The recent research using magnetic resonance imaging technology by Sally Shaywitz (2003) provides visual and definitive proof that research-based instruction for reading, writing, and spelling can train non-readers and even dyslexics to use more efficiently those parts of the brain that process reading. In other words, phonetic instruction that employs multisensory techniques of transmitting that instruction can help adult and child non-readers to use the appropriate parts of the brain for reading and writing, which good readers do automatically. The implications for changing current instructional practice in most schools in the United States are clear.

Your work must get out to administrators, teachers, and parents. But, also, you must apply your work to the classroom. Please, I implore you, join us in the trenches.

## REFERENCES

Bereiter, C. & Scardamalia, M. (2004). Learning to work creatively with knowledge. In E. De Corte, L. Verschaffel, N. Entwistle & J. van Merriënboer (eds), *Unravelling basic components and dimensions or powerful learning environments*. EARLI Advances in Learning and Instruction Series.

Brown, A. L. & Campione, J. C. (1986). Psychological theory and the study of learning disabilities. *American Psychologist*, 41(10), 1059–68.

Brown, A. L. & Campione, J. C. (1996). Psychological theory and the design of innovative learning environments: On procedures, principles, and systems. In L. Schauble & R. Glaser (eds), *Innovations in learning: New environments for education*, 289–325. Hillsdale, NJ: Erlbaum.

Brown, A. L. & Campione, J. C. (1998). Designing a community of learners: Theoretical and practical lessons. In N. M. Lambert & B. L. McCombs (eds), *How students learn: Reforming schools through learner-centered education*, 153–86. Washington, DC: American Psychological Association.

Campione, J. C., Shapiro, A. M. & Brown, A. L. (1995). Forms of transfer in a community of learners: Flexible learning and understanding. In A. McKeough, J. Lupart & A. Marini (eds), *Teaching for transfer: Fostering generalization in learning*, 35–68. Hillsdale, NJ: Erlbaum.

Chall, Jeanne, S. (1996). *Stages of reading development*, 2nd edn. Fort Worth, TX: Harcourt Brace College Publishers.

Chall, Jeanne S. (2000). *The academic achievement challenge: What really works in the classroom*. New York and London: The Guilford Press.

Fink, R. (1995). Successful dyslexics: A constructivist study of passionate interest reading. *Journal of Adolescent and Adult Literacy*, 39, 268–80.

Palincsar, A. S. & Brown, A. L. (1984). Reciprocal teaching of comprehension-fostering and monitoring activities. *Cognition and Instruction*, 1(2), 117–75.

Palincsar, A. S., Brown, A. L. & Campione, J. C. (1993). First-grade dialogues for knowledge acquisition and use. In E. A. Forman, N. Minick & C. A. Stone (eds), *Contexts for learning: Sociocultural dynamics in children's development*, 43–57. New York: Oxford University Press.

Report of the National Reading Panel: An evidence-based assessment of the scientific research literature on reading and its implication for reading instruction, 2000.

Scardamalia, M. & Bereiter, C. (1999). Schools as knowledge-building organizations. In D. P. Keating & C. Hertzman (eds), *Developmental health and the wealth of nations: Social, biological, and educational dynamics*, 274–89. New York: Guilford.

Shaywitz, Sally M. D. (2003) *Overcoming dyslexia: A new and complete science-based program for reading problems at any level*. New York: Alfred A. Knopf.

Snow, C. E., Burns, M. S. & Griffin, P. (eds) (1998). *Preventing reading difficulties in young children*. Washington, DC: National Academy Press.

Wolf, M. & Katzir-Cohen, T. (2001). Reading fluency and its intervention. *Scientific Studies of Reading*, 5, 211–39.

# 16     What successful adults with dyslexia teach educators about children*

*Rosalie Fink*

*Overview:* A major problem in teaching dyslexic children is their learned negativity toward reading, built from multiple frustrating and embarrassing encounters with printed text. Fink suggests going beyond goals that treat reading comprehension and fluency as if they are disembodied skills, and argues for the importance of the motivating forces of affect and interest. Reading, after all, is about the skill of getting information through text. Based on her in-depth study of successful adult dyslexics, Fink suggests several affective hooks to draw in reluctant dyslexic children, especially emphasizing their individual interests and passions and catering to them. This essay provides a reminder that in the end, one major purpose of studying dyslexia is to translate the research into effective strategies to help learning-disabled children become successful adults. *The Editors*

This essay analyzes development in 60 highly successful men and women with dyslexia and relates the boy William (Bernstein, this volume) to these adults' histories. The 60 men and women developed literacy three to four years later than normally developing peers (Fink, 1995/96, 1998a, 1998b, 2000a, 2000b; Mascolo, Li, Fink, & Fischer, 2002). They followed non-linear developmental pathways similar to a pathway found in children by Fischer and his colleagues (Fischer & Bidell, 1998; Fischer & Knight, 1990; Fischer, Rose, & Rose, this volume).

The men and women include professionals in a variety of fields that require sophisticated reading (i.e. law, medicine, business, and the arts and sciences). Among them are Dr Baruj Benacerraf, Nobel laureate in Immunology and Pathology; the late Professor Ann L. Brown, Harvard and University of California educational researcher; George Deem, New York City artist; Dr Florence

* The research for this essay was supported by a Spencer Postdoctoral Research Fellowship awarded through the National Academy of Education. I am grateful to the Spencer Foundation and the National Academy of Education for their generous support. I also wish to thank the late Jeanne Chall, Julia Feldman, Jennifer Natalya Fink, Gerald Fink, Kurt W. Fischer, Jane Holmes Bernstein, Susan Merrifield, Terry Tivnan, and Susan Vogel for their invaluable assistance. Finally, I wish to express my gratitude to the men and women who participated in the interviews and assessments. Without their courage, generosity, and candor, this essay would not have been possible.

Haseltine, author of *Woman Doctor* and Director of the Center for Population Research at the National Institutes of Health; Dr Robert Knapp, Harvard University oncologist and author of *Gynecological Oncology*; Professor Ronald W. Davis, Stanford University biochemist; and Professor Sylvia Law, New York University legal scholar. The book *Why Jane and John couldn't read – and how they learned* (Fink, 2006) describes the research and a number of the men and women who were highly successful in their careers despite their dyslexia. These men and women were interviewed and assessed individually in order to analyze how they developed literacy as children and how they read and write as adults.

A blossoming literature on adults with learning disabilities has emerged recently, showing successful adult outcomes as well as pervasive continuing difficulties in cognitive and affective domains (Blalock, 1981; Bruck, 1990; Felton, Naylor, & Wood, 1990; Fink, 1992, 1995/1996, 1998b, 2000a, 2006; Finucci Gottfredson, & Childs, 1985; Fowler & Scarborough, 1993; Rawson, 1968; Reder & Vogel, 1997; Roffman, 2000; Scarborough, 1984). Using different research designs, Vogel and Reder (1998a, 1998b) and Fink (1998a) independently documented achievement of high literacy in some adults with reading disabilities. Fink found three literacy profiles among highly successful adults with dyslexia – one group with a compensated profile and two groups with partially compensated profiles. One partially compensated group exhibited persistent ongoing weaknesses in spelling. The other partially compensated group was more severely affected, exhibiting ongoing limitations in an array of areas, shown by lags in word recognition, oral reading accuracy, spelling, and reading rate (see Fink, 1998a, 2000b, 2006 for details about methodology and results). Identification of the three profiles was consistent with the double deficit hypothesis (Wolf, 1997; Wolf & Ashby, this volume; Wolf & Katzir-Cohen, 2001).

The 60 men and women with dyslexia were selected (1) if they had achieved high success in a profession that requires complex reading and demands extensive training, skill, and responsibility; and (2) if they had met the Orton Dyslexia Society Research Committee's research definition of dyslexia (1994) and reported having had difficulties learning to decode single words and/or learn adequate reading and spelling skills, beginning by first grade and continuing at least until third grade. The participants between ages 26 and 50 had been diagnosed with dyslexia by learning-disabilities professionals using established assessment instruments. For those older than 50 (educated when documentation was less common), a case history of early and continuing difficulties in reading unfamiliar words, spelling, and writing constituted the "diagnostic signature" of dyslexia (Shaywitz, Fletcher, & Shaywitz, 1994, p. 7). The men and women were matched for problems and severity of dyslexia and concomitant traits, shown in Table 16.1.

Table 16.1. *Self-reported problems of the 60 participants with dyslexia.* *

| Problem** | # Males | # Females | Total |
|---|---|---|---|
| Single word decoding | 29 | 30 | 59 |
| Spelling | 30 | 29 | 59 |
| Discrepancy | 26 | 27 | 53 |
| Diagnosis/Remediation | 25 | 25 | 50 |
| Letter identification | 23 | 23 | 46 |
| Writing | 25 | 24 | 49 |
| Slow reading and/or writing | 28 | 26 | 54 |
| Memory | 26 | 26 | 52 |
| Laterality (left–right distinction) | 16 | 22 | 38 |
| Second language | 27 | 28 | 55 |
| Fine motor (i.e. illegible handwriting) | 19 | 17 | 36 |
| Familial dyslexia | 22 | 26 | 48 |
| *Mean number of problems per participant: | | | |
| | Males | Females | |
| Mean # of problems (SD) | 9.9 (1.3) | 10.0 (1.3) | |
| Range | 6–12 | 8–12 | |

**There were no significant differences between males and females.
$(t = 0.30, p = .767)$.

Many of these men and women were outstanding professionals in the top echelons of their fields. Fifty-nine of the 60 adults with dyslexia were graduates of four-year colleges or universities, and the majority had earned master's and/or doctoral degrees. They included 17 PhDs, 6 MDs, 4 JDs, 19 Master's Degrees, and 12 Bachelor's Degrees. One individual had attended but did not complete college.

### Late literacy

On average, these men and women developed basic fluency, or what Chall (1983) described as relative smoothness in reading connected text, between ages 10 and 11, approximately three to four years later than "normally developing" peers. In some cases they developed basic fluency even later. They vividly recalled "finally learning to read" as a milestone.

James Bensinger (physicist):

In fifth grade, I finally learned to read. We finally found a tutor, Mrs. King, who finally taught me to read. . . . it was a big change!

Amy Simons (attorney):

I didn't learn to read, to read very effectively, until I was in fifth grade.

Baruj Benacerraf (immunologist):

My problems were earlier. . . . And from about 11 or 12, I surmounted it; I surmounted my reading problem.


## Fischer's web-like pathway

The 60 individuals whom I interviewed and tested were successful in fields that demand high literacy levels, yet they were late literacy learners. Although they comprehend complex written materials as adults, approximately two-thirds of them show ongoing problems with spelling and other sound-analysis skills. Approximately one-third show severe ongoing problems with both orthographic and phonological skills despite their high reading comprehension levels. This ensemble of traits suggests that these individuals developed literacy in a way that was different from the "normal" pathway.

Classic models of reading suggest that in the normal pathway three main components initially develop separately in a forward moving, hierarchical, ladder-like structure in which one skill builds incrementally on another (Fischer & Knight, 1990; Fischer, Rose, & Rose, this volume; LaBerge & Samuels, 1974). A child who follows a normal pathway climbs the sequential rungs of a ladder and moves progressively forward from lower-level visual-graphic and sound-analysis skills to higher-level semantic skills (including symbolic and abstract reasoning and meaning-making). Later, as the "normal" individual progresses in development, these three elements become integrated in an almost seamless fashion so that reading becomes rapid, efficient, and automatic.

The 60 adults with dyslexia did not follow this normal, ladder-like pathway but learned to read through a different interest-driven pathway. Their skills did not become well integrated in a smooth, seamless, automatic fashion. For them, the elements of visual-graphic, sound-analysis, and meaning-making skills remained partly independent of each other and only partially linked or integrated. Instead of proceeding in a forward-moving, unidirectional manner from lower-level to higher-level skills, they learned reading skills through a web-like developmental pathway – a pathway that was messy at times, moving simultaneously forward and backward in a poorly integrated fashion.

These men and women had grappled with profound problems with letter identification, word recognition, and sound analysis. In the most extreme cases, some continue as adults to have difficulty with the most basic orthographic skill, namely, letter identification – particularly when distinguishing between similar-looking letters, such as *b, d, p, q, m*, and *n*, which are similar in feature form except for differences in orientation and direction of letter parts. Graphic artist George Deem, for example, who reads complex authors such as Proust and others, continues to have difficulty distinguishing *b* from *d* in new, unfamiliar words.

George Deem (graphic artist):

Yes, I am still involved with *b* and *d*. If there is a word that I don't know, and it has a *b* or *d*, . . . that gets me very mixed up because I have to look at another word that I already know to remember that the *d* goes that way and the *b* goes this way. Usually I look for the word *but*; *but* is my finder.

Some of these men and women continue to have difficulties translating letters into their corresponding sounds in adulthood. They tend to use phonological strategies, but not very effectively. For example, Charles Bean attempts to sound out new words through phonological analysis; the problem is that his phonological skills are unreliable.

Charles Bean (neurologist):

Phonics doesn't always work. Even though I'll read phonetically, my phonetic sounds don't always fit with everybody else's. I can't break it down. . . .

George Deem and Charles Bean both read sophisticated material for pleasure, including the work of Proust and various poets and novelists. How do they navigate the sophisticated material? Reading comprehension test results show that they comprehend effectively and construct meaning, a high-level skill, while still struggling with basic orthographic and phonological skills. Even in adulthood, when they encounter new, unfamiliar text, they follow a messy, web-like pathway, moving simultaneously back and forth between lower and higher skill levels (for details see Fink, 1992; Mascolo *et al.*, 2002).

## Development of high literacy

Despite their struggles, the 60 adults with dyslexia developed most of the salient characteristics of Chall's (1983) Stage 5, the highest level of reading development. The only Stage 5 characteristic that many still lack is rapid reading speed and automaticity. (On average, they still read slowly when their rates are compared to the rates of matched non-dyslexic adults.) When I tested them, results showed that the 60 individuals with dyslexia comprehended sophisticated text, achieving high scores on silent reading comprehension and vocabulary subtests on The Diagnostic Assessments of Reading with Trial Teaching Strategies (DARTT) (Roswell & Chall, 1992) and The Nelson-Denny Reading Test of Vocabulary, Reading Comprehension, and Reading Rate (ND) (Brown, Fischco, & Hanna, 1993). In 95 percent of cases on the DARTT, their vocabulary and silent reading comprehension reached ceiling (12.9 GE). And, on the ND their mean reading comprehension = 16.9 GE, a grade equivalent slightly above the fourth year of college.

## Avid reading

I was curious about how these adults had developed high literacy in the wake of their serious struggles with lower-level skills. I expected to discover extraordinary bypass strategies; presumably, continual frustration with basic skills would have led them to avoid reading and obtain information through other means. But, to my surprise they were avid readers.

Ann L. Brown (former educational researcher):

I became a very avid reader; I read my way through the local library.

Robert Knapp (gynecologist):

I went to the library and read a lot on my own.

Baruj Benacerraf (immunologist):

I read a lot! Always! I never avoided reading. Never! Never!

Even in cases where they felt profoundly alienated from school, they read a lot. Physicist James Bensinger, for example, was very depressed as a child because school was a painful place for him, so he shut off school and read.

James Bensinger (physicist):

So I did a lot of reading. When I finally learned how to read, I read a lot. I just shut off school. . . . but I did a lot of reading, actually.

## Personal interests

An important common theme emerged from their stories: their reading focused on a personally fascinating topic that captured their imagination and intrigued them. Driven by curiosity and a passion to know more, they read avidly to find out about their topic of interest, engaging in what Jeanne Chall called "reading to learn" (1983).

Ronald W. Davis (biochemist):

I became fascinated with nitrogen chemistry. So the way to understand that was to start reading chemistry books. So I got organic chemistry books and read as many as I could find.

Susan Cobin (headteacher):

I read lots of biographies. The first book I remember reading was a biography of Franklin Roosevelt. It was a key into reading, a step into reading for me. And I continued to read biographies. Lots of them.

Passionate interest in a topic that required reading provided the scaffolding these individuals needed to develop relative fluency and optimal reading comprehension ability. But how were they able to think about ideas and make sense from print when their basic decoding skills remained weak? How did they construct meaning, a higher-level skill, despite continuing problems with lower-level skills such as letter identification, word recognition, and phonological analysis? The key was that they relied on context – during childhood and, in some cases, into adulthood.

Baruj Benacerraf (immunologist):

Even today, when I can't figure out a word, I guess from the context. Yes, I guess what makes sense.

Alexander Goldowsky (museum coordinator):

I tended to be, you know, fairly context-driven. So I made assumptions very quickly based on context and usually substituted a reasonable word.

Barbara Bikofsky (special educator):

I used context a lot to guess at new words.

Cap Ellen Corduan (theatre set designer):

I get the gist of the story and . . . I have it pretty much right!

How did these individuals manage to guess right from context? According to schema theory (Anderson, 1983; Rumelhart, 1980; Snow, Burns, & Griffin, 1998), under certain conditions context-reliant reading is effective and accurate, especially when the reader possesses background knowledge and has a schema for the material. In the cases of these men and women, their deep knowledge of one particular schema supported their development of high-level literacy. Through avid, highly focused reading in specialized disciplines and genres, they developed deep background knowledge, becoming conversant with domain-specific vocabulary, concepts, themes, questions, and typical text structures. Extensive reading about a favorite subject enhanced their background knowledge and enabled them to gain practice, which fostered fluency and increasingly sophisticated skills. The redundant text material itself seems to have provided the requisite drill and practice that facilitated their reading development at optimal levels.

## Reading was captivating

Captivating – this word appeared repeatedly as individuals described their reading experiences. As children, these men and women were avid readers who were often transported by the reading experience. Getting "lost in a good book," they became completely involved, even transformed – by the characters and plot of a novel, for example, losing awareness of all else around them. This total immersion stemming from involvement and enjoyment is what Csikszentmi-halyi (1991) calls a "flow experience" – the feeling of being carried away by a current. When concentration based on enjoyment and interest is this intense, the result is a loss of self-consciousness, which can be very liberating, both emotionally and cognitively. For an individual with dyslexia, who ordinarily struggles with reading and, consequently, becomes anxious in many reading situations, such a flow-like experience is memorable and significant.

The men and women vividly recalled memorable, joyful reading of a particular genre.

Baruj Benacerraf (immunologist):

I read a lot, especially about the lives of famous scientists. Famous scientists and artists, too. I managed to read with pleasure, even though it took me longer. I always enjoyed reading even though it was tedious. I read a lot! Always! Reading . . . is one of my greatest pleasures.

Priscilla Sanville (arts educator):

I was amazed that I could be so locked in a book. It was like the discovery of how a book could take me somewhere different and take me into a world and characters that I could identify with.

Robert Knapp (gynecologist):

I always read history books. Beginning in grade school! And even today, I'm a Civil War buff. I love to read about the Civil War.

Despite early and ongoing travails with the most basic skills of reading, these men and women were transformed by their interactions with interesting, personally intriguing reading materials – materials that they frequently chose themselves as children.

### Gender differences

There were no gender differences in their literacy strengths and weaknesses, but a salient difference between the men and women was their favorite topics and genres, which followed traditional gender patterns (Fink, 2000a, 2000b). Of the 30 women with dyslexia, 23 preferred fiction, whereas 7 preferred non-fiction. Of the 30 men with dyslexia, 14 preferred fiction, while 16 preferred non-fiction. Gender differences in topics of personal interest reading were statistically significant (chi square $= 5.71$, $p = .017$) and mirrored the reading interests of "normally developing" readers (Whitehead & Maddren, 1974, pp. 24–5). Table 16.2 summarizes findings about gender and topics of high interest reading.

Table 16.2. *Gender and topics of high interest reading (by subject).*

| Women | | Men | |
|---|---|---|---|
| n = 30 | | n = 30 | |
| Novels | 23 | Novels | 14 |
| Biographies | 2 | Biographies | 2 |
| Science | 2 | Science | 5 |
| Social Studies | 1 | Social Studies | 6 |
| Cooking | 1 | Automechanics | 1 |
| No Data | 1 | Sailing | 1 |
| | | Poetry | 1 |

Gender differences in topics of high interest reading were statistically significant (chi square $= 5.71, p = .017$).

Women, more often than men, noted the "pull" of novels, especially those related to self-identity and relationship issues. They were particularly drawn to love stories, even where history was ostensibly the subject.

Ann L. Brown (former educational researcher):

I remember reading many historical novels; I read those avidly, particularly about the Tudor and Stuart Periods. Because mainly they were lovely love stories.

Jane Buchbinder (writer):

I loved novels. . . . I read Judy Blume books, like *Are You There God? It's Me, Margaret* and *Wifey*, which were really captivating.

Men, more often than women, were captivated by factual, information-loaded materials found in non-fiction texts.

James Bensinger (physicist):

. . . I knew certainly as early as fifth grade that physics was what I wanted to do. So I did a lot of reading. Ya know, I read magazines and books and just spent a lot of time, just reading about physics.

By "just reading about physics," James Bensinger developed the specialized vocabulary and conceptual knowledge of this discipline. His immersion in physics enabled him to develop specific scientific schemas for reading and thinking about physics. By acquiring detailed background knowledge in one field through avid, highly focused reading, he enhanced his ability to use the context to read, conceptualize, and engage in creative problem solving in physics. His prior knowledge from reading about physics enabled him to evoke sophisticated physics schemas that supported his ability to read complex, highly technical, abstract physics texts.

## Mathematics and science

How did these men and women fare when it came to studying science and mathematics? Due to their difficulties with reading, seven women and one man were explicitly advised not to take courses in science and mathematics. They vividly recalled being given this advice, even when they expressed interest and demonstrated ability in these subjects.

Dorothy Brown (special educator):

I wanted to be a scientist but wasn't encouraged; I was told to avoid science courses because of my learning disability.

Females who were interested in science were channeled into more traditional female courses, roles, and occupations under the apparent assumption that cloaked in these cultural costumes, their learning differences would be invisible and inconsequential. A woman from a science-oriented family reported that she had not been supported to pursue her scientific interests due both to her learning disability and her gender.

Maureen Jacobson (social worker):

Science is a favorite direction in my family; my father is a medical doctor. My brother, brother-in-law, and my husband are also doctors. But, being a girl, it wasn't anything taken seriously. I was never pushed towards the sciences or given any support even though I always wanted to be a veterinarian. So instead of becoming a vet, I became a social worker.

Ronald W. Davis was forbidden to take elementary algebra due to his reading difficulties and poor performance on intelligence and achievement tests taken under standard administration conditions.

Guidance counselor:

With an IQ of 90, you'll never pass elementary algebra. I forbid you to take it. Take shop instead; major in shop.

Davis' father was a carpenter and would have been happy for his son to major in shop and become a carpenter – just like Dad. Davis' parents hadn't gone beyond the eighth grade in their own education, so they didn't have the background to recognize his academic talents. But Davis was driven by intense curiosity about science. He wanted to go to college to become a scientist and knew that, to be accepted in college, you had to study algebra. Consequently, Davis disregarded the guidance counselor's advice.

Ronald W. Davis (biochemist):

I'm going to go and take the class . . . and I don't care if you don't want me to take it. I'll take shop, but I'm taking the algebra, too.

Davis borrowed an elementary algebra textbook during the summer and read it slowly and methodically in a manner typical of many individuals with dyslexia. Reading at his own slow pace, he ultimately mastered the algebra concepts.

Ronald W. Davis (biochemist):

Then I got a 95, the highest grade in the class.

Davis encountered serious obstacles at every stage of his education, from elementary school through graduate school, yet he persisted in surmounting them. He failed freshman English in college yet he was undaunted, approaching this setback in a positive, pragmatic manner.

Ronald W. Davis (biochemist):

So I researched all the English comp. teachers and figured one who would give me a passing grade, given my spelling abilities.

By researching the professors, Davis learned which teacher would be likely to understand his difficulties with spelling and grammar; he discovered ways to make things work for him and so navigated his way through the educational system. Davis passed freshman English the second time around and eventually graduated from college. His approach demanded the kind of persistence, reinterpretation, and adaptive behavior that Gerber and his colleagues (Gerber, Ginsberg, & Reiff, 1992) call "reframing." Davis reinterpreted his experiences of failure and engaged in appropriate behavior to cope with the obstacles and setbacks that inevitably occurred because of his struggles with literacy. Later, he earned a PhD in chemistry, becoming an internationally acclaimed scientist known for his groundbreaking research in biology and genomics. What carried him through were his persistence and his passionate interest and avid reading in a content area that he found fascinating: science.

## Implications of passionate interests

The 60 adults with dyslexia developed high-level literacy through avid reading about a subject of passionate personal interest. They were "turned on" to their topic, whether it was biology, biography, or love stories. They found materials that thoroughly engaged them – so much so that many reported flow experiences, as described by Cszikszentmihalyi (1991). Apparently their imaginations took flight as they discovered their own interests and sought relevant books that excited them.

But struggling readers frequently fail to find books that excite them. Indeed, we know from research that they are often downright disengaged while reading (Wolf, 1998; Wolf & Katzir-Cohen, 2001). These case histories suggest that, in order to entice seemingly "turned off" students into reading, we need to provide reading materials based on each child's interests and passions.

How can teachers ascertain individual interests? One way is by interviewing each child and administering an interest inventory. This involves inquiring about each child's family, hobbies, favorite books, movies, television programs, videos, and computer activities and then locating interest-based materials for the child. Personally interesting reading materials can provide the drill and practice necessary to create good readers. For struggling readers, interest-based materials can be used effectively in conjunction with standard texts and explicit phonological strategy instruction to help develop fluency and optimal literacy.

### Girls and boys

The men and women in these case studies tended to prefer different types of texts – on average, fiction for women, and non-fiction for men. This finding raises the question: how can we engage children with dyslexia in reading by using their preferred interests and genres without promoting gender stereotypes?[1]

An answer may lie in the way in which we approach reading with children. A child's gender conceptualization and knowledge of the world can be expanded through guided critical analyses and thoughtful dialogue about the reading material. The example of a girl who reads only romantic novels is illustrative. To support her optimal development, she should be not only allowed but also encouraged to pursue her fascination with love stories. One approach could be to find love stories in which the female protagonist is involved in a romance and at the same time also involved in a profession less typical for women. An example is the biography written by the daughter of Madame Curie, the first person to receive the Nobel prize twice, once in physics and once in chemistry (Curie, 1937).

Another approach is to reframe *the way* that the individual reads love stories. For example, we might ask students of both genders to consider what is meant by the conclusion, "She married a doctor and lived happily ever after." What was the quality of the couple's life twenty years later? Under what conditions did the woman live? The man? According to what assumptions? How fulfilling were

---

[1] Engrossing activities dealing with gender development are presented in a paper by Nancy Prosenjak (1999) and a brochure published by the National Council of Teachers of English entitled *Guidelines for a Gender-balanced Curriculum in English* (1998). In addition, teachers can consult *Great Books for Girls* (Odean, 1997), an invaluable resource that annotates over 600 books for children from ages 2 to 14. Heroines in these books are girls and women who are not passive but instead active, creative, articulate, and intelligent, meeting challenges, resolving conflicts, and engaging in exciting, active quests. Similarly, I also recommend *Great Books for Boys* (Odean, 1998). This annotated compilation of books for children ages 2 to 14 has been selected with the expressed purpose of raising boys who love to read and are compassionate and cooperative. The books listed and described in these resources present boys and girls with alternative visions of boyhood and manhood, girlhood and womanhood.

their lives, and why? The discussions we engage in, the views of gender that we express, can affect a girl/woman's developing view of herself and her own life possibilities. Such guided questioning can also prevent gender stereotyping in boys and men.

Many of the women whom I interviewed called their favorite books "trashy novels;" they seemed almost ashamed of the books they liked the most. Is there value in reading romantic fiction? Research suggests that the act of reading contemporary romantic fiction is associated with several positive outcomes (Radway, 1991). First, the romantic novel is easily accessible and understandable because of its relatively simple vocabulary, standard syntax, and familiar language style. Romantic fiction is reader-friendly and can break down important barriers to literacy – barriers that otherwise deter reluctant readers. Second, romantic fiction promotes the development of interpersonal relationships and attitudes of caring and empathy. Readers of romantic fiction can actively extrapolate information about successful intimate relationships and apply that information to their own lives (Radway, 1991, p. 193). Readers can develop what Carol Gilligan calls the perspective of care and relationship, a perspective in which the relational world is valued and highly regarded (Gilligan, 1982). This viewpoint is important for both girls and boys as they negotiate relationships in their lives.

Evidence from recent studies suggests that boys as well as girls yearn to develop sensitivity (Kindlon & Thompson, 1999; Pollack, 1998) and can benefit from education in an empathic perspective of care and relationship – a perspective developed in part from reading and analyzing romantic texts. Yet the case histories of successful adult dyslexics show that a majority of males prefer to read non-fiction. What are the values inherent in reading non-fiction texts? Non-fiction provides essentially unlimited, detailed information and exposure to the wider world – with virtually no boundaries of geography, history, time, space, or topic. By presenting vast amounts of information in numerous content areas (i.e. mathematics, science, social studies, art, etc.), non-fiction helps prepare readers for the world of work and citizenship. In addition, non-fiction texts educate from a variety of philosophical, religious, and moral perspectives. Through non-fiction, readers can learn about the perspective of justice (Gilligan 1982), or judging right from wrong. Guided critical reading is important, not only for helping students develop literacy skills, but also for expanding their notions of gender, increasing their knowledge of a content area, and developing their moral and ethical views of the world.

**Twin texts: fact and fiction together**

To facilitate broader text experiences regardless of gender on a topic of personal interest, educators can teach with twin texts. This duality entails the simultaneous teaching with both fiction and non-fiction books that deal with similar themes or topics. Camp (2000) has described how twin texts can be used in synchrony to deepen the classroom literacy program. Through compelling examples of twin texts and detailed explanations of their paired usage, Camp's work shows that, with the help of a teacher's skillful guidance with twin texts, students can learn to appreciate new genres that enrich their interest and deepen their understanding about a topic of personal passion.

### Mathematics, science, and civil rights

Some individuals with dyslexia in these case studies were excluded from higher-level mathematics and science courses due to their reading difficulties. Yet according to Moses and Cobb (2001) mathematical literacy should be a civil right. In their book *Radical Equations*, Moses and Cobb present a compelling case, carefully arguing that mathematics literacy is a civil right commonly denied to disadvantaged minority youth. Their argument links the denial of mathematics literacy directly to lack of access to one particular course: elementary algebra. Apparently, this course acts as a gatekeeper, effectively excluding large numbers of minority students from the opportunity to pursue higher education. Since algebra is a prerequisite to higher mathematics courses and college entrance, denying children access to ninth grade algebra essentially excludes them from study in most four year colleges. Moses and Cobb argue that disadvantaged African-American and other minority youth are consistently denied access to algebra based on discriminatory practices arising from unsound and unconstitutional assumptions about ability in American public schools.

Like many minority children, students with dyslexia are at risk for denial of access to algebra and other higher-level courses due to their learning disability. According to my interviews, individuals with dyslexia who were interested in science and mathematics were explicitly discouraged from taking higher-level mathematics and science courses because their difficulties with reading led others to the misperception that they would have difficulties with quantitative and scientific reasoning. Females with dyslexia experienced this response more frequently than males, a result consistent with research on individuals without learning disabilities (Wigfield, Eccles, & Radriguez, 1998).

Studies have revealed that women and men with and without dyslexia have succeeded in science and mathematics at the highest possible levels (Fink, 1992, 1995/1996, 1998a; Keller, 1983). The lofty goal of preventing a reading disability from inadvertently stunting an individual's cognitive growth in science or mathematics requires ongoing personalized analysis of each developing student's learning profile. As educators, we need to recognize that a problem with reading may obscure ability – even talent – in another area. The case histories discussed in this essay underscore the need to ensure that boys and girls with dyslexia are encouraged to pursue courses that tap into *all* their talents and interests (Bernstein; Rose, this volume).

This point leads directly to William's case. William's verbal responses, body language, and gestures led quickly to my main concern for William: that his intellectual curiosity, infectious smiles and laughter, and overriding upbeat attitude toward learning and life could change drastically for the worse if he is not encouraged to pursue his personal interests. In the brief taped interlude, William spoke about two intriguing interests – singing and geography. William's love of singing and curiosity about geography *can and should* be used as a hook into reading for him.

### Conclusion

My interviews with these 60 individuals with dyslexia revealed that they became hooked on reading by reading extensively, almost voraciously, in an area that fascinated them. Indeed, they were transformed by reading and experienced rapture or flow. Yet they also told me that they had struggled painfully, relentlessly – and almost lost their optimistic views and hopeful personalities – because they endured so much public and private humiliation and emotional pain. As educators, we have a responsibility to provide for enjoyment and joy in children's reading experiences. As Csikszentmihalyi so aptly proclaims, enjoyment "is not a hedonistic goal, but the energy that propels a person to higher levels of performance" (Csikszentmihalyi, 1991, p. 133), the motivator for building knowledge in general (Fischer & Connell, 2003). A large body of research shows that children need a balanced program that includes explicit skills instruction along with opportunities to read authentic texts. It is equally crucial that we simultaneously offer them rich, personally intriguing, reading materials based on their own interests. Otherwise, I fear that we may lose children like William forever.

REFERENCES

Anderson, J. R. (1983). *The architecture of cognition.* Cambridge, MA: Harvard University Press.
Blalock, J. W. (1981). Persistent problems and concerns of young adults with learning disabilities. In W. M. Cruickshank and A. A. Silver (eds), *Bridges to tomorrow: The best of ACDL*, 35–55. Syracuse, NY: Syracuse University Press.
Brown, J. I., Fischco, V. V. & Hanna, G. (1993). *Nelson-Denny Reading Test, Form H.* Chicago: Riverside.
Bruck, M. (1990). Word recognition skills of adults with childhood diagnoses of dyslexia. *Developmental Psychology*, 26(3), 439–54.
Camp, D. (2001). It takes two: Teaching with twin texts of fact and fiction. *The Reading Teacher*, 53(5), 400–8.
Chall, J. S. (1983). *Stages of reading development.* New York: McGraw-Hill.

Csikszentmihalyi, M. (1991). Literacy and intrinsic motivation. In S. R. Graubard (ed.) *Literacy: An overview of 14 experts.* The American Academy of Arts and Sciences.

Curie, E. (1937). *Madame Curie.* London: Heinemann.

Felton, R. H., Naylor, C. E. & Wood, F. B. (1990). Neuropsychological profile of adult dyslexics. *Brain and Language*, 39, 485–97.

Fink, R. P. (1992). Successful dyslexics' alternative pathways for reading: A developmental study. Unpublished doctoral dissertation, Harvard Graduate School of Education. *Dissertation Abstracts International*, F4965.

Fink, R. P. (1995/1996). Successful dyslexics: A constructivist study of passionate interest reading. *Journal of Adolescent and Adult Literacy*, 39(4), 268–80.

Fink, R. P. (1998a). Literacy development in successful men and women with dyslexia. *Annals of Dyslexia*, 48, 311–46.

Fink, R. P. (1998b). Successful dyslexics: A constructivist study of passionate interest reading. In. C. Weaver, *A balanced approach to reading instruction.* National Council of Teachers of English.

Fink, R. P. (2000a). Gender and imagination: Gender conceptualization and literacy development in successful adults with reading disabilities. *Learning Disabilities*, 10(3), 183–96.

Fink, R. P. (2000b). Gender, self-concept, and reading disabilities. *Thalamus*, 18(1), 15–33.

Fink, R. P. (2006). *Why Jane and John couldn't read – and how they learned.* Newark DE: International Reading Association.

Finucci, J. M., Gottfredson, L. S. & Childs, B. (1985). A follow-up study of dyslexic boys. *Annals of Dyslexia*, 35, 117–36.

Fischer, K. W. & Biddell, T. R. (1998). Dynamic development of psychological structures in action and thought. In R. M. Lerner (ed.), *Handbook of child psychology. Vol 1: Theoretical models of human development*, 5th edn, 467–561. New York: Wiley.

Fischer, K. W. & Connell, M. W. (2003). Two motivational systems that shape development: Epistemic and self-organizing. *British Journal of Educational Psychology: Monograph Series II*, 2, 103–123.

Fischer, K. W. & Knight, C. C. (1990). Cognitive development in real children: Levels and variations. In B. Presseisen (ed.), *The at-risk student and thinking: Perspectives from research.* National Education Association.

Fowler, A. E. & Scarborough, H. S. (1993). *Should reading-disabled adults be distinguished from other adults seeking literacy instruction? A review of theory and research* (Technical Report #TR93–7). Philadelphia, PA: National Center on Adult Literacy.

Gerber, P. J., Ginsberg, R. & Reiff, H. B. (1992). Identifying alterable patterns in employment success for highly successful adults with learning disabilities. *Journal of Learning Disabilities*, 25, 475–87.

Gilligan, C. (1982/1993). *In a different voice: Psychological theory and women's development.* Cambridge, MA: Harvard University Press.

Keller, E. F. (1983). *A feeling for the organism: The life and work of Barbara McClintock.* New York: Freeman.

Kindlon, D. & Thompson, M. (1999). *Raising Cain: Protecting the emotional life of boys.* New York: Ballantine Publishing Group, Random House.

LaBerge, D. & Samuels, S. J. (1974). Toward a theory of automatic information processing in reading. *Cognitive Psychology*, 6, 293–323.

280     *Rosalie Fink*

Mascolo, M., Li, J., Fink, R. and Fischer, K. (2002). Pathways to excellence: Value presuppositions and the development of academic and affective skills in educational contexts. In M. Ferrari (ed.), *The pursuit of excellence in education*, 113–46. Mahwah, NJ: Lawrence Erlbaum.

Moses, R. P. & Cobb, C. (2001). *Radical equations: Math literacy and civil rights*. Boston: Beacon Press.

National Council of Teachers of English (1998). *Guidelines for a gender-balanced curriculum in English*. 1111 W. Kenyon Road, Urbana, IL.

Odean, K. (1997). *Great books for girls*. New York: Random House.

Odean, K. (1998). *Great books for boys*. New York: Random House.

Orton Dyslexia Society Research Committee. (1994). Operational definition of dyslexia. In C. Scruggs (ed.), *Perspectives*, 20(5), 4.

Pollack, W. (1998). *Real boys: Rescuing our sons from the myths of boyhood*. New York: Henry Holt and Company.

Prosenjak, N. (1999). Reading across the grain of gender. Paper presented at the meeting of the Colorado Council of the International Reading Association, February, 1999.

Radway, J. A. (1991). *Reading the romance: Women, patriarchy, and popular literature*. Chapel Hill, NC: University of North Carolina Press.

Rawson, M. (1968). *Developmental language disability: Adult accomplishments of dyslexic boys*. Baltimore: Johns Hopkins University Press.

Reder, S. & Vogel, S. (1997). Lifespan employment and economic outcomes for adults with self-reported learning disabilities. In P. Gerber & D. Brown (eds), *Learning disabilities and employment*. Austin, TX: Pro-Ed Publishers.

Roffman, A. (2000). *Adults with learning disabilities: Life-long struggles*. Baltimore: Paul H. Brookes.

Roswell, F. G. & Chall, J. S. (1992). *Diagnostic assessments of reading with trial teaching strategies*. Chicago: Riverside.

Rumelhart, D. E. (1980). Schemata: The building blocks of cognition. In R. Spiro, B. Bruce & W. Brewer (eds), *Theoretical issues in reading comprehension*. Hillsdale, NJ: Lawrence Erlbaum Associates.

Scarborough, H. S. (1984). Continuity between childhood dyslexia and adult reading. *British Journal of Psychology*, 75, 329–48.

Shaywitz, B., Fletcher, J. & Shaywitz, S. (1994). The conceptual framework for learning disabilities and attention deficit/hyperactivity disorder. *Canadian Journal of Special Education*, 9(3), 1–32.

Snow, C. E., Burns, M. S. & Griffin, P. (eds) (1998). *Preventing reading difficulties in young children*. Washington, DC: National Academy Press.

Vogel, S. A. & Reder, S. (1998a). Literacy proficiency among adults with self-reported learning disabilities. In M. C. Smith (ed.), *Literacy for the 21st century: Research, policy, and practice*. Westport, CT: Greenwood Publishing (Praeger).

Vogel, S. A. & Reder, S. (1998b). Educational attainment of adults with learning disabilities. In S. A. Vogel and S. Reder (eds), *Learning disabilities, literacy, and adult education*. Baltimore: Paul H. Brookes.

Whitehead, F. & Maddren, W. (1974). *Children's reading interests* (Schools Council Working Paper No. 52). London, England: University of Sheffield Institute of Education, Schools Council Research Project into Children's Reading Habits.

Wigfield, A., Eccles, J. & Rodriguez, D. (1998). The development of children's motivation in school contexts. *Review of Research in Education*, 23, 73–118.

Wolf, M. (1997). A provisional, integrative account of phonological and naming speed deficits in dyslexia: Implications for diagnosis and intervention. In B. Blackman (ed), *Cognitive and linguistic foundations of reading acquisition: Implications for intervention research*. Hillsdale, NJ: Lawrence Erlbaum Associates.

Wolf, M. & Katzir-Cohen, T. (2001). Reading fluency and its intervention. *Scientific Studies of Reading*, 5, 211–39.

Wolf, Shelby A. (1998). The flight of reading: Shifts in instruction, orchestration, and attitudes through classroom theatre. *Reading Research Quarterly*, 33(4), 382–414.

# 17 Is a synthesis possible? Making doubly sure in research and application

*David Rose*

*Overview:* While most research on dyslexia focuses, not surprisingly, on reading, David Rose cautions against an overly narrow vision of reading and dyslexia. Borrowing the concept of double dissociation from neuropsychological lesion studies, Rose suggests expanding the horizon of inquiry into other skills and populations than those directly related to reading or reading difficulties. This broader horizon leads to better understanding of what makes dyslexic children different as well as which of their skills, broadly conceived, are relevant to the reading process. For example, many children with reading disabilities typically also function poorly on various non-reading tasks. More specifically, Braille reading in blind children highlights that being competent at reading comprehension and spelling requires ample exposure to print and skill at eye scanning (or finger scanning of Braille) – aspects of the printed world that are limited for the blind. From an educational perspective, this broader approach facilitates creating the most effective interventions, which must make use of children's relative strengths, remediate their weaknesses, and address a wide range of relevant skill areas.                    *The Editors*

From the outset, I want to confess that I am a recovering neuropsychologist. For the last fifteen years I have tried to abstain from the practice of neuropsychology in favor of my day job – the design of educational technology. I have not been entirely successful, however, because most of the students for whom my colleagues and I at CAST (Center for Applied Special Technology) have been designing educational technology present either subtle or dramatic neuropsychological problems. That emphasis is due in large part to the addictive influence of a number of mentors, many of whom contributed to this book or to the work cited in this book, and I am happy to acknowledge their sustaining leadership.

The question that I wish to address – "Is a synthesis possible?" – comes from the perspective of my present role as a consumer of neuroscience and cognitive science more than a producer. Such a question is very apt for our work at CAST, where we seek fundamental principles that are synthesized from research in order to provide the basis for designing learning environments to meet the needs of students with learning-related disabilities.

From that perspective I want to raise a caution – that while a synthesis may be possible, premature synthesis is often dangerous. For a developer of technology, where investments in programming and design are not theoretical but real and expensive, premature syntheses present considerable danger. Let me expand a little on this point from a neuropsychological perspective and then illustrate with some examples from the educational technology that we develop.

## Double dissociation

There has been much homage in the field and this book to Norman Geschwind (1965), and rightly so. He was a great synthesizer and teacher. But I also want to recognize a contemporary of his, Hans-Lucas Teuber of MIT (Teuber & Rudel, 1962; Teuber, 1978). He was a terrific complement to Geschwind because he continually raised questions about the generality with which people should interpret the various findings in neurological research. In particular, he continually raised the need for "double dissociation" in interpreting neurological findings.

Most readers are probably familiar with double dissociation, but I will risk a quick review for those who are not. Basically, double dissociation is a method for ensuring that conclusions derived from lesion research are properly interpreted. Let's look at a concrete example. Suppose you discovered a young man who had suddenly lost his ability to jump, and further that subsequent MRI scans of his brain revealed a lesion in area A. A potentially premature synthesis would be to conclude that area A is the "jumping center" of the brain. Instead, it would be critical to dissociate the jumping-related effects of that lesion from possible other effects: does it affect only jumping, or does it also affect other behaviors like running, squatting, or driving a car? If the lesion in brain area A results in disruptions that are not unique to jumping but extend also to other behaviors, then its function is clearly not limited to jumping. Instead both or all of a group of behaviors may have some function in common, and it is that function that is disrupted by the lesion.

Suppose, on the other hand, that the lesion in area A does indeed disrupt only jumping: further tests reveal no disruption in other specific behaviors, like running or driving a car. That finding would dissociate running and jumping to some extent: their functions would appear to be distinct. Teuber argued, however, that a further test is needed – a double dissociation – in order to draw appropriate conclusions.

That further test would examine whether a lesion in some other area might similarly affect jumping. In Teuber's terms, the question is whether the disruption in jumping caused by the lesion in area A is dissociable from the effects of a different lesion. It might turn out that lesions in some other area, or even in many or all areas, disrupt jumping. Those results would lead to a very different conclusion about the role of area A as a jumping center. The test that Teuber recommended was to identify a lesion that affected some other function (like running) but did not affect jumping – the double dissociation.

This double dissociation procedure may seem cumbersome, but failing to take such steps often results in faulty conclusions, including premature syntheses that bedevil the field. Unfortunately scientists and practitioners rarely practice double dissociation in analyzing the neuropsychology of learning disabilities and therefore arrive at problematic and often premature conclusions.

## Dissociation across tasks

This book does not deal with the kinds of specific lesion studies that spawned the double dissociation algorithm. Nonetheless, as a framework double dissociation can be of great help in interpreting what kinds of syntheses might be appropriate given the data. Thanks to the foresight of the organizers, the basis for a process analogous to double dissociation has been provided in the case studies of the four boys.

The tasks that the boys performed concentrate generally on learning disabilities, and specifically on reading abilities and disabilities. Fortunately, the case studies avoid common pitfalls by including a number of significantly different measures of reading ability (Bernstein, this volume; Appendix). In any complicated activity like reading, it is essential to provide such variety. Even more important from the standpoint of double dissociation, the case studies also assess behavior in other domains – on *non-reading* tasks. The Rey-Osterrieth Complex Figure and the tapping tasks, for example, are critical to interpretation of the reading performance because they allow us to investigate whether the observed disruptions in reading are in fact unique to reading, whether they are dissociated from disruptions in other tasks.

In fact, the disruptions in reading are generally not dissociated from disruptions in the other tasks. Students with reading disabilities often show performance deficits (or differences) on non-reading behaviors (Bernstein; Immordino-Yang & Deacon; Taylor; Wolf & Ashby, this volume; Wolf & Katzir-Cohen, 2001). The disruptions differentiate the students with reading disabilities from regular students, and they appear not only in reading tasks but also in non-reading tasks. This information is crucial for illuminating the link between neurology and function.

The fact that disruptions in reading abilities are often not isolated from disruptions in non-reading abilities receives too little attention in the learning disabilities literature. As a result, premature conclusions about the underlying causes or central deficits are often proposed. When researchers and practitioners pay attention to the finding that many students with reading disabilities are also more likely to have difficulties (in specific ways) on the Rey-Osterrieth or to have atypical finger tapping, they are less likely to arrive at a premature synthesis that ignores important data. The lack of dissociation of reading deficits from deficits in complex figure drawing, for example, leads to a focus on identifying underlying functions that are likely to be closer to the underlying reality of learning disabilities.

To be blunt, it is incumbent on learning disability researchers who identify "core" deficits in such tasks as naming or phonemic awareness to show they are dissociable from deficits in such tasks as finger tapping or drawing. If they are not, it is incumbent to take proper care in drawing conclusions.

The problem for researchers in reading disabilities is that the overlap (or lack of dissociation) between deficits in reading and deficits in other tasks is gigantic. Individuals with reading disabilities have been shown to have significant differences from other students on a very long list of behaviors that range from motor abilities to social abilities, from oral language abilities to strategic operations (see for example Duffy, this volume; Eden, Stein, Wood, & Wood, 1995; Immordino-Yang & Deacon, this volume; Lovett & Steinbach, 1997; Lyon, 1996; Pennington, 2002; Watson & Willows, 1995; Wolf & Ashby, this volume). To ignore the actual range of disabilities is to ensure very premature conclusions indeed.

As an example, an important question that I will return to later has to do with differences among media. In our increasingly multimedia world, a fundamental dissociation needs to be addressed: do students who have been identified as having reading disabilities perform normally (or better) when learning to "read" information in other media? Failing to carefully examine the abilities of students classified as "reading disabled" in other domains – like constructing meaning from images, video, or oral language – leads to premature conclusions that are problematic for instructional design. Most teachers and researchers assume that the core deficit in reading disability is limited to text or phonological analysis, leading to interventions that are focused on text and/or the sounds of words. In reality, the evidence across many tasks points to just the opposite conclusion.

Without careful investigation of the capabilities of children who are called reading disabled across a wide variety of tasks and media, researchers and practitioners are unlikely to achieve an accurate synthesis. Early evidence, both in this book and in countless other articles, suggests that descriptions of a child as reading disabled are usually inaccurate because the deficits expressed in reading have not in fact been dissociated from other deficits. An informed synthesis will require a great increase in carefulness in drawing conclusions.

### Dissociation across readers

Teuber would suggest a second way that more care is needed in drawing conclusions. It is not enough to examine merely whether the performance deficits of reading-disabled students are actually limited to reading. Researchers and practitioners need also to examine whether the observed deficits in students with reading disability are limited to those students. How do other groups of students with specific disabilities – *not* classified as reading disabled – perform on the same reading tasks? If they show no overlap in performance, then dissociation will have been demonstrated. If there is overlap among several or all tasks, we might learn something interesting about reading.

Here again, I appreciate that the organizers have provided the case study of Jonathan – not a classic reading disability. Teuber's point is that much can be learned about reading disability by specifically including such students in a study. It is imperative that the performances of a wide range of children be examined. In fact, most students with disabilities have trouble with reading. Their patterns of deficits in reading are highly instructive, both about reading disabilities and about normal reading.

Deaf students are a good example. Overall, deaf students have difficulty in acquiring literacy: the overall reading level of deaf students tends to plateau at about the fourth grade level (for example, DiFrancesca, 1972). That would seem to support the important role of knowing the sounds of language, as in phonemic awareness. On the other hand, closer examination reveals more interesting detail. First of all, the really surprising thing is that deaf students learn to read at all. If minor deficits in auditory processing or phonemic awareness are thought to underlie reading disabilities, then how can deaf children (who clearly go far beyond auditory processing difficulties, and would have to be considered profoundly disabled in phonemic awareness) learn to read at all? Many deaf children are strong and avid readers, showing no sign that their profound deficits in phonemic awareness are a liability at all.

In fact, what is important appears to be not the sounds of language but language itself. Preliminary work suggests that the best readers among deaf children are those who have been brought up in a family of signers (Padden, 1990; see also Petitto, Zattore, Gauna, Nikelski, Dostie, & Evans, 2000). With that rich background of language – visual, not oral – children have a strong foundation for learning to read. Without that foundation, they have difficulty in achieving full literacy.

Blind students are another example. What blind students show is that a person does not have to see the letters to learn to read: one can read with one's fingers. At the same time, blind students have difficulty with various aspects of literacy. They read slowly, for example, partly an artifact of the sluggishness of the hand compared to the eye (Millar, 1997). They have difficulty with knowing where they are in the text, a result of the inability to scan with the hand as well as the eye (Millar, 1997). They are also often notoriously poor spellers (Richard Jackson, personal communication). What that demonstrates is probably that the learning of conventional orthography is greatly aided by the sheer volume of practice that visual learners have compared to tactile learners. (There is less Braille around, anywhere, and fewer Braille teachers.)

Students with cerebral palsy and other motor disorders are particularly interesting examples. Contrary to prevalent folk wisdom, individuals with motor disorders have a much higher incidence of learning disabilities than the population as a whole (Billard, Gillet, Barthez, Hammet, & Bertrand, 1998; Frampton & Goodman, 1998; Robertson, Finer, & Grace, 1989; Robinson, 1973). One explanation that has been given is that the brain damage that has caused the motor disorder has also affected areas of the brain involved with reading. However, reading also requires action. Highly skilled reading requires highly skilled and strategic planning of those actions. From the control of eye movements that target the discriminant aspects of text to the control of mental operations that extract and synthesize meaning, highly skilled reading requires highly skilled and strategic planning, monitoring, and action (Case; Immordino-Yang & Deacon; Wolf & Ashby, this volume). The planning and operational deficits that are often central to motor disorders are also evident in the operations of reading.

Many reading researchers miss this point. As a result, the usual assessment of phonemic awareness, for example, hopelessly confounds perceptual tasks with operational ones. When the student is asked to "say cat without the 'c,'" we are not assessing sound awareness, but the capacity for fairly sophisticated operations on sequences of sounds. The operations or actions that these tasks require are the kinds of tasks that children with motor disorders usually fail.

Children with autism or Asperger's syndrome are similarly interesting. It is common, especially in Asperger's syndrome, to find children who are precocious readers, who are able to decode words at preposterously early ages with little or no instruction. Moreover, experiments have shown that they are not just "word calling" but have learned the phonics patterns that will allow them to decode novel and even nonsense words (O'Connor & Hermelin, 1994; Welsh, Pennington, & Rogers, 1987). What their early reading demonstrates is that decoding is a small part of reading, for in spite of their precocity in word reading, they are often strikingly disabled in comprehension (Welsh et al., 1987). These children demonstrate how separable the various aspects of reading are: decoding skills may be necessary, but they clearly are not sufficient for adequate reading (Campione, this volume).

The examples I have presented are merely illustrative. The specific reading abilities of many other types of students who have demonstrable non-reading disabilities are equally thought-provoking. Students with ADHD, Executive Function Disorder, emotional disorders, or even Down Syndrome provide a rich source of natural experiments that reveal what reading really requires of the learner. These comparisons provide essential background information from which to evaluate what is really unique among a group of students with reading disability.

What is the lesson from all these children with disabilities? First of all, they show that reading has many components, and that difficulties in reading do not come from a single source, but from many (Campione; Case; Fischer, Rose, & Rose; Immordino-Yang & Deacon, this volume; Waber *et al.*, 2001; Wolf & Ashby, this volume). From a double dissociation standpoint they demonstrate that reading difficulties in students with learning disabilities are not entirely dissociated from reading difficulties of other students with disabilities. Avoiding premature closure requires investigating the reading abilities and disabilities of a wide spectrum of students, looking for the dissociations that will indicate the discontinuities that characterize reading. Such dissociations are critical to avoid incorrect conclusions about the critical aspects of learning disabilities, and even of reading itself.

## Remedial technologies and the student with reading disabilities

Why is it important to identify accurately the critical aspects of learning disabilities? Let me express the importance from the perspective of our work at CAST. As developers of educational technology that is focused primarily on children with disabilities, all of us at CAST must understand what we are trying to address instructionally. There are two broad directions that developers of new technology usually take in addressing the needs of students with disabilities.

The first approach is to use the new technology as a tool for remediation or rehabilitation. In this approach, the technology is usually a part of an instructional or therapeutic milieu. The intent of the technology is to target especially effective and intensive instruction on the student's core area of deficient skills. The rationale for such an approach is obvious, and such interventions will in some way be essential.

But if the targeted area of deficiency, let's say phonemic awareness, is not actually the core deficit but is merely a very visible symptom of a more fundamental deficit, or if it is a core deficit for some students but not all, then the intervention will have mixed results. For example, the intervention may build phonemic awareness skills without having a major impact on the overall remediation of reading disabilities. Moreover, at least for some students we will have expended great time and energy – both teacher and student – on an incidental aspect of the problem rather than its core. The result will be the disappointment of lost opportunity and optimism for further intervention.

A modern example of such a remedial technology is Fast ForWord, by Scientific Learning Corporation, a program specifically developed to address the problems of students with reading disabilities. Fast ForWord has been developed from the work of Paula Tallal, and the product reflects the claims of

Tallal's research that the core deficit in reading disabilities is one related to auditory perception (Tallal *et al.*, 1996; Waber *et al.*, 2001). The program seeks to remediate, through extensive progressive practice in sound discrimination, the auditory processing problems that Dr Tallal's research identifies as central to reading and learning disabilities.

Fast ForWord is an impressive, and expensive, undertaking. The expense of developing (as well as purchasing) Fast ForWord is justified to the extent that it is successful in addressing the core deficit in reading disability across a large number of students. Apparently Fast ForWord is demonstrably effective with a subpopulation of children who have learning disabilities: the intensity and focus of instruction provided by the technology outstrips what a classroom environment can provide. Does it address the core deficits of the full population of students with reading disabilities? Undoubtedly not. It is interesting to observe the changing marketing claims made for the product – from early releases that were striking in their hyperbole to recent claims that are much more modest, and more admissive that the product does not work for everyone.

When marketed as a cure for reading difficulties, Fast ForWord will certainly disappoint many. When marketed as an important tool to address one of the root deficits in some students with learning disabilities, Fast ForWord may prove to be an excellent choice. Clear dissociation of the individuals for whom it will be helpful from those for whom it will not is an important pragmatic step. Proper research is critical in that step.

Fast ForWord is but one example of the remedial type of technology that is being developed for students with learning disabilities. I hope that other technologies, directed at other facets of reading disability, will be developed with the same zeal and marketing savvy that the founders of Fast ForWord have devoted to their product. Key to the development of other products will be a program of research that does not reach premature closure about the aspects of reading disability that it in fact addresses.

### Assistive technologies and Universal Design

The second approach that technology developers usually take to address the needs of students with disabilities does not focus on remediation, but instead concentrates on designing tools for communication and learning that are more responsive and supportive for students with disabilities than the usual tools. In this approach, various alternative technologies and techniques are provided that allow a student to succeed through scaffolds, alternative methods of representation or expression, and so forth.

When these technologies are provided to students so that they can overcome barriers inherent in existing technologies or curricula, they are called "assistive technologies." A program that reads text on the computer screen for blind students and students with learning disabilities is such an assistive technology.

Another approach, one pioneered by CAST and called Universal Design, is to design curricula and media that have alternative representations and supports built in at the outset for use by many different people. In WiggleWorks (© Scholastic), a reading program for kindergarten through third grade, each book is available in print and on compact disc (CD). On the CD versions, each book is highly flexible and customizable so that almost any student can find a presentation that is supportive and appropriate to his or her needs. Even a student with severe physical disabilities can turn the pages without having to use a keyboard or a mouse. More specifically for students with reading disabilities is a newer set of books, this time for middle schoolers, published by Scholastic as Thinking Reader. These books embed many different supports, all highly individualized, to help struggling readers as they read core literature in their middle school classrooms.

Whether through assistive technologies or Universal Design, we seek to provide a measure of success for students through support rather than through sustained concentration on their weaknesses. This approach has many advantages (Meyer and Rose, 1998; Rose & Meyer, 2002) but also is prey to problems of premature synthesis. I will describe one of these.

We have developed a program at CAST called the e-Reader, now called Aequus AspireREADER 4.0. It is an application, much like a word processor, which is designed to scaffold students who have difficulties in reading. With this program students read their text on the screen of their computer rather than in a printed book. While this setup has some disadvantages (computer screens are not as sharp as printed pages), there are enormous advantages in the level of support for reading that a student can access. For example, with the AspireREADER students can click on any word that they cannot decode and hear that word read aloud. Or they can have the sentences themselves read aloud while highlighting the words in time, with the speech providing multiple representations in visual and auditory modes. Or they can enlarge the text, get definitions for words, etc.

With these scaffolds, a student who has difficulty in decoding words can competently read almost any text. For the student in middle school or high school who does not yet read fluently, such a tool can help greatly in dealing with content textbooks in nearly all their subjects. Thousands of teachers all over the country have scanned their textbooks into digital versions so that they can provide adequate support for students with reading disabilities. This approach provides a crucial alternative to "dumbing down" the textbooks for the many thousands of students whose reading level is much lower than their conceptual level. The AspireREADER also acts as a browser. Students can launch to any web page and get support for reading the text on that page; they are not left stranded with text they cannot read.

Such an approach, however, assumes that the difficulties are entirely in the decoding of text. The assumption is that the problem is a reading problem – focused on the representation of language in text. If the problem of the reading-disabled student extends to understanding complex oral language, as it clearly does in many students, then our approach will not be sufficient. Nor will reading the sentences aloud by a human reader, for that matter. In our work with students, we have found many instances where by compensating for supposed difficulties we have not in fact helped the students much. The problem is that we have not understood the core deficit correctly because we have relied on premature syntheses in the literature.

## Coda

The question is: is a synthesis possible of cognitive science and neuroscience with educational practices for people with learning disabilities? The answer is: yes, dangerously so. For those of us who are faced with decisions about remediation and universal design, we need research that has been carefully designed to identify clearly what we need to address. Such research should include data that provides tests of double dissociation: a wide variety of reading and non-reading tasks done by a wide variety of reading-disabled and non-disabled students. Such research would be doubly careful, which is just exactly what we need.

REFERENCES

AspireREADER 4.0 (Computer Software). (2005) Pine Brook, New Jersey: Aequus Technologies.

Billard, C., Gillet, P., Barthez, M., Hommet, C. & Bertrand, P. (1998). Reading ability and processing in Duchenne muscular dystrophy and spinal muscular atrophy. *Developmental Medicine & Child Neurology*, 40(1), 12–20.

DiFrancesca, S. (1972). *Academic achievement test results of a national testing program for hearing-impaired students, United States, Spring 1971* (Series D., No. 9). Washington, DC: Callaudet College, Office of Demographic Studies.

Eden, G. F., Stein, J. F., Wood, M. H. & Wood, F. B. (1995). Verbal and visual problems in reading disability. *Journal of Learning Disabilities*, 28(5), 272–90.

Frampton, I., Yude, C. & Goodman, R. (1998). The prevalance and correlates of specific learning difficulties in a representative sample of children with hemiplegia. *British Journal of Educational Psychology*, 68(1), 39–51.

Geschwind, N. (1965). Disconnection syndrome in animals and man (Parts I, II). *Brain*, 88, 237–94, 585–644.

Lovett, M. W. & Steinbach, K. A. (1997). The effectiveness of remedial programs for reading disabled children of different ages: Does the benefit decrease for older children? *Learning Disability Quarterly*, 20(3), 189–210.

Lyon, G. R. (1996). Learning disabilities. *Future Child*, 6(1), 54–76.

Meyer, A. & Rose, D. H. (1998). *Learning to read in the computer age*, Vol. 3. Cambridge, MA: Brookline Books.

292    *David Rose*

Millar, S. (1997). *Reading by touch.* London: Routledge.
O'Connor, N. & Hermelin, B. (1994). Autism and reading. *Journal of Autism and Developmental Disorders,* 24(4), 501–15.
Padden, C. A. (1990). *Deaf children and literacy. Literacy lessons.* (Microfiche [1 card(s)], Paper. ED321069). Geneva, Switzerland: International Bureau of Education.
Pennington, B. F. (2002). *The development of psychopathology: Nature and nurture.* New York: Guilford Press.
Petitto, L. A., Zatorre, R., Gauna, K., Nikelski, E. J., Dostie, D. & Evans, A. (2000). Speech-like cerebral activity in profoundly deaf people while processing signed languages: Implications for the neural basis of human language. *Proceedings of the National Academy of Science,* 97(25), 13961–6.
Robertson, C. M., Finer, N. N. & Grace, M. G. (1989). School performance of survivors of neonatal encephalopathy associated with birth asphyxia at term. *Journal of Pediatrics,* 114(5), 753–60.
Robinson, R. O. (1973). The frequency of other handicaps in children with cerebral palsy. *Developmental Medicine & Child Neurology,* 15(3), 305–15.
Rose, D. & Meyer, A. (2002). *Teaching every student in the digital age.* Alexandria, VA: American Association for Supervision & Curriculum Development.
Tallal, P., Miller, S. L., Bedi, G., Byma, G., Wang, X., Nagarajan, S. S., Schreiner, C., Jenkins, W. M. & Merzenich, M. M. (1996). Language comprehension in language-learning impaired children improved with acoustically modified speech. *Science,* 271, 81–4.
Teuber, H.-L. (1978). The brain and human behavior. In R. Held, H. Leiber & H.-L. Teuber (eds), *Handbook of sensory physiology,* 879–920. Heidelberg: Springer-Verlag.
Teuber, H.-L. & Rudel, R. G. (1962). Behavior after cerebral lesions in children and adults. *Developmental Medicine & Child Neurology,* 4, 3–20.
*Thinking Reader (Computer Software).* (2004) Cambridge, Massachusetts: Tom Snyder Productions.
Waber, D. P., Weiler, M. D., Wolff, P. H., Bellinger, D., Marcus, D. J., Ariel, R., Forbes, P. & Wypij, D. (2001). Processing of rapid auditory stimuli in school-age children referred for evaluation of learning disorders. *Child Development,* 72, 37–49.
Watson, C. & Willows, D. M. (1995). Information-processing patterns in specific reading disability. *Journal of Learning Disabilities,* 28(4), 216–31.
Welsh, M. C., Pennington, B. F. & Rogers, S. (1987). Word recognition and comprehension skills in hyperlexic children. *Brain and Language,* 32(1), 76–96.
*WiggleWorks (Computer Software).* (1993) New York, NY: Scholastic.
Wolf, M. & Katzir-Cohen, T. (2001). Reading fluency and its intervention. *Scientific Studies of Reading,* 5, 211–39.

# Appendix
# Transcript and behavioral data from Profiles in Reading Skills (Four Boys)*

*Jane Holmes Bernstein*
*in collaboration with members of the MBB / Development Working Group of the Harvard Interfaculty Initiative on Mind, Brain, & Behavior*

*Francine Benes, Kurt Fischer, Jerome Kagan, Deborah Waber, and Maryanne Wolf*

### The children: the initial interview

*The four boys are all 9 years old. They are right-handed. Jonathan has not experienced difficulty in learning to read. The other three boys have.*

#### Jonathan
. . . . . . Well, I like to play sports. . . . . . . I like to play
     *[Jane Holmes Bernstein (JHB): You're a sportsman – OK]*
lots of different sports, like. . . . . . . I play baseball . . . and soccer. . . . . I want to play–LAUGHS–hockey and football but I can't–LAUGHS–
     *[JHB LAUGHS. Why can't you play hockey and football?]*
'cos I'll break too many teeth. . . . . . . DISINGENUOUS EXPRESSION* + GRIN!

FACIAL EXPRESSION: Bright, animated, mischievous.
INTONATION: Within normal limits: varies appropriately with content.
POSTURE: Arms on table, in "conversational space" with JHB.
GAZE PATTERNS: Gazes up when thinking/formulating remarks; focuses appropriately on JHB when making point.

INTERVIEWER COMMENT: Comfortable with himself, enjoying the attention. Fluent use of conversational language: turn-taking is smooth with appropriate "cross-cutting" of his and JHB's remarks. Socially aware, even

---

* The four boys' performances were shown on a film available to the participants in the conference that led to this book. This transcript describes their performances.

Table A1. *Demographic data for the four boys.*

|          | Age   | Grade                        | Mother's education | Father's education |
|----------|-------|------------------------------|--------------------|--------------------|
| Jonathan | 9–03  | 3rd                          | college            | college            |
| William  | 8–10  | 3rd                          | graduate school    | graduate school    |
| Brian    | 8–11  | 3rd                          | graduate school    | college            |
| Andrew   | 8–11  | 2nd (repeated 1st)           | 1 year college     | college            |

sophisticated: knows that his last remark will not be expected – waits for its effect on JHB!

## William

...... I'm really good at geography........ and ... hummm!... I'm really good at

     *[Maryanne Wolf (MW): yeah]*

singing........ I'm pretty good at lots of things actually.

     *[MW: Yes, I know that . . . that's what I hear] [Yeah! That's great . . .]*

FACIAL EXPRESSION: Bright, engaged.

INTONATION: Appropriately varied; matched to content of remarks.

POSTURE: Arms on table; in conversational space with MW.

GAZE PATTERNS: Looks up and to the side when thinking/formulating; focuses on MW appropriately when offering specific information.

INTERVIEWER COMMENT: Mildly anxious but very familiar with MW, whom he likes and who enjoys him. Elicits encouraging, soothing tone of voice from MW. Conversation moves smoothly between W and MW with appropriate cross-cutting of utterances.

## Brian

...... *[JHB: I guess you've got some friends to play with?]*

... Yeah....

     *[JHB : Do you have, er . . . who's your best friend? . . . do you have a best friend?]*

... Yeah....

     *[JHB: Who's that?]*

... My twin brother....

     *[JHB: Oh, you have a twin! Whoa! I can ask you about that. What's it like to have a twin?]*

...... */voices clash/* ... I like to have a twin because . . . because, when, like, nobody's, here to play with me I usually always play with my brother . . .

     *[JHB: Oh, right! And is he an OK brother or is he a pain-in-the-neck brother?]*

... He's an OK brother. ......

FACIAL EXPRESSION: Minimal change in expression.

INTONATION: Minimally varying, with atypical lifts and drops at the end of clauses.

POSTURE: Sits straight up. Responsive to questions but not interactive with JHB.

GAZE PATTERNS: More or less fixed on JHB: not an intense stare, but atypical nonetheless.

INTERVIEWER COMMENT: Conversation is notably dysfluent, the social interaction awkward (though not unfriendly). JHB is struggling to elicit information, needing to keep asking specific questions and/or to offer language for B to "choose from," and attempting to inject more animation into the interchange with somewhat exaggerated intonation (*Oh! You have a twin. ........*, etc.). B's speech output is unusually staccato: words are frequently uttered one by one with breath pulses not synchronized to the syntax of what he is saying. He answers rhetorical questions, miscues on language elements (*what is it like?* → "I like to . . ."), repeats the form of a question to cue his answer, and typically does not follow through with expectable information unless specifically queried.

**Andrew**

...... Captain Cat!! ... Cat.

*[JHB: Captain?. . . Cat?!] [Well, OK. Can you tell me a bit about Captain Cat? What's it about?]* ...

He joins the army (sing-song intonation)... and then Blond Hair.... er! ... army person ... plays with him ALL the time ....

*[JHB: oh!]*

...... and the sergeant there gets Blond Hair in trouble ...... because he wasn't doing his chores so he had to scrape the potatoes ......

*[JHB: oh, dear! (matching his dramatic intonation) ...... LAUGH ...... A lot of potatoes?]*

... Uh, yeah (dramatic sigh!) ...... And he let Captain Cat play with the ... the little scraps .....

FACIAL EXPRESSION: Big dramatic facial expressions to punctuate his storyline.

INTONATION: Wide range; theatrical description.

POSTURE: Sits back in seat, very comfortable.

GAZE PATTERNS: Within normal limits: focuses off and on JHB's face fluently.

INTERVIEWER COMMENT: Andrew's story is hard to follow in spite of its dramatic presentation which appears to be intended to punctuate and accentuate the narrative. Andrew seems unaware of his conversational partner's inability to follow him. He does not, however, have difficulty in interweaving his comments with hers, fluently responding to her queries on line.

### The tasks

*Task 1: rapid naming*

Narrator: *On this task the boy is to name the 50 items as quickly as possible: first colors, then letters, then objects.*
[**Note**: / marks the taking of a breath as the boys are reciting the items from the task.]

#### Colors
**Jonathan**
Black Red Yellow Green Blue / Red Black Yellow Blue Green
Yellow Green / Red Blue Green Black Ye . . . Red / Blue Yellow Black
Red Bl . . . / Black Yellow / . . . Red Yellow Green Blue Black Green Red. . . .
INTERVIEWER COMMENT: Unhurried but moves quickly through task. Performance is accurate with only occasional hesitations. Recites five to six items per breath pulse. Body relaxed. Hands quiet on table.

**William**
Black Red Yellow Green Blue / Red Black /Yellow Blue/ Green
Yellow . . . CLEARS THROAT . . . Green Red Blue / Green Black / Red Blue /
Yellow Black /
Red Black. . . um . . . Yellow Red Yellow . . . CLEARS THROAT . . . Green
Blue Black /Green Red. . . .
INTERVIEWER COMMENT: Starts by holding on to the side of the table with both hands. Shifts to tracking, pointing with the right finger item by item. Starts to recite items in pairs or triplets to give himself a rhythmic pattern to help manage the effort required.

**Brian**
Black / Red / Yellow / Green / Blue / Red / Black / Yellow / Blue / Green /
Yellow / Green / Red / Blue / Gr . . . Green / Black / Red / Blue / Yellow / Black /
Red / Black / Yellow / Red. . . . Yellow / Green / Blue / Black / Green /Red. . . . . . .
INTERVIEWER COMMENT: Sits absolutely straight up in seat, hands in lap. Does not change position throughout.

**Andrew**
Black Red Yellow . . . er! Green / Blue / Red Black / Yellow Blue . . . Green
(END OF LINE) . . . (4 sec pause) . . . Yellow Green Red . . . Red (Blue) Green
Black . . . Red Blue Yellow Black (END OF LINE) . . .

Table A2. *Tasks performed by the four boys. (Publications describing each task in detail are given at the end of this Appendix in the section References.)*

| | |
|---|---|
| Rapid naming | On this task the boys name 50 items as quickly as possible. The items are presented in a 10 column × 5 row array. The stimulus items for the whole task include: Colors – Letters – Objects – Numbers – 2 step (Letters, Numbers) – 3 step (Colors, Letters, Digits). The transcript includes only the trials for Colors, Letters and Objects. |
| Untimed reading | The boys read a list of words from the Letter-Word Identification subtest and then a list of non-words from the Word Attack subtest of the Woodcock-Johnson Psychoeducational Battery, Revised. The items listed in the transcript are those on which each boy is starting to make errors and/or to expend effort. |
| Timed reading | The boys read a list of words and non-words (Torgesen's Reading Efficiency Task) as quickly as they can – for 45 seconds. The items in the transcript are those on which each boy is starting to make errors and/or to expend effort. |
| Paragraph reading | The boys read an paragraph at approximately 3rd grade level from the Gray Oral Reading Test, 3rd Edition. (Performance not formally scored, but time is recorded.) |
| Motor tapping (P. H. Wolff) | On this task the boys are required first to tap in time with a metronome and then to continue the same tapping rhythm when the metronome is switched off. There are 10 conditions for the whole task: Right alone, Left alone, alternating Right and Left hands (R – L – R – L) at two different tapping rates and asynchronous alternation (R – both – R – both; L – both – L – both) at three different tapping rates. In the transcript the photos of the boys show them doing the fastest alternating hand condition and the slowest asymmetric alternation condition only. (Individual scores not available.) |
| The Rey-Osterrieth complex figure | The boys are required to copy a complex geometric figure using 5 different colored markers in a predetermined order – the Copy condition. Having copied it, they are given a new piece of paper and asked to draw it from memory – the Immediate Recall condition. Approximately 20 minutes later, following interpolated activity, they are asked to draw what they can remember – the Delayed Recall condition. The "Organization," "Style," and "Accuracy" of the boys' performances for these two conditions are discussed in the transcript, as determined by the Developmental Scoring System for the ROCF (Bernstein & Waber, 1996). |
| Handwriting sample | The boys are required to write "I like pizza", first with their right – preferred – hand and then with their left. |
| Debriefing | The boys are asked which task they liked the most and encouraged to discuss their experience. |

(6.5 sec pause) . . . Red Black Yellow Red Yellow . . . /*mild expletive*/ . . . I mean, Green Blue Black . . . . . . Green Red . . . . . .

INTERVIEWER COMMENT: Starts off comfortably with arms crossed on table; some fidgety movement in feet/legs. As proceeds, the struggle to retrieve words leads him to sharply raise his arms (in exasperation?) – he starts to hold on to the edge of the table with considerable tension. Legs are no longer moving. Nods head sharply when cannot find word (attempt to physically "release" the word?).

### *Letters*

**Jonathan**

o a s / d p a / o s p d /
s d a p / d o a p s / o /
a o s / a s / d p o d a /. . . . . .

INTERVIEWER COMMENT: Leaning on arms on table. Mildly fidgety fingers.

**William**

o a / s d / p a / o s / p d /
s d / a p / d o / a / p s o
a / o / s a s d p o / d a /. . . . . .

INTERVIEWER COMMENT: Tracking along lines left to right item by item with right index finger. Left hand follows across items.

**Brian**

o / a / s / d / p / a / o / s / p / d /
s / d / a / p / d / o / a / p / s / o /. . . . . .

INTERVIEWER COMMENT: Sits upright, still throughout. Speech pattern: one breath per letter.

**Andrew**

o a s d p / a o s p / d /
s d a p d . . .(5 secs.) . . . / o a p s o /
a / o / s . . .a / o / s . . .a s d→b p o d→b a→s . . . I mean, a. . . .

INTERVIEWER COMMENT: Initial mild fidgetiness in feet/legs. Sits comfortably: no obvious tension. Performance is slow.

### *Objects*

**Jonathan**

book chair dog hand star / chair book / dog / star / hand
dog hand book star / hand book / chair star dog / book . . .

INTERVIEWER COMMENT: None

Table A3. *Performances for rapid naming tasks.*

| Task | Colors | Letters | Objects | Numbers | Two-set | Three-set |
|------|--------|---------|---------|---------|---------|-----------|
| Mean/SD | 41.6/11.9 | 24.4/5.1 | 41.6/8.4 | 25.0/4.8 | 30.1/6.4 | 33.6/7.4 |
| Jonathan | 44 | 35 | 56 | 29 | 36 | 37 |
| Andrew | 86 | 67 | 127 | 94 | 97 | 102 |
| William | 73 | 33 | 52 | 43 | 46 | 48 |
| Brian | 45 | 29 | 44 | 30 | 35 | 32 |

Score = Latency in seconds to name 50 items
*Note:* Only Color, Letter, and Object conditions are presented in this transcript.

**William**
book chair / dog hand star / chair / book dog / star hand /
dog hand book star / hand book / chair star / dog book . . .
INTERVIEWER COMMENT: Smooth reading. Tracks each word with right index finger. Left hand anchors page.

**Brian**
book / chair / dog / hand / star / chair / book / dog / star / hand /
dog / hand / book / star / hand / book / chair / star / dog / book . . .
INTERVIEWER COMMENT: Reads with his "one-breath-per-item" pattern. No obvious tension.

**Andrew**
book . . . [4 secs.] . . . chair dog / hand star . . . [4 secs.] . . . chair . . . [3secs.] . . . book / dog . . . [4.5 secs.] . . . star hand /
dog . . . [4 secs.] . . . hand . . . b . . . book . . . [3 secs.] . . . star hand . . . [2 secs.] . . . book . . . (omits 'chair': [4 secs.]) . . . star . . . [4 secs.] . . . dog / book . . .
INTERVIEWER COMMENT: Sits straight, concentrating hard. Subvocalizes in longer pauses.

*Task 2: untimed reading – words and non-words*

*Untimed reading: words*
Copyright © 1989 by The Riverside Publishing Company. *Letter-Word Identification* (words) and *Word Attack* (non-words) subtests reproduced from the *Woodcock-Johnson Psycho-Educational Battery – Revised*, by Richard W. Woodcock and M. Bonner Johnson, with permission of the publisher Narrator: *This task involves single word reading with no time constraint. The segment*

*highlights the items on which each boy had difficulty. Checkmarks indicate correct performance.*

### Jonathan
Reads items correctly to the word experiment: He says ex . . . ex-pe. . . experiment . . .

### William
Reads one page of words accurately. We turn to a new page: Big whistling, laughing, groan at sight of what he clearly perceives as more challenging words!! But he is willing to try. . . . . . .

JHB responds to his willingness and validates his reaction. [*JHB: "Who-oa!! Take a deep breath!!. . .Here we go. . . . . . ."*]

William gets hold of both sides of the editor's desk on which the materials are placed and proceeds, holding on quite firmly: . . . . . . should ✓ island ✓ correctly ✓ since ✓ personality: per . . . son . . . al . . . i . . . ty . . . . personality experiment ✓

### Brian
about: a . . . bout part ✓ knew ✓ because ✓ faster ✓ whole ✓
[NEW PAGE]
For should, he says: shouted. . . . show-der . . . showder. For island: iz-land . . . izland For correctly: ke . . . ko . . . . . .
    [*JHB: "Tricky, huh?"*]
. . .Yeah . . .
    [*JHB: "Do your best"* quietly]
. . . crocodile . . .
    [*JHB: "OK. Try the next one."*]
. . . For since: sign-ge
    [*JHB: "have a go at the last two then?"*]
. . . For personality: per . . . persel
    [*JHB: "all right"*]
. . . For experiment: (sub voce: I've seen that word!
    [*JHB: "oh, yeah?"*])
. . . . ex . . . pertmental (whispered) . . . experimental . . .

### Andrew
Using his finger to keep his place, word by word.
get ✓ was ✓ i. . . . get ✓ was ✓ his ✓ when ✓ For fixed: fexed must ✓
[NEW PAGE . . .]

about ✔ part art-ay knew ✔ because ✔ For faster: ferter . . . f . . . ar . . . ter For whole: wole
[NEW PAGE]
For should: sholed For island: izland For correctly: cried For since: sign . . . signed For personality: pers . . . . . . persON. . . .
[*JHB*: "*OK. Try that last one.*"] For experiment: eraser . . .
    Table of results appears after the next task.

*Untimed reading: non-words*
Narrator: *This task involves the reading of non-words with no time constraints.*

**Jonathan**
For grawl: growl loast ✔ sluke ✔
    . . . . . . [*JHB*: "*Try those . . .*"]
For thrept: thre-ept wheeg ✔ mibgus mib-gus ✔ For splaunch: splanch For quantric: kwun . . . kwon-tric lindify ✔

**William**
For snirk: serink . . . snerink . . . snerik For yosh: yoash tayed ✔ For grawl: grow ('ow' as in <u>owl</u>) For loast: lo . . . . . . loast For sluke: snulk . . .

    . . . . . .[*William was very amused at his own efforts; JHB shared the joke: "You can't tell me that you don't know what these mean – right?! 'Cos nobody else does either!"*]

For thrept: threp . . . thrept For wheeg: weg For mibgus: mibg For splaunch: splench L A U G H S For quantric: kwəntray
        [*JHB shares laughter.*]
For lindify: linedrif . . .

**Brian**
zoop ✔ lish ✔ For dright: . . . . . . dr . . . . draik . . . draight For jox: jok For feap: . . . f . . . feap gusp ✔
        [*JHB*: "*OK! Will you try another page of these weird ones?*"]
NEW PAGE
For snirk: s. . . k . . . i . . . skit For yosh: usk For tayed: tell For grawl: . . . g . . . r . . . grə . . . aller For loast: lo . . . lost For sluke: sluk . . .

**Andrew**
zoop ✔ lish ✔ For dright: bringth jox ✔ feap ✔ For gusp: gjoops
NEW PAGE
For snirk: sn . . . snirk yosh ✔ For tayed: . . . t . . . tell For grawl: growled For loast: lost For sluke: sluk . . .

Table A4. *Performances for untimed reading tasks.*

| Task | Words "Letter-Word Identification"<br>Standard score / percentile | Non-words "Word Attack"<br>Standard score / percentile |
|---|---|---|
| Jonathan | 115 / 83rd | 103 / 57th |
| Andrew | 81 / 10th | 89 / 22nd |
| William | 95 / 37th | 91 / 26th |
| Brian | 86 / 18th | 88 / 21st |

*Note:* The segments were selected to demonstrate the child's range, especially the upper end.

*Task 3: timed reading – words and non-words*

*Timed reading: words*
Narrator: *On these tasks the boys must read the items as quickly as possible.*

**Jonathan**
Reads to grade level without difficulty. Hands quiet on table.

**William**
great ✓ space ✓ For short: . .snort river ✓ For crowd: crowed plot ✓ For overt: . . . o-fer
For glide: gild people ✓ almost ✓ strong ✓ For hardly: harleyed . . . hardy
For flint: final-ul
healthy ✓ famous ✓ For extent: exciten . . .
INTERVIEWER COMMENT: Tracking item by item with his finger; left hand holds onto and anchors page. Occasionally uses left hand to maintain place in the line while right finger moves on.

**Brian**
father ✓ open ✓ shoes ✓ money ✓ great ✓ For space: special For short: [*misses completely*] river ✓ For crowd: cower . . . coward For plot: peepul . . . people . . .
INTERVIEWER COMMENT: Sits straight, motionless.

**Andrew**
time ✓ neck ✓ For dear: "skip!" For able: abble For fine: find For date: bi-ate . . . bə. . . bate For work: worm jump ✓
    [*JHB: "Keep going!" – to next column*]
. . . Oh! . . . For kind: kid long ✓ For then: they . . .

INTERVIEWER COMMENT: Using pen in right hand, tracks item by item down column.

Table of results appears after the next task.

*Timed reading: non-words*

**Jonathan**

tive ✓ For poth: po . . . eth barp ✓ For shlee: sh-lee For meest: mee-t . . . mee-eet stip ✓ For plin: plin . . . pline skree ✓ frip ✓ sline ✓
INTERVIEWER COMMENT: Comfortable, relaxed.

**William**

For pate: pat . . . . pate nup ✓ For bave: brave herm ✓ For chur: chew For dess: dress For knap: nat tive ✓ poth ✓ For barp: parp For shlee: sheel For meest: mest . . . meest stip ✓ plin ✓ For skree: streak For frip: flip . . .
INTERVIEWER COMMENT: Tracking item by item with right hand; hanging on grimly to the side of interviewer's desk with left hand.

**Brian**

For ni: ni . . . ni . . . ni . . . For ko: o . . . ko For ig: i . . . g . . . ig om ✓ pim ✓ For baf: bafe din ✓ For wum: wə . . . o . . . wə . . . . . . om
For lat: late For fet: fate pate ✓ (does not recognize similar sound pattern) For nup: nə . . . ape For bave: brave . . .
INTERVIEWER COMMENT: Sits straight up; no body movement.

**Andrew**

For ga: da ip ✓ For ta: tə . . . a For ni: nə . . . i . . . ni ko ✓ ig ✓ For om: . . . . . . om pim ✓ baf ✓ For din: bine For wum: wom For lat: let . . . lat fet ✓ For pate: pet . . .
INTERVIEWER COMMENT: Tracking item by item with pen in right hand. Left hand pulling at ear. Frowning with expression of great concentration on his face.

*Task 4: paragraph reading*

Narrator: *The boys are asked to read the following paragraph, formatted as presented, which is at approximately a 3rd grade reading level.*

It was time to get up and go to school. The children made their beds and dressed. One child said, "I can't find my red shoes." Mother said, "Then you'll have to wear the brown ones instead." The other child said, "I've lost my blue book." Father said, "I saw it on the floor last night." When the children were ready at last, they helped Father look for the car keys. Mother kissed them all good-bye and said, "Have a nice day."

Table A5. *Performances for timed reading tasks.*

| Task | Words | Non-words |
|------|-------|-----------|
| Mean/SD | 48.5/2.8 | 23.1/13.8 |
| Jonathan | 56 (57) | 27 (30) |
| William | 45 (52) | 21 (29) |
| Brian | 37 (43) | 13 (17) |
| Andrew | 24 (33) | 11 (14) |

Score = # items read correctly in 45 seconds; # items attempted in parentheses.
*Note:* The behavioral episodes were selected to demonstrate the child's range, especially the upper end.
Material from the Gray Oral Reading Test, 3rd Edition, 1992, is reproduced with permission of PRO-ED, Inc.

## Jonathan

It was time to get up, and go to school. The children made their beds and dressed (*upwards pitch*) . . . . . . dressed (*downwards pitch*). One child said, "(*with appropriate intonational expression for dialogue*) I can't find my red shoes." Mother said, "(*expression*) Then you'll have to wear the brown ones instead." The other child said, "(*expression*) I've lost my blue book." Father said, "(*expression*) I saw it on the floor last night." When the children were ready at last, they helped Father look for the car keys. Mother kissed them all good-bye and said, "(*expression*) Have a nice day."

*Number of seconds to complete the paragraph: 38*

## William

It was time to get up and go to school (chopped breath). The children made their beds (breath) and dressed (breath). One child said, I-can't-find-my-red-shoes, mother said, then you'll have-to wear the brown ones instead. The other child said, I've lost my brown . . . ones, I've . . . okay . . . I've lost my blue book. Father said, "I saw it on the floor last night." When the children were ready AT LAST (emphatic: big grin), they helped their father look at . . . look for the car keys. Mother kissed them all good-bye and said have-a-nice-day.

*Number of seconds to complete the paragraph: 40.*

## Brian

It / was / time / to / go . . . get / up / and . . . go to school. The children made. . .their beds . . . an . . . an-d . . . dr . . . dressed. One / ch – child said . . . I / can't find / my / red shoes. Mother . . . said then you'll / have / to wear / the brown . . . brown ones . . . in / stead. The other . . . children said I / lost / my / blue / book.

Father said / I / saw / it / on the / floor . . . last night . . . when the children were . . . read-ing at / last. They / helped / father / look / for / the / car keys. Mother / kissed / them / all good – bye . . . and said . . . have / a / nice / day. (no expression).

*Number of seconds to complete the paragraph: 70.*

**Andrew**
(*Hands together on table*) It was time . . . to get up, and . . . t . . . (*picks up pen in R hand; starts tracking along line word by word*) . . . go . . . to . . . school. The . . . children (*tracks with pen from end of first line to beginning of next line; transfers pen to L hand; tracks across second line word by word*)
made. . . their . . . beds . . . and . . . dressed . . . on . . . children said . . . I can . . . I can't . . . find
(*At end of second line, moves pen back to beginning of the third line – seems unsure of his position – looks back to end of second line; takes thumb nail to end of the second line, moves it down one line and moves thumb deliberately along the third line from left to right to the beginning of the fourth*)
brown . . . (*apparently realizes that this does not make good sense; moves up one line*)
my . . . red . . . shorts . . . mother said . . . they . . . then the-then you have . . . to . . . wear . . . the . . . (*tracks with left hand from right to left along the line*)
brown . . . ones. Inside the . . . oth-er . . . children . . . sa . . . said I lost . . . my (*tracks back along line*)
blue book . . . father . . . said . . . I . . . saw . . . it . . . on . . . the . . . floor . . . last . . . night. (M*oves to left without tracking; misses the sixth line completely; continues using the pen to track word by word*)
look for the ca-ar keys mother . . . kissed them . . . all good – bye . . . and . . . said . . . have . . . a . . . nice . . . day.

*Number of seconds to complete the paragraph: 112.*

*Task 5: motor tapping*

Narrator: *On this task the boys are required to tap in time with an audible metronome beat. They must maintain the beat when the metronome is switched off half-way through the trial. The first condition involves alternating sides – left hand, right hand, left hand and so on. The second condition involves an asynchronous rhythm, both hands, right hand, both hands, and so on.*

*The tracings illustrated next to the picture of each boy represent his ability (or inability) to maintain performance in stable fashion over time. The upper tracing is the right hand, the lower tracing the left hand. The tracings are a schematic representation of what is actually a series of points with each point representing the deviation in time of each tap from the target pattern. The interested reader is referred to Wolff (1993) for details of the procedure.*

### *Alternating hand tapping*
**Jonathan**
INTERVIEWER COMMENT: Concentrating visually on his hands with great intensity. Occasional heavy sighs.

**William**
INTERVIEWER COMMENT: Extremely anxious expression. Legs moving rhythmically. Watches computer screen displaying the tracing to his left: "I hate it when it does this!! . . . . . . When's it going to say it?" (waiting for the computer generated voce to tell him to stop).

**Brian**
INTERVIEWER COMMENT: Simply sits quietly, apparently unconcerned, concentrating on tapping his fingers as required.

**Andrew**
INTERVIEWER COMMENT: Tightly compressed lips, intense concentration. Starts by holding hands above the keys with index finger pointing downwards; spontaneously shifts to tapping with ball of index finger.

### *Asynchronous hand tapping*
**Jonathan**
INTERVIEWER COMMENT: Big sighs. Slight head bobbing to rhythm of hands on keys. Shifts spatial position of finger on key for the hand doing the double tap.

**William**
INTERVIEWER COMMENT: Head and upper trunk beating up and down with rhythm of fingers on keys. Marked overflow movements in mouth musculature. Some associated leg movement. Desperate intonation: "When's it going to say it? . . . . . . Dave?. . . . . . Can't you warn me?"

**Brian**
INTERVIEWER COMMENT: Still. Concentrating on hands.

**Andrew**
INTERVIEWER COMMENT: Legs swinging in time with hands. Intense concentration. Starts to subvocalize with rhythm.

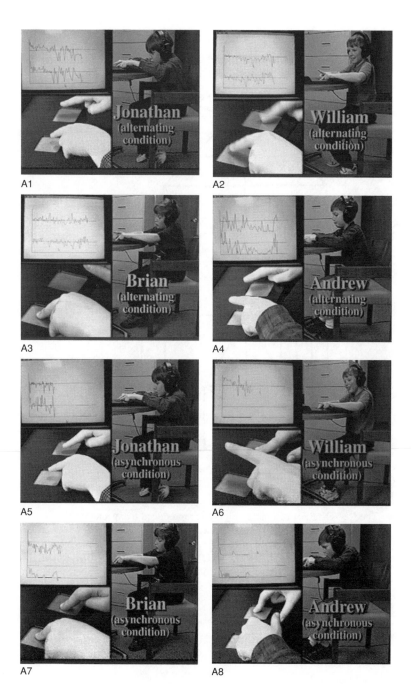

Figure A1 Jonathan's alternating hand tapping task. A2. William's alternating hand tapping task. A3. Brian's alternating hand tapping task. A4. Andrew's alternating hand tapping task. A5. Jonathan's asynchronous hand tapping task. A6. William's asynchronous hand tapping task. A7. Brian's asynchronous hand tapping task. A8. Andrew's asynchronous hand tapping task.

*Task 6: The Rey-Osterrieth complex figure – figure copying and recall*

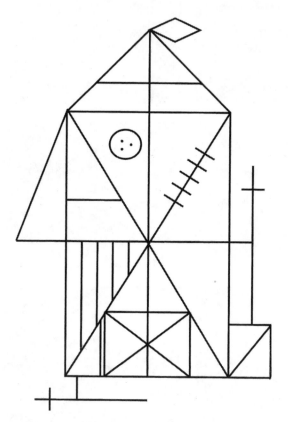

Figure A9  Rey-Osterrieth complex figure.
The Rey-Osterrieth Complex Figure is reproduced by special permission of the Publisher, Psychological Assessment Resources, Inc., 16204 North Florida Avenue, Lutz, FL 33549, from the Rey Complex Figure Test and the Recognition Trial by John E. Meyers, Psy.D. and Kelly R. Meyers, B.A. Copyright 1992 by PAR, Inc. Further reproduction is prohibited without permission of PAR.

**Jonathan**

Figure A10A  Jonathan's copying of Rey-Osterrieth figure.

Figure A10B  Jonathan's immediate recall of Rey-Osterrieth figure.

Figure A10C  Jonathan's delayed recall of Rey-Osterrieth figure.

# William

Figure A11A  William's copying of Rey-Osterrieth figure.

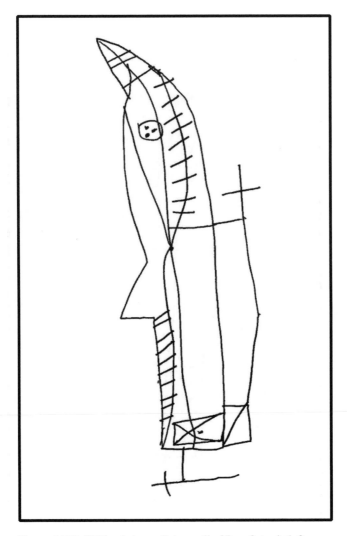

Figure A11B  William's immediate recall of Rey-Osterrieth figure.

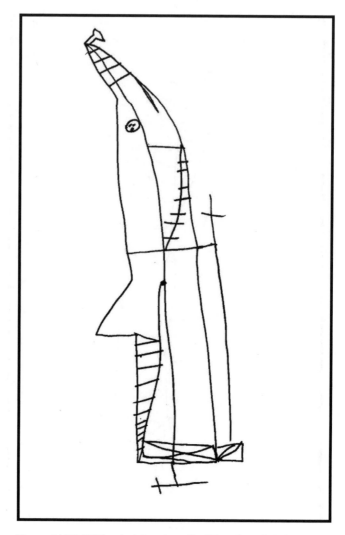

Figure A11C  William's delayed recall of Rey-Osterrieth figure.

**Brian**

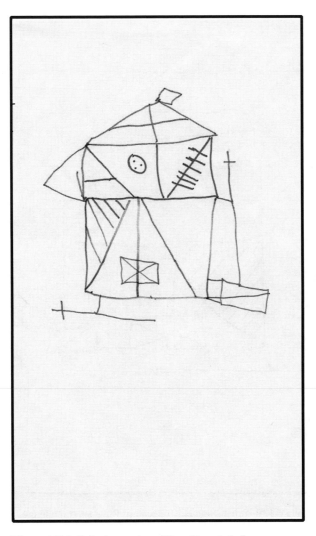

Figure A12A  Brian's copying of Rey-Osterrieth figure.

Figure A12B  Brian's immediate recall of Rey-Osterrieth figure.

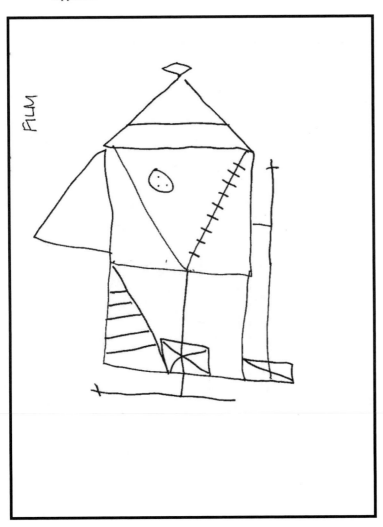

Figure A12C  Brian's delayed recall of Rey-Osterrieth figure.

**Andrew**

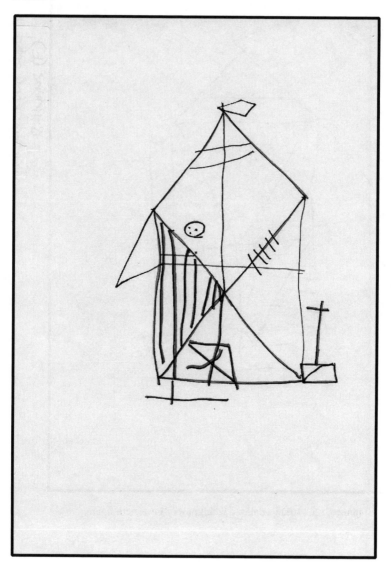

Figure A13A  Andrew's copying of Rey-Osterrieth figure.

Figure A13B  Andrew's immediate recall of Rey-Osterrieth figure.

Figure A13C  Andrew's delayed recall of Rey-Osterrieth figure.

Table A6. *Performances for Rey-Osterrieth complex figure organization and style.*

| | Copy | | Immediate recall | | Delayed recall | |
|---|---|---|---|---|---|---|
| Condition | Organization | Style | Organization | Style | Organization | Style |
| Jonathan | 9 | C | 5 | C | 4 | C |
| William | 3 | OC/IP | 4 | P | 5 | P |
| Brian | 7 | P | 7 | P | 7 | P |
| Andrew | 5 | OP/IC | 6 | Int | 4 | Int |

*Organization* scores range from 1 to 13 (the normative data were collected from children in kindergarten through 8th grade).

*Style* categories are as follows: C = configurational; Int = intermediate; P = part-oriented. For the Copy condition only, the Intermediate category is split into OC/IP = Outer configuration/inner part and OP/IC = Outer part/inner configuration.

Accuracy

| | Copy | | Immediate Recall | | Delayed Recall | |
|---|---|---|---|---|---|---|
| | Structural Elements | Incidental Elements | Structural Elements | Incidental Elements | Structural Elements | Incidental Elements |
| Condition | n = 25 | n = 39 | n = 25 | n = 39 | n = 25 | n = 39 |
| Jonathan | 25 | 39 | 21 | 31 | 21 | 31 |
| William | 25 | 37 | 19 | 33 | 19 | 37 |
| Brian | 25 | 38 | 22 | 35 | 22 | 35 |
| Andrew | 25 | 37 | 20 | 19 | 15 | 19 |

*Accuracy*: Structural elements include the base rectangle of the figure and the diagonals and diameters within it. Incidental elements include the internal details of the base rectangle and the elements that are attached to the outer perimeter of the base rectangle.

### Task 7: handwriting sample

Narrator: *Each boy was asked to write "I like pizza."*

**Jonathan**

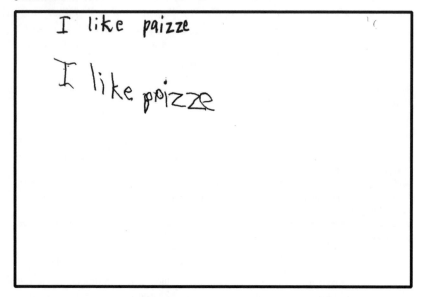

Figure A14  Jonathan's handwriting sample.

**William**

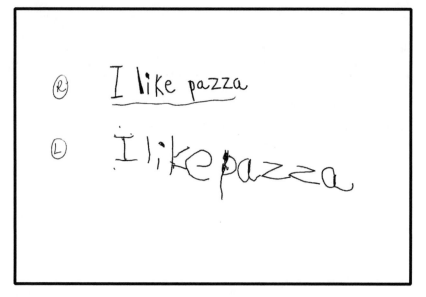

Figure A15  William's handwriting sample.

**Brian**

Figure A16  Brian's handwriting sample.

**Andrew**

Figure A17  Andrew's handwriting sample.

*Task 8: debriefing*

## Jonathan

The one I liked the best was the reading. . . . . . I mean, the drawing one.

[*JHB: The drawing? You liked that? You draw well and you've got a good memory?*]

Well . . I'm really not like Monet. . . . . . or a Picasso. . . . . . I just like to draw . . . . . .

INTERVIEWER COMMENT: Conversational interchange, the back-and-forth of question, comment, and answer is quite comfortable. As in his initial conversation with JHB, Jonathan's expression indicates that he is well aware of the – mischievous – impact of his words!

## William

. . . . . . And . . . reading the things [gesturing]. . . . . . like, the things, the colors, the numbers, the letters, the others. . . .

[*JHB: Yes, right! What do you think was hard about that?*]

. . . Hum-m-m. . . just . . . my mind needs more . . . like . . . time to process . . . what's on the sheet . . . of paper . . .

[*JHB: Do you have the feeling like your mind can think it but your tongue can't say it quickly enough?*]

. . .Yes . . .

[*JHB: What does it feel like?*]

. . . Sometimes it's like that. Sometimes my mind just needs a little extra time to say (with soothing, encouraging intonation). ."Oka-ay . . . what's that? . . . Oka-ay . . . remember . . . . ." . . . like . . . stuff like that . . . . . .

INTERVIEWER COMMENT: Conversational interchange is, as was the case with Jonathan, comfortable. William's insecurity in word retrieval is clearly evident even in this short segment. Of note here is his response to *JHB*'s potentially leading question. Although he initially assents to her suggestion, he goes back to his own previous description and amplifies it with his own explanation.

## Brian

. . . . . . the best one I liked was like the numbers, and the colors . . .

[*JHB: You do that really well, right? . . .*]

. . . PAUSE . . .

[*JHB: . . .What about that complicated design?*]

. . . That was kind of easy.

[*JHB: Yeah? You can remember things pretty well?*]

Yeah. . . . . . . PAUSE . . .

[*JHB: What's hard for you?*]

...... the hardest ... um-ding (sic) was ... reading those words that weren't true. ...

INTERVIEWER COMMENT: With Brian, JHB needs to ask questions, make encouraging comments, to keep him going. There is no back-and-forth rhythm in conversation. Brian's speech output pattern is regularly paced in a staccato fashion and with minimal expression.

**Andrew**

...... Er! ...the one where you did with T H I S hand (gestures) and T H I S hand was ...

  [*JHB: Yes*]

... this hand was easy ... this one was a little bit harder! (exaggerated intonation) ...

  [*JHB: You did it very nicely and, you know, since you're not a leftie, we don't expect you to be perfect.*]

and I think er! ... the reading thing was er!. .. good.

  [*When you read the stories?*]

Yeh.

INTERVIEWER COMMENT: Andrew engages in conversational interchange easily with his and JHB's remarks overlying each other as soon as their import is grasped. Again in the face of a leading question from JHB, he does not fully agree but tries to distinguish what he thought he was doing.

## REFERENCES

RAPID NAMING

Denckla M. B. & Rudel, R. G. (1976). Rapid automatized naming (R.A.N.): Dyslexia differentiated from other learning disabilities. *Neuropsychologia*, 14, 471–9.

Wolf, M. (1991). Naming speed and reading: the contribution of the cognitive neurosciences. *Reading Research Quarterly*, 26, 123–41.


READING WORDS AND NON-WORDS: UNTIMED

Woodcock, R. W. & Johnson, M. B. (1989). *The Woodcock-Johnson Psycho-Educational Battery, Revised*. Allen, TX: DLM Resources. Letter-Word Identification subtest.

Woodcock, R. W. & Johnson, M. B. (1990) *Woodcock-Johnson-Revised Tests of Achievement*. The Riverside Publishing Company. Word Attack subtest.


READING WORDS AND NON-WORDS: TIMED

Torgesen, J. K., Wagner, R. K. & Rashotte, C. A. (1999). *Test of Word Reading Efficiency*. Austin, TX: PRO-ED Publishing, Inc.

PARAGRAPH READING

Gray Oral Reading Test, 3rd edn, 1992. Austin, TX: PRO-ED.


MOTOR TAPPING

Wolff, P. H. 1993. Impaired temporal resolution in developmental dyslexia. *Annals of the New York Academy of Sciences*, 682, 87–103.
Wolff, P. H., Michel, G. F., Ovrut, M. & Drake, C. (1990). Rate and timing precision of motor coordination in developmental dyslexia. *Developmental Psychology*, 26, 349–59.


REY-OSTERRIETH COMPLEX FIGURE

Bernstein, J. H. & Waber, D. P. (1996). *Developmental scoring system for the Rey-Osterrieth complex figure*. Odessa, FL: Psychological Assessment Resources, Inc.
Osterrieth, P. A. (1944). Le test de copie d'une figure complexe. *Archives de Psychologie*, 30, 206–356.
Rey, A. (1941). L'examen psychologique dans le cas d'encéphalopathie traumatique. *Archives de Psychologie*, 28, 286–340.

# Index